WOT! NO ENGINES?

First edition, published in 2002 by

WOODFIELD PUBLISHING
Woodfield House, Babsham Lane, Bognor Regis
West Sussex PO21 5EL, England
www.woodfieldpublishing.com

© Alan Cooper, 2002

All rights reserved.
No part of this publication may be reproduced
or transmitted in any form or by any means,
electronic or mechanical, nor may it be stored
in any information storage and retrieval system,
without prior permission from the publisher.

The right of Alan Cooper
to be identified as author of this work
has been asserted by him in accordance with
the Copyright, Designs and Patents Act 1988

ISBN 1-903953-18-9

Wot! No Engines?

Royal Air Force Glider Pilots
& Operation Varsity

Alan Cooper

Woodfield Publishing
~ WEST SUSSEX • ENGLAND ~

My thanks to Harry Clark, without whom this book would never have been published. He flew in a glider on Operation Varsity as a member of the Second (Airborne) Battalion, Ox & Bucks Light Infantry and it was he who bought to my attention of the fact that half the glider pilots on Operation Varsity were from the RAF; that 61 of them had made a one-way trip, and that very little had ever been written about them, despite the wealth of the histories of World War II.

I am honoured to have been able to tell their remarkable story.

Alan Cooper, 2002

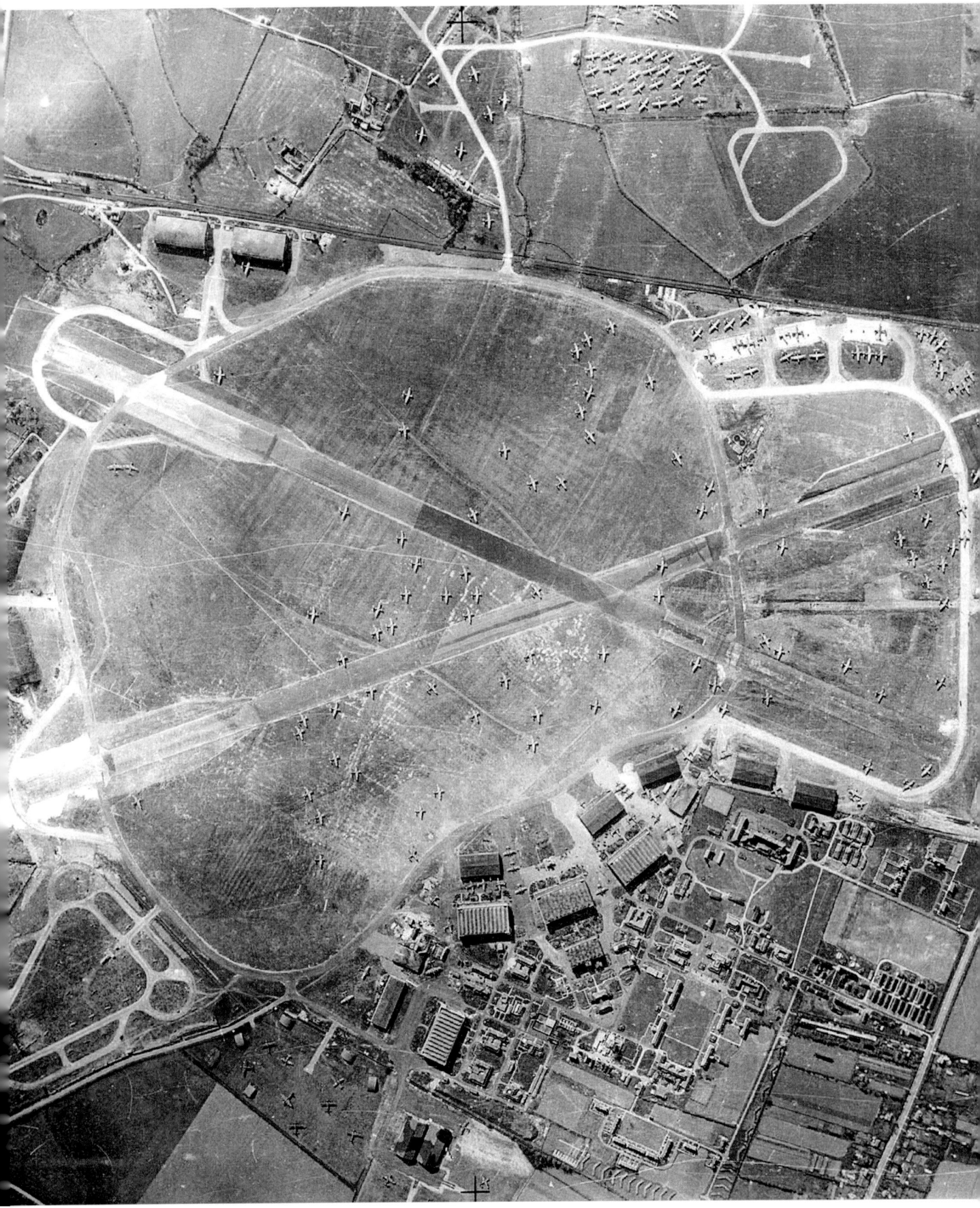

Practice glider landings at RAF Brize Norton, 1944 [Alec Waldron]

Contents

Introduction		9
CHAPTER 1	THE FIRST GLIDERS	11
CHAPTER 2	GLIDERS AT WAR	15
CHAPTER 3	EARLY GLIDER OPERATIONS	21
CHAPTER 4	FURTHER GLIDER OPERATIONS	29
CHAPTER 5	AIRBORNE INVASION	35
CHAPTER 6	WOT!... NO ENGINES?	45
CHAPTER 7	FLYING & GLIDER TRAINING	51
CHAPTER 8	PREPARING FOR VARSITY	67
CHAPTER 9	GLIDER TUGGING	91
CHAPTER 10	CROSSING THE RHINE	95
CHAPTER 11	OPERATION VARSITY: THE PLAN	99
CHAPTER 12	PREPARATION FOR VARSITY	101
CHAPTER 13	D-DAY – 24TH MARCH 1945	105
CHAPTER 14	PERSONAL MEMORIES OF OPERATION VARSITY	117
CHAPTER 15	THE MEN THE GLIDERS CARRIED	163
CHAPTER 16	AFTERMATH	169
CHAPTER 17	POST-MORTEM	203
CHAPTER 18	SOUTH-EAST ASIA	215
CHAPTER 19	FURTHER PLANNED OPERATIONS	217
CHAPTER 20	REUNIONS	221
Appendix	STATISTICS, BIBLIOGRAPHY & ACKNOWLEDGEMENTS	227
Index		243
Postscript	THE ORIGINS OF 'MR CHAD'	246

RAF Horsa Gliders and Albemarle tugs ready for take off, 1944. [Alec Waldron]

Introduction

This book is primarily about the RAF pilots who were seconded to the Glider Pilot Regiment in 1944/45 following the devastating losses suffered by the regiment during the ill-fated Operation Market-Garden at Arnhem in Holland in September 1944.

The RAF pilots, many of whom had trained abroad under the Empire Flying Training Scheme, had returned to the UK in the hope of flying single-engine fighter aircraft such as the Spitfire or Hurricane, twin-engine fighter-bombers such as the Mosquito or Beaufighter, or four engine heavy bombers such as the Lancaster or Liberator. Most of them were understandably horrified when they found themselves 'volunteered' to fly gliders, something that they had never intended to do, and after the disastrous losses at Arnhem, something that they very much hoped they would not be asked to do...

Despite their misgivings, they went on to play a very important part in the largest airborne operation of World War II, Operation Varsity, the crossing of the Rhine on 24th March 1945. Their contribution has been hitherto largely overlooked by historians, and it is hoped that this book will go some way towards making up for this oversight.

Varsity was an immense and ambitious plan, involving over one million men in total. Masterminded by Field Marshal Sir Bernard Montgomery, it called for the concerted effort of many branches of the Armed Forces. The Royal Air Force was to be heavily involved, not only providing glider pilots but also supplying aircraft and crews to tow the gliders to their landing zones, fighter aircraft as escorts, bomber aircraft to weaken enemy positions in the target area before the main attack commenced, and air-sea rescue aircraft to pick up survivors.

The glider pilots would work side-by-side with the airborne forces of the British Army, whom they would be carrying into action. They would also work in close co-operation with the US Air Force and Airborne divisions, who would be mounting their own, separate attacks. The airborne troops were to form a bridgehead on the east of the Rhine to facilitate ground forces crossing the river into Germany.

Despite assurances received from their commanders that enemy anti-aircraft fire would be negligible on the day of the attack, in reality the gliders came under heavy and accurate fire, both in the air and after they had landed, and casualties were heavy, particularly in the first wave of landings.

In the course of researching this book, Alan Cooper has interviewed dozens of survivors, and their first-hand stories of the events of 24th March 1945 make for fascinating reading. There are many tales of individual bravery, lucky escapes, tragic misfortunes, odd coincidences and bizarre occurrences – the like of which can only happen in the heat of battle, when every moment is literally a life and death situation.

Here, in their own words, the veterans of this, the greatest ever glider-borne military operation in history, have been given the opportunity to place their memories on record and to pay tribute to the lost comrades they left on the battlefield near the German towns of Hamminkeln and Wesel over 50 years ago.

Along with the recollections of the Royal Air Force glider pilots, there are also many contributions from Army pilots of the Glider Pilot Regiment, men of the RAF tug squadrons, and the airborne troops who were 'passengers' in the gliders. Even after so many years, the respect they have for each other's skills is very much in evidence. Operation Varsity was very much a team effort and the level of co-operation between the various elements of the Armed Forces involved is to be greatly admired.

Despite the initial losses, history records the operation as a success; the Rhine was breached and the last chapter of World War II had begun, the ultimate downfall of Hitler's forces now a certainty, thanks in no small part, to the contribution of the RAF pilots seconded to the Glider Pilot Regiment.

Wednesday 24th March 1999: Former RAF glider pilots John Herold, Cy Henson and Len MacDonald plus author Alan Cooper (with bugle) pay tribute to the 61 RAF Glider Pilots killed during Operation Varsity, of whom 48 lie in peace at the Reichswald War Cemetary, Kleve, Germany. [Hilda Cooper]

CHAPTER 1

THE FIRST GLIDERS

The concept of flying without man-made power is not a new phenomenon. History shows that men were experimenting with, and flying, natural flying machines over 200 years ago. As early as 1709, an unmanned flying machine was designed and flown; it was said to have flown like a glider and was surely the first in its field. In the same year, a Portuguese priest built the world's first hot air balloon. However, it was 1853 before the first manned flight by a glider was recorded.

In 1883, in the USA, a glider invented by George Caley was built and flown in California. A number of books around about this period were also written on the progress in building flying machines.

In 1900, Americans Wilbur and Orville Wright flew their first glider, which was unmanned and controlled from the ground like a kite. In 1901, on their second glider they added a front elevator for ascending and descending with the pilot controlling the wing warping by control cables attached to his body leaving his hands free to control the front elevator. By later use of a movable rudder in place of the fixed one and in conjunction with the wing warping, turns were made possible.

The first manned glider was built in 1909 in Australia. In the same year, Lieutenant John Dunne of the Royal Engineers Balloon section, designed and successfully flew a glider. By this time, many men in many countries were building gliders and in 1911 the idea of military gliders arrived with the formation of the Air Battalion of the Royal Engineers.

During World War I, powered flight was considered most important, but after the cessation of hostilities, the Treaty of Versailles prohibited Germany from having military aircraft. The Germans began to build gliders and gliding turned into a national sport. In 1929, only ten years after the end of WWI over 50,000 Germans were members of gliding clubs. It was to prove an excellent training ground for many Luftwaffe air aces such as Adolf Galland.

Between August 31st and September 7th 1922, at Gersfeld, Germany, S/Ldr Wright of the Royal Air Force was investigating the conditions under which successful soaring flights had been carried out. At the request of the Secretary of the Royal Aero Club, he went along with a Cpt Sayers, acting as one of the Aero Club representatives. Before leaving the UK he was given a letter from the German Embassy requesting that every assistance should be given. On arrival at Gersfeld on the 31st August 1922, he met General Waitz, who was in charge of the organisation responsible for the soaring competitions. It was soon apparent that they were not very welcome, but the letter from the German Embassy in London enabled them to have passes to visit Wasserkuppe Hill and the gliding centre. The unwelcome greeting they received went further when Dr Ing Ursihus, editor of *Flugsport* and an active supporter of the Rhön Soaring Club was not willing to assist more than was necessary.

On the day that Wright arrived, a Mr Royce of the *New York World* and a former WWI pilot hired a glider which had been built by the local village carpenter and made a very good straight glide of 800 metres. The fee to fly the glider was

2,000 marks plus a guarantee of 10,000 marks in the event of the machine being totally wrecked. Some German students sent Wright and Sayers a note saying they would like them to attend a conference on soaring flight at another hotel in the village. No secret was made of what Germany had achieved with regard to research into aeronautics and this 'fraternisation' did not please Dr Ursihus who promptly left the room.

Another flight was made by Mr Royce, this time for a period of 4 minutes and travelling for a half a mile without losing height. The owner of the machine was severely censured for allowing foreigners to use it and was prevented from using it again.

On 3rd September 1922, Wright found several shed doors open and was able to make examinations of a number of machines housed there until he was discovered by the carpenter Herr Espelawl, who had arranged with Wright to hire a machine. Espelawl explained that Berlin had issued instructions that Wright was to be watched and that he was not to be allowed to see any of the machines. He was advised by Herr Espelawl to leave Gersfeld as soon as possible as things could get worse.

When Wright arrived back at the hotel he was told that he was forbidden to fly over the area and immediate steps would be taken if he disobeyed the order. They decided to leave for Cologne the next day. It was evident that there were bitter feelings against the Bavarians and Prussians by the remainder of the Germans in the village, but the Bavarians held the power and respect and no one dared question their decisions.

In 1929 the decision was taken to form the British Gliding Association and the London Gliding Club and in 1930 the London Gliding Club was inaugurated. The first founder member was F/O (later Grp Cpt) Edward Mole, holder of British Gliding Club certificate No 6.

In 1930 C.H. Lowe-Wylde founded the British Aircraft Company and began to build gliders. Within five weeks he had built his first glider, the BAC 1, a copy of the German Zogling primary trainer.

It was then that Barbara Cartland – later a Dame of the British Empire – came into the

The Barbara Cartland glider (above). Barbara Cartland and Flying Officer Ewen Wanliss fly the first ever air-mail glider from Manston to Reading in 1931 (below).   [Dame Barbara Cartland]

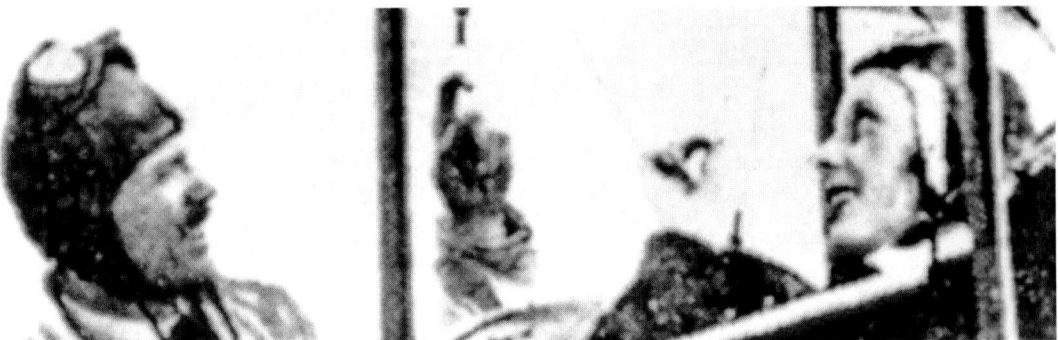

picture. She, along with two RAF officers, thought the idea of towing gliders from an aeroplane to be a good commercial project, particularly in the financial recession at that time. A glider was very cheap to build and Barbara had one built by Lowe-Wylde – the BAC VII – a two-seater version of the BAC IV.

In 1931, as Barbara Cartland's glider was being built, the *Daily Mail* newspaper offered a £1,000 prize for the first glider to cross the English Channel. In the rules of the competition they did not specify a particular method of launching a glider and it was thought by Barbara and her colleagues that if a glider could be towed to 12,000 feet over England, from there on it would be easy to free glide across the Channel and into France. The Germans had already experimented with towing gliders but it had not been attempted before in the UK. Lowe-Wylde thought they should enter and take up the challenge, but Barbara believed that with so many taking part in the event, it would become nothing more than a publicity stunt.

Barbara Cartland's glider had her name written in red letters on both sides of the fuselage and right across the under surface of the wing. The pilot of the towing aircraft was F/O Ewan Wanliss. It was towed via a quick-release hook fitted on the wing centre section above the head of the towing aircraft's pilot. To avoid the towing cable fouling the tail unit, a long steel tube, which had to be supported by a large cradle, was mounted above the tug's rudder. Because of this, it was decided not to enter the Channel crossing competition, but instead to fly inland.

On the 20th June 1931 they took off from Manston airfield, turned their back on the Channel and headed for Reading to become the first aeroplane-towed mail-glider. Barbara sat in the open cockpit of the towing aeroplane with F/O Wanliss, the release hook just above her head. F/O Mole was the glider pilot. For take off it was a perfect, calm and sunny day. Wanliss was a little worried, as it had been suggested that a weight at the back of the towing plane might cause it to turn turtle. However, without any problems they reached Reading aerodrome, a journey of about 100 miles. Here the Mayor was waiting of them and Barbara handed over a letter to him.

The 'Barbara Cartland' glider took part in many rallies that summer and carried a passenger, her agent Ian Davison, who had a letter from the Lord Mayor of London for the Mayor of Blackpool.

During the flight to Blackpool the glider raced an express train and won with ease.

Later, the 'Barbara Cartland' set a record by hand-launch with falling flight of four and half miles, but on landing from a second flight it was blown over in a gale near Brighton and was completely wrecked.

In 1984, at Kennedy Airport in the USA, Barbara received America's Bishop Wright Air Industry Award for her contribution to the development of aviation.

The first man to cross the Channel in a glider was Lissart Beardmore, a Canadian who crossed it the day before the *Daily Mail* competition, which was won by a German – Robert Kronfeld. Afterwards he said, "I think a new epoch in air travel has begun."

The Air Ministry, however, decided otherwise and stopped glider towing, believing it to be too dangerous. In England, gliders returned to hand-launching but in Germany they did not forget what had been proved by the experiment – as we were later to learn to our detriment.

In 1932, the Russians went even further by building the world's first passenger transport glider.

In 1933, with the rise of Hitler and the Nazi party, came the German Gliding Research Institute, who produced a high altitude meteorological research glider. Out of this came the first assault glider of WWII.

In 1938, the German Glider Force was created and in 1939, just after the war had begun, a special storm unit was formed, equipped with DFS 230 assault gliders.

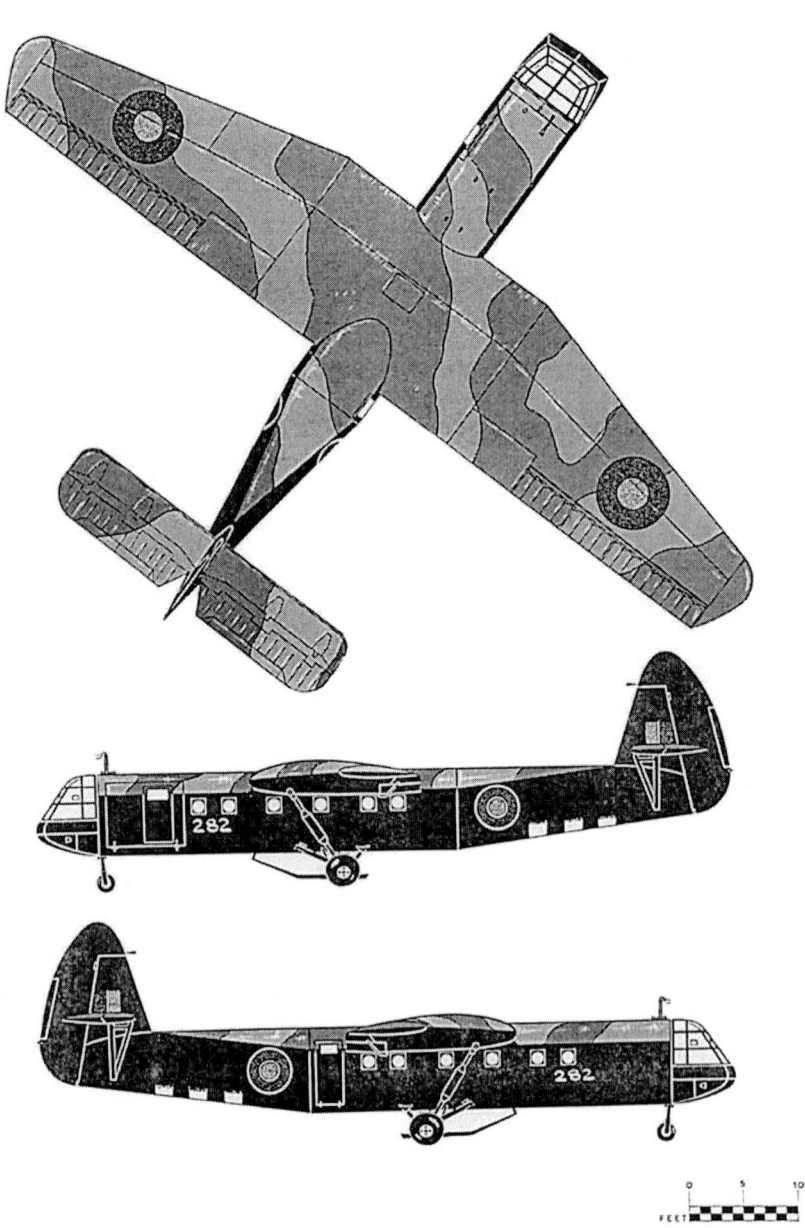

The Airspeed Horsa glider. [George Burn]

CHAPTER 2

GLIDERS AT WAR

Following the German invasion of Poland, both the United Kingdom and France declared war on Hitler's Germany on 3rd September 1939.

Preparations in Germany for the first glider-borne assault began in November 1939, but it was well into 1940 before all the problems connected with this had been overcome. In November 1940, a special unit, Storm Unit Koch, was formed under Cpt Koch and named No 1 Wing of the Air Landing Group.

On 10th May 1940 Germany invaded Belgium, Holland and Luxembourg spearheaded by glider and parachute troops. This frontal assault was on a fort in Belgium, which could have proved an obstacle to the advancing German Panzer forces. Hitler himself convened the plan to capture the fort along with three bridges, which was successfully achieved without great loss of life for the attacking troops and thus became the first glider-borne assault in history.

The Germans had been first to exploit the possibility of using gliders to deliver troops to a target and deal with it quickly.

June 1940 saw the evacuation of the B.E.F at Dunkirk. The United Kingdom was now on its own, as the French had requested, and been given, an armistice from the German forces. France was to be occupied for the next four years.

On 22nd June 1940, Prime Minister Winston Churchill sent a memo to the Chief of Staff:

"We ought to have a corps of at least 5,000 parachute troops. I hear that something is being done to form such a corps but I believe, only on a small scale. Advantage must be taken of the Summer to train these forces who can none the less play their part meanwhile as shock troops in Home Defence. Pray let me have note from the War Office on the subject."

A training unit for airborne troops followed at Ringway airfield, near Manchester (now Manchester Airport) although there was nobody with any experience of parachuting or gliders. General Wavell had, on 10th September 1936, witnessed the Russian Army dropping 1,200 men, 150 machine guns and 18 light field guns, and two weeks later, near Moscow, the dropping of 5,200 men. When he returned to the UK he reported: "If I had not witnessed this descent, I could not have believed such an operation possible."

Major, later Lt Col, John F. Rock of the Royal Engineers was ordered to take charge of the military organisation of British Airborne Forces. One of his colleagues from the RAF was Wg/Cdr L.A. Strange DSO, MC, DFC and Wg/Cdr, later Gr/Cpt Sir Nigel Norman Bt CBE.

The parachute instructors were at first from the Army and RAF but later entirely from the Physical Training Branch of the RAF, which still applies today. The Central Landing School was formed and in September became the Central Landing Establishment, however, it was conspicuous mainly for the almost total lack of the equipment necessary to train parachute soldiers, glider pilots and air-landing troops. There were only four aircraft available for use in training, including Whitley Mk IIs.

On 4th September 1940, a conference was held at the Air Ministry on the subject of the deployment of Airborne Troops. The tactics used by the Germans were mentioned, in that they started their attacks with parachutes, followed by airborne troops and with heavy bombing in the vicinity of the drop zone. The question of dropping heavy equipment was also discussed. The use of gliders for heavy equipment and the carrying of troops was also mentioned.

(a) Was it possible for gliders to land personnel safely, without shock and without unnecessary impediments on a given spot.

(b) The use of gliders was preferable to the use of aeroplanes because of the employment of aeroplanes for landing or parachuting troops, in the RAF, immobilise valuable equipment that was urgently required for other purposes. The use of bombers for this purpose would reduce the scale of a bombing attack, the construction of gliders on the other hand, could be undertaken by the wood-working industry and would not interfere with aircraft production.

(c) Gliders with light wing-loading could be landed at low speed and in a small space, and no need for an aerodrome, on good authority it was supposed that gliders could be economically built which could land at 40mph, and carry 40 men.

During September 1940, an order was made for 400 Hotspur gliders to be built by Harry Lebus (an East London furniture manufacturer) and Waring and Gillows. They were to be available by the middle of August, 1941.

The prototype took to the air on 5th November 1940. It was designed to carry 8 men and a cargo of 1,880lbs and had a wingspan of over 45 feet, a length of over 39 feet a fully laden weight of 3,598 lbs. It was made mostly of wood.

A test flight of the Hotspur I took place on 21st January 1941. It was flown by F/O Davie and F/O Kronfeld.

On 19th September, a Glider Training Squadron was formed at RAF Ringway with Tiger Moths as glider tugs and Kirby Kite gliders for training.

The army supplied the first men to be trained as glider pilots.

When it was realised that the Hotspur would not come up to the required standard, it was re-assigned to a training role. Over 1,000 were built, but were never used on operations.

In December 1940, the Glider Squadron moved to RAF Thame, Oxfordshire, there they used the Tiger Moth and later the Hawker Hector aircraft for towing.

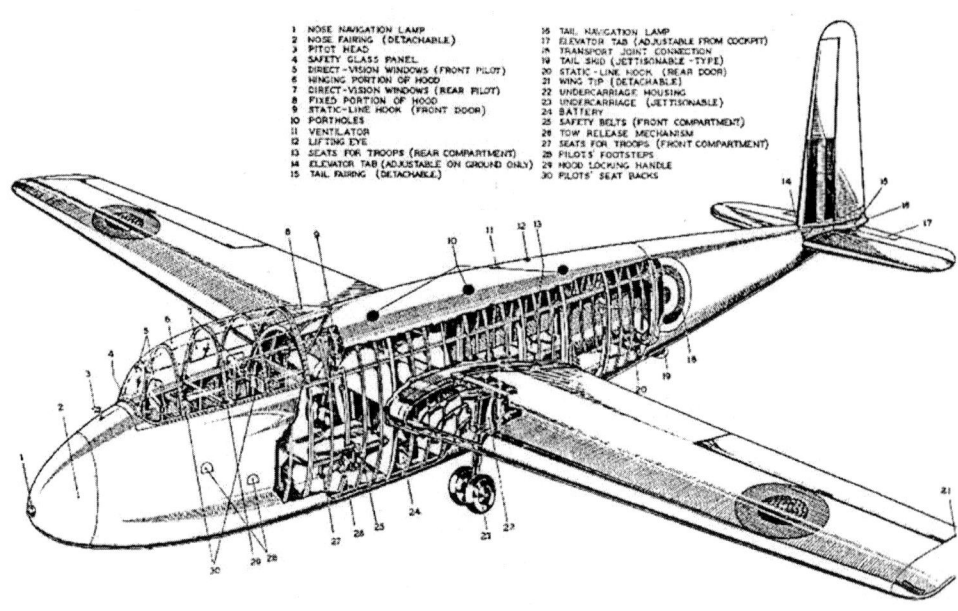

The Hotspur Mk.II glider. [George Burn]

On the 11th December 1940, another conference was held at the Air Ministry by the Vice Chief of the Air Staff. It went on to say that the original request by Churchill for 5,000 army parachutists and 360 glider pilots by Spring 1941 had been modified to 500 parachutists but it was clear the glider pilot project would not be realised. Glider pilots would have to be skilled as pilots and navigators if they were to accomplish the towed flight safely in heavy gliders and make spot landings at previously unknown points. They would need to reach heavy bomber standards in skill and should, in general, be RAF or seconded army pilots, employed constantly in flying until an air-borne operation was staged.

The specification for a military troop-carrying glider, capable of carrying 25 men and having two pilots, was taken up in December 1940.

In February 1941, an order was made for 400 to be built. This was the Horsa Mk I and later Mark II, designed by A.E. Ellison and Airspeed's Technical Director Hessel Tiltman in 1940. In all 2,960 Horsas were built in WWII.

The Airspeed factory at Portsmouth was the first factory to be bombed in WWII. Just after the design office had been moved to de Havilland's at Hartfield, the Portsmouth factory was destroyed in a lone raid by a JU87 bomber. Other firms involved in glider building at the time were General Aircraft and the Birmingham Coach Works.

The Horsa was made in six sections known as 'barrels'. Each barrel was assembled on a rotatable rig, which made it possible for the operatives to remain at floor level throughout the assembly. The sections were then lap-joined at the bulkheads which, together with the longerons and stringers, resulting in a fuselage of exceptional strength.

The Horsa's fuselage was circular, made of plywood and attached to numerous circular ribs of stouter wood. It had an 88-foot wingspan, was 67 feet long and weighed 15,250 lbs. There were seats down the length of each side, also made of light wood, each provided with a safety harness which fitted over the shoulders of the wearer while a belt encircled his waist. The floor was

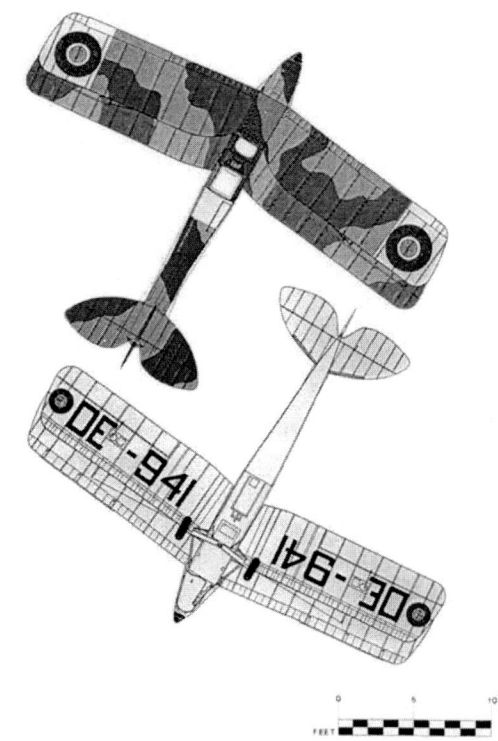

corrugated to prevent slipping. The glider had two entrances, one on the port side near the nose and the other on the starboard side at the stern of the fuselage. The entrance to this slid up vertically and the whole tail unit was detachable to enable the quick unloading of jeeps, anti-tank guns and other equipment. The tail could also, if necessary, be blown off by a dynamite cartridge, although this did hold a risk of fire.

If there was a need to ditch in the sea (as did happen on all glider operations) the glider, being made of wood was capable of remaining afloat for up to 24 hours.

The pilots sat side by side with the first pilot sitting on the left. The controls were similar to a power driven aircraft, except, of course, there were no throttles. The tow release lever was painted red. There was also one in the tug aircraft to release the rope after the glider had released from the tug aircraft. For flying at night or in cloud there was an instrument called a Cable Angle Indicator, nicknamed the 'Angle of Dangle'. This was connected to the tow-rope and the slightest movement caused the two illuminated white lines in the face of the dial to move.

On take-off, the glider was pulled by the tug aircraft until the rope became taut and the two took to the air. The glider pilot would choose the time to cast off.

The correct position for a glider whilst being towed was either slightly above the tug (high tow) or slightly below (low tow) but never directly behind, where the tug's slipstream would cause the glider to oscillate so violently that the tow-rope would very soon snap. The rope was attached to the tow aircraft and to the glider by a bolt and shackle device. The rope on the Horsa was three and three eighth inches in width, 350 feet long and was waterproof. Within the rope was a telephone wire which connected the glider pilot with the tug pilot.

Horsas – and the later Hamilcars – were fitted with large flaps, enabling them to dive at a comparatively steep angle if necessary, in order that they could be brought down to the ground quickly after being cast off.

All pilots wore Mae Wests in case of ditching, but were not equipped with parachutes.

In January 1941, 15 members of the RAF with experience of flying a Sailplane (one of the current aircraft at the time) were posted in as glider instructors. They had to quickly train themselves not only as instructors in glider flying but also to double as tug pilots.

The first 12 pupils were from the army but were later joined by sixteen RAF bomber pilots. One of the 12 army pilots was Corporal Strathdee of the 1st Dragoon Guards, later killed on Operation Freshman in Norway.

After some disagreement, it was decided at a meeting at the Air Ministry on 7th September 1940 that the glider pilots would come from the army. Some 80 army personnel with previous flying experience were selected and attached to the squadron's Army Co-operation Command for initial training on powered aircraft. The pupils varied considerably in their flying experience and in their medical and educational standards. The amount and method of training given by the army squadrons also varied considerably . In consequence, the general training progress was unsatisfactory. On 11th December 1940, at a meeting at the Air Ministry but attended by War Office representatives, the Chairman ruled that glider pilots would require the highest order of piloting skill and experience. It was agreed that glider pilots would have to go through Elementary Flying Training School and more advanced flying training, and that they should be airmen.

As a result of the meeting the 80 soldiers were transferred back to the army. This however proved to be extremely complicated and led to serious discontent amongst the personnel concerned. Individual cases were still under discussion in February 1942. A start was made in giving training to over a 100 RAF personnel. Many accepted this willingly but there was feeling amongst others that they had been 'down-graded'. This batch contained about 70 Canadians, and it was among these that the discontentment was most pronounced. In the early months, pep talks were necessary to restore morale, but some of the most prolific grumblers were released from glider training. They would undergo 10 weeks at RAF/EFTS on a course of a 100 plus hours on Tiger Moth aircraft and the Miles Magister. This would include navigation, meteorology, aerobatics, cross country flights and night flying, also 14 hours in the Link Trainer. The minimum pass mark was set at 80% in all subjects.

This was followed by 8 weeks at a Glider Training School flying Hotspurs, and a further 4 weeks converting to the Horsa and Hamilcar.

To qualify for the Glider Badge a pupil must:

a. Have completed a total of not less than fifteen hours on service gliders, of which not less than eight must have been solo.

b. Be able to fly a service type glider reliably and accurately by day in clear air and solely by instruments, and land consistently well.

c. Be able to execute correctly all normal manoeuvres appropriate to the service type of glider on which trained.

d. Have carried out successfully a cross-country flight on tow of not less than one hour's duration terminating with a release landing at an aerodrome other than the aerodrome of departure.

e. Be able to pinpoint his position whilst on tow.

f. Be able to make a spot landing from a height of three thousand foot, the arrival time to be within a period of one minute of the estimated time of arrival, the glider pilot having made all the preparations for the flight himself.

g. Be able to fly consistently well with the aid of instruments alone, whilst on tow.

h. Have passed satisfactory the examination test in subjects dealt with in the course by ground instruction.

On 24th August 1941, the Director of Plans held a meeting at the Air Ministry at which the following points were made:-

(i) Experience with Hotspurs indicated that it would not be necessary for glider pilots to be drawn from fully trained operational bomber pilots.

(ii) There would be great advantage if glider pilots were to fight as soldiers and able to take part in the land battle.

(iii) The provision of glider pilots by the RAF would immobilise a large number of pilots who could be usefully employed for other purposes, and there was no likelihood of the RAF being able to provide the 800 pilots required by the War Office at that time.

These points were put to the Army Council in an Air Council letter dated 29 August 1941, and the Army Council agreed in principle, on 24 September 1941, to provide glider pilots on condition that these were subtracted from the quota being supplied by the Army to the RAF for aircrew duties.

There was great tension between the Army and the RAF at this time, with RAF personnel frequently referring to Army personnel as 'Brown Jobs'.

In September 1941 the prototype Horsa was flown by George Errington from Fairey's Great West Aerodrome, now London Heathrow Airport; the tug aircraft was a Whitley.

For obvious reasons, gliders soon became know as 'matchboxes' by the 'glider-riders' or airborne troops.

German glider landed very near to Tavronitis bridge, Crete, 1941. [Alan Cooper]

Maleme aerodrome, Crete. [Alan Cooper]

CHAPTER 3

EARLY GLIDER OPERATIONS

In April 1941, Germany was looking for a base in the Eastern Mediterranean to conduct an air war against England and it was decided to invade the Greek island of Crete, 100 miles long and 40 miles wide. The invasion had the codename Operation *Merkur* (Mercury).

On 20th May 1941, Germany tried out her newly-formed glider assault regiment in an assault on Crete. Of the first 1,900 troops despatched, 750 were taken by glider, the rest by air landing transport and small sea craft. The gliders were detailed to attack the airfield at Maleme. Although this part of the operation went smoothly, for the paratroopers it was a different story, one in four being killed before he reached the ground. The gliders used were DFS-230s, 72-ft wingspan monoplanes with a length of 37 feet, capable of carrying 10 men and towed by JU52s. The German glider pilots landed in the mud and shingle, touching down wherever they could, ploughing through bushes, olive trees and shallow stone walls until they stopped.

Having made a successful landing, the gliders then came under heavy fire from the ground and the commanding officer of one of the senior glider detachments, Major Braun, was killed before leaving his glider as machine gun bullets tore into the canvas sides of the DFS 230 glider.

Eventually the island was taken by the Germans, but out of the 22,000 troops it took to do so some 6,000 were killed and many more wounded – losses of more than 30 per cent. Among those killed were several senior officers who had helped to form the division. Of the 500 transport aircraft employed, over half were destroyed.

Graves of German paratroopers, Crete. [Alan Cooper]

The targets on the morning of the 20th were Maleme and Canea and in the afternoon Retimo and Heralion. It took another 'Dunkirk' by the Royal Navy to get the troops out of Crete, over half the force of 42,500 being evacuated to Egypt. 17,500 men were killed, wounded or taken prisoner.

German losses were so great that Hitler forbade any more large-scale airborne assaults. Although airborne troops increased in Germany, the concept of a parachute division did not.

General Student dubbed Crete "the grave of the German paratroopers."

However, despite the losses, Germany had succeeded in taking Crete and Churchill wrote that this was a sad story. He was annoyed that he had allowed himself be swayed by arguments against the use of airborne troops. Gliders had been produced only on a small scale so far and there were practically no parachutists or glider pilots. A whole year had been lost, he confessed.

On 30th August 1941, the question of providing and training of glider pilots was written in a secret memo. It went on to say that the policy had been for glider pilots to be provided by Bomber Command. This was based on the belief that a high degree of skill was required to fly the larger gliders. However, experience with Hotspur gliders indicated that the standard required was not as high as had previously been thought.

Subject to confirmation of this by experience with Horsa gliders, it was proposed that pilots should be trained *ab initio* at Elementary Flying Training Schools from which they would pass to a special glider training unit. It was estimated that the course would take 14 to18 weeks and that provided an early decision was given, the training of 400 pilots could be completed by July/August 1942.

The source was another problem if they came from the army they could also be fighting soldiers as well as glider pilots, if they came from the RAF it would mean a large number of personnel being employed for no other role than as glider pilots. In view of the manpower requirements, it would be impossible to tie up RAF pilots for this role without affecting the expansion programme. The employment of Bomber pilots would immobilise a large proportion of the bomber force, and at a time when it was needed the most. The Air council decided that it would be a mutual advantage if the pilots came from the army and not the army and air force.

Pilots required for service in the Middle East, it was decided, should be trained in India from army and Indian sources.

On 14th November 1941, at a meeting at the War Cabinet, the question of tank-carrying gliders was discussed. The Hamilcar had a wingspan of 110 feet a weight of 36,000 lbs,

Crashed German glider, Crete, 1941. [Alan Cooper]

could carry a load of a seven and half-ton tank or two Bren gun carriers, had a range of 500 miles and needed 1500 yards to take off. The tug for this glider would be a Stirling bomber. The prototype was expected to be ready by December 1941.

A training programme began in December for 400 army glider pilots and a Gliding Training unit was divided into two training schools on the 1st December. Later this expanded to five, along with two operational Training Units and a Glider pilot instructors school.

On the 21st December, a Glider Pilot Regiment was formed from volunteers. Lt-Col Rock was appointed commanding officer of the 1st Battalion and in January 1942, forty officers and men were sent to an RAF Elementary Flying School for flying training. One of the volunteers was Major, later Brigadier George Chatterton, a former pre-war RAF pilot. After an accident in 1935 he was discharged from the RAF but recalled for ground duties at the start of WWII. He then joined the army and went to France. After evacuation from Dunkirk, he volunteered for the GPR was accepted and appointed to be second in command under Rock. The glider pilots, as well as flying the glider, had to be fully trained soldiers who could fight on the ground after landing. Another recruited by General Browning was Lieutenant Ian Murray who had served in the Grenadier Guards with Browning. He was to make the rank of lieutenant colonel and command the second battalion the Glider Pilot Regiment.

The question of the type of aircraft suitable to be used for towing was also a contentious subject. The Whitley, Hector and Master were pressed into service. The Hector and Master had been used to tow the Hotspur glider but were not suitable for towing the larger and heavier Horsa.

In February 1942, Wg/Cdr Tom W. Kean, AFC of Flying Training Command, who had begun his RAF career as a carpenter rigger in 1925 and qualified as a pilot in 1933, was given the task of opening five Glider Training Schools and a Heavy Glider Conversion Unit. Thame, Croughton, Weston-on-the Green, Stoke Orchard and Shobden were all operating by June, and the Heavy Unit at Brize Norton by July. He became, and remained, the Chief Instructor at Brize Norton until March 1944, then at North Luffenham, where the Heavy Conversion Unit moved in August 1944.

On 29th April 1942, the establishment of an Airborne Division was decided. It would consist of a parachute brigade, a glider-borne brigade and a few dozen special gliders to carry light tanks. It would be commanded by the 41-year-old Major General Frederick Browning, husband of novelist Daphne du Maurier. Direct comparisons were made between a British and German Airborne Divisions.

The British would consist of:

Headquarters Airborne Division

38 Wing RAF (Parachute Exercise Squadron and Glider Exercise Squadron.

Two Parachute Brigades each of three battalions with a brigade strength of 2,000.

One Air Landing Brigade

Divisional Troops

Glider Pilot Regiment (Glider Pilots)

Regimental Headquarters and six companies (Total 800 approx.)

Total divisional strength approx 10,800.

In comparison the Germans had a total divisional strength of 18,000 and 6,600 parachutists; in Britain there were 3,500. Air landing troops numbered 2,000 in Germany and 1,600 in Britain.

In June 1942 it was decided to use the Albemarle, a fast medium bomber with a tricycle undercarriage, as a troop carrier and glider tug.

In October 1942, John Rock, the man who had done so much to progress the airborne cause, and in particular the glider, was tragically killed. The rope on the Hotspur glider he was flying broke in flight and as Colonel Rock attempted to land the glider in the dark it struck a telegraph pole and the sandbag which was used for ballast broke free, crushing Rock and his co-pilot. Rock's injuries were so severe that he died two days later.

On 19th May 1942, Tom Kean had his first flight in a Hotspur at Ringway: 45 minutes flying blind, testing the use of two adapted petrol gauges for maintaining position on the tug. The flight was flown with a pre-war Austrian expert, Robert Kronfeld, Chief Test pilot at the Glider Development Unit at Ringway. He flew again on the 17th June, testing equipment and lights on the tug. A few days later he flew his first solo flights, first with a light load and a then a full load.

It was decided to set up the Heavy Glider Conversion Unit, which initially was expected to be formed at Shobdon under the Army Co-Operation Command. Early in 1942, Flying Training Command was told to plan and consider the practicability and feasibility of the complete flying training of the Army pilots going from Elementary Flying Training School to Heavy Glider Conversion Units.

The advantage of one continuous phased programme under one command were immediate apparent. During the planning stage Tom Kean flew to Shobdon before it became a glider training school and reported back to the C-in-C's conference at the Air Ministry that he thought Shobdon was quite unsuitable for an Heavy Glider Conversion Unit. Later Little Rissington was also mentioned but found to be unsuitable, particularly for night flying, as it was often affected by low cloud. Also a hump in the middle made it impossible to see if all the take-off run was clear.

The Air Officer Administration rang the C-in-C and told him that Kean thought that Shobdon was unsuitable. Everyone at the meeting thought that Kean had blighted his career, but when the C-in-C came in with his Senior Air Staff Officer (SASO) he listened to what Kean had to say and then asked him what he thought was the most suitable place. The reply was 'Brize Norton.'

In response, the Commander-in-Chief simply said, 'Examine it.'

In 1942, the nucleus of the HGCU had formed at Shrewton under the Army Air Corps, but in 1943 transferred to Brize Norton under Flying Training Command.

On 15th July 1942, RAF Brize Norton was to acquire a unique role when it became No.1 Heavy Glider Conversion Unit, with an aircraft establishment of 56 Horsas and 34 Whitley Mk V tug aircraft.

On 23rd August, Tom Kean visited Brize Norton and had his first flight in a Horsa and later the same day flew a Whitley, towing a glider. On the 28th he again visited the HGCU at night and flew two night-trips in a Horsa and as before, but at night, he flew a Whitley, again towing a Horsa. The Chief Instructor at the time, Peter May, was in the back of the Whitley and left Tom to it. The entry in Tom's log book recorded: "Full marks to May, who sat so far back that he could not have helped me had it been necessary."

They had never flown together before and Tom wondered if he would have been quite so trusting had the roles been reversed. Somehow, Tom doubted it, but Peter greatly impressed Tom.

There were frequent accidents soon after training began. Some of the Whitley tug pilots became very reluctant to fly at night because of the dangerous situations which could develop soon after take-off. There were times when the glider climbed too quickly so that the tow ropes lifted the tail of the tug and so caused the Whitley to dive towards the ground, no matter how hard its pilot pulled back on the control column to raise the elevators. In an emergency, if he reacted quickly enough, the tug pilot could reach across to the starboard side of the cockpit and release the tow-rope, but it did mean crash landing in total darkness. In August a number of Whitleys crashed either on take off and or soon afterwards.

On 2nd September a Miles Master DL 425 towing a Hotspur HH 518 glider crashed. The Master flew into the church steeple at Witney and the crew was killed; the Hotspur crew was unhurt.

In September 1942 crashes were common and morale was very low at Brize Norton.

Squadron Leader Reg Leach, with 700 flying hours and unaware of the existence of Horsa gliders, found himself in the right hand seat beside the first of 133 men of the Glider Pilot Regiment over a period of ten months in which he flew 137 hours 40 minutes during the day and 30 hours 50 minutes at night. It took a long time to build up such a tally on Horsas, as each flight took an average of only 25 minutes and many lasted only 10 minutes: take off, circuit, release, approach and land. After landing came a wait of 10 minutes while a tractor towed the glider back to the take-off point.

The Force was to quartered on Salisbury Plain near Netheravon aerodrome and its satellite at Shrewton, where the Glider Pilot Regiment was to be quartered.

With Rock's death, Chatterton took over the 1st Battalion of the Glider Pilot Regiment.

And so came, on 19th November 1942, the first British glider-borne operation: codename Freshman.

The Germans occupied Norway in April 1940 and immediately took over the Norsk Hydro Electric Company's heavy water plant at Vermork. It was vital that this plant was destroyed, as the Germans were working on atomic research with the aim of producing the first atomic bomb.

In September 1942 plans were being made for a glider-borne attack on the plant by volunteer specialist troops. The object of the operation was to destroy stocks of heavy hydrogen and to damage the hydroelectric works in Southern Norway. The area was mountainous, 80 miles from the west coast and 65 miles due west of Olso. The plant was built on a plateau of rock 1,000 feet above the valley bottom.

It was calculated that a party of 16 to 25 parachutists, allowing for casualties in the drop, would be sufficient to carry out the operation. Various methods of getting the troops there were discussed, by flying boat was one an by parachute was another, although there did not appear to any suitable dropping zones within 15 miles of the objective. Dropping men into water in special waterproof suits was yet another idea, but this was discarded for a number of reasons. Dropping into snow was another concept, but this would mean waiting until January 1943 and would require all the members of the party to be expert skiers.

Delivery by glider seemed possible, although no suitable areas had been found for landings. The conclusion, on 13th November 1942, was that the only practical ways were by flying boat or a skiing party introduced by glider or parachute when the country was under thick snow from January onwards. However, it was eventually decided to use two Horsa gliders towed by two Halifax aircraft. The best time would be between the 18th and 26th November. The trip involved flying some 400 miles in the dark.

The Halifaxes were from 295 and 297 Squadrons and the personnel code name was 'Washington Party'. The party was under the control of Gr/Cpt Tom B. Cooper DFC and Squadron Leader P.B.N Davis, the adviser on glider tactics and the supervision of the training of the glider pilots. The first two glider pilots chosen for this operation were St/Sgt Malcolm Frederick Strathdee, formerly of the 1st Dragoon Guards (one of the first 16 ex-RAF Bomber pilots who volunteered in February 1941) and Sgt Peter Doig, who were to fly glider DP-349, a Mk 1 Horsa towed by Halifax A-Able, flown by Squadron Leader A.M.B Wilkinson, DFC. The second glider HS-114 would have two former bomber pilots at the controls – Pilot Officer Norman Arthur Davies, aged 28, from Melbourne, Australia (also one of the first four glider pilots trained) and Pilot Officer Herbert John Fraser, also 28, from Bendigo, Australia, both members of the Royal Australian Air Force. They would be towed by Halifax W7801 B-Baker flown by F/Lt Arthur Roland Parkinson, age 26, from Lachine, Province of Quebec, Canada with Pilot Officer Garard Walter Sewell De Gency, who was only 20 years of age. Gr/Cpt Cooper was down to fly with Squadron Leader Wilkinson on this operation. The gliders would carry between them 30 Royal Engineers from 9th Field Company (Airborne) and 261st Field Park Company (Airborne), who were stationed at Bulford Camp. In October they were posted to the Glider Training School at Shobden for training for the operation.

The party would take off from RAF Skitten, a satellite of RAF Wick and the nearest airfield in the UK to Norway, but still 400 miles from the Drop Zone (DZ).

On 16th November the two Halifaxes arrived at Crimond airfield from RAF Waddington, along with three gliders. However, the Halifaxes were found to be unserviceable and it would take some hours to put the problems right. On the 17th they set off for RAF Skitten. It would appear that there was a problem with Parkinson's crew, as Squadron Leader Wilkinson's flight engineer Sgt James Falconer, aged 20, was transferred to Parkinson's crew at the last moment.

At 1740 (5.40pm) on the 19th November, S/Ldr Wilkinson, with Gr/Cpt Cooper aboard as second pilot, took off from Skitten, towing Horsa DP-349, flown by Strathdee and Doig with 15 Royal Engineers aboard. The officer in charge of the RE party, Lt Methven, only aged 20, was already the holder of the George Medal. The second Halifax, piloted by Flt Lt Parkinson and Glider HS-114 flown Davies and Frazer took off at 1810 (6.10pm) carrying 14 Royal Engineers. At 23.41 (11.41pm) the operations room at Wick received a signal from Parkinson, asking for a course back to base. He was given a direction finding over the North Sea. At 23.55 (11.55pm) a signal came in from Wilkinson's Halifax saying that his glider had been released into the sea. The radio direction finding showed him to be over mountains of southern Norway but the glider had been released many miles from the landing zone area.

The Rebecca receiver in the Halifax had become unserviceable, which meant navigating with the use of maps and in thick fog. Finding the intended release area proved impossible. With the Halifax now running on reserve fuel tanks and being affected by severe icing, both Halifax and glider began to lose height near Stavanger. The rope was released and DP 349 crash landed in the snow-covered mountains at Fylgjedal. Incorrect maps of the area in Norway were one of the reasons why this release failed. Lt Methven, the leader of the Royal Engineers and

The very first intake of the Glider Pilot Regiment, including Sergeant Peter Doig. [Alec Waldron]

five other members of his party, along with both glider pilots Strathee and Doig, were killed in the crash. Four others were seriously injured. The injured were taken away by the Germans to Stavanger hospital, where they given poison by doctors before being thrown into the sea, weighed down by heavy stones.

The second Halifax, flown by Parkinson, which had radioed for a route back to base, was troubled by icing and both tug and glider began to lose height until the ice-covered rope eventually snapped and the glider crashed into the mountains north of Helegoland. Both glider pilots Davies and Fraser were killed, as was one of the Engineers. The remaining 14 survived, but were soon captured by the Germans, who arrived quickly and later shot them.

The Halifax managed to clear the first mountain tops but collided head-on with the next range. All the crew were killed and buried very crudely by the Germans. When the Norwegians asked if they could give them a proper burial, their request was refused and they were forbidden to go near the graves. A Norwegian report said that the pilot was believed to be a New Zealander – at any rate he had a very dark complexion.

On 25th January 1943 Strathdee and Doig were recommended for the DFM by Major General Browning; this was endorsed by Admiral Lord Louis Mountbatten on 19th March 1943. However, neither of their headstones has the DFM marked on it, and as they were killed in action it must be presumed it was not awarded. Only the Victoria Cross or a Mention in Despatches can be awarded posthumously. Strathdee had been an RAF pilot and wore RAF wings on his battledress and not the wings of a glider pilot. The story is that the Air Ministry refused his plea to fly in the Spanish War and so he resigned his commission in the RAF.

In 1945, troops of the 1st Airborne Division Engineers flew to Norway to discover what had happened three years earlier. The bodies that had been buried so badly and without any care were exhumed and re-buried with full military honours in cemeteries in Norway.

The Germans involved in the murders were rounded up and brought to trial before a War Graves Tribunal in Oslo. A number of them were found guilty. Two were sentenced to death and two to life imprisonment, including the officer commanding all German forces in Norway.

Gr/Cpt Tom Cooper was killed testing a jet aircraft on 5th March 1949, just before his 41st birthday. He was buried in Boscombe Down Cemetery.

On 19th December 1942, Tom Kean took over as Chief Instructor from Peter May. His deputies were F/Lt Hughes and F/Lt Hill (both later became squadron leaders). Peter May went to 296 Squadron from Brize Norton and worked closely with George Chatterton in preparing the invasion of Sicily. Sadly, this was an operation he was not to return from.

The 31st December 1942 saw Squadron Leader Reg Leach's shortest flight – and nearly his last. The Horsa in which he was instructing, with Sgt Russell as his pupil, was being towed by an Albemarle aircraft at a height of just 300 feet when the rope broke and they were forced to land in a ploughed field just beyond the boundary of RAF Brize Norton.

Reg's longest flight lasted for two hours and involved both navigation and cloud flying without the benefit of a two-angle indicator, which was not then fitted to the HGCU Horsas. This was on 19th April 1943, with Sgt Clarke under instruction. They were towed up through 10/10 cloud at a point north-east of Didcot, flew in a north-north-westerly direction, then east and finally south-south-east before descending and breaking cloud near Luton. At this time there was no means of communication between Horsa and Whitley and so they were unable to direct the pilot of the tug, F/Sgt Symonds. Fortunately, he was a good map reader and navigator and could recognise their position and tow them back to base. At this time, S/Ldr Leach decided to give some of his glider pilots navigational exercises after separating from the tug. With only two or three persons on board, the Horsa had a very flat angle of glide and at an indicated 80mph lost height at about 350 feet per minute. It was therefore possible to release from the tug at a height of about 7,000 feet when about 20 miles out and arrive back at Brize Norton with height to spare for a safe approach and landing. He did this several times, map-reading his way home on each occasion.

How high the gliders could be towed was also something worth investigating. On the 2nd December 1942, accompanied by Sgt Hotchkin, Reg was released at a height of 11,600ft, while still climbing, which is believed to be a record at that time. On the 26th January 1943, this time with Sgt Higgins under instruction, Reg reached 12,100 feet, a new record and thought to be unsurpassed by a Whitley/Horsa combination. The entry in Sqn Ldr Leach's log book read: "Very cold. –15C."

As they progressed, glider pilots were given loads to carry. They were sometimes 'dud' loads of heavy concrete blocks, lashed to the floor, but mostly they were 'live' loads provided by the Ox & Bucks Light Infantry. A full load of 35 men unarmed was the equivalent of 28 armed men. The men were lined up at attention and then marched briskly into the glider. They sat on benches along both sides of the fuselage, aft of the door. There were no parachutes for them or for the two-man crew. On one occasion Reg Leach saw men standing at the open door and looking downwards as they swayed away in a climb. The pilots enjoyed a favourite prank when carrying a full 'live' load. After releasing at a distance from Brize Norton at 7,000 ft and killing time before landing, the pilot would dive the glider to gain speed and then pull back on the control column to go into a climb. As the speed fell away he would gently point the nose downwards to create a little negative 'g' and all the men behind would rise slowly towards the top of the cabin. Then, with hard pull on the control column, they would thump back into their seats!

The stalling speeds were as low as a 43mph when light and 55mph when heavy, using full flap, so thanks to these huge flaps there was a possible speed range between 60mph and 190 mph when approaching to land.

S/Ldr Leach left 1 HGCU on the 20th July 1943.

In February 1944, the HGCU moved to RAF North Luffenham. Tom Kean was still the Chief Instructor until August 1944 when he handed over to S/Ldr John Sidebottom and left for a course at the Empire Central Flying School, Hullavington.

CHAPTER 4

FURTHER GLIDER OPERATIONS

In 1943 the Halifax began to come into operation as a glider tug, replacing the Whitley, and with the Germans beaten in North Africa thoughts began for the invasion of Sicily. Major General Hopkinson commanded the 1st Air Landing Brigade in which there were two companies of glider pilots under Lt-Col Chatterton and Major M. Willoughby. In April 1943, Colonel Chatterton was told that there was to be a glider-borne night assault on Sicily on 9/10th July 1943. This alarmed Chatterton, as there was so little time to prepare and his pilots were so inexperienced. The role of tugs and gliders would be shared with the Americans, and it was a case of take it or leave it for Chatterton – if he did not go along with this, he was to be relieved of his command.

The Americans were using the small Waco CG-4A, renamed the Hadrian FR-556 with an all up weight of 7,500lbs which could carry 13 troops plus two pilots, one Jeep and six men, or one 75mm Howitzer gun and six men. It was made of tubular metal and fabric-covered wood, which was easy to strip and store. The first of its type arrived in the UK in February 1943 and underwent its first trial flights on 9th February 1943. It was known that the Dakota could tow the Waco and that there would be no problems with other aircraft. The Americans had originally ordered 26,000 of these gliders, which was subsequently reduced to 6,000. In July 1943 the first Hadrian glider was towed across the Atlantic under the code name Operation 'Voodoo' – the first of over 1,000 supplied to the RAF – the remainder being delivered by sea in packing cases.

It was said that the Hadrian was designed to take the General Purpose vehicle (Jeep) which would fit exactly in its fuselage. The nose of the glider was hinged for direct loading of equipment and unloaded by the use of two small ramps.

The planned involvement for airborne troops in Operation 'Husky' – the invasion of Sicily – was for the British 1st Air Landing Brigade to arrive in gliders behind the invasion beaches on the south-eastern coast, capture a bridge called the Ponte Grande, near Syracuse, assist in taking the port and silence a coastal battery.

The American pilots of the 51st /52nd Troop Carrier Wings who were to fly in the American troops, and also tow most of the British gliders, had little experience of night flying and were in the main, pilots from civil aviation backgrounds, few having seen action or flown through flak. The approach route, designed to avoid the anti-aircraft guns of the Allied naval convoys carrying the sea-borne assault troops, involved three sharp turns while the pilots were flying over the sea in the dark.

The British were to use the Horsa glider, which could carry 31 troops and had a large Perspex-covered cockpit with four clear view panels, one in front of each pilot and one on each side, which could be opened. In the cockpit on a central panel was an air speed indicator, artificial horizon and rate of climb indicator; underneath was a turn and bank indicator and altimeter; on the right hand of the pilot a VHF TR9 radio was fitted. The undercarriage was a tricycle with a nose wheel and two main wheels on two separate triangular frames of tube contraction, which pivoted on brackets attached to the

The cockpit of a Hadrian glider. [Alec Waldron]

fuselage. This could be released after take off by pulling a release control in the cockpit, the landing being made on a wooden metal-faced skid under the fuselage and a small tail-skid.

The flying speed was between 130 and 140 knots, depending on the tug being used and the load being carried. The landing speed was 70 to 80 knots, once again depending on the load being carried. The troops sat on plywood seats, 23 facing each other down the sides of the glider with four at the at the rear facing forward. Three more could be seated on the starboard side, opposite the forward loading door, making 31 in all. Originally 2,400 Horsas were ordered, but by June 1943 this was reduced to 1,250 and thereafter by 20 a month. The Horsa could carry two jeeps or one 6-pound gun or one 40-mm gun. The rope used for towing was about 350 feet in length and attached to strong points in the centre of the glider.

The art of glider 'snatching' started in the USA before WWII with a system developed to allow an aircraft to snatch a mailbag from the ground without landing. A small cable winch was fitted inside the fuselage of an aircraft with the cable running through guides to an external extended arm and attached to a hook. When the hook engaged a loop on a mailbag on the ground, the bag was 'snatched' into the air – a simple system but the one that was developed to become glider snatching. This would prove invaluable in retrieving gliders from operational zones. It was later used successfully in Europe to recover crashed gliders from Normandy.

In February 1943, 295 Squadron received their first Halifax V aircraft.

It was soon realised that Horsa gliders would have to be used in large numbers because of the limited resources of the Waco. The problem now was how to transport them to North Africa in sufficient numbers? To move them by ship was not an ideal solution. They would take up a great deal of space in the hold of a ship – space that was needed for heavier and more urgent cargo. However, towing them all the way seemed a doubtful proposition. It was once again Gr/Cpt

Tom Cooper and S/Ldr Wilkinson, both involved in Operation Freshman, who proved with a series of 10-hour cross-country flights around the UK that the Halifax could tug an unloaded Horsa 1,400 miles and still land with fuel in its tanks. Twenty three Halifaxes, fitted with bomb-bay fuel tanks, were prepared and taken on charge by 295 Squadron at Porthreath. The gliders were picked up from Netheravon and flown to Porthreath.

For the trip, each glider carried three glider pilots, because of the physical and mental strain of maintaining the right position to prevent the tow-rope snapping over such a long distance. They had to deliver 30 Horsas to Salle, near Casablanca. The first tug/glider combo to take off was attacked by a fighter. With the tow-rope parted, the Halifax was shot down and the glider ditched. The glider crew, Major Alastair Cooper and St/Sgts Dennis Hall and Anthony Antonopoulos were safely picked up later by the Royal Navy within twenty four hours of ditching. Cooper was soon once more at the controls of a glider, and this time landed safely in North Africa.

The second combo to take off was successful, the glider being flown by Colonel Chatterton, Sgts P. Attwood and H. Flynn. The codename for this glider delivery was Turkey-Buzzard.

It was an unwritten law among glider/tug crews that if the tug aircraft had a problem he should always tell the glider pilots before casting off the tow-rope and order the glider to cast off before releasing the rope.

On the 7th of July, 27 gliders had arrived at Sale but the next stage of the journey involved 350 miles to the airfield at Froha and then on to Kairouan, which entailed flying over mountains as high as 7,000 feet. The first arrived on the 28th June, twelve days before the invasion of Sicily was to begin.

A setback came on 20th May 1943 when Air Commodore Sir Nigel Norman Bt, AOC No.38 Wing, was killed when the Lockheed aircraft in which he was travelling, bound for North Africa, crashed when the port engine failed. The aircraft had already landed on one occasion for instrument repairs. Sir Nigel had been lying on a portable bed, the only area left available to him, when the aircraft hit the ground. He was thrown violently against its side and killed immediately when his neck was broken.

Allegedly, he was once asked "Why must you always want 100%?" by a high ranking officer. His reply was not recorded, but the way he conducted himself implies that he believed it the only way to achieve victory, and would perhaps have been his reply if it had been recorded.

Although the Horsas arrived safely, there were still not enough of them. The US-built Wacos

Two Hotspur gliders. [Alec Waldron]

would have to be used to make up the shortfall – and in great numbers.

It was down to the British glider pilots to locate and assemble them at Oran airfield. Thirty were assembled and training undertaken by very inexperienced American glider pilots.

The first operation, codename Operation Ladbroke, took place on 9/10th July. It was carried out entirely by glider-borne troops, led by Brigadier Hicks. Their objective was the Ponte Grande bridge near Syracuse. They were to be borne by 147 Waco and Horsa gliders towed by 109 Dakotas flown by American pilots plus seven Halifaxes and 21 Albemarles flown by pilots from the RAF. They were to release between 9:10 and 10:30pm, the Wacos from 1,900 feet and Horsas from 4,000 feet.

There were many problems to surmount. Seven gliders failed to clear the North African coast and those that did discovered that over the Mediterranean, gale-force winds had made the sea very rough with white wave tops of foam. Despite some being blown off course, 90% reached the south-eastern tip of Sicily then swung Northeast on a prescribed zig-zag course in search of the glider release point off the coast near Syracuse.

Up to 115 aircraft, carrying 1,200 men started on that last leg of the journey, but few found the proper release point. Of the 147 aircraft carrying the paratroopers that set out from Tunisia, 23 failed to return and 37 were badly damaged, 81 men were killed, 16 were missing presumed dead and 132 wounded. Those killed included 57 glider pilots.

Nevertheless, the use of gliders was thought to have been worthwhile and much had been learned for future airborne operations in which gliders would be involved.

During the main assault, 54 gliders landed in Sicily, but only 12 on their correct landing zones. A further 69 landed in the sea with a loss of 326 men, when the gliders were released too early, because, it was said at the time, the American pilots in the C47s decided they could not cope with the heavy flak and prematurely turned back towards North Africa. It is also said that resentment was so high among the British troops towards the American tug pilots that when they got back to Tunisia they were confined to camp to avoid a lynching.

One of those released to soon was Colonel Chatterton with Brigadier Hicks aboard. When he realised he was not going to make the shore, he made for a black patch ahead, which he hoped was an island. When he had almost reached it, his glider came under fire and then a searchlight found him. Chatterton realised he was making for a steep cliff. He put the glider into a stalling turn and plunged downwards. The glider struck the waves. While still under the umbrella of the searchlight and subsequent machine gun fire, they decided to swim for it and left the wrecked and waterlogged glider. They reached the beach safely and joined up with the SAS, taking 150 Italians prisoner. Colonel Chatterton was awarded a DSO for this operation. Out of this came the policy that all glider pilots should be capable of handling all types of arms and of fighting on the ground as efficiently as the troops they were transporting.

Major-General Hopkinson, commander of the first Airborne Division and planner of Operation Ladbroke was one of the first to fall in the water. He hung onto a piece of wreckage until picked up by HMS *Keren*.

Another problem for those that managed to survive the weather was the anti-aircraft fire from German and Italian gunners who succeeded in scattering the formations far and wide.

On 13th July the next glider operation to Sicily began, Operation Fustian, the objective to take a bridge at Primosole, over the River Simeto. A small force was to take the guns of the Royal Artillery in Horsa and Waco gliders, with US paratroopers being taken in Dakotas.

The operation went wrong when Allied naval forces mistakenly opened fire on the force and a number of aircraft were shot down. The naval forces had recently been subjected to attacks by enemy aircraft and thought they were just defending their patch. It was night time and hazy over the coast and a considerable number of the airborne force were off course and flying in the danger zone – a belt of five miles wide running along the coast of Sicily. Most of the gliders reached the shore, where the landing zones were clearly visible, although according to one glider pilot, St/Sgt White, the enemy anti-aircraft fire with tracer was far brighter than the landing markers set out by the Independent Parachute Company, who were acting as Pathfinders for the first time. White was able to land successfully 27 minutes late, landing through the fire without casualties only a hundred yards from the bridge, the gun and jeep he carried were both in action the following day.

One of the casualties was S/Ldr Wilkinson, an expert in the art of glider towing who had taken part in the first attempted glider operation to Norway. He met his death over the hills of Sicily flying a Halifax with a Horsa in tow to attack the bridge at Ponte Grande.

Another fatality was Major Alastair Cooper. The tug that was towing him was hit at 500 feet by anti-aircraft fire and blew up in the air. In attempting to land his glider, he hit the side of a hill not far from the target. With him was Lt Col Charles Crawford, the man in charge of the force of artillery that was being dropped and his headquarters staff.

In August/September 1943, glider ferrying operations to North Africa under the operational code name 'Elaborate' continued, with 295 Squadron based at Porthreath being once again the towing squadron.

F/O Arthur Norman, who had already taken part in several successful long tows in this period of Operation 'Elaborate', was flying Halifax HS-102 and towing a Horsa glider in the area of the Bay of Biscay when he was intercepted by no less than eight JU88 fighters, which manoeuvred into position to mount an attack. As cloud cover could not be reached, the glider pilot, Lt J.R. Prout and his crew of Sgts Hill and Flynn asked to cast off in a pre-arranged plan and successfully ditched their glider into the sea. The area was WSW of Cape Finisterre and the time 12:07pm. The enemy fighter unit was from 13/KG and the JU88 that attacked Norman was flown by Oblt Dieter Meister.

The attack on the Halifax lasted fifteen minutes, during which time Norman succeeded, with skilful airmanship and coolness, in enabling his rear gunner Sgt Grant to bring effective fire on the enemy aircraft, one of which was seen to break away with smoke pouring from it. It would appear that it had to ditch, as the pilot was seen

Two Albemarle glider tugs. [Alec Waldron]

later wallowing in the sea in the area of the attack.

During the attack, Norman continued to throw the Halifax all over the sky, but despite this the aircraft was badly damaged, with the wings, both starboard engines, fuel tanks and tail unit all having been hit by rockets from the attacking JU88s. A piece of the starboard inner propeller smashed through the fuselage and into the aircraft. A large hole appeared in the starboard wing and petrol poured out, leaving a white trail behind. Inside the Halifax, the emergency rations were scattered all over the floor and the flight engineer's parachute was shot to pieces.

Suddenly, they were able to slip into the protection of a cloudbank and assess the damage, and they realised that during the evasive action by Norman, the tow-rope had been attached. This had helped to keep the offending fighters at bay and became quite a lethal weapon if they came too close.

With its short runways, a landing at Gibraltar was out of the question, so they decided to make for their original destination of Sale in Morocco. Miraculously, they successfully reached Sale, and Norman was promptly recommended for and later awarded the DFC and Sgt Grant, the rear gunner, the DFM.

The ditched Horsa crew was soon picked up by Air Sea Rescue, thanks to the accurate plotting and signalling to base of their position by Norman and his crew.

Dramatic pictures, taken by attacking German aircraft, show Norman's Halifax under attack and finally, Prout's Horsa glider ditched in the sea. [S/Ldr C Goss]

CHAPTER 5

AIRBORNE INVASION

In May 1943, the 6th Airborne Division was formed under the command of Major-General R.N. Gale DSO, OBE, MC, with Lieutenant General F.A.M Browning in overall command.

It was the middle of 1943 that training of airborne troops for the invasion of Europe began, along with the arrival of the United States 101st Airborne Division in August 1943.

The 6th Airborne was stationed at Salisbury Plain and formed along with the 3rd and 5th Parachute Brigades. New parachute battalions were formed from county regiments on a regional basis. The glider troops of the 6th Brigade were the 2nd (Airborne) Battalion Ox & Bucks Light Infantry, the 1st Battalion Royal Ulster Rifles and the 12th (Airborne) Battalion Devonshire Regiment.

Glider training went on steadily with larger and larger formations taking to the air. By November 1943, exercises with as many as 40 gliders taking part were successfully mounted and the methods of marshalling larger formations and putting them on the right route for the targets was being worked out, and now could be tried on a reasonable scale.

In January 1944, Air Vice Marshal L.N. Hollinghurst CB, CBE, DFC was appointed to command the squadrons of the Royal Air Force, now in several groups. No 38 Wing had now expanded and became 38 Group. This meant that some Stirling and Halifax squadrons from Bomber Command could be made available for glider towing.

This expanded to such a degree that on 24th April 1944 an entire airborne division – the 6th – took to the air thanks to the united efforts of the Royal Air Force and the United States Troop Carrying Command. They did not know it at the time, but this was a dress rehearsal for what was to happen six weeks later – the invasion of Normandy on 6th June 1944.

In August 1943, the area of Caen, Normandy, had been studied for the use of airborne troops. For various reasons, parachute troops were used in most instances instead of gliders, but where areas were deemed suitable for glider landings, they were to be used instead of parachutists.

It was decided that 38 Group would not be large enough to carry the planned invasion force, so another airborne group was formed – No 46 – on 17th January 1944, under the command of Air Commodore L.A. Fiddament CB, OBE, DFC and equipped with Dakotas from the United States.

Number 38 Group had 264 aircraft, 150 Horsa and 70 Hamilcar gliders, and 46 Group five squadrons of 150 aircraft and 200 Horsa gliders, making a total of 414 aircraft and 420 gliders, which would take the 6th Airborne Division to Normandy on Operations 'Tonga' and 'Mallard'.

There was still a need for a larger glider to carry heavy equipment. General Aircraft Ltd of Hanworth Air Park, Feltham, tendered successfully for the Air Ministry Specification X27/40 contract and work commenced on the GAL Hamilcar in May 1941. They first produced a half-scale airframe, which was towed by a Whitley, but the aircraft suffered a heavy landing and was written off. The full size aircraft was too large to be flown off the park at Hanworth, so it

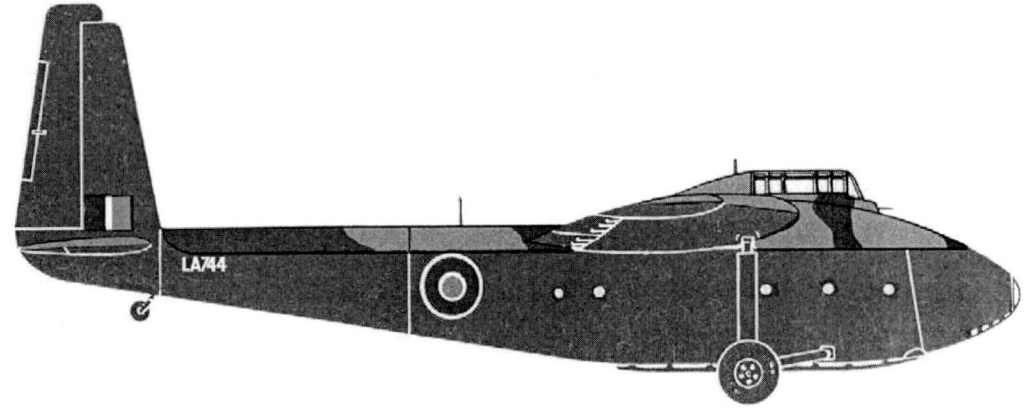

The Hamilcar. [George Burn]

was taken by road to Yorkshire to be assembled and test flown in March 1942. The Lancaster was a suitable tug aircraft, but the RAF could not spare Lancasters for this role. As the engines of the Stirling tended to overheat, the only other aircraft suitable was the Halifax.

The Hamilcar was a high wing monoplane of wooden construction with plywood and fabric. It was 68ft long, had a 110ft wingspan and a loaded weight of 36,000lbs. Unlike the Horsa, it was a transport glider, able to carry two Bren gun carriers or one seven and half ton Mk VII tank. It had a crew of two pilots, sitting in tandem, with dual controls set on top of the fuselage above the main cargo compartments. The nose of the glider hinged sideways to allow vehicles to be driven straight in and out. The bulk of the glider was built at the Birmingham Railway Carriage & Wagon Company, the Co-operative Wholesale Society Ltd and AC Motors Ltd and erected at RAF Lyneham and RAF North Luffenham.

On a training flight from Tarrant Rushton, a Hamilcar missed the runway and demolished a building. The rapid deceleration caused the tank being carried to be catapulted forward at a speed of about 85mph, which surely gave it the land speed record for a British tank!

Early in 1944, the Halifax designated for tug duties was modified for the dropping of parachutists in addition to its glider towing airborne duties. The mid-upper turret was removed, a glider towing hook was fitted under the rear turret and a paratroop hatch cut in the floor.

In April 1944 at Tarrant Rushton they were busy with mass take-offs of aircraft and gliders and a demonstration was arranged for General Eisenhower, during which Halifax/glider combinations were made airborne in minutes and after release came into land accurately, and in a small area.

For a considerable time up to the Autumn of 1944, there was a basic training output of 40 army glider crews per month. Personnel involved at this time were:

	RAF Personnel
1 Elementary Flying Training School (4 flights)	400
2 Glider Training Schools	1,300
1 Heavy Glider Conversion Unit	1,400
Total	**3,100**

On 8th May 1944, General Eisenhower designated the 5th June 1944 as D-Day.

Mass take-offs of Halifax/Horsa or Halifax/Hamilcar combinations were practised as a good discipline. Gliders were placed along the runway while the Halifaxes were positioned each side of the runway, connected by their towropes to their individual gliders. On being given the 'go' signal, the Halifax moved down the runway, taking up the slack in the tow-rope, and after checking with the glider pilot they were ready for take off. The Halifax began to roll down the runway with the glider lifting off and moving into the high tow position and then the next combination began to move into take-off position and started to roll. So it went until all had taken off. The average take off time was 45 seconds.

In May 1944, the King, Queen and Princess Elizabeth watched a mass glider landing. Also in May 1944 came an instruction for Training and Employment of Glider Pilots.

Organisation

(1) In order that Glider Pilots, who are highly trained air specialists and not first line troops, be properly controlled and employed after they reach the ground and have discharged their duties as glider pilots, they must be organised into units.

(2) Taking the squadron as the basic unit, the Glider Pilots are divided up, for purposes of control, into flights. Thus, a Troop Carrier Group can organise a Glider Pilot Organisation similar to a ground force company with the Group Glider Officer in the Troop Carrier Group as Glider Pilot company Commander.

(3) For purposes of administrative and tactical control, a headquarters higher than Group will be set up, comparable to the Infantry Battalion headquarters, and the personnel for this will be set up by the Wing Glider Officer. Since it is not contemplated that these Glider Pilot Units will remain in the combat area more than a few days, a complete staff is not necessary for the successful operation of the Glider Pilot Organisation. Where the tactical situation warrants, the Wing Glider Officer will take in a jeep and personnel suitable for his needs.

Action

(1) Immediately upon landing, all glider pilots will assist in unloading the supplies and/ or equipment in their gliders.

(2) All glider pilots will then proceed, with the troops in their gliders, to the assembly area of the airborne unit they carried and upon arrival at the airborne assembly area, the

Glider pilots in the cockpit of a Horsa glider. [Alan Cooper]

glider pilots will assemble into their organisations, then proceed as a unit, under the command of their own Senior Glider Pilot, to the Glider Pilot Wing assembly area.

(3) Flight and Squadron Commanders will have in their possession, prior to take-off, a complete and accurate roster of all the glider pilots in their particular unit. When the units have assembled and moved to the Glider Pilot Wing assembly area, all Glider Pilots not present or accounted for, either as killed, wounded, prisoner of war or down en-route, will be considered as a missing in action and will be carried as such. Upon the return of the Glider pilot, so carried, to his unit, the Unit Commander will appoint a board of three commissioned officers, at least one of whom will be of field grade, to investigate all such absences, and if a satisfactory explanation is not forthcoming, disciplinary action will be taken against subject officer.

(4) The Glider Pilot Wing Headquarters should come in with the first glider lift and set up in an assembly area previously designated at the Glider Pilot briefings. Upon arrival at the Glider Pilot Wing assembly area, the Glider Pilot Group Commanders, having previously determined the status of their organisation (effective strength, equipment and supplies) will report to the Glider Pilot Wing Commander, and will submit a report twice daily thereafter until evacuated.

(5) Having determined the status of his Wing, the Wing Glider Officer will report to a previously designated staff officer of the Airborne Commander in the area, charged with the responsibility of co-ordinating glider pilot activities. Upon the establishment of the Airborne Division's Command Post, the Glider Pilot Wings will come under the control of the Division Commander. Each wing will, at this time, send a liaison officer to the Division Command Post until such time as his particular wing is evacuated to its home stations.

(6) During this time the Glider Pilot Units are in the combat zone, they will be considered as attached to the airborne unit with which affiliated and used at the discretion of the Airborne division Commander; co-ordinated by an airborne officer named and known to both airborne and glider officer and glider organisations by working through the glider officer in charge to obtain glider pilots, if required, for such duties as the defence of Command Posts, the control of traffic, the policing and maintenance of order in captured towns, the guarding of prisoners of war, the preparation and maintenance of landing zones, the collection of supplies, and the establishment, operation and protection of supply depots. When the tactical situation permits, Wing Glider Officers will provide a glider pilot guard to protect gliders from damage by civilians and/or army personnel until such time as glider pilot evacuation is possible. Except in cases of extreme emergency, the glider pilots will not be committed to action, and then only in a defensive role.

Evacuation

(1) Evacuation of glider pilots will be given the highest priority possible in a plan of the appropriate field order. All units or organisations concerned in glider pilot evacuation will be instructed as to their duties and responsibilities prior to mission.

Equipment

(1) All glider pilots committed to an operational mission will be equipped as herein as set forth in paragraph 4 and 5. All previous lists of equipment for glider pilots are hereby rescinded.

(2) Any glider pilot transferred, on temporary duty for an operational mission, between organisations of this command will; be equipped by parent organisations as herein-

after stated, and will have in his possession, at the time of transfer, all items of this equipment.

(3) A release of its items, hereinafter listed, to airborne units, will be accompanied only through a responsible glider pilot in charge, who will obtain adequate receipts.

(4) Clothing worn:
    a. Infantry Combat suit.
    b. Infantry combat boots.
    c. Helmet Steel complete with liner.
    d. Cap, wool
    e. 2 ID or dog tags

(5) Equipment carried.
    a. Pistol Belt
    b. Webbing suspenders
    c. Field Bag containing:
- 2 days K rations
- 1 days D rations
- Sleeping bag
- Halazone tablets
- 3 field heating units
- First aid pouch
- First aid dressing
- 1 Shell dressing
- 1 .45 pistol
- 1 .30 Carbine with 75 rounds of ammunition (for co-pilots)
- 1 Sub-Machine gun with 150 rounds of ammunition (for pilots)
- 2 grenades
- Compass
- Gas mask
- Flak suit
- Entrenching tool
- Trench knife
- A Mae West when flying over or landing near water.
- Flak suits and Mae Wests to be left in the gliders after landing and will be reclaimed with the gliders at a later date.

For the D-Day landings, 38 and 46 Groups contributed a total of 362 aircraft plus 61 in reserve and 1,120 gliders. Of these, 70 were Hamilcars towed by Halifaxes of 298 and 644 Squadrons.

Gliders were to feature on a number of operations during the D-Day landings.

Operation 'Coup de Main' was a glider-borne assault to capture the River Orne and the Caen Canal bridges in Normandy, France.

The role of 644 and 298 Squadrons was to tow and release the Horsa gliders at 6,000 feet and then fly to Caen and bomb a powder factory. The gliders were released at 4,500 feet owing to cloud.

The overall airborne codename for this was 'Tonga'. The two 'Coup de Main' glider units were to take the River Orne and Caen Canal bridges. Operation 'Deadstick' and the other glider unit was to capture the coastal gun battery at Merville, along with the 9th Parachute Regiment on the evening of the 6th. Two hundred and fifty six gliders, including Hamilcars carrying tanks, the first to be transported into battle by glider in the history of warfare, were to be used in Operation 'Mallard'. Both ops were carried out successfully – but not without heavy casualties and losses of aircraft.

The 'Coup de Main' team had Air Vice Marshal Leslie Hollinghurst as overall commander, with Brigadier George Chatterton commanding the glider pilots. Sqn Ldr Wright was in charge of intelligence maps and photographs and Flt Lt Tommy Grant DSO was flying instructor to the glider pilots.

The flying, by Sgt James Wallwork DFM and his second pilot Sgt Johnnie Ainsworth in Horsa No 91, was described by Air Marshal Sir Trafford Leigh-Mallory, who in 1943 was appointed Commander in Chief of the Allied Air Forces for the invasion of Europe, as amongst the finest of the war. Wallwork was able to land his glider within 47 yards of the Benouville Canal Bridge (later known as Pegasus Bridge). It was 16 minutes past midnight on the 6th June 1944, and the bridge was taken with only two men being killed. The attack was led by Major John Howard. Both Jim and Johnnie were hurt in the landing when they went through the Perspex nose of the glider. Johnnie had a broken ankle

The bust of Major John Howard, which occupies a place of honour at Pegasus Bridge. [Alan Cooper]

and badly sprained knees and Jim a cut on his head. He was recommended for the DFM on 7th June and this was endorsed by General Montgomery on 16th June. Beside the name of General Montgomery, his recommendation carried those of many other famous names of WWII, including Major General Gale, Lt General Horrocks, and Air Marshal Cunningham. The pilots had no assistance from the ground, the approach being achieved by the use of a direction indicator (a gyro compass) and a stop-watch, as their angle of approach was too steep for the standard P.4 compass.

One member of the Ox & Bucks Light Infantry that Jim carried in the back of his glider that night was Wally Parr. Many years after the war, Wally was reading an article in the *Eagle*, the Glider Pilot Regiment magazine, when he realised that the article was about the glider in which he had flown to the Rhine Crossing. He had written in chalk on the front 'Lady Irene II'. On the operation to Normandy in June 1944 he had written on the front of Jim's glider "Lady Irene I".

The assault on the Merville Battery was planned with parachutists going in first, followed by three Horsa gliders, carrying further Paras and Royal Engineers.

The dropping would be preceded by bombers attacking the gun battery and then Ouistreham where a further battery and flak positions were located. Seven Horsas were pulled by Dakotas of 271 Squadron and four by Albemarles of 295 Squadron. The three that were to land on the

The Benouville (Pegasus) Bridge in 1993, before its replacement. [Alan Cooper]

WOT! ... NO ENGINES?

An aerial reconnaissance photograph of the Benouville (Pegasus) Bridge, taken the morning after the attack, shows the amazing accuracy of the glider landings in 1944. [Alec Waldron]

DZ, near the battery were pulled by Albemarles from 297 Squadron.

Operation Mallard took off between 6.40 and 7.35pm – 256 gliders and tugs carrying troops of the 6th Air Landing Brigade. A number of the Horsas ditched into the sea en route, but all 38 Hamilcars landed safely with their history-making cargo of tanks.

In addition to the troops, 7,000 tons of supplies were delivered by glider at Normandy.

Besides the Hamilcars, 320 Horsas took part in operations Deadstick, Tonga and Mallard in June 1944 during the invasion of Normandy.

By the end of June, Halifax towing squadrons had carried out 51 successful and three aborted operations without any losses.

On 20th June 1944, General Eisenhower approved the organisation of the First Allied Airborne Army. This was composed of the British 1st Airborne Corps, consisting of the 1st and 6th Airborne Divisions, 1st Special Air Service Brigade, the 1st Polish Independent Parachute Brigade Group, the US 18th Airborne Corps, the British 52nd Lowland Division, 9th US Troop Carrier Command and 38 & 46 Groups RAF.

American-built gliders were to be used for this operation. Fourteen Waco gliders, flown by members of the Glider Pilot Regiment and towed by the RAF, set off on 5th August 1944, their passengers French SAS troops, codename Dingson, their target near Lorient, France. The operation was a success, with all but one of the gliders making a safe landing, and of the 20 pilots who set out, 18 returned within 11 days and the remaining two later, having been injured in landing.

This was followed by Operations 'Dragoon' and 'Bluebird' on 15th August 1944. The British element of four Waco and 36 Horsa gliders would take part and land in the south of France. The Horsas would be flown by the Glider Pilot Regiment and the Wacos by American pilots. Once again, it was a success, with only one casualty, Sgt Jenner of the Glider Pilot Regiment.

On 9th October was Operation 'Molten', when 32 Horsas were ferried to Italy and 27 made it in 10 hours.

The next major airborne operation was Operation 'Market-Garden' at Arnhem, Holland on 17th September 1944; the largest ever airborne operation up to that time.

The plan was devised by Field Marshal Bernard Montgomery, commander of the 21st Army Group, which included the First Canadian and Second British Armies. His plan was to cut off the Germans in the western part of the Netherlands, outflanking the border fortifications of the Westwall and putting the Second Army across the major water obstacles in the Netherlands and in a position to drive deep into Germany along the North German plain. His idea was for one 'full-blooded' thrust north-eastwards into Germany and Berlin, which he argued to the Americans, would prompt the German high command to capitulate.

Ever since Normandy, Eisenhower had been seeking an opportunity to use the idle airborne troops – these elite forces were burning a hole in the Allied commander's pocket. Montgomery's plan was daring and not without appeal but there were fears, as one senior British officer put it at the time, that the objective might be "a bridge too far."

The airborne landings themselves, caught the Germans by surprise and were a great success, but the troops were some distance – six to eight miles – from their primary objective of the bridge over the Rhine.

The operation was, in the main, carried out by parachute drops by 50 American Wacos accompanied by 38 Horsas and Wacos of General Browning's Corps. HQ were to land in the same area as two of the 82nd US Parachute Regiments, south of Nijmegen and to the north of Eindhoven. The British 1st Airborne Division parachute and glider landings of 345 Horsas and 13 Hamilcars were the most successful made by either side during the war so far. One major problem for General Urquhart, however, was that the gliders carrying the reconnaissance armoured jeeps failed to arrive, having crashed en route. It was to have been their job to forge ahead and seize the Bridge at Arnhem.

The airborne troops were supposed to capture and hold the bridges for four days before being relieved by a link-up with the allied land forces. However, despite a magnificent effort, the operation ultimately faltered when the planned rendezvous failed to materialise. Many of the airborne troops were killed or captured.

Of the 10,000 men of the 1st Airborne Division who set out, Urquhart lost 7,578 men, of these 229 Glider pilots were killed and 469 wounded or taken prisoner. They had, at Arnhem, flown in 658 gliders with 4,500 men, 95 guns and jeeps, some of the guns being 75mm Pack Howitzers with their tractors.

Jim Wallwork, who ended up at a hospital in Worcester, was returned to his regiment three weeks before the Arnhem operation, where for the first time the Glider Pilot Regiment fought as an infantry battalion.

The USAF lost 424 aircrew, the RAF 294 aircrew and RASC despatches. Seventy-four RAF transport aircraft were lost – 47 Stirling tug aircraft and 27 Dakotas. In all, 29 Hamilcars were used at Arnhem.

These losses, in particular the glider pilots, would create a serious shortage for the action that was to come in 1945...

Mass glider landings, Normandy, 6th June 1944. [Alec Waldron]

No 6 RAF Glider Pilots Course – 'B' Flight – 4th Nov 1944 – RAF Brize Norton (Left to right)

Back Row: Sgt A Logie (KIA) | F/Lt R Gray (KIA) | Sgt J Nearns. | F/O J Freeman (KIA). | Sgt A Stredwick. | F/O A Ledbrook (KIA) | F/O J Leyland | Sgt P Green | F/O E Hart | Sgt L MacDonald.
Centre Row: 1. Sgt A Love (KIA). | 5. Sgt A Huggett. | 9. F/O Parsons. | 10. Sgt D Matthews.
Front Row: F/O E Cook (KIA). | Sgt J Simpson. | F/O C Lee. | Sgt W Foy. | F/O Lodge. | F/Sgt T Laidlaw (KIA). | F/O R Grub. | FlO J Haig (KIA). | Sgt F Meek. | Unknown.

CHAPTER 6

WOT...! NO ENGINES?

On 3rd July 1944, a memo was sent to the Assistant Chief of Air Staff by the Director of Operations. It said that the War Office estimated there would be a difficulty in providing enough soldiers to train as glider pilots. It was suggested that the deficiency might be met by drawing on the present surplus of RAF pilots. The question remained whether, in the future, glider pilots were to be soldiers or airmen. A meeting was arranged for 12th July at the Air Ministry in King Charles Street, London, on the agenda the future provision of glider pilots. At that time, there were 1,400 glider pilots in the UK. The rate of casualties in Operation Overlord (D-Day) had been below expectations, and in view of this the proposal to transfer 10,000 men from the RAF deferred list to the Army, many of whom were likely to volunteer for glider pilot training, the War Office was now satisfied with the monthly intake of 135 men per month from their own resources. But it was for consideration whether the Air Ministry wished to train any RAF pilots to fly gliders.

The Glider Training Schools run by the RAF for the Army at that time employed some 1,500 RAF personnel. The suggestion was that if the RAF's surplus of trained pilots were retrained as glider pilots, the Glider Schools and Elementary Flying Training School could be closed down, with a consequent manpower saving, because the trained RAF pilots could go straight to the Heavy Glider Training Schools. However, if the elementary schools were closed down, there would be no flow of trained glider pilots to replace men loaned by the RAF should they be required to return to duties on powered aircraft. The rates of pay would also be an issue, as the rate of pay for glider pilots was far below that of comparable ranks of trained pilots in the RAF.

The meeting came to the conclusion that things should be left as they were for two months, during which time the War Office would endeavour to build up a reserve of pilots, and that further information would be forthcoming on which to base a firmer estimate of probable casualty rates.

On 31st July, a memo was sent out to the Vice-Chief of Air Staff from the Assistant Chief of Air Staff. He went on to say that a situation had arisen in the Army's Glider Pilot Regiment. They required 40 replacement crews at two men each per month. This would involve about 135 volunteers being found from the Army per month.

They would undergo training for six to eight months and require about 1,500 RAF personnel to train them. In comparison, for RAF pilots to convert to glider pilots would only take four to six weeks. He concluded that the current state of affairs could carry on for a very long time, owing to the numbers already in training.

He went on to say that previous policy had been that the Army should find personnel for glider pilot duties because it was believed to be an advantage if glider pilots were fighting soldiers as well and able to play an active combat role after landing. This policy had now changed and the War Office thinking was now that glider pilots should only know enough about land fighting to be able to defend themselves in an emergency, get clear of the battle zone and return to their units as quickly as possible.

On 12th July it was suggested that the RAF could help the Army out by 'lending' them some of their surplus pilots.

There were several objections from the Army with regard to this proposal, the main one being that this would eventually lead to the majority of glider pilots being airmen, with a consequent wasting away of the Glider Pilot Regiment, of which the Army was justly proud (and of which, incidentally, C.I.G.S was Colonel-in-Chief).

It was proposed that in two months time the RAF should begin to provide replacement glider pilots and that they should be seconded to the Glider Pilot Regiment for periods of 18 months to two years, with the option of transfer if they wished, so that their recruitment would not involve the disappearance of the regiment.

On the 26th September, after Arnhem, where 229 glider pilots had been lost and over 400 wounded or taken prisoner, there was a serious shortage of glider pilots which was being resolved by RAF pilots going on a 4 week conversion course followed by 2 to 4 weeks operational training.

An enquiry was made to the RAF delegation in Washington.

a. Whether USAAF could provide glider pilot training for up to 250 RAF ex-flying training schools crews each of 2 pilots.

b. Date on which course could commence.

c. Length of course.

d. Whether training would be to operational standard.

e. Whether crews could be trained in time to ship to and arrive in India early January 1945.

The RAF pilots would either be sent from the UK or taken from volunteers already at Canadian flying training schools. It was hoped to find 500 volunteer pilots from Flying Training Schools in Canada. The war in the Far East was also a consideration for the need for more glider pilots.

On 11th October, Wg/Cdr Kean was told to report to Flying Training Command Headquarters on the 12th. Here, he was told to form a new Heavy Glider Conversion Unit, No 23 and to train 90 crews by 12th January 1945. That night he flew up to East Moor and then to Harrogate, where a large number of surplus RAF pilots were stationed at a Personnel Reception Unit, without any hope of operational training or active service in the war. The pilots were assembled at the Majestic Hotel, Harrogate on the morning of 13th October to hear Wg/Cdr Kean's appeal for volunteers to fly gliders. Remarkably, the Wingco managed to get enough volunteers for glider pilot training. Tom Kean told them that

RAF Hawker Hector glider tug. [Alec Waldron]

he admired them for their courage, not only agreeing to fly gliders instead of fighters or bombers, as many had hoped to do, but also for volunteering for the unenviable task which they knew they must perform, especially in the full knowledge of the terrible losses incurred at Arnhem.

By 1st November, No 23 HGCU was formed at Peplow, with Seighford as its satellite. Flying instructors spent a fortnight at Hockley Heath learning glider training methods on Hotspurs and were then ready to convert to Horsas. The towing aircraft would be flown by ex-bomber pilots. They were each given a 35 minute familiarisation on Albemarles by Wg/Cdr Kean, including stalling, feathering, and asymmetric flying, before being sent off to perform two solo flights.

The training of these pilots was completed by 12th January 1945, when Kean returned to Hullavington to complete the second part of his training course. When this was completed, he was posted to No.1 Glider Training School at Croughton as Commanding Officer for three months. He then flew out to Palestine for a Staff College course.

Brigadier Chatterton was ordered to train a glider force of at least 2,000 gliders in preparation for an operation to fly across the Rhine.

His only avenue for replacements for those lost at Arnhem was the RAF. He went to see the Director of Training RAF Air Chief Marshal Sir Peter Drummond, who agreed to transfer RAF trained pilots into the Glider Pilot Regiment on a fifty-fifty basis.

Len Macdonald, having completed his flying training in Miami, USA, came back to the UK with no thought or intention of flying gliders. However, in October 1944, he found himself along with some 200 other RAF pilots at the Majestic Hotel, Harrogate, Yorkshire, where, as Len remembers it, they were "told in no uncertain terms that they had 'volunteered' to fly gliders." This was followed by a glider course at 21 EFTS on Tiger Moths, heavy glider conversion on Horsas at 21 Heavy Glider Conversion Unit, Brize Norton and then operational training.

GPR pilot's wings.

RAF pilot's wings.

For some, the training was to be fatal. On 3rd November 1944, at No 5 Glider Training School, Shobdon, there was a fatal collision in the air between two gliders. Sgt J.W. Walker was killed and Sgt J.F. Boon later died in hospital; both were from No.9 Glider Pilot (RAF) course. On 5th December a glider crashed again at Shobdon. P/O E.R. Bird was found unconscious after the crash and suffered multiple injuries. On the 6th LAC Nightingale was hit by the wing of an incoming glider and sustained cuts and lacerations to his face.

An order was given on 16th November 1944, that all RAF glider pilots under General Browning were to wear khaki battledress for working dress and RAF service dress on all other occasions.

The question of some form of military training for RAF glider pilots was also discussed.

Len Macdonald remembers undertaking an RAF battle course with the RAF Regiment in August 1944 – but this was not part of any glider pilot training scheme – it was just to keep 'sprog' pilots occupied. As Len remembers it, the only glider pilots to receive battle training after 'volunteering' for gliders were those who had actually volunteered – they got a 14 day course on small arms at Fargo and a week of assault courses and field training at Bridgnorth. The majority, who like Len himself had certainly not volunteered, got none.

While on operational glider training in November 1944, Len was ordered to get down behind a Bren gun situated in a pool of water by an Army instructor. Len was wearing RAF Blue Battledress and no protective covering at all. His request to go and get a groundsheet to lie on was refused so he, in turn, refused to accept the order. The matter was referred to the RAF Commanding Officer in charge of the base, who said, "For God's sake issue them with overalls!"

On 12th December 1944 the AOC of 38 Group, Air Vice-Marshal J.R. Scarlett-Streatfield CBE, visitedEarls Colne to interview RAF Glider pilots.

On 1st January 1945 the RAF Element of the Glider Pilot Regiment was formed at Headquarters, No 38 Group, Transport Command.

Personnel of the RAF Element of the Glider Pilot Regiment would be attached in accordance with the terms of Army Orders 167 of 1941 and Air Ministry Order A774/41 to the units of the Glider Pilot Regiment under arrangements to be made by the A.O.C 38 Group in consultation with the Commander Glider Pilot Regiment. The wings of the Glider Pilot Regiment were to be commanded by Army Officers with the RAF officers as second in command. Of the Squadrons and Flights of the Glider Pilot Regiment, half were to be commanded by Army officers and half by RAF Officers, the seconds in command to be officers of the opposite service of the Squadron or Flight Commanders.

On 2nd January 1945, Exercise 'Quiver' took place. It was becoming apparent that many crews, according to HQ 38 Group, were depending on Radar aids for navigation to an excessive degree, owing to the availability of this aid during the majority of their flights. Consequently, they had lost confidence in their ability to navigate by dead reckoning (DR) and normal navigation methods. The exercise was to take place at the Station Commander's discretion, when other commitments permitted.

The object of the exercise was for crews from all squadrons to locate a pin-point target (Rockall) after a DR navigation flight without radar aids, and thus increase the confidence of the navigators in their own abilities.

On 31st January 1945, 450 aircraft and 5,500 personnel were involved in training glider pilots of which 900 were Army and 750 RAF. The aircraft consisted of 300 four-engine, 446 two-engine, 373 one-engine and 1,900 gliders.

On 21st February 1945 the whole airborne forces situation was discussed. The cost of airborne forces to the Army and RAF was complicated to assess because it was necessary to estimate what effect the aircraft and personnel would have had on other operations if they had not been allotted to airborne forces training and operations.

The cost of airborne forces arises from:

(i) The high quality of the army personnel required and the subsequent adverse effect on the fighting efficiency of the units from which they were drawn.

(ii) The heavy training commitment.

(iii) The relatively small number of days during which airborne forces perform the special role for which they have been trained.

Indeed, owing to the expense of training and equipping airborne divisions, it had become a clearly accepted principle that these valuable formations should be withdrawn as soon as they had performed the special tasks for which they were trained and should not be allowed to be drawn into the general melee of the subsequent conventional land battle.

The various airborne operations that had taken part in the war so far were discussed: Holland, Crete and Tunis by the Germans; Sicily, D-Day and Arnhem by the Allies; and the operations in Burma by Wingate's Chindits, dropping small airborne forces and airfield construction groups before flying in normal army units by conventional means.

The aim of the Sicily and Overlord airborne operations had been to cut communications, hold certain vital points and spread alarm and despondency among the enemy, thereby gaining some measure of tactical initiative in preparation for the main amphibious landing.

The Arnhem operation was to lay an airborne carpet across a series of waterways, thereby securing bridges over which the main armoured forces could safely follow up. German intentions

RAF Tiger Moth flight trainer. *[Alec Waldron]*

in Holland during 1940 had been more or less similar. The tactics of the Germans at Crete were that the airborne forces should secure an airfield, allowing the remaining forces to be flown in and followed up subsequently by amphibious forces.

The aims of airborne operations were:

(i) To prepare the way for amphibious operations and secure certain tactical features;

(ii) To prepare the way for the main advance across geographical obstacles and to forestall enemy demolition of bridges, etc;

(iii) To harass the enemy's communications and to force his diversion of effort and finally a general withdrawal.

On 24th February 1945, the Vice Chief of Air Staff had been in discussion with the War Office over the number of glider crews that had to be maintained to meet the requirements in Europe and South East Asia Command, and for the time being, to agree with them a figure of 1,030 glider crews as the number that would have been trained and ready for action by 1st April. This figure included 884 RAF crews, that had been handed over from time to time out of surplus aircrew trainees. But plans had to be made for a continuation of the war beyond June 1945 and for the return of a number of these pilots to the RAF. Discussions took place to try to avoid this, as it would cripple the glider force at a time when it could possibly be brought into action.

However, the way it worked out on paper was that two RAF men were required on a permanent basis to provide airborne assault lift for one soldier, whom they may have to carry into battle once or maybe twice in a year.

The RAF had loaned something like 1,600 RAF pilots to fly gliders at a time when it was facing a considerable deficiency amongst its own crews due to heavy losses in Bomber Command.

On the 28th February 1945, calculations showed that on the basis of the German war continuing to the end of September 1945, there would be a deficiency of trained pilots by June 1945.

This would reach 1,580 by the end of July 1945. There were, at this time, approximately 1,776 RAF Glider pilots, of whom 1,068 (534 crews) were in the UK and 708 (354) crews in South East Asia.

To make good the projected shortage of trained pilots it was planned to withdraw 1,500 of these glider pilots during June and July 1945 to meet RAF requirements. It was not feasible to replace this number with trained army glider pilots between February and May 1945, so the intention was that all RAF glider pilots should begin to be withdrawn from glider duties to Air Force duties at the rate of about 250 a month commencing in May 1945. If the War Office could not release 1,500 RAF Glider pilots during June and July they should, it was suggested, at least release the second pilots of all the RAF glider crews, some 888 pilots.

In the light of the altered circumstances of the war, it was thought to be a fantastic extravagance to employ two fully qualified RAF pilots as a glider crew, especially if the UK were to lose large numbers of these crews in future airborne operations. The RAF also thought it a luxury to have a second pilot in a crew where there was already one fully trained RAF pilot.

However, the Glider Pilot Regiment believed that if they could retain the 888 pilots, they could make up the deficiency from the other sources such as the Admiralty and thus avoid setting up any additional glider pilot training capacity.

On 3rd March 1945, the debate over glider pilots continued.

If 1,776 army glider pilots were to be trained, the programme would have to start on 1st August 1945 and would employ some 10,000 RAF training personnel for ten months.

The following was agreed:-

(a) The War Office would have to be told of the latest position of RAF pilots and make it clear that the loan of RAF pilots as glider pilots was a key factor in the Air Ministry's calculations.

(b) The War Office would have to be pressed for consideration for the release of 888 RAF second pilots as already suggested.

(c) The War Office would have to be informed that there was no prospect of replacing any of the exiting 1,776 RAF glider pilots out of RAF resources at the end of their operational tour.

(d) The Air Ministry should offer to leave existing training facilities (some 5,400 RAF personnel) at the disposal of glider pilot training (basic and /or operational flying maintenance) and invite the War Office to work out with the Air Ministry the best overall method of employing these training facilities.

The Director of Operations (Tactical) did not think of a second pilot as a luxury, particularly when launching large waves of gliders with 10 to 25 soldiers in each glider against important objectives. It was most desirable that the glider passengers or freight should not be lost owing to the first pilot becoming incapacitated. There was also a psychological benefit as far as the soldiers were concerned. Furthermore, during a long tow, the second pilot assisted, as it was physically tiring for one pilot; he also assisted with advice after cast-off. Nevertheless, there was a strong case for accepting just one pilot if he was a fully qualified RAF pilot and he recommended that the War Office should give this favourable consideration.

The breakdown of glider pilots in March 1945 was:

Northwest Europe RAF Glider pilots Operationally trained in 38/46 Group Squadrons	Total 415
Completed flying training and Army training at Fargo and now under operational training	Total 86
Completed flying training and undergoing Army training at Fargo	Total 33
Overall Total	**534**

On 8th March 1945, the possible deficiency of basically trained pilots by June 1945, on the basis of the war continuing after June 1945, was once again considered and discussed.

Wg/Cdr Kean AFC completed his training of RAF pilots on 12th January 1945, exactly on schedule and then returned to Hullavington to complete the second part of his Empire Central Flying School course. When this was completed, he was posted to No 1 Glider Training School at Croughton, as Commanding Officer.

CHAPTER 7

Flying & Glider Training

As soon as the war with Germany was announced by Prime Minster Neville Chamberlain on 3rd September 1939, the Dominions came in to support their mother country.

There was an immediate requirement to train large numbers of aircrew in as short a time as possible, but with the UK under attack by the Luftwaffe and with limited training facilities available, it was proposed that pilots be trained overseas.

A message was sent to the Prime Minister of Canada, Mackenzie King. Similar messages went to Australia and New Zealand outlining the problem and the proposals to solve it.

Thus the Empire Training Scheme came into being and four training schools in the UK were immediately transferred to Canada:

No.31 – Kingston, Ontario
No.32 – Moose Jaw, Saskatchewan
No.33 – Carberg, Manitoba
No.34 – Medicine Hat, Alberta,
This later rose to 14.

Talks began with the USA when the aircrew situation in 1940 became acute. At first the British were told that all the US training schools were fully occupied training their own crews, but several schemes were soon put into operation.

First to arrive were the British Flying Training Schools, followed by two other schemes, the Towers Scheme (named after Admiral Towers) and the Arnold Scheme (named after General Arnold, Chief of Staff of the US Army in 1941).

There were six BFTSs, at which 7,000 RAF and 400 USAAF pilots were trained:

No.1 – Terrel, Texas
No.2 – Lancaster, California
No.3 – Miami, Oklahoma
No.4 – Mesa, Arizona
No.5 – Clewiston, Florida, and
No.6 – Ponca City, Oklahoma.

John Crane flying a Harvard flight training aircraft at No.3 BFTS – Miami Oklahoma USA. [John Crane]

The instructors were civilians and the schools took 200 cadets per week for a period of 20 weeks training.

The Towers scheme was designed to train flying-boat pilots and pilots for the Fleet Air Arm. This was also extended to take RAF observers, wireless operators and flight engineers.

An agreement was also made with South Africa, which provided seven Elementary Flying Training Schools (EFTS), and seven Service Flying Training Schools (SFTS).

Every Flying Training School cadet's ambition was to win his wings and become a fighter pilot. With luck he would progress to an advanced unit in the UK, then to an Operational Training Unit and finally join a fighter squadron. Their dreams were all of Spitfires and Hurricanes.

• • • • • • • • • • •

In 1939, Phil Johnson was a telephone engineer at the GPO, a 'reserved' occupation.

When the Local Defence Force (later the Home Guard) was formed, it was more or less compulsory for those in a reserved occupation to enlist, and Phil duly did so.

He received a little military training at the local cattle market, where his GPO work inspector doubled as captain in the LDV.

"If you failed to turn up on Sunday morning with the LDV," he remembers, "you would be up in front of the inspector Monday morning!"

Weapons training took place at their local Territorial Army ranges using .22 and .303 rifles. Overnight duties, carried out on a rota basis, involved guarding various telephone exchanges, armed with Canadian Ross rifles with only two or three rounds per man.

Phil had volunteered for pilot duties with the RAF, but his call-up was delayed due to his involvement with GPO work on the many airfields being built for the Americans. It was April 1943 before he received his call-up papers.

Basic training was followed by ground work in preparation for flying duties, theory of flight, engines, Morse code, semaphore, Aldis lamp work, meteorology, navigation and map reading, aircraft and ship recognition etc, before ever seeing or getting into an aircraft.

By August he was flying a Tiger Moth aircraft, followed by more flying training at Heaton Park and then boarding the liner *Queen Mary* for a journey across the Atlantic to the USA.

The two-seater Tiger Moth trainer, made of wood and metal with a fabric covering, became one of the most famous trainer aircraft in the world. Many were made in the UK and the Commonwealth and a number sent to South Africa for the Empire Training Scheme.

It had a maximum speed of just over 109 mph and was ideal for training as it could cope with the heavy-handed as well as those with a light touch.

• • • • • • • • • • •

No.1 BFTS in Terrell, Texas was one of the six set up in 1941 to train pilots for the Royal Air Force. It commenced operations on June 9th 1941, at Love Field, Dallas, moving to Terrell, 32 miles east of Dallas. The airfield was ready in August 1941. The aircraft used were Stearman PT-18s, Vultee BT-31As and North American AT-6As loaned by the Army Air Corps. The instructors, both flying and ground, were American civilians.

The first two courses to arrive started flying at Love Field, and the third was the first to arrive at Terrell. In all, there were 27 courses trained at No.1 BFTS, although the last two did not graduate at the school, which closed soon after VJ Day, in August 1945.

Initially, courses were of around 50 students, and four courses of these numbers were in resident at any one time. With No.13 Course this was doubled in strength and only three courses were there at any one time. Also starting with No.13 course, a small number of US Army aviation cadets joined each course, up to and including No.19 course, after which student strength reverted to being British only.

The American cadets arrived after having some 100 hours flying training at civilian primary schools before leaving for the UK. Most of those from the early courses, who were accepted for aircrew training before the grading system began, had in fact, never been off the ground before. Courses 1 to 6 arrived before the USA entered the war and were mostly civilians who wore civilian clothes when off the camp, except for a few 'special' occasions. In the beginning, there were only 4 RAF permanent staff at Terrell: a wing commander, a squadron leader, a flight lieutenant and a sergeant. Later, numbers grew considerably, as special staff were added and eventually totalled 15.

With the appearance of the American cadets, a number of US Army officers and enlisted men joined to the staff of the school. From No.10 Course, a Cadet Officer/NCO disciplinary system was inaugurated, and things began to move away from the rather free-and-easy ways of the early days.

Flying was carried out as the first part of the advanced training on the AT 6 Harvard, an aircraft that was also made in great numbers and in many countries. It had a top speed of 210mph. The total number of hours to be flown was increased from the original 180.

The elimination rate was around 40% – much the same as at the US Army schools, a but some were sent to Canada to continue their pilot training there, whilst others re-trained as navigators or wireless-operators. In all, about 2,200 cadets passed through No.1 BFTS, including some 150 Americans.

No.1 Course graduated on 2nd November 1941, and the last to actually complete their training No.25 course, on 24th August 1945.

During the life of the school, 19 cadets were killed in flying training and one other died of illness. All are buried in the BFTS plot at Oaklands Memorial Cemetery, Terrell, where a permanent Memorial, Plinth was dedicated at a ceremony on 16th April 1942 by Viscount Halifax, then British Ambassador to the USA.

On return to the UK, many of those trained at Terrell were killed in operations against the enemy – members of courses number s 4 and 7 particularly.

Many were awarded decorations for bravery, at least 50 DFCs and DFMs were awarded to Terrell graduates. One, Flt Sgt Arthur Aaron, was awarded the Victoria Cross. The hospitality over an average six months that a course lasted was extended to everyone in the local community many friendships were long lasting and continue to this day.

• • • • • • • • • •

No.3 British Flying Training School was at Miami, Oklahoma.

Phil Johnson trained there on No.19 Course, from December 1943 to June 1944, when he got his wings having put in 220 hours flying and, in his estimation, ten times that amount on ground school subjects. Then it was back to the UK via Canada to Harrogate PDC.

• • • • • • • • • •

As a schoolboy, Gordon Procter lived in Purley, Surrey, close to Kenley and Biggin Hill aerodromes, where he avidly watched the Gloster Gladiators of the Royal Air Force. Over the hill was Croydon Aerodrome where his father took him and his brother to watch the comings and goings of the Imperial Airways Hercules, Heracles and Hannibal aircraft, and, less frequently, those of the German and French airlines.

Gordon Procter

AARON, Arthur Louis, VC DFM

Acting Flight Sergeant, No.218 'Gold Coast' Squadron, Royal Air Force Volunteer Reserve.

Arthur Aaron was born 5 March 1922 in Leeds. In 1941 the Aircrew Selection Board recommended him for pilot training in the RAFVR and in November 1941 he commenced his journey to the Number 1 British Flying Training School at Terrell, Texas, arriving December 1941. Aaron was awarded his pilot's wings in June 1942 prior to his return to the UK, and postings followed to an initial bomber training unit on Wellington and Stirling aircraft.

On 17 April 1943, his operational posting was to Number 218 'Gold Coast' Squadron, 3 Group, RAF Bomber Command at RAF Downham Market, Norfolk and later that month he was dropping anti-shipping sea mines near the Frisian Islands off the Dutch and German coasts. Over the next 3½ months he completed a further 18 operations, the majority of which were against heavily defended targets in Germany. These included Dortmund/ Essen, the Ruhr and Hamburg. His aircraft was damaged on a few occasions by anti-aircraft fire and on one occasion was set on fire by an incendiary bomb dropped by a bomber flying above. For his actions on that occasion in October 1943 he was awarded the DFM. The citation read: *"...a fire was started to the rear of the bomb doors. The wireless operator and flight engineer managed to control the outbreak. Meanwhile, flight Sergeant Aaron pressed home his attack on the target undistracted by the perilous situation in his aircraft."*

On his 20th operational flight on the night of 12 August 1943, Sergeant Aaron and his crew took part in an attack on Turin. Although never proven conclusively, it is thought to have been another British bomber which mistakenly fired upon Aaron's Stirling, although official records state that when approaching to attack the bomber received devastating bursts of fire from an enemy fighter. Three engines were hit, the windscreen shattered, the front and rear turret put out of action and the elevator controls damaged, causing the aircraft to become unstable and difficult to control. The navigator was killed and other members of the crew were injured.

A bullet struck Sergeant Aaron in the face, breaking his jaw and tearing away part of his face. He was also wounded in the lung and his right arm was rendered useless. As he fell forward over the control column, the aircraft dived several thousand feet. Control was regained by the bomb aimer, F/Sgt Alan Larden, at 3,000 feet. Though unable to speak, Sergeant Aaron made it clear to the F/Sgt Larden by signs that he wished to take over the controls. A course was then set southwards in an endeavour to fly the crippled bomber, which had all but one engine out of action, to Sicily or North Africa.

Sergeant Aaron was assisted to the rear of the aircraft and treated with morphine. After resting for some time, he rallied and insisted on returning to the cockpit, where he was lifted into his seat and his feet placed on the rudder bar. Twice he made determined attempts to take control and hold the aircraft to its course, but his weakness was evident and with difficulty he was persuaded to desist. Though in great pain and suffering from exhaustion, he continued to help the bomb-aimer fly the plane by writing directions with his left hand. Five hours after leaving the target, the aircraft's fuel began to run low, but soon afterwards the flarepath at an aerodrome at Bone, Algeria was sighted. Sergeant Aaron summoned his failing strength to direct the F/Sgt Larden in the hazardous task of landing the damaged aircraft in the darkness. Four attempts were made under his direction; at the fifth, Sergeant Aaron was so near to collapsing that he had to be restrained by the crew and a near perfect landing with undercarriage retracted was completed by the F/Sgt Larden, who had never landed an aircraft before.

Nine hours after landing, Sergeant Aaron died from exhaustion. Had he been content, when wounded, to lie still and conserve his failing strength, it is thought that he would probably have recovered.

His citation concludes: *"In appalling conditions he showed the greatest qualities of courage, determination and leadership and though wounded and dying he set an example of devotion to duty which seldom has been equalled and never surpassed."*

F/Sgt Larden RCAF was later awarded the CGM (flying).

Extract from *Victoria Cross - Bravest of the Brave*, by Horsman & Taylor, Woodfield Publishing, in press.

(above) F/Sgt Arthur Aaron VC DFM – a graduate of No.1 BFTS, Terell, Texas USA

(left) Aaron's Stirling crew. F/Sgt Larden centre.

His father had served in WWI with the Lancashire battery of the Royal Artillery and wanted Gordon to follow in his footsteps. He told many stories of his three years in the trenches at the Somme, Paschendale and Arras. Instead, Gordon volunteered for aircrew late in the summer of 1942 and before his 18th birthday. He had to wait until 18th January 1943 before becoming an aircrew cadet.

His first two months were spent at a block of flats at Regents Park and then on to ITW (Initial Training Wing) at Stratford-on-Avon. He spent a short time flying Tiger Moths from Wolverhampton, but the weather was so bad that nobody was allowed to fly solo, which worried Gordon in case it affected his future potential as a pilot.

From there he moved to Heaton Park near Manchester to await a boat to the USA. The departure was from Liverpool on 26th August 1943, the ship the *Mauritania*. The crossing was rough with huge waves crashing over the top of the ship and damaging one of the additional gun emplacements on the deck.

On arrival they were shipped to a reception camp at Moncton, New Brunswick, Canada, where they stayed for a month until September 1943, when selection came for the Flying Training Schools. Gordon was delighted to be told that he was going to Falcon Field, Mesa, Arizona, the home of No.4 BFTS.

To get there involved a seven-day train journey, he remembers, with one of the two washrooms on the train being out of action.

He arrived at Falcon Field on 6th October 1943 and remained there until 17th April 1944 with a nucleus of RAF Officers, American Instructors, excellent food (and a lot of it) and a stand-in mother and father in Phoenix who looked after three cadets during their stay. Looking back, Gordon now thinks that this was probably the happiest time of his life, so much so that his home in the UK is now called 'Falcon Field'. He has returned to the USA in the years since the war and paid his respects to the 23 cadets who died during training there.

On 17th April 1944 Gordon received his wings and a commission in the Royal Air Force.

The trip home to the UK, in direct contrast to the outward trip, was very peaceful, the sea like a millpond with not a wave in sight. He had high hopes on his return of flying a Spitfire, Hurricane, Mustang or Tempest, having trained on single-engined aircraft.

On his return he had various postings, one as assistant flying control officer at RAF Benson before being sent on leave. Little did he know that all his contemporaries around the UK at various RAF bases were also being sent on leave at that time.

His next posting came as a shock – to No.5 Glider Training School, Shobdon. The airfield was six miles from Leominster in Herefordshire. At its height there were over 1,000 people based at Shobdon. As he arrived he realised it was not a bad dream when he saw rows and rows of Hotspur gliders lined up on the runway.

• • • • • • • • • •

Rick Brown trained at No.6 BFTS (Ponca City) at Oklahoma, believing – as did all those he trained alongside in the USA – that his destiny was to become a top scoring fighter ace. Their illusions encouraged by the fact that in their final training in the USA was on single-engined trainers.

However, on their return to the UK in the autumn of 1944, it was soon obvious that this was not to be the case. The only 'crack at the Hun' they would get would be via the Glider Pilot Regiment. As Rick remembers it, they took the opportunity to get themselves killed readily enough – although some went kicking and screaming!

• • • • • • • • • •

The famous Welsh rugby star Bleddwyn Williams also trained as a pilot at No 4 BFTS in Arizona on course 18 and qualified on single-engine aircraft. When he arrived back in the UK he expected to continue flying training with an Advanced Flying Unit, but was informed that the Army had an acute shortage of glider pilots after the great losses at Arnhem and soon he, like Gordon Procter, found himself heading for Shobden in Herefordshire.

It would appear that those who volunteered to become glider pilots fared somewhat better than those who were conscripted in that they received a full training programme.

Those first volunteer pilots received training at Shobdon and then Brize Norton, plus infantry training on Salisbury Plain.

Those who didn't volunteer, it would seem, became second pilots and had little training, more-or-less going straight to operational units.

• • • • • • • • • • •

Len Macdonald also trained at No.3 BFTS at Miami, Oklahoma, flying the Fairchild PT-19, a Canadian aircraft with a maximum speed of 132 mph, fully aerobatic and easy to handle, and also in the North American Harvard. It was never his intention to fly gliders.

In October 1944 he found himself on parade with another 200 RAF pilots at the Majestic Hotel in Harrogate. When the roll-call was completed they were addressed by an officer who said those famous words that everyone who has served in the armed forces has heard – 'You lot'.

"You lot have just volunteered to fly gliders," was said with a certain amount of relish, and at a single stroke got rid of 200 RAF aircrew, who, at the time, the RAF did not know what to do with.

What followed was a glider course on firstly Tiger moths at 21 Elementary Flying Training School and then heavy Glider Conversion on Horsa gliders at 21 HGCU at RAF Brize Norton.

• • • • • • • • • • •

John William Rayson, known as Johnny or 'Titch' to his friends in the RAF, was born at Bexhill-on-Sea in 1924 and educated at Abingdon, incidentally, where he lives today. He joined the RAF on a short University Course, at Clare College Cambridge in 1942. In 1943, he reported to the Air Crew Recruits Centre at Regents Park, London then returned to Cambridge to the initial (square bashing) training that everyone has to go through. In May 1943 he underwent flying training at No.9 BFTS (Anstey) Grading School, flying Tiger Moth aircraft. In June he went to Heaton Park, awaiting the trip across the Atlantic which took him firstly to Monkton, New Brunswick, Canada and then in August 1943 to No.3 BFTS at Miami, Oklahoma, USA for primary and advanced flying training. He was awarded his wings and a commission as a pilot officer in the Royal Air Force in January 1944.

On his return to the UK in November 1944 he was seconded to the Glider Pilot Regiment.

• • • • • • • • • • •

David Richards was also at No.3 BFTS, on No.18 Course, returning to the UK in May 1944. Another there at the same time was John Perry who, after preliminary training in the UK, flying Tiger Moths, went to No.3 BFTS where he trained alongside US Cadets, flying Fairchild PT-19s and North American AT6s, anticipating eventual conversion to fighters. The US cadets were already moving on to Mustangs as the next progression towards becoming fighter pilots. But when David returned to the UK in the Spring of 1944 he found there was a glut of fighter pilots and with a second front opening up in June 1944, the only opening seemed to be on four-engined aircraft.

He volunteered for the Fleet Air Arm, hoping to stay on fighters, but after Arnhem it was glider pilots that were needed, so he volunteered for transfer to the Glider Pilot Regiment and was accepted.

• • • • • • • • • • •

Ron Watson trained at No.1 BFTS at Terrell, Texas on No.20 Course and remembers flying cross-country to Wichita Falls.

• • • • • • • • • • •

Cyril (Cy) Henson joined the RAF in August 1942 as an under training pilot. His initial fighter training was under the Towers Scheme, conducted by the US Navy at Detroit and then Pensacola.

John Love joined the RAF in October 1942, aged 18 and after the Initial Training Wing at Torquay and grading school at Theale near Reading, he sailed to Canada on the *Ile de France*. He flew Cornells at Elementary Flying Training School in Assiniboia in Saskatchewan, then Harvards at No.34 SFTS at Medicine Hat, Alberta, Canada. He received his wings and was commissioned in July 1944.

When he arrived back in the UK in September 1944, it was obvious that the Empire Training Scheme had done its job well as there were plenty of pilots 'surplus to requirements'.

• • • • • • • • • • •

F/Sgt Billingham joined the RAF in February 1943. After ten months waiting he arrived at the Air Crew Recruiting Centre at Lords Cricket Ground, St John's Wood in North London. He was then posted to No.5 Initial Training Wing at the Coorak Hotel, Torquay – B-Flight of No.4 Squadron – and stayed there until June 1943.

After gathering at Heaton Park, Manchester, he boarded a ship at Gourock, Scotland, sailing through the Suez Canal, then stopping at a transit camp at Port Tewfik. From there he went on to Durban and No.1 A/S Baragwanath, near Johannesburg, an Elementary Flying Training School, where he trained on Tiger Moths from 4th December 1943 to 19th February 1944 and then on to advanced training on Harvards from February to 4th August 1944 when he gained his wings and sergeant's stripes. On one occasion he flew to Vereenigiging with his instructor, F/O Guthrie. When he failed to spot the town, Guthrie grabbed the controls and did a ninety degree bank, pointing to the name of the town marked out on the ground in huge letters for all to see, but particularly for his pupil!

The return sea voyage to the UK entailed zig-zagging around the ocean on a Dutch ship, *Niuew Amsterdam*, via Freetown, Sierra Leone, taking 16 days to reach Gourock in Scotland. Also on board were thousands of Italian prisoners of war.

• • • • • • • • • • •

William Davies from Newport, Monmouthshire (now Gwent) was soon known as 'Taff' Davies in the armed forces. He went along to his local labour exchange in 1942 and said he would like to fly with the RAF. A medical followed. A few weeks later he was told to report to an address in Penarth. It turned out to be a large house, where he was given a further and much fuller medical and a test in English and maths. This was followed by a number of interviews by RAF officers, the outcome being that he was passed for training as a pilot. The training scheme was for pilots, navigators and bomb aimers – if you failed on one, you had the chance to train for one of the others. He received his call up papers in January 1943 and reported to the Air Crew Receiving Centre at Lords Cricket Ground.

Here he was kitted out and marched to the billets. His group was billeted at No.6 Hall Road, St John's Wood, a large block of flats, where they were given elementary military training such as drill, PT and route marching plus the usual inoculations and dental treatment.

The only fly in the ointment for most of the recruits was that, before they could move on, they were required to be able to receive Morse code at four words a minute both via radio and on the Aldis lamp.

"Most of us hadn't a clue about Morse code," he remembers, "and we went around all day for weeks going dot-dash-dot-dash in our heads. So far, everyone had got through and the Air Crew Reception Centre was interesting, with something going on and somewhere to go. For pay we had to go to Regents Park Zoo, Hampstead Heath for route marches, Seymores Hall for lectures and back to Lords for anti-gas training. At Hall Road there was a clocking and in and out system like in a factory."

Here Bill stayed until 6th March 1943, when he was posted to No.4 Initial Training Wing at Paignton, Devon. The course was 12 weeks in subjects such as navigation, theory of flight, armaments, meteorology, signals and hygiene. Their billets were hotels on the sea front and the schooling done in the Country Club.

The drill parades were on the sea front. From there he moved to No 9 Elementary Flying School at Ansty, near Coventry, on 24th June 1943. The flying training was to be carried out in a Tiger Moth aircraft – a time for butterflies in the stomach – he would soon know if he would take to flying or not. Each instructor had two pupils. Bill's instructor was a Warrant Officer, an unflappable man whose criticism was always to the point but never nasty.

For his first flight Bill was strapped into the rear cockpit with his parachute on plus helmet and goggles. The aircraft trundled down the grass runway at first quite bumpy and then, as the aircraft picked up, becoming smoother. As they reached flying speed, the aircraft touched the ground once or twice and then they were up. There was no sensation of speed or height – it felt to Bill as if they were hovering.

For half an hour they flew for air experience. It was the only flight Bill was to have for pleasure – from then on it was hard work. As they came down for landing, Bill realised he had made the right decision – flying was for him. He completed the compulsory 12 hours, but did not go solo. Nevertheless, he was told to continue flying training as pilot. Now came a promotion from Aircraftman 2 to Leading Aircraftman and a weekly pay increase from three shillings (15p) to seven shillings and sixpence (38p) – quite a jump!

After 9 days 'embarkation leave' he reported to Heaton Park, Manchester, a sort of embarkation camp. Here you were allocated your draft. Most drafts went to Canada or the USA, about one in seven went to South Africa or Rhodesia. Bill went to South Africa, being kitted out with tropical clothing, often said in jest to be a cruel deception to make the men think they were going to hot climates when in fact they were going to the North Pole! The pith helmets issued were the same as those worn by troops in the Boer War or in India. When they actually arrived in Africa, however, the sun helmets were taken back.

On 10th September 1943, Bill's draft left Heaton Park for Gourock on the Clyde to board a troopship. At each posting, small groups of men would band together and become friends and when they were split up, another band would form at the next posting. That is how it went on time and time again. At Gourock, the train stopped at the dockside and the men were taken out to the large ships lying in the very wide river Clyde on a small paddle steamer.

Bill's ship was a former liner, *Llangibby Castle*. "Being Welsh," he laughs, " this sounded like a home from home!"

The idea, once aboard, was to get a cabin with a porthole, but they found themselves going down and down into the ship, well below the waterline. At each deck, troops were allocated a space and eventually it was their turn. They entered a large room with a low ceiling which, when the ship was in service as a liner, had been the mail room. Here 100 men were housed.

"At one end of the room was a pile of hammocks and all over the ceiling were hooks on which to sling the hammocks. We soon discovered that it was far from easy to get into a hammock in the first place and there were many comical scenes as we struggled to learn this trick, only to find that when you finally did get into it, it closed up around you like a banana! The sailors told us they used two pieces of wood about 18-inches long, one at each end of the hammock, then it would stay open along its whole length. Unfortunately, there was no wood available, so we stayed like bananas for the entire trip..."

At meal times the men sat 18 to a table. Two men from each mess, armed with a bucket and a large cauldron, collected the food for their mess from the galley. There were only two meals a day and foods like corned beef had to be cut into 18 pieces with a blunt knife.

After sailing at dusk they found themselves next morning off the coast of northern Ireland in a convoy of 16 liners in lines of four, stem to stern. The *Llangibby Castle* was at the rear of the four in their line. Guarding the convoy were nine destroyers and a merchant type aircraft carrier.

They sailed on across the Bay of Biscay and through the straits of Gibraltar. They were told that they were only the second convoy to pass through since the Germans had been pushed out of North Africa. When they arrived at Port Said, they had been at sea for 16 days. At the end of the Suez Canal they were given the order to start disembarking. Each man had two kit bags, which were in storage in the hold of the ship, and retrieving them tuned into chaos. They were taken ashore in small 'lighters', and once ashore they boarded three ton trucks and travelled a few miles into the desert on the Cairo-Suez road to a tented transit camp. They were given 100 Egyptian piastres, worth about £1 and called by the troops 'ackers'. The camp was called a 24-hour transit camp but they stayed there three weeks. Bill remembers that the rations were the same every day.

"Breakfast was small eggs and a thick slice of bread covered in margarine, which somehow resisted melting in the heat. The mug of tea was hot, sweet and strong – the best part of the meal. For lunch it was a piece of cheese and strong onions plus more tea. This was eaten out of mess tins and the tea drunk out of a large china mug. The evening meal was stew. The rumour was that this was made from camel meat and local natives! The dessert was dried fruit that had been soaked and boiled then covered with custard. All this had to be put in one mess tin, putting bread in the middle to separate the stew from the dessert, followed by a quick dash to your tent to eat it before it all soaked into one. As it was, by the time you got back, your food would be covered in flies. If you stopped to kill one, there would be ten more."

After three weeks it was back to port to board another ship, this time the *Highland Brigade*, where conditions were much as before.

It was now very hot and very uncomfortable below decks at night.

After a week they arrived at Aden, where they docked for 24 hours and then sailed on into the Indian Ocean, next stop Mombassa for a 24-hour layover before crossing the equator where the usual rituals were held and enjoyed by all.

As they approached Durban, they could hear someone singing. It was a lady dressed in white and singing through a loud hailer. Her repertoire was endless, including 'The White Cliffs of Dover'. She was there throughout the war and, it was said, never missed a convoy.

The next day they boarded a train through the Johannesburg mountains until they finally reached No.2 Air School in the Transvaal. Here they stayed for a month. The food was good and they had the use of a large outdoor swimming pool. In December 1943 they split up. Bill went to No.3 Air School Wonderboom near Pretoria, the capital of South Africa. They were now part of the South African Air Force or Afrikaans. Some of the ground crew were RAF and a few RAF instructors but in the main the majority were South African Air Force. They wore khaki uniforms with each instructor having four pupils. The courses divided into two parts – six weeks elementary training and six weeks advanced. At any one time, an instructor would have two elementary pupils and two advanced.

The elementary pupils flew in the morning from about 6.30am to 10.00am followed by classwork in the afternoon. The advanced pupils flew from 10am. The mixture of pupils was 50/50 RAF and SAAF.

The South Africans all spoke English and Afrikaans and all were to be commissioned once they had their wings. The RAF pupils would be mostly sergeants – only a few would be given commissions. The airfield at Wonderboom was grass and the aircraft Tiger Moths. Bill did not hit it off with his instructor, a Lieutenant in the SAAF, who ranted at him from the time he took off to the time he landed. Every time Bill was coming in to land the controls were snatched away. Bill began to lose heart and it looked as if he was going to be washed out.

Then came a breath of fresh air. He was given a chance to fly with a new instructor, another Lieutenant in the SAAF, but they got on straight away. After an hour Lt Ogilvie asked, "Taffy, can you land this aircraft?"

"Certainly!"

"Then go ahead – and don't kill us!"

At last Bill could feel he was really flying the aircraft. After he had landed successfully, Ogilvie simply said, "Well done!"

A further two hours went by and Bill was given a solo test. After that, things just got better and better as he progressed into 1944.

Soon his progress test came, flying with Flt Lt Chubb RAF. Everything seemed to go okay in his test, flying steep turns, side slipping, spinning and practising force landings. He was told at the end that he was okay and to carry on.

Next day he started aerobatics, doing three loops and two stall turns. Things carried on progressing until February 1944 when he did his first night flying solo, formation flying and a two-hour cross country. The night flight was, as Bill describes it, 'interesting'. He was flying with Lt Peart SAAF and the officer in charge of flying Lt De Beere also SAAF.

The rules for night flying were that no more than three aircraft were allowed on the circuit at one time, but on this occasion there were four. The pilots of these aircraft thought that De Beere was under the weather, having been drinking when he said, "Send the four up and off to bed we can all go!"

Bill's instructor said he was not keen and told Bill to keep his eyes open. The flarepath consisted of a large paraffin flame called the 'money flame' aim for, and a row of smaller paraffin flares along the landing run. Landing was to be with the flames on your left.

Bill recalls, "The money flame gave you just enough light to touch down and an instrument in the aircraft called the 'glide path indicator' helped you down. Very much like a set of traffic lights, it was marked orange on the top, green in the middle and red on the bottom. Red meant you were to low, whereas orange meant you were too high."

Bill took off and did a circuit and prepared to land. He could see the position of the other three aircraft from their lights having been the third to take off.

"I was watching the air speed, rate of descent, wings level not slipping or skidding, glide path showing green, no-one in my way... However, the coloured boys on duty that night had built a fire just to the left of the money flare to sit around to keep warm. I must have wandered slightly left as I checked the instruments and when I looked up again at the flare path I was lined up on their camp fire and not the money flare. As I came in along the line of flares, I could see people running by the light of the fire, so I opened up and went around again!"

His second attempt at landing was successful.

By the time the end of the course came he had 89 flying hours in his log book and was classed as 'average'.

He was posted to No 27 Air School Bloemmopreit, near Bloemfontein, Orange Free State in March 1944. Here pupils flew Harvards, which had a single 450 hp Pratt & Whitney radial engine, variable pitched propeller and low wing retractable undercarriage. Bill remembers:

"The new camp was larger as was the airfield and the air filled with the noise of powerful engines. The training was the same, four pupils to each instructor. In the Harvard the pupil sat in the front and the instructor in the back, the reverse to the Tiger Moth. The Harvard had a plastic hood which you could cover yourself with, but for landings and take off it had to be open in the event of a crash to avoid being trapped in the cockpit. The engine was primed and the hand throttle opened slightly while on the port wing an airmen wound up a large starting handle inserted into the side, near the Harvard's engine. When the engine started the handle was disengaged and removed.

"There was a set series of checks before take-off. T.M.P.F.F – 'T' for throttle, 'M' fuel mixture lever in the full rich position, 'P' propeller pitch lever in the fully fine position, 'F' fuel gauges showing enough fuel, 'F' flaps up.

"You taxied downwind of the airfield, swinging the nose of the aircraft from side to side to see where you were going, owing to the fact that it was not possible to see straight ahead over the engine. You stopped at the downwind end, at right angles to take off, which would be into the wind. Then you got on the RT [Radio Telephone] set and called the control tower. The call sign was 'Pulpit' and the aircraft was in a squadron code called 'Rascal'.

"The landing series of checks was U.M.P.F.F U – Undercarriage, Mixture rich, Pitch fine, Fuel gauge and Flaps down."

After five hours of flying with an instructor, Bill flew solo. The effects of G were something new after the Tiger Moth.

"Any violent movement, for example steep turns and the blood was pushed from your head and down into your body. You had difficulty in seeing and very often black out came. You did not actually lose consciousness but just could not see. But after a few days of aerobatics this became a normal thing."

All that remained now was the passing out parade. Of the four pupils each instructor had, two would pass out and the other two who were half way through their training would go on wings parade as guard of honour. Thus Bill went on parade twice – once as a guard of honour and once to receive his wings. As each pupil's name was called, he would march out to the front and stop two paces from the officer presenting the wings, who would then pin them on the pupil's left breast. After shaking hands, the pupil would take a pace to the rear, salute again and then march back to the ranks.

Bill received his wings from the Chief of the South African Police.

When they got back to their billets, they changed into a tunic, which already had wings and the three stripes of a sergeant sewn on. It was now August 1944 and they were due to leave for the transit camp at West Lake, near Cape Town the day after passing out.

The journey, by train took two days. Having sleeping accommodation on the train was a new experience for many.

Bill remembers:

"Many of the men thought they were due to be sent to India at this juncture in the war but no… it was back to the UK – and on the fourth largest ship in the world at that time, a Dutch liner called the *New Amsterdam*. When they boarded the ship they discovered that 5,000 Italian of prisoners war had already been aboard for some days. They had been captured in North Africa, some of them years earlier, and now that Italy had capitulated, they thought they were going home… The part of the ship they were on was wired off.

"The ship had an American crew and American gunners. On this ship there were no hammocks but bunks which folded down when not in use. I was in the former cinema, which had a high ceiling. I was seven bunks up from the ground. With the *New Amsterdam* being so fast, it did not need an escort so we sailed alone."

The coast of Ireland soon was seen on the port side and they docked at Gourock on 15th September 1944. After disembarking they boarded a train headed for No.7 PRC (Pilots Reception Centre) Harrogate, Yorkshire. At the end of September they were sent home for 14 days leave. During this time the Battle at Arnhem took place, although Bill remembers that the only thing on their minds was their new status as pilots.

"We were asked at Harrogate what type of flying we would like to go into. I opted for ground attack, having done well at bombing and ground to air attack in South Africa."

The PRC was based in a large Harrogate Hotel which had been taken over by the RAF. When Bill arrived back from leave, one of his pals pointed to a large black board in the foyer of the former hotel. There was a list of names, including Bill's, announcing a posting to the RAF Regiment Depot near Bridgnorth, Shropshire.

Here they found themselves on a two-week infantry-style course.

• • • • • • • • • •

John Herold also trained in South Africa. He had joined the RAF as a regular in 1937 at the age 16 as a 'boy entrant'. He trained as a photographer at the School of Photography, Farnborough, after which he was posted to Calshot with the rank of Aircraftman 1st Class.

When the war started, John was at Invergordon with 201 Flying Boat Squadron. He then joined a fighter Squadron – No.16 – and went to France with the BEF. After the fall of France and with most of the squadron's aircraft missing, the survivors beat a hasty retreat to the UK…

In 1942 John was selected for aircrew training and in February 1943 he set sail for South Africa. He trained at Kronstad and Kimberley on multi-engined aircraft and was awarded his wings and a commission at the end of 1943. Like many others, he returned to the UK to find a glut of young pilots, all trained under the superb Empire Flying Training Scheme.

• • • • • • • • • •

Flt Sgt Wilson graduated as a pilot on the 22nd September 1944 at No.4 BFTS at Saskatoon, Saskatchewen, Canada, with the following rating:

Flying – 3rd equal on course
Ground School – dismal.

He returned to the UK on the SS *Mauritania* and duly reported to the centre at Harrogate and the Majestic Hotel, which he found to be cold, ill-lit and depressing.

• • • • • • • • • •

Jim Rudkin was trained on Harvards at Dunnville, Canada during the summer of 1944. He was under no illusions how difficult it would be to become a fighter pilot, not only because the war was coming to an end but because the course was extended, not once, but twice.

He received his wings at Dunnville in August 1944, followed by a five-week stay at Moncton, New Brunswick, an indication that there was no rush to get him back to the UK. He eventually returned on the *Ile de France* to Greenock and then to Harrogate on the 12th October 1944.

• • • • • • • • • •

Ivan Lancaster was born and grew up in Lancashire until he was 12 years old, when his family moved to Ely, Cambridgeshire.

When the war broke out, he was 15 years old and joined the Air Training Corps. He visited two Bomber stations, Mildenhall and Waterbeach. While he was there, he saw "the dark and nasty side" of a bomber station during wartime when two Stirlings and one Wellington crashed. But he did manage to get a flight in a Stirling...

When he commenced his studies as a trainee surveyor, he was not aware that it was a 'reserved occupation', so when his 18th birthday came around, he kept quiet about his occupation and volunteered for aircrew. The usual initial training followed, after which two students, including Ivan, were called for immediate service under the Pilot, Navigator and Bomber scheme. They were given leave and then told to report to the Aircrew Reception Centre at St John's Wood, London. After the war when Ivan met the other man, he was surprised to find he had failed his flying training.

After further initial flying training he went to No.3 BFTS at Miami, Oklahoma. As with 95% of successful pilots, he graduated as a sergeant pilot. He was recommended to fly *(1) fighters at low level, (2) fighters at a medium level or (3) fighters at a high level*, and confidently expected to do so when he returned to the UK. However, he also was to end up at the Majestic Hotel, Harrogate, Yorkshire...

• • • • • • • • • •

KENNETH ROSS joined the Air Defence Cadet Corps (the forerunner of the Air Training Corps) in Glasgow at the age of 15.

"We met for two evenings a week," he remembers, "and were required to wear made-to-measure RAF-style uniforms. We were taught various topics such as signals, theory of flight, meteorology and so on. At weekends we went to a flying boat base at Rhu, near Helensburgh on the West Coast of Scotland and flew in Sunderland flying boats.

He trained at No.3 BFTS and received his wings on 15th April 1944, with a score of 77% along with the Right Honourable Sir Peter Shore MP, coming 33rd out of the 95 cadets who passed.

He felt this was not to bad for a boy who had left school at the age of 14 and without any qualifications. Within days he was boarding a train back to Moncton, Canada.

Here they remained for a week or two and then from Halifax, Nova Scotia, they left on a large troop ship bound for Liverpool. He recalls that the food was barely adequate and they bought eggs and bacon from the crew of the ship. After a spell at home he reported to Harrogate.

• • • • • • • • • • •

Stanley Weston left Heaton Park and embarked on the *Queen Elizabeth* for Canada in August 1943. From Moncton he joined No.35 EFTS at Neepawa, Manitoba and flew Tiger Moth Mk IIs, which had a Perspex hood over the cockpit to protect the instructor and the cadets from the elements. After six weeks training he was posted to No.17 SFTS at Souris, Manitoba. As a 98% RAF course, No.102 found themselves most unwelcome, as the instruction staff of the Royal Canadian Air Force had worked their socks off to complete course 101 in order to obtain a spot of leave. Over 40% of the course were washed out in the first six weeks.

Stanley and the remainder finally passed out on 22nd September 1944 – he also ended up at Harrogate on his return to the UK.

• • • • • • • • • • •

John Barnsley joined the RAF in 1942, and having passed the aircrew selection board at Weston-Super-Mare was given a service number and sworn in.

He reported to the Aircrew Recruit Centre St John's Wood and after the usual induction procedures he was posted to No.4 Initial Training Wing at Paignton, Devon. Here he received all the ground training necessary before taking to the air, and he remembers 'a lot of marching'. He was then posted to Wesfords, near Leicester for his initial flying training and his first encounter with a Tiger Moth. Then he was off to Canada via New York on the *Queen Mary* and then by rail to Moncton, New Brunswick, a holding depot. After 6 days on the boat and 4½ days on the train, he arrived in Saskatchewan.

The course ended on 12th December 1943 and after leave over Christmas he was posted for advanced training to Dauphin, Manitoba, a school for twin-engined aircraft, which John wanted to fly. What was to be an 8-week course turned into a 28-week course, because, he was later to discover, of the glut of pilots in the UK.

His total flying hours to pass for his wings were 202 – of this 65 were at Elementary Training School on the Cornell basic training machine. At Service Flying Training School he flew 137 hours in a Cessna monoplane (roughly equivalent to the RAF Oxford) and in an Anson for advanced navigation and beam approach training.

He finally left Canada on 28th August and arrived in Harrogate on the 6th September. At Harrogate life was very boring and the future black, so much so that when the Royal Navy asked for RAF pilots John immediately volunteered. However, this was at about the time of Arnhem and the sudden shortage of glider pilots, so understandably John heard nothing more from the Navy.

• • • • • • • • • • •

In 1942 Ken Scolding was in a reserved occupation, but by August 'the powers that be' relented and allowed him to join the RAF...

After a week at St John's Wood he was posted to No.2 Initial Training Wing at Cambridge. At this time he was also married and had a daughter. His next move was to Marshal's Flying School – or to give it its official title, No.22 EFTS. Here he flew twelve and half hours on Tiger Moths but failed to go solo, thought to be essential for grading as a pilot. By this time it was May 1943, however, and despite this shortcoming he was graded as a pilot and found himself at Heaton Park awaiting a boat to Canada. In June 1943 he left on the *Empress of Scotland* (which had, in peacetime been the *Empress of Japan* – not considered a good omen by the crew). To escape the hunting packs of U-boats, they had to seek shelter in the fog banks off Newfoundland, being unescorted at the time. Below decks were German prisoners from Rommel's Afrika Korps. As Hitler had told them in one of his infamous speeches that no ship crossed the Atlantic without being sent to the bottom there was some concern below decks.

They were due to disembark at St John, New Brunswick, but instead hugged the coast and landed at Newport News, Virginia. The German prisoners were handed over to the Americans and were treated with contempt, which did not please the British guards who had been looking after them since leaving the UK. They told the Americans in no uncertain terms that the Afrika Korps were better soldiers than they would ever be.

After a twelve hour train journey to Monkton they were put on another train to No.33 EFTS at Caron, Saskatchewan. This journey took four days and three nights. The weather was hot and the billets looked after by civilians who were very good. From his log book Ken notes that he took 12 hours to fly solo, not in a Tiger Moth but a Cornell. Much to the excitement of his room-mates, the first time round he failed to land and he had to go around again. Bets were hastily laid as to whether or not he would prang the aircraft. Fortunately for him, he landed in one piece, even remembered to raise the flaps while taxiing.

He had flown 33.05 hours dual and 31.30 hours solo, daytime but only 20 minutes solo at night. He feels he was lucky not to have been remustered as a navigator. From Casron he was posted to No.35 SFTS at North Battleford, Saskatchewan, where he flew Oxfords and after 5 hours 20 minutes went solo – the second lowest time of the course. It is very cold in this part of Canada – good practise in the snow, without a visible horizon, for instrument flying.

On the 23rd December 1943 he was presented with his wings and went to Winnipeg for Christmas leave. While there, he received a telegram to say that he had been given a commission. He had been a sergeant for one day only!

He travelled to New York to await a boat home and stayed in some of the best houses on Park and 5th Avenues and thanks to the generous hospitality of his American hosts, his stay did not cost him a penny.

The journey home was very rough and he remembers that the ship, the *Neuw Amsterdam* "rolled like tub". He was not sorry to see the coast of Scotland.

On arrival at Harrogate, orders were posted, with some staying in the UK and others posted to India. The list was in alphabetical order. His friend went to India and he stayed in the UK.

He was posted for a refresher course on Tiger Moths at No.6 EFTS Sywell, Northamptonshire.

He was billeted in the town and able to have his wife with him for a few days. He flew 23 hours days and 10 minutes nights on this course. He had forgotten how dark the UK could be in the blackout and found one circuit at night and having to land on a goose-neck flare-path quite enough.

• • • • • • • • • •

Stanley Kent – who became known as 'Duke' – started his RAF service a couple of days after the war started. He had already been through the Short Service Commission selection process. He was told that the RAF had enough pilots under training and his only hope of flying was to train as an air gunner, which at the time were urgently needed.

He completed his training as a wireless operator/ air gunner and was posted to No.3 Group Bomber Command in June 1940. He completed a tour of operations (at that time 25), but just before he had completed his tour, he was sent to Malta in October 1940, for attacks on the Italian Fleet. This short visit turned into a tour, and with the island running out of ammunition, food, fuel and aircraft he was despatched back to the UK via the Suez Canal. His entire crew was recommended for the DFM.

On arrival back in the UK he was sent as an instructor, without any training, to a unit about to commence crew training for flying Mosquitoes.

After a few months he was given a commission and, while on leave in London, he met a senior RAF officer with whom he had flown in Malta. After some discussion, he was posted to a Special Duties Flight, flying Liberators. When his tour with this unit was completed, he requested to go for pilot training. Having been on 'heavies' and been flown around by someone else, he was now only interested in flying attack fighters. He was a good shot and an average pilot and because he was aware of the 'air gunner's angle' he felt he had a good chance.

• • • • • • • • • •

John Perry was posted to No.3 BFTS. Here he met John Rayson, Ken Ellwood and a number of other cadets who were to join him later in the GPR. Having been awarded his wings, he returned to the UK in the Spring of 1944. He found that there was a surplus of fighter pilots and after the opening of the second front in June 1944, the only way to get into any action was to convert to four engine aircraft. He volunteered for the Fleet Air Arm with a view to staying on single engine aircraft, but the disaster at Arnhem put paid to that. John volunteered for the GPR and was naturally accepted. At Brize Norton he was joined by his second pilot, Pete Read and given the shortest haircut he ever had in his life. It was so short that his newly acquired blue beret fell over his ears!

On arrival at 'B' Squadron, he was kitted out with Khaki battledress, a blue shirt and Pegasus insignia.

"That way," he remembers, "we had a foot in each camp."

How did glider flying training compare with powered engine aircraft?

• • • • • • • • • •

Joe Kitchener joined the army in January 1939 and transferred to the Glider Pilot Regiment in February 1942 from the Royal Artillery.

At Elementary Flying Training School, Joe flew 70 hours on Tiger Moths and 22 hours on Magisters. He then was posted to Kidlington

Ken Ellwood. [Ken Ellwood]

Glider Training School where he flew 56 hours on Hotspurs and then at a Heavy Glider Conversion Unit at Brize Norton where he flew 9 hours on Horsas.

His Glider pilot wings were awarded in April 1943, having flown a total of 157 hours.

At EFTS, after 12 hours he flew solo on Tiger Moths. An extension could be given if it was thought a man could make it if given extra time. Those who failed were returned to their former unit.

He went on to see service in North Africa and Italy, on D-Day and at Arnhem.

• • • • • • • • • •

Edgar (Eddie) Raspison was called up for service with the Royal Scots Fusiliers and was posted to the 6th Battalion and shipped off to France in 1940. He was in luck, missing the evacuation at Dunkirk, and came back from France via Le Havre on the same ship, the tramp steamer *Amsterdam* that he had sailed out on from the UK. On his return, he transferred to the Royal Army Service Corps and was promoted to Corporal. He was then approached to train as an army glider pilot and was called forward to the Aircrew Selection Board at Padgate. However, it was not flying gliders that he first encountered but initial infantry training under a Guard's warrant officer.

His flying training started at No.3 EFTS at Shillingford, Oxford, and began his flying training on Tiger Moths with a maximum 12 hours before he went solo. Much groundwork was involved, with map reading, air navigation and the Link Trainer flying simulator. After 54 hours dual instruction and 44 hours solo flying the course was moved to No.5 Glider Training School at Shobdon near Hereford in March 1943.

It was here that he had a sobering experience when he flew a Magister into high tension cables, getting away lightly with a cut lip and a cut on one leg.

• • • • • • • • • • •

Fred Meek, along with 110 RAF and American cadets, passed out as a sergeant pilot on his 21st birthday at No.3 BFTS and returned to the UK on the Dutch ship *Nieuw Amsterdam* with other ex-cadets and about 6,000 members of the Canadian army.

After training with No.15 EFTS at Carlisle, he returned to Harrogate where he had been posted on his return to the UK. Here he and others were called to a meeting in the local cinema to be addressed by a St/Sgt from the Glider Pilot Regiment, asking for volunteers, and telling them that those who did would be made first pilots.

Fred did not volunteer but was posted to No.5 Glider course at 21 EFTS at Booker. The course lasted two weeks and then he was posted to No.21 HGCU at Brize Norton where he crewed up with his first pilot.

• • • • • • • • • • •

In America they were late in picking up on the use of gliders in war.

Getting the powers that be interested enough to do something about obtaining gliders was the first problem. No one seemed to know the type of glider was required. It was only when the Waco Aircraft Company offered a fifteen-place military glider on the lines of the German DFS-230 that things started to take off. The Waco CG-4A glider was accepted as the combat glider of the United States Army.

Just as Churchill had done in 1940, General Arnold commanded, in 1942, that ten thousand gliders be produced within six months in preparation for a second front in 1943. The officer ordered to make this happen was stunned, as there were, at that time, no plans or factories set up to build gliders. However, the second front did not materialise in 1943, so the order for ten thousand gliders was rescinded.

The training of glider pilots in America was similar to those in the UK. Pupils were assigned to elementary flying schools and flying done on Piper Cub or a similar light aircraft. This lasted for 40 hours, when pupils were transferred to elementary glider schools.

By 1943 the Waco was being produced in great numbers, but in August 1943, in front of the Mayor, members of the council and other prominent people at St Louis, Missouri, a Waco glider lost a wing over the city and crashed, killing all on board. Hardly a good omen.

After training, US glider pilots received silver wings with a G in the middle and were placed in holding pools until Troop Carrier Command received the required numbers of C47 groups to which each could be assigned.

They then started to learn the technique of flying while being towed, flying in formation and night flying.

RAF Hadrian glider. [Alec Waldron]

CHAPTER 8

Preparing for Varsity

It was October 1944, when Cy Henson found himself at Harrogate, a pilot officer with 450 hours in his log book. When one day he visited the orderly room he found they were compiling lists of volunteers who wanted to get into operational flying. He put his name down on the understanding that one possibility was the Fleet Air Arm. Having been trained under the Towers Scheme by the US Navy at Detroit and Pensacola, Cy felt he stood a chance. It was then that he found out that the list was for glider pilots after the losses at Arnhem the month before. He soon realised his mistake and was shocked, to say the least, at having volunteered. His argument was that it would be far better if he went to the Fleet Air Arm. The 'powers that be' agreed, but as they had had so few volunteers for gliders, his name could now not be removed from the list. His outrage was exacerbated by the fact that two others pilots who volunteered had been taken on by the FAA. His protest was still going on when he was posted to Bridgnorth, along with 30 others, for military training.

This course, he was glad to record, only lasted two weeks and contained the usual foot stamping that all drill instructors seem to revel in. He had, over two years, suffered all manner of indignities with the thought that one day he would be a pilot. These two weeks, he thought, would not in any way make him into a soldier, especially as the instructors showed little interest in training them to do anything useful, but merely seemed intent on making their life as uncomfortable as possible.

On one occasion, on the assault course they were made to crawl along a drainpipe, about 15 feet long with water and mud flowing through it. At the end of the pipe, a corporal was feeding thunder-flashes inside as fast as he could, smothering the occupiers with mud and water.

"If you saw one before it went off and pushed it under the water, the result of the explosion was even worse and deafening," Cy recalls. "This was the highlight of the day for the instructors."

One thing Cy did learn about himself during those weeks was that if pushed hard enough he could learn to hate and that given enough excitement and the right circumstances he could probably learn to kill. Today, in hindsight, and being generous after fifty years, he thinks this was probably the aim.

It was at Bridgnorth that he first came into contact with the 'hairy blanket' style battledress with RAF ranks in blue, RAF wings, and a blue beret as worn by the RAF Regiment.

The group was divided into first and second pilots and the induction into gliders was training on Hotspur gliders at No.1 Glider Training

Cyril 'Cy' Henson – 1945.

School based at RAF Croughton, near Brackley, Northamptonshire. The course was of ten hours and Cy went solo in under two. Even on gliders it was great for him to be flying again, having not flown for three months, although it was vastly different after flying Harvards. When he cast off from the Miles Master tug aircraft he found the experience exhilarating, and the glider surprisingly manoeuvrable during the first few minutes that one had before seeking to return to the airfield.

"All in all, a very pleasant experience," he remembers.

From there he went to 23 Heavy Glider Conversion Unit at RAF Seighford, where he was introduced to the Horsa glider and also checked out the American Hadrian glider. Here he did just ten hours night and day over two weeks and was teamed up with his co-pilot, Sgt Ken Wright, RAF whom he had known at 34 SFTS. They were to remain as a crew until after Operation Varsity.

Soon after a short leave they were back with the Army, this time the Glider Pilot depot at Fargo, on Salisbury Plain, and all signs of life as members of the RAF were said goodbye to for the time being. They managed, at least, to attempt to fire most small arms, including the Projector, Infantry, and anti tank (PIAT) guns. One experience with this last weapon was enough for Cy, who hoped he would never have to repeat it, although the soldiers he carried in the gliders thought very highly of this weapon.

While on the firing ranges, where live shells were flying around, a small Army Observation aircraft came over. When Cy looked back, all he saw was a puff of smoke, no aircraft, just a pile of debris coming down through the air. The expression 'friendly fire' had not been invented at the time.

On 24th January 1945, Cy was posted to RAF Great Dunmow, Essex and G Squadron of the Glider Pilot Regiment.

They were issued with their own side-arms. Cy had a 9mm Browning automatic revolver, which he had great fun firing at all manner of targets. Marching around the perimeter track, 5 miles in 50 minutes with full pack, was a regular

RAF Glider pilots in battledress. Earls Colne, 1945. (l to r) Matcham, Newton, Barnsley, Elliott, Bruce. [John Barnsley]

feature of the day. This was combined with a lot of flying – mainly circuits with heavy loads, cross country flying on tow behind Stirlings and a number of mass landing exercises.

He was usually lucky in being able to land early at the far end of the runway, before space ran out and the chance of collision increased, often followed by sound of shattering woodwork as glider hit glider.

Rumours of an impending operation were rife at this time.

● ● ● ● ● ● ● ● ● ● ●

John Barnsley also undertook a course at Bridgnorth and was introduced to unarmed combat by the RAF Regiment. On 1st November, he was posted to Shobdon where he met his first glider.

The basic training was on a Hotspur towed by a single-engined Miles Master Mk.II usually used for training fighter pilots. The Hotspur could carry eight troops, although with all their equipment it was difficult to get them all in.

No time was lost getting into the air and on the day after arrival he made several flights. Out of the 14 days he was at Shobdon, he flew on seven – a total of 32 take-offs and landings. His longest time in the air was 50 minutes, but mostly the flights were of only ten to fifteen minutes.

From Shobdon he was posted to Brize Norton Heavy Glider Conversion Unit. One of the first things here was the crewing up of pilots. This was done in the usual aircrew fashion with everybody in a large room being told to 'sort them selves out into crews'. John was lucky, he remembers, that Sgt Danny Bruce found him. They got on very well, having both been trained in the USA as fighter pilots. They flew on six days, 18 take offs and landings, the towing aircraft a Whitley bomber. At one time three crews were detached to RAF North Luffenham, in Rutland as the weather was starting to deteriorate at Brize Norton. They were taken up to 8,000 feet, staying up as long as possible.

Back at Brize Norton they were introduced to the 'Hadrian' the re-named American Waco CG4 glider. It carried two pilots and eight men or a jeep. It was made of tubular frame and canvas and was so light it could be pulled about by two men. John is glad to say they only flew this glider on two occasions. The main glider at Brize

RAF Glider pilots on parade at Brize Norton, 1944. Major Dale (Hamilcar pilot) centre. [Ken Ashurst]

Norton was the Horsa Mk.I. John had no trouble in converting to a 'motor-less aircraft' as they were called in the flying log-book.

At Brize Norton, one afternoon was spent learning to throw grenades and fit fuses – something John never expected to do on an RAF Station.

He was then posted to Hampstead Norrey, near Newbury, where the training on gliders (towed by Albemarles) was limited, owing to bad weather, giving more time for infantry training. John found the PIAT gun great fun but caused some consternation in damaging one of His Majesty's aircraft with it.

On 27th December, after Xmas leave, he was posted to 'B' Squadron under Major Ian Toler, whom he found to be an extremely nice man. At first there was also an RAF squadron leader, but when it was found that the army and RAF could work together in harmony, he soon vanished. The RAF pilots saw little of the GPR pilots who it would appear were billeted away from the camp.

It was 15th January before flying began, when John, F/O Shannon and Sgt Elliott took off in a Horsa Mk II on an endurance test. The main purpose of this flight, although not realised at the time, was to ascertain if the Halifax tug could get them to the Rhine and return without running out of fuel. They were assured by the flight engineer on the Halifax that they still had plenty of fuel on their return.

A number of cross country flights followed and one Friday in March they were sent to Colchester ranges with 1500 rounds of ammunition, rifles, and two or three Bren guns. The ammo was soon used up and they entrained to camp for a weekend pass to London.

On another trip to the Fingringhoe ranges they used 2-inch airborne mortars and rifles.

"No instruction was given as how to fire the mortars," John recalls, "but as they seemed fairly straightforward we just got on with it, which did not seem to please the range warden."

They had to shoot at a plywood tank, but failed to hit it. The warden was not pleased and made them do it again, which they duly did and this time were successful. Again, the warden was not pleased.

"You were only supposed to hit it," he shouted at us, "not destroy it!" says John.

● ● ● ● ● ● ● ● ● ● ●

Kenneth Ross undertook a course at Salisbury Plain, learning to strip, assemble blindfolded and use under all sorts of conditions the small arms used by the army – the bazooka (PIAT), Bren gun and mortar.

Rifle practice was done on the rifle ranges at Bisley. Ken also learned about laying and clearing land mines, setting booby traps and the fusing and throwing of grenades. They dug slit trenches in snow-covered, frozen earth and crawled through water and mud while real bullets flew overhead and the earth around exploded.

They were taught by battle-trained experts how to kill quietly and silently but above all else how to stay alive. The instructors were from the Guards who had the uphill task of changing pilots into fighting soldiers in three weeks. No time was wasted on useless drill.

From Reveille at 6.30am until 'lights-out' at 10pm they toiled at Salisbury Plain. Night training exercises were carried out by the use of the compass.

Their uniforms were confusing – camouflage jackets with RAF wings and Airborne Pegasus shoulder flashes.

Glider training was undertaken from airfield to airfield using the American Waco, but more often the Horsa. Early in his training, Ken became second pilot to the Flight Commander of the unit, Flight Lt L. Halley DFC, who had completed a tour on Bomber Operations. They flew together for most of the remainder of their time on gliders.

Just as the RAF glider pilots were learning to fly a glider being towed by a bomber, so the bomber pilots had to learn how to tow a glider. A snapped tow-rope was not an unusual occurrence.

"It is one thing to tow a car along a road for a few miles, but quite a different thing to tow a heavy and unwieldy glider for hundreds of miles," remembers Ken. "Not only do they move laterally to each other but also vertically and if a glider got into the slipstream of the tow plane it was buffeted all over the place. Often turbulent air was encountered when a plane was towing a glider and the two aircraft did not always encounter the turbulence simultaneously. The outcome meant violent stresses on the tow-rope which simply snapped."

Kenneth Ross and Flt Lt Halley only once experienced a snapped rope. They were flying over Lincolnshire at a height of about 5,000 feet when the rope parted and they had to glide downwards.

Circling, they descended slowly and picked out a large field, towards which they headed. They made a long, flat approach, holding off until the last moment.

"We touched down as lightly as a feather," Ken recalls, "ending up close to the boundary of the field."

In the adjacent field, less than fifty yards away, but with backs towards them, half a dozen agricultural workers toiled away, completely unaware of their presence.

"We opened the glider windows and shouted 'Hello!'" says Ken with a smile. "I will never forget the look on their faces they turned towards us. They must have thought we were part of a German invasion force!"

• • • • • • • • • • •

Ivan Lancaster remembers being assembled at Harrogate to be told that the Army needed volunteers as a glider pilots.

"Needless to say, they were booed off the stage," he recalls, "although a few RAF pilots did volunteer…"

Some ten days later they were again assembled.

"This time we were told 'you either volunteer or be transferred to the army as privates and sent to the Far East in the infantry' – quite a threat," says Ivan.

Having reluctantly transferred to the Glider Pilot Regiment, Ivan underwent battle training with the RAF Regiment and then the army followed by flying training on Hadrian (Waco) and Horsa gliders. Then he was sent to Fargo Camp, Salisbury Plain with 100 other pilots for infantry training.

"Just before Xmas 1944 came the news that there would be no leave as civilians would need all the available transport," he recalls.

On the evening the announcement was made there was uproar and subsequently it transpired that a number of pilots had acquired a load of explosives and set off to blow up Stonehenge, only a few miles away.

"They were intercepted half way to Stonehenge and no action was taken against them, but the following day leave passes were issued and we all left Fargo for good," Ivan remembers.

Then came a posting to 'B' Squadron of the Glider Pilot Regiment at Earls Colne, Essex. Here they continued battle training and flying Horsas.

"Glider crews were usually both Glider Pilot Regiment or both RAF. In the case of the latter it would be an RAF officer with a sergeant as a second pilot. Co-operation between the Army and RAF on the squadron was very good," Ivan recollects.

• • • • • • • • • • •

Within a few days of John Rudkin arriving at Harrogate and the Majestic Hotel, came a visit by Wg/Cdr Kean, with the message that volunteers were needed to fly gliders to replace the men lost at Arnhem.

"He intimated that if we didn't volunteer we would end up flying gliders anyway," says John, "so after a short discussion with friends I put up my hand and volunteered."

He was only one of ten who did so.

"My greatest fear was ending up with a ground job," he says, "and I reasoned that even at the end of a tow-rope I would, at least, be flying."

He was posted to RAF Croughton where he adapted quite well to the Hotspur glider, but before this, he had to also do a two-week stint at RAF Bridgnorth with the RAF Regiment…

Upon arrival they were left in no doubt by the Regiment F/Sgt what was expected of them.

"Time was at a premium," recalls John, "a tragic situation, as there were between 40 and 50 pubs in Bridgnorth – there were 30 in one street alone, or so the story goes."

They fired sten guns at wooden figures which suddenly popped up as they walked through the woods, fired rifles in mock section advances. Once, on night exercise, they were made to spend the night in an old building with very little roof and a concrete floor. Somehow, they managed to sneak off for an hour at a local hostelry and on the way back to their 'lavish' accommodation, they raided a haystack to provide themselves with a little bedding.

"It was still the most uncomfortable and certainly the coldest time I ever spent in the war," recalls John, "certainly after the central heating of the billets in Canada."

One of the instructors was a Sir Michael Bruce, the older brother of Nigel Bruce, who for many years was Dr Watson to Sherlock Holmes played by Basil Rathbone. He had served in WW1 but been recalled to the RAF in 1941. He was the senior weapons instructor at Bridgnorth and at 54 years old, considerably older than the men he was meant to instruct.

"Everywhere you looked at Bridgnorth there were ranges for every kind of weapon and ditches in which men were meant to lie and hope for the best," remembers John."

Even colder conditions were to follow at Fargo…

Like Cy Henson, John was introduced to the PIAT gun (bazooka) which he describes as 'a monster'.

"We fired in alphabetical order. A chap named Bradley was the first in the trench to fire it – and his first reaction afterwards didn't inspire any of those to follow with confidence – He climbed out clutching his shoulder shouting a number of obscenities!"

With the help of the weapons instructors they soon got used to the 'kick' from the 'monster', but to be effective against a tank, you had to wait until it was only 25 yards away.

"Something we all hoped would never happen," laughs John.

It was then on to Fargo where it was bitterly cold and there was no fuel for the stove in the middle of the hut. They slept in their clothes and flying kit but still could not get warm. Eventually they got some fuel from the local American compound – illegal but worth it.

With this behind him, John moved on to RAF Peplow, Shropshire, seven miles south of Market Drayton. Here he learned to fly a Horsa glider towed by an Albemarle.

It was also here that they were introduced to khaki battledress.

"The commanding officer insisted that if you were on night flying duty and the weather bad, you stayed up all night – and if it cleared to permit flying even for an hour before dawn, then this you did," John recalls.

"On one occasion, very close to Xmas, I was scheduled for night flying on a night when there was also a mess dance. To my great delight it was foggy that night – a real pea souper – so I was able to get to the dance.

"The usual bus load of girls came and everything was going fine when, I was sent for by the officer in charge of flying. He met me at the door of the mess and said, 'Tell everyone on night flying to get cracking.' I returned to the dance floor and rounded up a few very disgruntled pilots whose remarks cannot be put into print! The fog had lifted and so flying was on – even though we would not have passed a breath test, if there had been such things in those days. All went well, although at one stage my co-pilot was asleep…"

By the time they landed, the party had finished so they returned to their billets for a good sleep.

"Getting home on leave in those days took for ever," John recalls, "24 hours to get to Grantham, trains being delayed in the fog and a long hold up at Birmingham during an air raid. I eventually made it home for Xmas Eve."

In January 1945 he was posted to Great Dunmow in Essex. Here he spent two months flying Horsas, keeping fit and undergoing infantry training.

John Crane. [John Crane]

During this time, he took part in a massive assembly of gliders, which turned out to be a rehearsal for the operation ahead.

• • • • • • • • • •

When John Crane arrived back in the UK from the USA, having trained at No.3 BFTS, he was at first posted to Harrogate then Whitley Bay, Padgate, Disford and finally March in Cambridgeshire, where for a while he became a fireman on the railways, living in civilian billets. He was then posted back to Harrogate and followed the same route as many others into the Glider Pilot Regiment.

Several short courses followed, on Horsas at Brize Norton, then to Bridgnorth, followed by Fargo, where he remembers being required to disembowel dummies with fixed bayonet whilst uttering war cries.

"That didn't go down too well with RAF pilots," he laughs, "we hadn't joined the RAF to train as infantry."

He was then posted to F Squadron at RAF Broadwell, Oxfordshire, flying Horsas towed by Albemarles or Dakotas. The training flights were mainly over the Cotswolds and Southern England. There was also a mass landing on Broadwell aerodrome. He was paired up with a Flight Officer Arnold, John at the time was a F/Sgt.

• • • • • • • • • •

From Sywell, Ken Scolding went to Bridgnorth with the news that he was to fly gliders.

"Some of the younger pilots were up in arms," he remembers, "and went to see the Commanding Officer. But it was of no use ... gliders it was."

Sgt John Crane and Sgt Ray Bowes with Horsa glider. [John Crane]

As for Ken, he thought that after the disaster at Arnhem, there would be no more gliders.

From Bridgnorth, Ken went to Fargo.

"Battledress and boot cleaning until you could see yourself in your toe caps," he laughs. "The NCOs were not terribly polite – 'never seen such a shower in my life' – 'you 'orrible lot' etc – but we were taught to strip a Bren gun and then put it together again with out having any bits left over."

In November 1944 Ken was posted to Shobdon and introduced, as he describes it, to 'the dreaded glider' – the Hotpsur.

"The controls were so stiff that after 15 minutes it felt like you had been flying for two hours," he recalls.

After 5 hours and 35 minutes dual, and 3 hours 30 minutes solo, he was declared a proficient glider pilot. The course consisted of 12 dual tows daytime, and 4 dual tows at night, 10 daytime tows solo and 2 night-time tows solo.

"Flying any glider at night was frightening," Ken remembers, "but with the Hotspur it could be suicidal."

He describes Flt Lt Sir Michael Bruce as "a complete nutcase" but remembers Shobden as the first place I saw the Army and RAF working together.

In November 1944 he was posted to No 21 HGCU at Brize Norton and introduced to the Horsa Mark 1 and the Hadrian (Waco) gliders. After 1 hour and 45 minutes dual on the Horsa he flew as first pilot and after 30 minutes on the Waco he again flew as first pilot. After 2 hours and 5 minutes days on the Horsa dual and 45 minutes solo, and 30 minutes dual and 20 minutes solo at night, his instruction on the Horsa was complete.

"Thank God," he says, "having had 1 hour dual and 10 minutes solo on the Waco I did not have to fly it at night."

In February 1945, he was posted to RAF Rivenhall and became a member of 2 Flight of 'A' Squadron GPR under Cpt Tony Turner, whose reputation was 'fireproof'. The Squadron Commander was Major Hugh Bartlett, captain of Sussex County Cricket Club, the Wing Commander was Lt-Col Billy Griffiths, the

Major Hugh Bartlett, S/Sgt Roy Howard DFM, Lt-Col Billy Griffiths and an RA F/O glider pilot. [Ian Toler]

England wicketkeeper and later Secretary of the MCC.

They flew nearly every day, sometimes twice. When not flying, they were trained by Tony Turner in the use of plastic explosives with an instantaneous fuse for felling trees, booby traps and how to avoid them, and house-to-house fighting.

Many exercises were flown from one airfield to another, to see how many gliders could be put down into a small area.

"For those landing first it was easy," recalls Ken, "but for those at the rear of the stream it was a problem to first locate a space and then to land in it and not on top of another glider."

Releases from 8,000 feet, flying with ballast of 3,000lb – about half the load of a Horsa – were also carried out.

They then got wind of an operation afoot…

At Fargo in February 1945, at the end of the course, P/O Wilson remembers they were invited to a shooting competition – RAF v Army – and the RAF won, taking top marks on the rifle, Bren and Sten gun, and only being beaten on hand guns.

"We left with big smiles on our faces and a V sign for the army instructors," he laughs.

He was posted to RAF Great Dunmow and 'K' Squadron, flying Hotspurs towed by Miles Masters until the 12th March and then Horsas towed by Halifax B III tugs day and night.

● ● ● ● ● ● ● ● ● ●

David Richards joined 'F' Squadron at RAF Broadwell in January 1945. He admits to being an unwilling 'volunteer' to the GPR. He flew 10 hours at RAF Croughton, then a Heavy Conversion course at Seighford, where they completed 5 hours by day and 2 hours by night on Horsas and a 'brisk' one hour on Wacos.

"Today," David feels, "this would be considered a do-it-yourself crash course. The instructors were all Tiger Moth instructors from EFTS and had less total flying time on gliders than the course pilots, who at least had 10 hours flying Hotspurs."

After joining 'F' Squadron, time was spent building up experience with loaded circuits and landings, a good deal of cross country flying and several 'Balbos' or mass-formation exercises and landings. These culminated with a loaded dress-rehearsal called 'Exercise Vulture 4' – when they actually carried the Air landing Brigade, David carrying the Battalion HQ of the Royal Ulster Rifles, including its CO.

Also in January 1945, Cy Henson was posted to 'G' Squadron at Great Dunmow.

"The living quarters were no better than Fargo, but the reception was better," he recalls.

He was issued with his own 9mm Browning revolver, which he "put to good use on anything that resembled a target".

"The motorbike was very popular for getting to the local hostelries," he remarks, "needless to say there were one or two minor accidents, but nothing very serious."

● ● ● ● ● ● ● ● ● ●

Alan Hoad remembers arriving at Bridgnorth, a camp consisting of wooden huts with not an aircraft in sight, where he was introduced to a tough-looking Irish Lieutenant christened 'Arnhem Joe'.

"Off duty he was quite a nice chap," recalls Alan. "There were also about a dozen corporals who had been taken off glider training to teach the RAF pilots ground combat. They were upset at being taken off flying and the RAF pilots were not too keen on flying gliders, so things did not start off on a good footing."

On one occasion there was a demonstration of mortar firing in a shallow valley near the camp.

"During this demonstration, 'Arnhem Joe' had just ordered the range to be reduced when a stray dog appeared and tried to attack the mortar, Alan continues. "In the confusion, the range was not reduced but lengthened, so the next salvo of bombs fell on the road. The RAF pilots shouted out that the Air Force would get the army out of trouble if it came to the real thing. This went down like a lead balloon and next thing, the mortars were turned around and the RAF pilots were shelled. The RAF pilots soon became Olympic sprinters! The casualty rate for this kind of demonstration was meant to be only one per cent!"

From here all the first pilots were sent to train on Hotspur gliders and the second pilots on Tiger Moths, later all meeting up again.

Alan crewed up with a Pilot Officer Miles Hardie at Brize Norton, with whom he had trained in America. Here they trained on Horsa Mk IIs towed by Whitley bombers.

"The weather was terrible for our first flight," Alan remembers, "in fact, all aircraft were grounded, but somehow the order had not filtered through to us or the pilot of the Whitely, who was the 'press-on' type anyway. He didn't turn back and after two hours we reached the airfield and started the approach to land.

"We were down to 300 feet and could at last see the runway, when suddenly the instructor shouted that we were going the wrong way and took over from Hardie. He turned the glider through ninety degrees. From the ground it must have looked like the Keystone cops – we saw the flight commander run across the runway, followed by an off duty airman. It was anything but funny at the time. We hit the ground at a speed of 80mph between the station commander's house and a hanger – right in the middle of the CO's cabbage patch! On we went, through the hedge and across the road. We managed to miss an old lady, a van and a cyclist. The glider ended up with its nose in one roadside ditch and its tail in the other."

The nose was ripped loose in the impact and Alan, who was standing up front, was hit in the back of the leg.

"Luckily, I got away with only a graze," he says. "In the event no one was badly hurt."

The following day Hardie went solo with Alan in the second pilot's seat. After a spell on night flying and a short time on Hadrians (Wacos), they finished the course.

At Hampstead Norris, in January 1945, they continued with further ground combat training and practice mass landings.

"The idea was to get as many gliders into a given space as possible," Alan recalls. "The ground instructors were all from the Army Glider Pilot Regiment and had been on active service. The ground training got tougher, with cross-country route marches. One exercise was to cross rolls of barbed wire, which entailed one man throwing himself on the wire and the remainder running over. The last man over pulled the man on the wire off and to his feet. Everyone had to do it without exception."

They finally arrived at an operational squadron where the tug aircraft were Albemarles. However, things did not begin well…

"The first combination to take off suffered a burst tyre in the tug aircraft. The glider cut itself lose but the aircraft tried to turn back, failed to make it, stalled, hit a tree which took the wings off and then hit an empty bomb dump. One pilot was killed, one had a fractured skull and another had fractured legs. Two pilots who had gone up for the ride were thrown out of the side – not a good start, but things soon improved."

After further training, six pilots, including Alan, were transferred to No.1 Wing. Within hours, they were on their way to Great Dunmow and 'G' Squadron of the Glider Pilot Regiment.

Here they found Stirling bombers taking off on supply-dropping missions and a camp of some 2,000 men.

On 6th March, airborne troops began to arrive.

• • • • • • • • • • •

Fred Meek was crewed up with Pilot Officer John Haig and trained on Horsa and Hadrian gliders in both day and night flying, towed by Whitley bombers. They were given ground instruction about loading both types of glider and all crews were given foot drill by RSM Brodie and his staff of the Glider Pilot Regiment. From Brize Norton they were posted to Hampsted Norris to fly Horsas, this time towed by Albemarles. By this time Fred had been declared 'unfit for overseas service'. He therefore concluded that No.5 Course, which he was on, must be destined for the Far East.

On completion of the course he was posted to RAF Great Dunmow as part of 38 Group. Others went to airfields which previously had been occupied by 9th USAAF who had now gone to France.

On arrival, Fred was interviewed by the Station Commander, Gr/Cpt MacIntyre, who seemed to consider glider pilots something of a novelty. After being given leave, he was posted to 'G' Squadron under Major M. Priest and CSM Harper. The tug aircraft were Stirlings from 190 and 620 Squadrons which, apart from towing gliders, were working with the SOE in Norway and France.

In December 1944, they suffered their first casualty when Sgt R. Poole (who slept in the next bed to Frank) and his crew were shot down over Oslo.

In January, they were issued with battledress uniforms with RAF insignia. The tug crews were being used as Bomber support in France with the 21st Army Group and Frank went up in a Stirling on a bombing exercise.

"It seemed very odd to see the massive bomb doors open and only a 12lb bomb drop out!" Fred remembers.

By this time, 'G' Squadron was divided into four flights, two commanded by Army captains and two by RAF flight lieutenants.

In March, training started using heavy blocks of concrete instead of troops, to get used to flying with a full load on board.

On 14th March Fred took part in 'Exercise Vulture', with a live load of 28 men of the Air Landing Brigade on board. He recorded a total flight time of 2 hours 40 minutes in mass formation followed by a landing back at base.

• • • • • • • • • •

Phil Johnson, having completed his flying training in the USA, arrived back in the UK in 1944. When he arrived at Harrogate he found his name already on a list to be a Glider Pilot and was shortly on his way to No.1 HGCU at Brize Norton with about 20 others. He remembers that two of them were killed when their Whitley tug crashed shortly after take off. After some flying here Phil went on to Hampstead Norris where he remembers they clipped the trees on take off. After five or six flights, they moved on to 'D' Squadron at Weatherfield, arriving just before Xmas 1944.

Here they did a lot of cross-country marches and map reading with compasses. However, the runway at Weatherfield began to break up so they moved to nearby Gosfield, near Halstead, Essex. When the Americans moved out, they moved to Shepherds Grove.

• • • • • • • • • •

Len Jordan started his glider training at Zeals, near Gillingham, Wiltshire. From there he was posted to the HGCU at Fairford, Gloucestershire, where the serious training on Horsa IIs began.

"The one thing disturbing here was being towed by Albemarle aircraft," Len recalls. "The glider pilots thought that *they* were unlucky ones – not so! They were safer than the men in the tug aircraft by whom they were towed, who wondered each time on take-off if they would clear the perimeter fence! Mind you, glider flying at night following that shallow 'V' of tail and faint wing lights of the Albemarle wasn't a picnic either. Hardly the most comforting way of spending those winter months in 1944."

After a four-day leave Len's next posting was to Fargo Camp, Salisbury Plain, on Boxing Day 1944.

"This proved even more exhausting than the training at Bridgnorth with the RAF Regiment," says Len. "The airborne instructors set out to prove they could be tougher than the regiment instructors at Bridgnorth. They soon convinced everyone that the cushy days in the RAF were over – for a while at least."

Night manoeuvres in January 1945 followed.

"Not the best way to remember Salisbury Plain," Len recalls. "Unexploded mortar bombs being thrown, assembling, stripping and firing Bren guns on freezing nights. It certainly made me pleased that I hadn't joined the Army."

Len Jordan at the controls. [Len Jordan]

Further training with Sten guns, rifles, mortars and the PIAT anti-tank gun followed with the Grenadier Guards.

In January 1945 Len was posted to Shepherd's Grove and 'D' Squadron of the GPR, where the tug aircraft were Stirlings. Here he joined up with an old friend, F/Lt Len Halley DFC, an ex-Lancaster pilot and instructor from Newfoundland, Canada. At 'D' Squadron Len became his deputy flight commander. The squadron commander was Cpt Barry Murdock, who had taken part in a number of previous glider operations, including D-Day and Arnhem – a very experienced soldier and in Len's opinion "a grand fellow… as were the rest of the army pilots."

Many exercises and cross country flying followed, including one mass exercise to Earls Colne, Essex, where they all landed, formed up in line down the runway and were inspected by the 'top brass' of the Army. On another occasion and another mass exercise the four flights of 'D' Squadron were required to fly in a box formation and then land in four quarters on the runway.

"This proved to be a bit of a shambles," recalls Len. "Some gliders overshot or undershot and others collided with each other. It was a case for those who got down without mishap to get out quick and look for a safe haven."

Len's co-pilot was Sgt Norman Cambridge, who hailed from Kent. Len encouraged him to take control of the glider as often as possible during training and in Len's opinion, "he probably did a better job of it then I did!"

● ● ● ● ● ● ● ● ● ●

Tony Wadley was posted to 'C' Squadron at Tarrant Rushton in January 1945 as a second pilot to a Sgt 'Tug' Wilson, who hailed from Doncaster. This was short-lived, as he was very quickly re-posted to 'A' Squadron at Rivenhall, flying Horsa IIs towed by Stirlings.

He also remembers a mass landing exercise at Great Sampford airfield, near Saffron Walden, Essex, involving several squadrons.

"A large part of our evening leisure time was spent at 'The White Hart' and 'The Spread Eagle' in the nearby town of Witham, with an occasional foray into Chelmsford or Braintree," he recalls.

● ● ● ● ● ● ● ● ● ●

Geoffrey Atkinson was posted to 'F' Squadron at Broadwell after three short glider conversion courses at Shobdon, Brize Norton and Hampstead Norris. Having been in the Officer's Training Corps at school and also the Home Guard, Geoffrey was well acquainted with the way the army did things as opposed to the RAF. Soon after his arrival at the squadron intelligence office, an army subaltern was posted elsewhere and Geoffrey was appointed to the job. With it came a 350cc Matchless motorbike. Another perk, as a member of Squadron HQ, was to be excused runs and marches, which he describes as "a diabolical institution".

Sid Edwards was posted to 'B' Squadron in the Autumn of 1944, having been in the RAF for about four and half years. He had undertaken his pilot training at No.1 BFTS, Terrell, Texas. Although he found it vastly different to his previous time in the RAF, he began to like the life of a soldier. He was to become the co-pilot to St/Sgt Eddie Raspison of the GPR.

• • • • • • • • • •

Bleddwyn Williams left Shobdon and was posted to Hampstead Norris, where he paired up with his second pilot, Sgt Graham Richmond, who hailed from Cumbria. After qualifying on the Horsa I they were posted to No 18 Flight of 'A' Squadron GPR.

He found the mass cross-country lifts a nightmare, the last one before Operation Varsity in particular, when the exercise took them out over the Cotswolds. While they were away from Rivenhall, a fog came down over the whole area, leaving each tug and its glider to find their own way home to base. Due to an inspirational decision by the tug pilot, Bleddwyn and his crew were able to touch down in safety, whereas all around them chaos reigned. The tug took them down to a height where Bleddwyn could just see the main railway line running from Liverpool Street Station in London to the east coast. This line ran quite close to Witham station and the camp. He released the tow-rope, approaching Witham station before turning to port along the approach road to the camp. A turn to starboard over the officers' mess enabled him to touch down on the runway.

"It was," he remembers, "a heart-stopping experience, but one that would stand me in good stead for what was to come shortly."

• • • • • • • • • •

Having been brought up in the Welsh countryside, Eric Ayliffe was graded a first class shot in his infantry training. He also found the "so-called field craft" enjoyable. Even a little previous poaching experience was put to good use. Tracking wild animals and heeding the alarm call of a blackbird were second nature to him. His sentiments were, "If I cannot fly, then why not become a good infantryman?"

When he was first detailed to join the GPR, he was disappointed, and wished he had transferred to the Fleet Air Arm. Since his schoolboy days his only wish had been to fly with the RAF. Along with many others, he objected to 'losing his engines' – only to be reminded that he had volunteered to fly his Majesty's aircraft and a glider was an aircraft – so who could argue?

After his original misgivings, he was pleasantly surprised to find that he enjoyed the comradeship of 'F' Squadron of the GPR.

Bleddwyn Williams.

Tug/Hamilcar combination in training over Dorset – 1945. [Bob Randall]

• • • • • • • • • • •

After a two-week course at Bridgnorth, John Rayson was posted to No 5 Glider Training School, flying Hotspur gliders, and then to Brize Norton and 21 HGU flying Horsas and Hadrians. It was here that he met his second pilot, Sgt Priddin.

In January 1945 he was posted to 'B' Squadron at Earls Colne, flying Mark I and Mark II Horsa gliders. He remembers the procedure for flying through cloud:

"When in cloud, the glider had to fly at a level lower than the tug aircraft. This was accomplished by the aid of an instrument called the 'cable angle indicator' – or as most people called it 'the angle of dangle' – which in theory allowed you to fly the glider on tow when you couldn't see the tug aircraft. A cord, attached to the tow-rope and to the back of the instrument, would only work when you were in low tow."

On 7th March he took part in 'Exercise Riff-Raff II', which lasted two hours. This involved a mass landing of about 120 gliders at Great Sampford, where gliders had to land as close as possible in order that they could all be accommodated. 'Exercise Riff-Raff I' had taken place on 2nd March, when large combinations of Halifax-Horsa flew to Great Sampford and Hamilcars to Earls Colne. One Hamilcar had a full load with a Locust Tank, another was half laden with a Bren gun carrier and the remainder unloaded.

Twelve Halifax-Hamilcar and 12 Halifax-Horsa combinations were involved. Two Hamilcars were forced to land on route, one near Alconbury and the other in the vicinity of Polebrook. They were tugged too close to each other and were compelled to take avoiding action. In each case, the rope broke under the strain. In the case of the Polebrook glider, the landing was completely successful, no damage being sustained. In the other case the rope became wrapped around the undercarriage and could not be released, and although a good landing was made, the loop of rope became caught and subsequently damaged the undercarriage.

On 10th March, John took part in 'Exercise Ian I' – 2 hours and 40 minutes – another mass landing. On the 12th 'Exercise Ian II' took place, again 2 hours 40 minutes. On the 14th was yet another mass landing, using a heavy Horsa Mark IIs, this time called 'Exercise Vulture' – 3 hours and 40 minutes.

"About 120 gliders were flying in pairs in line astern," John remembers. "A problem occurred in that the tail-enders were flying faster than the leaders, so by the time we got to the aerodrome we were all bunched together. It was a terrifying sight, as nearly all the gliders were released from their tugs at the same time and were weaving about all over the sky."

One dived directly in front of John and he had to make a violent turn to avoid a collision. The Horsa IIs were loaded with heavy equipment, and the Horsas Is with troops and light equipment. The gliders landed at Keevil and the tugs at Harwell, owing to poor visibility.

"Within five minutes all the gliders had landed," John recalls, "but the last one could not find any room to land and crashed into two other gliders and a hut. Both pilots suffered broken legs."

On or about 14th March 1945, a firm decision was made to mount the operation with a 'Y' date of the 24th March.

On the 17th Exercise 'Nosmo', another mass landing similar to the others, took place.

• • • • • • • • • • •

Jack Newton had been posted to 'B' Squadron at Earls Colne where the tugs were Halifaxes of 296 and 297 Squadrons.

On 17th March 1945, he flew as second pilot to F/Lt Mike Stringer. His log reads:

'17 March 1945 – Horsa RZ 152 – Ex Token 03.35 hrs.

He understood, and still does today, that exercise 'Token' was a dummy run for Varsity. During the trip, Jack did see the coast of Belgium as six Stirling-Horsa and six Halifax-Hamilcar combinations made their way via Cap Gris Nez to the Rhine in the neighbourhood of Xanten. The force was escorted by fighters and the glider pilots carried side-arms, ammunition parachutes

Hamilcar loaded with concrete slabs used in training..   *[Bob Randall]*

and Mae Wests in case they had to ditch into the sea.

Operation Token was a rehearsal for Varsity with 21 British and 22 American serials. Six British parachute serials were flown by three groups of 52nd Troop Carrier Wing. Each was represented by an element of the aircraft. Each double tow glider serial was represented by an element of two tug aircraft and four gliders. Each single tow glider serial was represented by an element of four tug aircraft and four gliders. The route was the same as that to be used on Varsity, up to the command assembly point.

• • • • • • • • • •

F/Lt Jack Halley and his second pilot Kenneth Ross were summoned into an office on 16th March. The room was full of 'gold braid' officers. They were asked if they would go on a flight of vital importance which must not be discussed with anyone on their return. They agreed and next day they were driven to an airfield where a glider and tug awaited them. They were a solitary combination of Horsa and Stirling and flew for four hours, seeing no other aircraft in the sky. It was, Kenneth remembers, "a glorious flight. As smooth as silk under a clear blue sky."

Their flight entered in Kenneth's log book as 'Exercise X', which he found out (in 1989!) was part of Operation Token, a secret exercise which involved flying beyond Brussels to within sight of the Rhine and back. The object was to test towing speeds and times and check the effectiveness of the beacons which had been located at various points along the route and at the break-off point, where the main streams for the Rhine Crossing were to turn to their respective targets.

Each glider was ballasted to 'full load' with concrete blocks to test the fuel consumption of the tug aircraft while pulling such heavy loads. The crews used for Token were to be the crews that would be the 'lead serials' – as they were called – for Varsity. The flying time for this exercise was 4 hours.

The record for two of the tug squadrons involved on Token were as follows:

620 Sqn at Great Dunmow, 17th March 1945. Two aircraft successfully completed Exercise Token, towing loaded gliders.

190 Squadron 17th March 1945. Group Exercise Token carried out by W/C Roberston and F/Lt Le Bouvier. This exercise met with some disapproval including Lt-Col Ian Toler DFC, who thought it was a foolish experiment and could possibly give the enemy an insight to the allied intentions.

Jack's father joined the army in 1941 and Jack the RAF in 1942. His father served in the 8th Army and their leaves never coincided. They did not meet up again until 1945 when Jack had reached the age of 21. The last time he had seen his father he was only 17.

On 21st March there was a ground exercise to test communications and the operation room procedure between, stations and groups.

• • • • • • • • • •

Bill Davies did not mind his infantry training on the principle that if he had stayed at Harrogate he "would have been there for ages, kicking my heels". He remembers one amusing incident:

"On one occasion while training, the RAF Regiment Corporal fell us out for a smoke break and as we lay on the grass smoking two elderly ladies came by and asked the Corporal if we were Germans. The Corporal replied yes we were. One lady then said 'they do look different to us, don't they – rather nasty and vicious looking.' The Corporal replied: 'They are nice and tame now – I keep them busy' – and off the two old ladies went!"

A spell on Tiger Moths at No 21 EFTS at Booker, Buckinghamshire followed.

"We had trained on Tiger Moths in South Africa, of course," recalls Bill, "so after a half-hour check out of the aircraft we were allowed to fly around solo to our heart's content. But on one occasion while flying in tandem with a pal, we got lost. In South Africa we were used to clear visibility and so few roads and railway lines – it was much easier to navigate than in the UK. We were lucky enough to spot another Tiger Moth with two people in the cockpit, one of them obviously an instructor. He indicated for us to follow him and a few minutes later he pointed down and then shot off. Sure enough, below was a control tower and windsock, the obvious signs of an airfield. The only problem, was it Booker or another field?"

It turned out to be RAF Denham who gave them directions to Booker.

"We crossed the railway line just after take off, went to the right and then straight to Booker, so home we came," laughs Bill.

At No.21 HGCU at Brize Norton, he paired up with Sgt Wally Martin, who became his second pilot. They remained together for the whole of their time with the GPR. They found the Horsa glider large after a single-engined aircraft. Bill describes the cockpit as "like being in a large plastic Easter-egg."

The first thing he noticed was no top plane as on the Tiger Moth and no low plane as on the Harvard he had flown in South Africa.

"The wings were so far back it felt as if you were in a flying cabin. The other thing was the tricycle undercarriage… no three point turn landings with a Horsa! If the glider was to be loaded with troops there was a sliding door on the port side for them to enter by way of a small ladder. If the load was a jeep and gun or a tank, the nose swung aside, two ramps were put in place and the vehicle was driven into the glider, whereupon the nose was swung back again."

The tug aircraft that Bill was mainly acquainted with was the DC-3 or 'Dakota', as it was affectionately known.

"A ground crew man would have two bats with which he signalled to the tug to take up the slack on the tow-rope and then you were ready for take off," Bill continues. "The tug set off down the runway and you were soon airborne, just above the tug aircraft. When the tug came off the ground, you then began to climb. There were two positions relative to the tug in flight. One was the high position, where you looked down on the tug aircraft and the second was the low position when you looked up at it. We preferred the high position."

Bill remembers the first flight he and Wally had in a Horsa:

"We flew around the circuit and when the instructor – a warrant officer – was ready to start his landing, he pulled a lever and we came away from the tug aircraft. He turned to approach, selected flaps down and then put the stick forward. Down went the nose, whereupon our feet were pointing down at the ground! As we came into land, he pulled the stick back and we landed like a huge bird!"

After two hours instruction they were left to fly solo until they went on night flying. The next time they had an instructor was when they flew the Hadrian glider, made of tubular steel covered with fabric.

"It was a much smaller glider and could only carry a jeep or a gun and not both as could the Horsa," remembers Bill. "It didn't have flaps but spoilers, which were like small hooks on top of the mainline and spoilt the airflow over the wing. But we found that the Hadrian stayed airborne much longer than the Horsa."

The course finished on 29th November 1944 but it was marred when a glider flew into a hill while night flying, killing two of their pals.

This was followed by a posting to ORTU (Other Ranks Training Unit) at Hampstead Norris near Newbury, Berkshire. Here they took

The Pegasus badge worn by Airborne troops. [Author]

a two week course practising mass landings and take offs known as 'Balbos'.

After this they went on leave, and while on leave Bill received a posting to 'E' Squadron GPR at Blakehill Farm, Near Cricklade, Wiltshire.

Here he was issued with khaki battledress emblazoned with Pegasus badges worn by all airborne troops (known to RAF wags as the 'flying donkey' or the 'airborne smock'). From day one Bill found it enjoyable and felt at home with the GPR. The squadron was commanded by Major Peter Jackson DFC, whose grip on the squadron, as far as Bill was concerned, was perfect.

"Both RAF and GPR pilots were of course used to different kinds of discipline than that used for men *en-masse*," he recalls. "This was self-discipline. If you wish this to succeed, you must trust the men; and if you wish to check up on them it must be done discreetly.

"For instance, on one occasion the CO came on parade and said 'Gentlemen need a haircut' – no more, just that. By the time the next parade came around, everyone who needed a haircut had had one and the CO did not need to check that this had been done."

They did not use a rifle range but had a valley in the hills, which had been sealed off from the general public. The targets were tins or small boxes.

"This way the men got used to having weapons fired at them rather then one man firing at a time on the ranges," Bill recalls.

They became proficient on all manner of weapons, even spending a few hours on the six pounder gun. The squadron was split into two flights and mixed between RAF and GPR, which help to mould them into one squadron.

On 21st January 1945, Bill's flight was posted to Oxford. Here the instructors were a captain, a sergeant-major and two sergeants from the Coldstream Guards.

"Their normal job was to train University Students," says Bill, "but at this time they did not have any students to train. The flight was sent there to keep them occupied. The billets were in the cellars of the Blue Boar Inn, Blue Boar Street, Oxford. A very convenient billet to say the least!"

No.1 Flight (RAF and Army), Tarrant Rushton 1945.

Here all manner of infantry training was carried out, such as orienteering, when the men would be taken out in a truck to be dropped off in the middle of nowhere, with instructions how to get to a another point, where the truck would again pick them up.

"Sgt Lamb, one of the instructors, told us towards the end of the course that if our drill was up to scratch he would march us through Oxford," Bill recalls, "but in the end he had to say that our drill was not up to the standard of the guards and he, being a guardsman, would only march in public with men of guards standard… although he did condescend to say he was pleased and proud of our improvement on the course."

On 5th February 1945 they returned to Blakehill Farm and back to flying gliders. On one of the mass (Balbo) landings they had a narrow escape.

"Having landed I shouted to Wally to get out and watch others landing," says Bill. "As we went to go from the cockpit and into the body of the glider there was a tearing sound followed by the wingtip of another glider coming through the fuselage of our glider, cutting a gash of about 15 feet."

On another occasion a glider had just taken off when the tow-rope came away from its tug.

"They were not very high at the time, so the glider pilots had to think quickly," says Bill. "They turned towards the airfield and came in over the control tower, which was a square, flat-topped building with a hand rail around the observation deck. At the time, the top brass were up there watching the flying.

"The glider pilots had forgotten that the tow-rope was hanging down. As they were coming in from behind and not having an engine, their approach went unnoticed, so the officers on the control tower roof were surprised, to say the least, when the tow-rope snagged on the handrail and a long length of it went whirling across the airfield."

On 14th March came another Balbo, and this time they were told to take their personal gear including their rifles, as if they were going into combat.

"We were issued with long fighting knives," Bill says, "although before the final take-off we were ordered by the CO to hand them back in again. We took off and were flying for three hours, landing at Tarrant Rushton, Dorset. This was a large camp with over 3,000 people living in the woods, including 400 WAAFS. Its call sign was 'Cheekbone'. It had three runways. Operations had been carried out from there in 1944 to Normandy and Arnhem. The Ox & Bucks, who took Pegasus Bridge, had flown from Tarrant Rushton. It should not have taken three hours to get there – our assumption was that the route chosen was similar in distance to a trip to the Continent."

On 19th March they packed their gear and went to RAF Birch.

● ● ● ● ● ● ● ● ● ●

John Herold did not volunteer, but was 'selected' to fly gliders on his return to the UK. At Brize Norton he teamed up with his second pilot, Sgt Jones from Liverpool, who he remembers as "dour but with a dry sense of humour and an excellent companion."

They were posted to 'A' Squadron at Rivenhall. During infantry training they had to learn quickly, not only to defend themselves but to fight as airborne troops.

"The GPR pilots were a rugged lot and fully understood the dilemma that the RAF pilots found themselves in, having been trained to fight in the air and now facing a war on the ground," recalls John, "but they did a wonderful job and gave us a lot of confidence."

From 'A ' Squadron they were posted to 'C' Squadron at Tarrant Rushton. They achieved proficiency on a heavily-loaded Horsa but John remembers one difference was very apparent:

"Once the flaps were down, the speed built up alarmingly and the nose pushed down, which did not happen on a lightly-loaded Horsa, in which the speed did not increase, even if the glider was pushed into the near vertical."

On 20th March, the whole squadron of Hamilcars and Horsas, towed by 296 & 644 Squadron Halifax tugs, flew off for RAF Woodbridge, Suffolk.

• • • • • • • • • • •

After training in Canada on Harvards and taking a short course on dive bombing, air-to-air tactics and gunnery in which he received a higher than average assessment, Frank Haddock returned to the UK and was given the choice of converting to twin or multi-engined aircraft.

He opted to remain on single engines, but life seemed to drag on through the spring and summer of 1944, with two flying refresher courses and a spell in the control tower but no progress towards advanced flying.

While in London on a weekend leave, Frank met an old friend with whom he had done his initial training who was now in the Fleet Air Arm with the rank of sub-lieutenant. They retired to the bar of the Charing Cross Hotel and his friend mentioned to Frank that the Navy were looking for RAF pilots to transfer to the FAA for training on Seafire aircraft.

However, when Frank returned to his unit, his appeal for a transfer fell on deaf ears. Instead, he was posted from the control tower to undertake a short battle-training course with the RAF Regiment. This was followed by a refresher course and then a posting to the Heavy Glider Conversion Unit at Fairford.

The new arrivals were assembled in a hangar. Some were Bomber captains who had just finished a tour, qualified flying instructors or men like Frank who had recently arrived back from training in the USA. He was approached by F/O Cecil Law and they crewed up for the next eleven months.

This was followed by a course at Fargo, the depot of the GPR, near Amesbury, which Frank describes as follows:

"The weather at Xmas time 1944 was sub-zero, with all the water in the camp frozen at night. The stoves were stoked up with anything that would burn and when the shell of the stove got red hot all the beds were dragged in a spoke formation around it, and full flying kit was donned before getting into bed. But by 4am, when the fire had died down and the fuel for it had been exhausted, there were moans and groans all around the Nissen hut, complaining about the cold. To make matters worse, the food was usually dished up cold. The main meal of the day consisted of a thin slice of meat and two boiled potatoes in a watery gravy.

"The drill parades were, to say the least, humorous, with most of the squad ending up on their backsides because of the slippery surface."

At the end of the course they were posted to 'D' Squadron at Weatherfield.

"After a long train journey from Wiltshire we were met at Braintree station by a convoy of trucks and taken to a deserted airfield where we learnt from the few RAF men left that the squadron had moved to Shepherds Grove, near Bury St Edmunds some two weeks before – a slight lack of communication somewhere along the line! So it was back onto the trucks for a miserable trip in pitch blackness across East Anglia to Shepherds Grove, where we arrived at about midnight. But we were well received by 'D' Squadron and soon given hot food and accommodation.

"Bearing in mind that we were the first RAF pilots to be attached to the GPR, and therefore an unknown quantity, and even a novel one, we received a very warm and sincere welcome from the Army pilots and once having changed into khaki battledress we soon blended in.

"The losses at Arnhem were self evident, with huts containing 18-20 beds occupied by only four or five men. This brought home the true cost of Arnhem – over 698 Army glider pilots killed or captured, despite the heavily-censored press having played down the true casualties."

After some weeks of training, Frank and Cecil were posted to 'C' Squadron at Tarrant Rushton for conversion to Hamilcar gliders, but on arrival they found some confusion. 'C' Squadron consisted of four flights of twelve Hamilcars but also a flight of Horsas – so they stayed on Horsas.

"Within three weeks the rumour got around of an impending operation," recalls Frank, "and we were kitted out with new battledress and weapons, mostly the new Mk II Sten gun with a wooden butt and a six inch bayonet, more a spike than a bayonet. We were also issued with a dagger and sheath, worn strapped to the leg, and hand grenades, ammunition and a field dressing each. Time was so short that we couldn't test the Sten guns on the ranges but had to go out into the woods at night and fire a few rounds off."

On 21st March 1945, 'C' Squadron moved out 48 Hamilcars and 12 Horsas towed by Halifaxes of 298 and 644 Squadrons and left for RAF Woodbridge, just north of Ipswich, Suffolk. This was an emergency landing ground with a single runway 3,000 yards long and 200 feet wide, ideal for 120 gliders – with the Hamilcars to be towed off in line astern formation, carrying their ten ton loads.

• • • • • • • • • • •

Having qualified as a pilot at the time of Arnhem and being a flight lieutenant, 'Duke' Kent requested an interview, having heard about the call for glider pilots. At the interview he was told that if he took on the glider pilot role he would be given the very top priority for further training on fighters. With this assurance, he threw himself into becoming a glider pilot.

"For fully trained RAF pilots," he was told, "flying a glider is comparatively easy, although you will be required to fly a glider into a battle zone, carrying jeeps, guns and men through the smoke of battle to land in obstructed areas, etc etc…"

With all this in mind, during training Duke never flew a loaded glider or attempted to land a fully loaded glider in an obstructed area or experienced any attempt to simulate a battle area. Many of the men, unlike Duke, had never experienced flak, an aircraft explode in front of their eyes, smoke haze, machine gun fire from the ground or aircraft descending out of control from all angles.

The only training consisted of a series of mass landings – 'Balbos' as they were called.

Duke felt the ground training given was totally inadequate, but determined that they would become first class soldiers whether they liked it or not. Many hours were spent in the billets stripping and assembling a Bren gun in the

Glider pilot training, Fargo Camp, Salisbury Plain – 1945   *[Alan Cooper]*

Sgt Colin Miller in front of a Hamilcar glider.

dark. Sten guns would be stripped down and placed in a pile in the middle of the room, the lights put out, or a blindfold put on, and the guns assembled as quickly as possible.

However, time on the ranges was paltry. The Bren gun was fired once or twice only, the Bazooka once and the Sten guns once or twice plus a few rounds fired with a rifle. When Duke had been a gunnery instructor with the RAF, his trainees would spend a whole day firing '303' Browning machine guns, rifles and shotguns from the aircraft gun turrets.

To achieve the same with the GPR would mean a lot of practise and familiarity under a variety of conditions, but the men were only allowed to throw a grenade from behind a pile of sandbags or fire a bullet lying on their stomach while looking at a pile of sand. As far as Duke was concerned, this was woefully insufficient before sending inexperienced RAF pilots into a ground war. Many situations could occur that the RAF pilots were not aware of.

He had the advantage of having flown in hostile conditions with Bomber Command over the Ruhr, he had been blown up in Malta and experienced being attacked from the air day and night. He had trained in armaments and could drive most types of vehicles. He tried his best to air his views but found they fell on deaf ears.

For his troubles Duke was promoted to squadron leader and made a squadron commander, but a few days before the impending operation he was sent on a company commander's course to the School of Infantry at Warminster.

● ● ● ● ● ● ● ● ● ● ●

Dennis Mills joined the RAF as apprentice in January 1938, so unlike many airmen who volunteered or were called up he was a regular who had decided to make a career of the RAF.

In 1940 he volunteered and was accepted but because of a shortage in his civilian trade – wireless and electrical – he had to wait two years before being released in 1942.

In 1944 he returned from pilot training believing that his next move was to an Operational Training Unit.

"But it was gliders I was destined for," he says, somewhat ruefully.

He went through the same training procedures as had many others. One thing he remembers at Fargo, the depot of the GPR, was that he was only allowed to wear Army denim battledress in freezing mid-winter weather.

"On arrival we were told that no one on the depot wore greatcoats and that going sick was a waste of time as there wasn't a medical officer," he says.

He and his co-pilot, Art Pogson, whom he has now lost touch with, were posted to 'D' Squadron at Shepherds Grove and then on to 'C' Squadron at Tarrant Rushton. This was the only squadron to operate with the giant Hamilcar glider, but there was also a Horsa flight, to which Dennis and Art were attached.

After his crash in training, Eddie Raspison had a spell on leave. He was recalled for another glider course at Stoke Orchard, near Cheltenham. From there he went to Stoney Cross in the

New Forest where conversion to the Horsa glider commenced.

In June 1944, came D-Day and Eddie's first operation, in which he carried men of the of Royal Engineers and a jeep and trailer. The landing was without incident, in a small field, with one wing coming to rest on a haystack.

In no time at all he was back in the UK via a tank landing craft.

In September came Arnhem, and again he flew as second pilot to Norman Jenkins. They went in on the second day of the operation, landing in a field of turnips in the area of Ossterbeek. This time they carried two Polish troops with a jeep, a 6-pounder anti-tank gun and a motorcycle. Sadly, both Poles were shot by a sniper operating from a church tower as they left the glider. Eddie and Norman got rid of the sniper with the Poles anti-tank gun, although they had been lucky as the gun was fitted with a flash eliminator, which should have been removed before firing high explosives. Eddie lost contact with Norman and on reaching the riverbank was lucky enough to get aboard one of the assault boats being operated by the Royal Engineers. On the other side he was again lucky in getting a lift on the upper deck of a jeep-cum-ambulance and there in the town met up with some of his comrades. He did not see Norman again until he reached the UK. He got back to the UK in a Dakota via Eindhoven.

• • • • • • • • • • •

One of the problems that engineers faced in planning for Operation Varsity was that, with a greater number of gliders allocated to each airfield than ever before, glider parking presented a problem. Over 7,000 square feet of surfacing material was required for each glider. The problem was solved by using rolls of square mesh track, from which individual hardstand areas were made – 77 feet long and 21 feet wide. The apron method of glider parking used a distance of 100 feet wide and 70 feet long for each glider, with 20 feet between the nose and tail which allowed for trucking and loading space. The hardstand area made a saving of 5,383 feet of material as compared with the apron method.

The Hamilcar.

Wing Commander Bill Angell DFC (2nd from right) and crew. [Bill Angell]

Halifax tug and Horsa glider combination. [Charles E. Brown]

CHAPTER 9

Glider Tugging

In October 1940, a flight was formed to tow gliders and for parachute dropping experiments. The flight was to be known as the Airborne Forces Development Unit.

It was October 1941 before the unit got its first Halifax bomber for use on parachute dropping trials. In November 1941, three further Halifaxes were received and a fifth followed soon after. All were modified for glider towing. By May 1942, Horsa and Hotspur glider trials were complete.

295 Squadron was involved in these early operations under 38 Wing of Army Co-Operation Command. At first they were equipped with Whitleys and a mixture of Hotspur and Horsa gliders.

In 1943 it was decided to expand 38 Wing to Group status, consisting of 9 Squadrons of Albemarles, 1 of Halifaxes and 4 equipped with Stirlings. The Halifax squadron was number 298 and formed at Tarrant Rushton in November 1943. It had a complement of 17 Halifaxes and 7 Horsa gliders.

The main function of 298 was to train with the new Hamilcar glider, the largest glider ever used on operations. It had a 110-ft wingspan and was 20 feet high.

Besides glider training and operations 38 Group also had a role supply dropping to the SOE and SAS behind enemy lines and also tactical bombing operations.

In March 1944, 644 Squadron was formed from 298 Squadron.

Another squadron involved in glider operation was 196 – equipped with Stirlings. Wg/Cdr Bill Angell DFC had joined the RAF pre-war. On the outbreak of war he was given a staff job and then a ground instructor's duties. He returned to flying 1943 and, after a refresher course, he was posted to 196 Squadron in October 1943. At this time 196 Squadron was operating from Witchford, flying Mk III Stirlings, however, within a week they were withdrawn from bombing operations and moved to a non-operational airfield near Leicester and joined No 38 Group for duties with the Army Airborne Forces.

The Stirling was fitted with a towing hook for glider towing and an intercom connection. Early in 1944, the Stirling Mk III was replaced by the Stirling Mk IV, which additionally had a hole in the fuselage floor for despatching parachute troops and equipment.

At the same time, training began in the techniques of glider towing, parachute dropping and low-level supply dropping.

By March 1944, No 38 Group's Order of Battle was nine Squadrons, each with 26 aircraft and 50 gliders plus 1 Squadron of 20 aircraft and 70 Hamilcar gliders. In the main, most of the crews were experienced Bomber Command aircrew. The motto of the group was *'A Noble Pair of Brothers'*, which signified the two groups 38 and 46 working together. No 46 Group operated with Dakotas.

Experience acquired in towing gliders came from local towing flights. As this experience increased, 196 began to fly in Squadron formation, then in Station formation and finally in Group organised simulated operational exercises. The aim of these flights was to give practise and experience to both tug and glider pilots of rapid take off and formation flying, and more importantly, experience of mass landings with the aim of landing as many gliders as possible, safely into a specified area, in as little time as possible.

It was the tug pilot's responsibly to get his glider pilot to a release point in relation to a landing zone at the right time to enable the glider to make its operational approach and landing. He was assisted in this by the bomb aimer, using specially adapted techniques and accurate map reading who kept the glider pilot informed as to his ground position. As Bill remembers it, there was a continuous two-way flow of information between glider and tug crews. The glider pilot himself decided when he would make the release from the tug aircraft.

On exercises, in reasonable weather conditions and after much practise, this was not a difficult decision to make – but at night or in bad weather and over enemy territory, in operations such as Normandy, Arnhem and the Rhine crossing, flying the approach to the prepared release point was anything but easy.

Bill Angell made two operational tows, both in fair weather and in daylight – Operation 'Market-Garden', the Arnhem assault and Operation 'Varsity', the Rhine crossing. Both were, in his opinion, successful.

Between these major airborne operations, his flying consisted of practise glider towing and parachute troop dropping combined with operational work, consisting of night-time parachute drops of members of the SAS and Free French over occupied countries organised by the Special Operations Executive (SOE).

John Gray served with 644 Squadron, flying Halifaxes and was based at Tarrant Rushton where he carried out a variety of operations but mainly glider towing. He was destined to tow a Hamilcar across the Rhine in March 1945.

● ● ● ● ● ● ● ● ● ● ●

Ron McQuaker completed a tour of bombing operations with 158 Squadron, flying Halifaxes. After a period as an instructor, he joined 298 Squadron, also based at Tarrant Rushton. When 644 Squadron was formed out of 298, he was transferred over. He soon found that taking off with a full bomb load was easy compared with taking off with a loaded glider in tow.

"Take-off often consisted of a series of swerves going down the runway," he recalls, "particularly when the glider was the Hamilcar, a huge machine, often carrying a tank and a 6-pounder gun."

He found the Horsa more manageable to tow.

● ● ● ● ● ● ● ● ● ● ●

Doug Coxell trained as a pilot in Terrell, Texas with No.1 BFTS. Following twin-engine conversion on Oxfords and Operational Training on Albemarles, he joined 297 Squadron in February 1944. Operational flying followed, with supply drops to the SOE and then the landings at Normandy and Arnhem before converting to Halifaxes. Bombing operations followed at Weburg and on targets between Rees and Wesel in February 1945.

On 7th March 1945, Earls Colne, the home of 296 and 297 provided 12 Halifax-Hamilcar and 12 Halifax-Horsa combinations to take part in a mass landing at Great Sampford in Exercise 'Rif-Raff'. The Hamilcar combinations led, with a briefed speed of 135 knots, followed by the Horsa combinations with a speed of 145 knots – the object being a mass arrival over the Landing Zone. Unfortunately, the Horsa stream caught up with the Hamilcar stream and chaos reigned, the formations scattering.

At Tarrant Rushton 644 and 298 Squadrons flew four-hour shifts night and day in order to train. Gr/Cpt Tom Cooper, the station commander, would only cancel glider tugging if the glider could not see the tug.

● ● ● ● ● ● ● ● ● ● ●

Jimmie Stark joined the RAF in June 1940, having volunteered (there was no conscription in Northern Ireland, his birthplace).

After training he joined 35 Squadron at Linton-on-Ouse in 1941, followed by a period with 58 Squadron and then 76 Squadron. A period as an instructor followed, then he joined 298 Squadron flying Halifaxes and towing Horsa gliders.

On D-Day in June 1944 he towed a Hamilcar, followed ten days later when he dropped by parachute a jeep and a 25-pounder gun. In September 1944 he towed a Hamilcar to Arnhem.

When Jimmie arrived at 298 he was pleased to find they were operating with Halifaxes, which meant he did not have to learn to fly another type of aircraft. However, the art of glider towing proved to be completely different from the bombing operations he was familiar with.

Each day, a glider was towed by tractor into position, whereupon the Halifax pilot would position the tug in front of the glider. The towrope was connected and when a signal was received that everything was okay the pilot slowly opened the throttle to take up the slack. The rear gunner in the Halifax would give the pilot the word that the rope was taut and the pilot would then open the throttle further and head off down the runway. The glider, being the lighter of the two, became airborne before the towing aircraft. It was the glider pilot's responsibly to keep the glider as low as possible so that it did not lift the tail of the tug aircraft and thus make it more difficult for the tug to get airborne.

"If the tail did lift," Jimmie remembers, "it would take the strength of Samson to get the Halifax off the ground."

This only happened to Jimmie on one occasion at Tarrant Rushton which was fortunately on a hill, and after take-off Jimmy was able to correct the problem.

Once airborne the tug/glider combination climbed to about 1,000 feet and then turned to do a circuit of the airfield. On the downwind leg, the glider pilot released his aircraft, turned into wind and made a landing on the airfield. The tug pilot flew and dropped the tow-rope in an appointed place, did another circuit and came in to land. They then taxied back into position where another glider was waiting and the whole procedure was repeated time and time again until all the gliders and their pilots had had a turn.

The SOE operations were worked in between the airborne operations and training. These trips often involved a jeep or six to eight men being dropped. As Jimmie remembers it, "with such a load in the bomb bay, the aircraft had the aerodynamics of a pregnant hippopotamus."

For a large operation, the gliders were parked in tow lines on the runways and the tug aircraft parked either side of the runway with the leading tug parked on the runway ahead of the leading glider. The left combination would take off first then the right, and so on.

"The two leading aircraft would be flying in still air and have very little difficulty," remembers Jimmy, "but the following aircraft in the 'glider trains' would often hit the slipstream of the aircraft ahead, in which case a wing would stall and the pilot would sweat like a pig hauling the wings and the aircraft back up again. The trick was to fly slightly to the left or right of the line, where there was still air."

• • • • • • • • • • •

Jack Cottam joined the RAF in 1941 at the age of 19 and undertook his Elementary pilot training at Marshalls in Cambridge. Two years later and now 21 he went to Neepawa, Canada, as a flying instructor, training pilots under the Empire Training Scheme. After two years in Canada he was posted back to the UK and joined 575 Squadron. On 26th February 1945 he reported to Down Ampney, the home of RAF Transport Command and the airfield that 575 were operating from at the time.

The role of the squadron at this time was glider tugging with Dakota aircraft.

Jack Cottram and Dakota. [Jack Cottam]

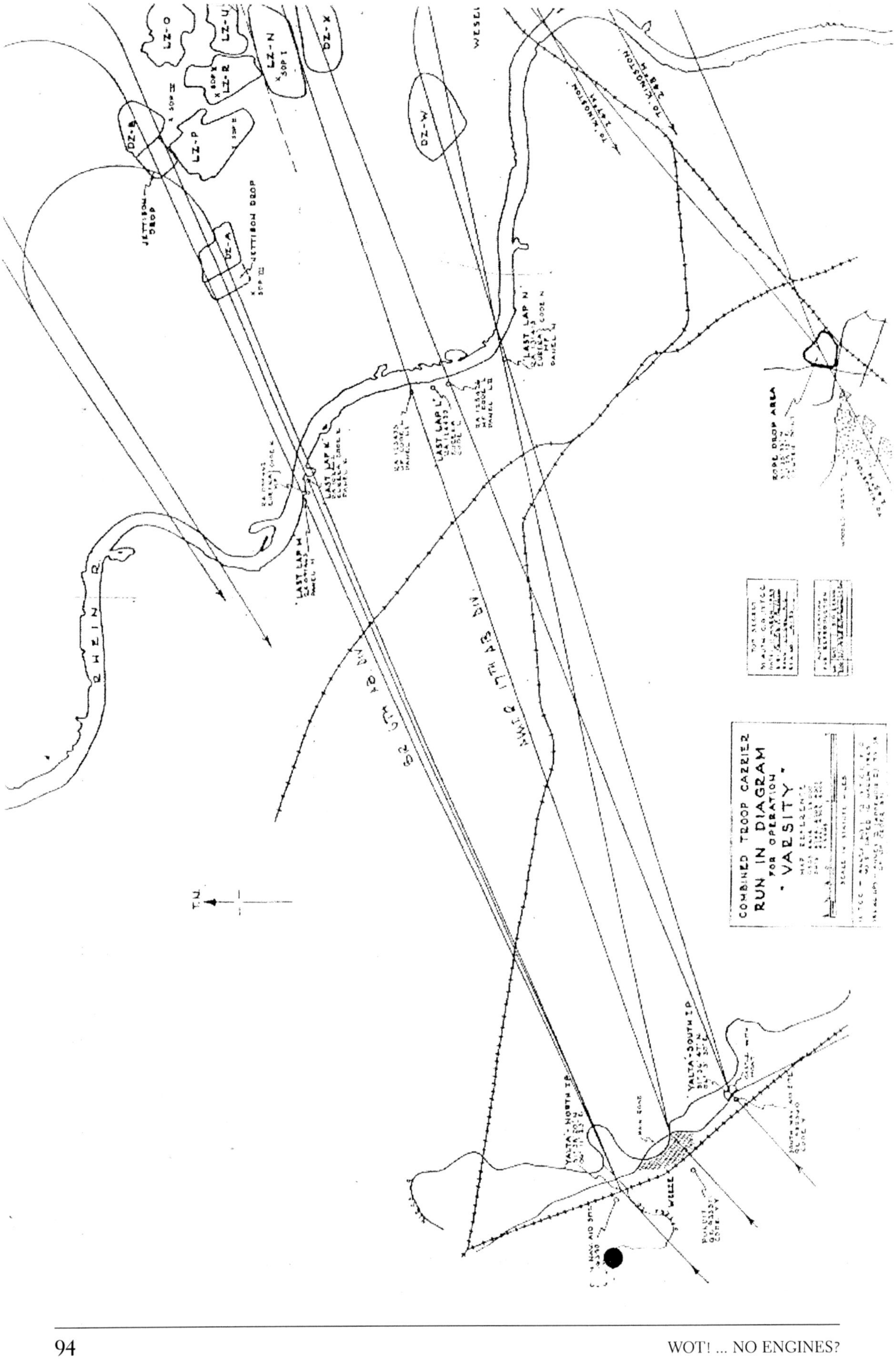
COMBINED TROOP CARRIER
RUN IN DIAGRAM
FOR OPERATION
"VARSITY"
RHEIN R.
DZ-A
DZ-B
DZ-W
DZ-X
LZ-O
LZ-P
LZ-R
LZ-N
JETTISON DROP
LAST LAP M
LAST LAP K
LAST LAP L
LAST LAP N
YALTA - NORTH IP
YALTA - SOUTH IP
WESEL
ROPE DROP AREA
TO KINGSTON

CHAPTER 10

Crossing The Rhine

After the Treaty of Versailles of 1919, the Rhine was denoted the frontier between Germany and France for a 100 miles from Switzerland to Karlsruhe. The river is a huge natural obstacle, protecting the German heartland, and crossing it became a major objective in the latter stages of World War Two.

The first troops to cross the Rhine in WWII were the First French Army who fought their way over on 19th November 1944.

At SHAEF (Supreme Headquarters Allied Expeditionary Force) HQ at this time there were already plans to cross into Germany via the bridges over the Rhine.

On 17th October 1944, General Omar Bradley moved the US 9th Army to the left flank of his 12th Army Group with the possible aim of crossing the Rhine in the Emmerich-Wesel area. The area was examined closely with a view to the use of airborne troops to assist the advance and was found the most suitable for this type of operation. The important defensive feature on the German bank was an area of high wooded ground straggling north west of Wesel, known as the *Diersfordter Wald*. Apart from this, the Rhine plain was flat so the *Wald* dominated the river and the flats to the west. It provided a natural protective ridge in front of a lesser river to the east, the Issel, where the Issel Bridge and a small town called Hamminkeln lay beside a road and railway line. This vital area, including the heights, was to be the object of the airborne army.

Two lessons learnt at Arnhem governed the selection of LZs and DZs and methods of landing.

(a) That it was preferable to land smaller forces of gliders, providing they contained tactical groups, on or adjacent to the objectives, rather than to make massed glider landings some distance away.

(b) That if the greatest advantage was to be taken of the initial surprise, the division must be landed in its entirety in one operation.

• • • • • • • • • •

On 7th November 1944 a Planning Staff Study for operation was put in place. The idea was to assist the advance of the 9th US Army of the Central Group by seizing bridgeheads on the east bank of the Rhine in the vicinity of Emmerich and Wesel.

The Central Group of Armies would halt on the west bank of the Rhine in order to allow time for regrouping and build-up of troops and supplies prior to executing a deep thrust into Germany.

It was the intention of the Central Group to seize a bridgehead on the east bank of the Rhine after regrouping and build-up of troops and supplies had been completed.

The bridgehead would be required to be approximately 5 to 10 miles wide and approximately 5 miles deep so that bridging operations could be undertaken relatively unhindered by artillery fire. Ground forces would require the assistance of Airborne Troops for the seizure of the bridgehead.

The Rhine Plain was 50 to 10 miles wide, flat and a rather featureless area. Water meadows extended on both sides of the river and the land closely resembled the Dutch Polder area. The banks of the Rhine were high and reinforced against the risk of flooding. The possible Dropping Zones for parachutists (DZs) and Landing Zones for gliders (LZs) between Emmerich and Wesel were virtually unlimited, therefore not a restricting factor in selecting the best area for an airborne bridgehead.

An ideal area for a bridgehead appeared to be east of Emmerich, starting at the sluice gate and following the course of the Rhine canal around a bend and thence to Alter-Rhine and back to the Rhine. This area was three quarters of a mile deep and two and a quarter of a mile wide and included one existing passenger ferry. There were three good approach roads to the west bank of the Rhine, while on the east bank there were six tracks and secondary roads into the position, but only one road out. This was the lateral road running east and west. The main west-east railroad between Emmerich and Wesel also ran through the area.

A second area considered for an airborne bridgehead was that east of Rees from the Alter-Rhine to the railroad, along the road, and back to the Rhine. This area was 5 miles wide and had an average depth of 3 miles. No existing ferry sites were in the area, but there were 12 approach tracks and roads to the west bank. The east bank had numerous tracks and secondary roads, and at least four good road exits into the position.

To establish an airborne bridgehead in either of the above two areas, two airborne divisions would be required. It was felt that the southern area was the best of the two areas.

At Wesel, there existed a road bridge and railroad bridge across the Rhine.

Operation Varsity had the following disadvantages from the Allies' point of view, which had to be countered by speed of action and accuracy of execution:

1. The element of surprise would be lost as landings had to take place in broad daylight, the gliders landing after the parachute drop. The whole area of operations was occupied by enemy troops who would be alerted before the arrival of gliders. This was unfavourable in comparison with Normandy, where initial mass landings took place at night, and Holland, where there were no enemy troops in the vicinity of the Landing Zones. To avoid a concentration of enemy fire on the LZ it was agreed that several LZs should be used, with gliders landing simultaneously on all of them, thus dispersing the enemy's attention and fire and making it difficult for enemy commanders to judge where the main effort was to be concentrated. To enable troops to reach their RVs and capture their objectives, it was agreed that gliders should land as near to them as possible and touch ground in the shortest possible time after release.

2. Enemy troops were known to be in the area of Landing, the latest information gave their disposition as follows:

DIERSFORDTER WALD
Artillery positions overlooking the Rhine.

HAMMINKELN
In the immediate vicinity of 6 Brigade Air landing, landing zones 'O', 'U', 'R' and its first objective - occupied by one Battalion of enemy parachute troops, billeted in houses and farms, which in many cases were changed into strong points.

HAMMINKELN RAILWAY STATION
In the immediate vicinity of bridges over the River Issel, the station was a supply point for enemy troops.

In the whole area of landings enemy troops withdrawing from the line of the River Rhine under pressure of our own ground forces, whose attack would start at dusk on Day 1, had to be expected.

Enemy reserves might arrive and even if weak, could seriously affect landings.

The overall codename for the crossing of the Rhine was Operation 'Plunder' – the 21st Army Group plan.

The US 9th Army's task was to make an assault across the Rhine in the area of Rheinberg, to secure a bridgehead at the junction of the Ruhr and Rhine rivers at Bottrop-Dorsten and to be prepared to advance to the general line inclusive of Hamm-Munster while protecting of the right flank of the Second Army.

The Second Army's task was an assault across the Rhine in the area of Xanten and Rees and to establish a bridgehead at Borken-Aalten-Doetinchhem-Hoch Elten.

The plan was to subsequently advance on a three corps front north-east towards Rheine. There bridging operations were to be centred on Xanten and Rees.

The First Canadian Army was to assist in broadening the apparent frontage of assault by carrying out feints along the Rhine to the left of the Second Army. Then hold securely the line of the rivers Rhine and Maas from Emmerich westwards to the sea and later to advance into eastern Holland and protect the left flank of the Second Army.

Within Operation Plunder there were five separate operations (see Table 1 below).

The British 6th Airborne Division was under the command of Major-General E.L. Bols DSO and the 6th Air Landing Brigade under Brigadier R.H. Bellamy DSO whose job it was to seize the bridge and contain the village of Hamminkeln. This would be the first air landing of the battle.

The Air Landing Brigade Group were given the task of seizing the bridges over the Issel. The 2nd (Airborne) Battalion Oxfordshire & Buckinghamshire Light Infantry, The First Battalion of the Royal Ulster Rifles were the unit given the task. They had to clear the area required for the Division HQ (12th Airborne Battalion Devonshire Regiment) to seize and hold the road junction and railway crossing and finally to seize and hold the village of Hamminkeln.

At this time, the Allies were being held on or about Germany's Western frontiers.

(1) Germany had succeeded in denying to the Allies the use of the port of Antwerp for more than eight weeks after its capture by them, imposing on them an enormous problem of supply and transportation.

(2) The German armies in the west, although severely shaken by the Battle of France and the rout that followed it, had made a remarkable recovery and were fighting with renewed vigour and determination in defence of the Reich.

(3) Germany, by using emergency measures, has so far succeeded in maintaining the flow of reinforcements from the replacement army to the armies in the field.

(4) The German Command had been able, by exploiting the ample and comparatively undamaged road and rail networks in Western Germany to switch its limited reserves of men and material from one sector of the front to another, as and when each successive Allied threat had claimed priority.

Since the Battle of France, the Allies had made three major attempts to rupture the German western defences and so gain a quick conclusion to the war.

On 28th November, General Montgomery met up with General Eisenhower at Zonhoven. They agreed that the situation at this time was not good. The American army was very short of ammunition and the rifle platoons under strength. A meeting was arranged for 7th

Table 1: Operation Plunder

Unit	Codeword	Formation	Task
30 Corps	Turnscrew	51st Highlanders	Assault on Rees
12 Corps	Widgeon	1 Commando Brigade	Assault on Wesel
	Torchlight	15 Scottish Div	Assault in the area of Xanten
16 US Corps	Flashpoint	30 US Div 79 US Div	Assault South of Wesel
17 US Corps	Varsity	6th British Airborne Div 17th US Airborne Div	Airborne Landings Diersfordt area

December 1944 at Maastricht. Two main factors were put forward by Montgomery at the meeting:

(a) The western front in the Ruhr. If it were cut off from the rest of Germany, the enemy's capacity to continue the war would be greatly diminished.

(b) It was essential that a mobile war was forced on the Germans by the Spring or early Summer. They had little transport, little petrol, and tanks that could not compete with the Allies in a mobile battle. Once the war became mobile, it was the end for the Germans.

His recommendations were:

(a) The Ruhr must be the main objective.

(b) The main effort must be made in the north because only there was the landscape suitable for a mobile battle.

In December, the Special Service Group was renamed the Commando Group. Also in December came German counter-attack in the Ardennes. Their plan was to strike with three armies through the Ardennes Forest, to cross the Meuse River and recapture Antwerp, which would cut off four Allied armies in the north. This battle continued until the 16th January 1945.

On 9th March 1945, Field Marshal Von Kesselring returned to Germany from Italy and was made Commander-in-Chief West, in place of Von Rundstedt. His orders were to hold the Western Front until the Eastern Front forces were up to strength. This would then enable him to launch a counter-offensive. However, on 9-10th March, he had only 55 Divisions with an average of 7,000 men per division against the Allies 85 Divisions.

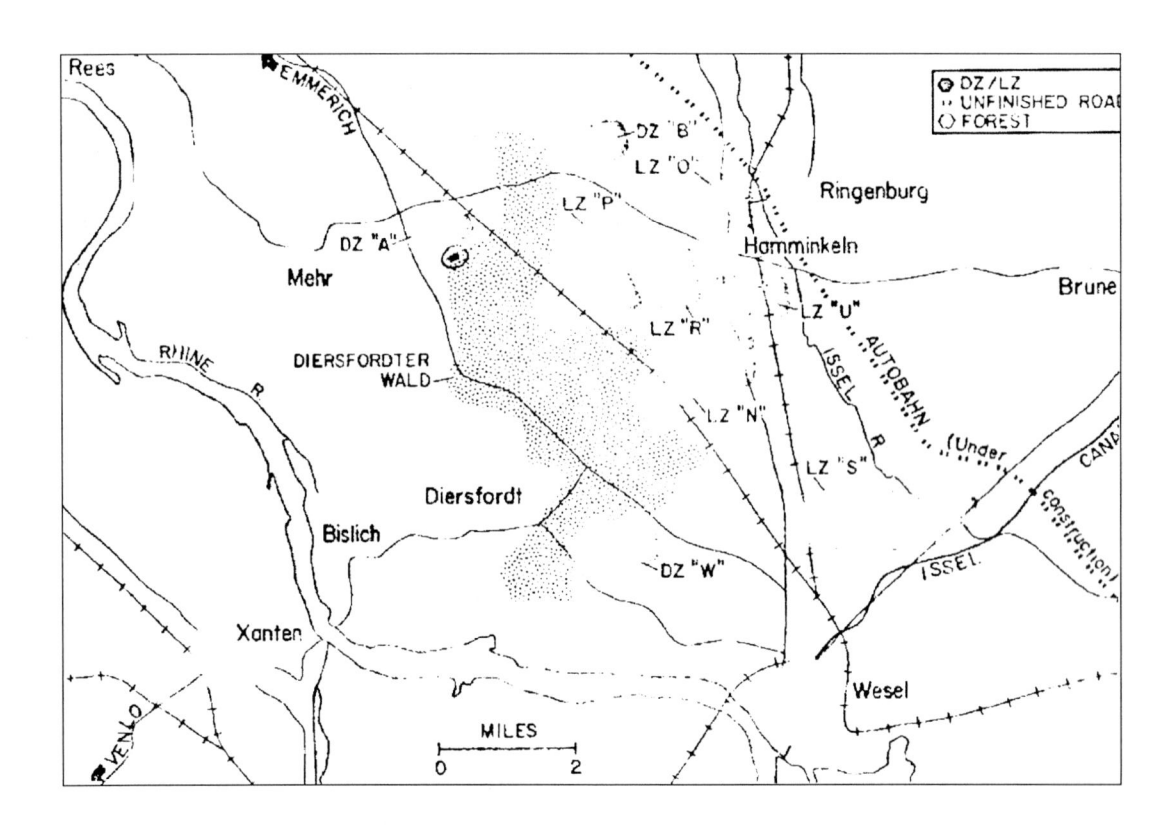

CHAPTER 11

Operation Varsity: The Plan

On 7th February 1945, General Montgomery said: "We are going into the ring for the final and last round; there will be no time limit; we will continue fighting until our opponent is knocked out."

The first intimation of Operation 'Varsity' was in a letter from AVM J.S. Scarlett-Streatfield CBE, AOC of 38 Group to the AOC of 46 Group on 12th February 1945, in which he suggested that as the operation might consist of one lift, 46 Group would be asked to produce their full strength and might and to operate from two airfields in East Anglia.

On 23rd February it was decided to allocate the maximum number of aircraft possible to Varsity, retaining only a minimum of aircraft for a transport role. 2TAF were requested to cut down their scheduled requirements to the barest necessities, to which they agreed on the 26th February, indicating that their minimum would be 35 Dakota aircraft.

On 28th February 1945, at a conference at SHAEF, the final plans for Plunder and Varsity were discussed. Troop Carrier and Air Force operations were discussed and 46 Group decided they could provide 120 aircraft.

The General Army Plan made by General Dempsey for Plunder envisioned a crossing of the Rhine by the 2nd British and 9th US Armies and establishing a bridgehead on the east bank of the Rhine in the area between Emmerich and Wesel, prior to executing a deeper thrust into Germany.

The Airborne Plan – Operation Varsity – devised by General Brereton, was to assist the advance of the 2nd British Army and 9th US Armies in their forthcoming attempt to obtain a bridgehead on the east bank of the Rhine by carrying out an airborne drop some five miles east of the Rhine, thus permitting the ground forces to capture their bridgehead across the river relatively unhindered by artillery fire.

The date set for the airborne operation was 1st April 1945, with the proviso that it may be brought forward to 15th March. The attack by ground forces was scheduled to commence before D-Day but the airborne attack would not be carried out until the hours of daylight on D-Day. The timing was set between 1000 and 1400 hours, depending on weather conditions.

The airborne troops would be under the control of General Lewis H. Brereton who in 1944 commanded the US 9th Air Force and in 1944/45 the First Allied Airborne Army. He had served in WWI as a Lt-Col and had been awarded the French Croix de Guerre.

The Airborne Troops to be employed were:

(a) 6th British Airborne Division
(b) 17th US Airborne Division
(c) 13th US Airborne Division in reserve.

The troop carrying lift would be carried out by 9th Troop Carrier Command, 38 Group, and 46 Group.

On 1st March 1945, a meeting was held at HQ Transport Command by the deputy AOC-in-Chief and the AOC 46 Group.

It was decided to provide 20 Dakotas as a reserve for 46 Group by 14th March and No.24 Squadron to provide 10 aircraft and crew from 15th March onwards to operate in 46 Group.

On 9th March, a directive was issued from Montgomery's Headquarters, defining his intention to Cross the Rhine north of the Ruhr and secure a firm bridgehead with a view to developing operations to isolate the Rhur and to penetrate deeper into Germany.

On 17th March, at a conference, a general plan was made. The 2nd Canadian Army, using 30th Corps, 12th Corps and its Commando Corps together with 16th US Corps, would obtain a bridgehead over the Rhine in the area of Wesel.

The 1st Allied Airborne Army would support this by landing East of the Rhine and attacking the enemy from the rear.

In order to safeguard the passage of the airborne force over Wesel on D-Day, the first objective of the Commando Corps was to capture Wesel itself. They were, however, very lightly armed and a bombing attack immediately prior to their assault on the town was considered by the Army to be essential. The task of the bombing was given to Bomber Command.

The flak between Emmerich and Wesel was not a limiting factor in the selection of the LZs and DZs for an airborne operation between Rees and Wesel. The concentration of flak was west of the Rhine near Emmerich and was likely to move to the east bank as the German army was pushed back into Germany.

Hamminkeln Railway Station, 1945.

CHAPTER 12

Preparation for Varsity

In preparation for Operation Plunder and Varsity a number of allied bombing raids were arranged.

The attacks were divided into three sections;

(1) Creation of a Ruhr interdiction line.

(2) Attacking enemy transportation system west of this Ruhr interdiction line.

(3) Preparation of the planned battle area.

The brunt of the air fighting in north-west Europe had been borne for at least two years prior to 1945 by the strategic air forces – in particular RAF Bomber Command and the 8th US Air Force. By striking at targets inside Germany they ensured that the main air battle took place away from the area of land operations.

This was particularly true of the period of the crossing of the Rhine in 1945. Highly successful campaigns against Germany's oil facilities and transportation system had made it essential for the enemy to retain what was left of their air forces for the defence of the Reich. The attacks on oil and transportation had also had a marked effect on the mobility of German armed forces.

The main feature of Luftwaffe operations in 1945 had been their lack of support for their ground forces, as they concentrated their remaining fighter aircraft well inside Germany for the defence of strategic targets. There were about 800 day fighters within striking range of both the Varsity and Naples II areas. However, of these a maximum of 450-500 aircraft might be serviceable and available to oppose the airborne landings, provided they were prepared for it and not committed elsewhere at the time.

The jet aircraft the ME-262 was stationed within range and it was believed that 30 of them could be mobilized quickly. They were armed with 30mm cannons and could inflict heavy damage on lightly escorted transport aircraft and gliders, but despite their superior speed they had been successfully prevented from attacking bomber formations by the concerted action of a greater number of Allied fighters.

With adequate escort, the transport aircraft and glider trains should be able to get to the appointed areas without much interference from the ME-262.

If a tactical surprise could be achieved, as in the case of Operation Market-Garden, fighter opposition against the initial landings might well be negligible. In any event, it was thought that Allied fighter cover should be sufficient to render abortive any enemy attempts to interfere with the approaching flights and actual drops. The enemy's main attack was expected to be directed against grounded gliders and concentrated troops on the ground.

The Air Marshal Commanding 2nd Tactical Air Force (2TAF) as Air Commander was responsible to the Supreme commander for all air operations in the SHAEF area, and would therefore be responsible for the co-ordination of all air operations in support of Varsity. It was at this level that requests were made to the agents of the Combined Chiefs of Staff (Chief of the Air Staff and Commanding General USAAF) to divert strategic bombers from their normal role.

This included escort of the troop transport aircraft and gliders from bases in England and France on route to the 2TAF area by RAF

Fighter Command and 9th US Air Force Fighters. In addition, air-sea rescue and diversion attacks would be provided by RAF Coastal Command with attacks and re-supply missions by heavy bombers of the 8th US Air Force. The AOC of 83 Group was responsible for all tactical air operations in the assault area.

The Ruhr Interdiction Line was a plan to isolate the Ruhr from Central and Southern Germany. This isolation was to be achieved by a drawing a line of interdiction, running in a rough curve southward from Bremen to the Rhine at Koblenz. Along this line were 18 railway bridges and railway viaducts, the destruction of which, it was estimated, would put every main railway line leading out of the Ruhr to the rest of Germany out of action. The three lines running through the targets to Bielefeld, Altenbeken, and Arnsberg were calculated to carry 50% of the rail traffic out of the Ruhr and were of greater importance than the others.

Some of these targets had previously been attacked but the damage inflicted had been repaired. On 21st February, a series of attacks was begun against these selected targets, which continued up to 20th March.

Some 40 attacks were made by heavy and medium bombers on bridges and viaducts. In addition, a number of fighter-bomber attacks were mounted on these same bridges, harassing attempts to repair the damage already done. Of these bridges and viaducts, ten were destroyed, two very seriously damaged and two others damaged but possibly passable by the 24th.

Bridges at Vlotho and Colbe were impassable for some of the time during this period.

The two bridges at Nuwied and Dottesfield were not included as targets, as they were within the range of artillery firing from the Remagen bridgehead. The approach lines had been cut at, and south of, Sigen.

Attacks on the viaducts included one on 14th March by 617 Squadron – the Dambusters – when S/Ldr Jock Calder dropped the first 22,000lb 'Grand Slam' bomb at Bieldfeld.

The Arnsburg railway viaduct was also attacked by 617 Squadron using 'Grand Slam' and 12,000lb 'Tallboy' bombs on 19th March. A 100ft section of the viaduct was severed, rendering the three main routes connecting the Ruhr with the rest of Germany impassable.

On 6th March Wesel – where German troops were concentrated – was attacked by 87 Lancasters of Bomber Command.

On 11th March, over 1,000 bombers attacked the railway centre at Essen, dropping over five thousand tons of bombs – the heaviest load of bombs ever directed onto a single target in one raid. This record was broken on 12th March when over 1,000 bombers dropped 5,487.2 tons of bombs.

On the 21st March, No.83 and 84 Groups succeeded in cutting German railway lines in 41 places, while No.2 Group by day attacked 17 towns close to the Rhine and by night any transport that could be seen. No 84 Group attacked the village of Zwolle, the depot of the German parachute troops, and also the HQ of the German 25th Army at Bussum, Holland, scoring direct hits with rockets and incendiary bombs. Also on the 21st and 22nd, 10 German airfields received over 2,700 tons of bombs from the 8th US Air Force, these airfields had been built for attacks on the UK in 1940/41 and had large concrete runways with excellent facilities for sustaining a strong air effort.

Strong Allied fighter forces swept the area of the airfields, strafing the fields and parking shelters, attacking fuel dumps and other ancillary airfield installations, while 52 German aircraft were shot down in combat and 116 destroyed on the ground.

Later reconnaissance photographs showed the attacks were very successful, the runways and landing areas were cratered and rendered at least temporarily unusable. The effectiveness of these attacks would be shown later on 24th March by the small scale of resistance by the German Air Force to the Allied sorties on Operation Varsity.

On the 23rd March 121 and 126 Wings of 83 Group attacked the anti-aircraft positions which were beyond the range of the Second Army artillery.

Over 115 attacks were made on the enemy transport system west of the Ruhr Interdiction Line, involving 6,916 effective sorties by heavy bombers and 3,582 by medium bombers during which 31,635 US tons of bombs were dropped. These operations resulted in claims for the destruction of 1,060 motor transport, 183 locomotives and 3,522 railroad cars. 338 rail cuts were made.

During the period from 21st to 23rd March, air attacks were directed against the communication centres within and close to the proposed battle area. Air attacks were made on a large number of known enemy barracks, camps and other military positions and on the airfields likely to be used by the German Air force in operations against the forthcoming operation.

Some 43 attacks were made by the 8th and 9th US Air Force and Bomber Command and Second Tactical Air Force. 3,471 sorties were flown by heavy and medium bombers and 8,508.25 tons of bombs dropped on rail centres and road junctions in the assault area. The fighter-bombers flew 2,967 sorties by day and there were 204 sorties by Mosquitoes by night.

The excellent weather conditions aided the precision and power of these attacks in the immediate preparation for the battle on the 24th. Clear skies and excellent visibility prevailed for most of these three days over the battle area and beyond, permitting accurate bombing at both medium and high altitude and the easy picking out of targets of opportunity. However, smoke from German towns and villages and other targets attacked, but above all from smoke generators in use by the Allied ground forces, was the one real serious handicap to the bombing force and often prevented clear observation of results achieved.

These smoke canisters were set off by the Pioneer corps to screen from the enemy troop movements and activities on the western bank of the river with a pall of smoke 10,000 yards in length.

The remains of Wesel after the RAF and USAAF bombing raids – March 24th 1945. [Mike King]

Hamilcar gliders and their Halifax tugs lined up and ready to go – 24th March 1945.

CHAPTER 13

D-Day – 24th March 1945

On 17th March it was decided to use the Commando Corps to safeguard the passage of the airborne force on D-Day by taking the town of Wesel. They were lightly armed, however, and a bombing attack immediately prior to their assault on the town was considered to be essential. The task of bombing was offered to Bomber Command, who were asked to bomb Wesel by night immediately prior to the assault by the Commando troops.

On 19th March, RAF station and Squadron commanders were briefed at Headquarters 38 Group and the operation commenced on 21st March 1945. Airborne formations were ready to take off as from 24th March 1945.

On 20th March, HQ 12 Corps assumed operational command of 52 (Lowland) Infantry division. Troops available to 12 Corps for Operation Plunder included 29 divisions of British and US troops, including two Airborne divisions and came to more than a million men. Units involved were:

- 7th Armoured Division
- 15th (Scottish) Infantry Division
- 52nd (Lowland) Infantry Division
- 53rd (Welsh) Infantry Division
- 4th Armoured Brigade
- 34th Armoured Brigade
- 1st Command Brigade
- 115th Infantry Brigade
- Elements of 79th Armoured Division

Due to the lessons learned at Arnhem, it was decided to drop the airborne troops in close proximity to the start lines of the ground assault with the object of widening and extending the bridgehead as quickly as possible. The airborne landings could only be made in daylight and owing to the take-off aerodromes being located in the UK and the Paris area, it was calculated that P-Hour could not be before 10am. On the other hand, a night assault by the ground troops was required, for reasons of surprise and to give maximum cover from enemy fire during the initial crossing of the river.

The British gliders were briefed to fly at a height of 2,500 feet for the whole of the outward journey and the US gliders at 1,500 feet on the early part of the journey, decreasing to 600 feet above ground level at the dropping and landing zones.

The crossing would have the support of a Bomber Command attack on Wesel, after which it was estimated it would take about 12 hours for the resulting smoke and dust to settle. This was essential if the airborne forces arriving at 10am were not to fly in blind.

On 19th & 20th March, 6th Airborne Division moved to the airfield transit camps.

On 21st March 1945, General Montgomery visited General Simpson's US 9th Army HQ in Munchen Gladbach to go over the final details for Operation Plunder.

On 22nd March, in the German village of Walbeck, Montgomery called 'O' Group to give the final orders. That night the US Third Army under General Patton crossed the Rhine south of Mainz and into the German heartland.

On 23rd March 1945, Montgomery issued the following message to the armies:

"On the seventh of February I told you we were going into the ring for the final and last round; that there would be no time limit and that

Horsa gliders ready for take-off. [Alec Waldron]

we would continue fighting until our opponent was knocked out. The last round is going very well on both sides of the ring – and overhead.

"In the West, the enemy has lost the Rhineland, and with it the flower of at least four armies – the Parachute Army, Fifth Army Panzer Army, Fifteenth Army and Seventh Army; the First Army to the south is now being added to the list.

"In the Rhineland battles, the enemy has lost 150,000 who have been taken prisoner, and there are many more to come; his total casualties amount to about 250,000 since the 8th February.

"In the East, the enemy has lost all Pomerania east of the Oder, an area as large as the Rhineland; and three more German armies have been routed. The Russian armies are within about 35 miles of Berlin. Overhead, the Allied Air Forces are pounding Germany night and day.

"It will be interesting to see how much longer the Germans can stand it. The enemy has been driven into a corner; he cannot escape. The complete and decisive defeat of the Germans is certain; there is no possibility or doubt on this matter.

"The 21st Army Group will now cross the Rhine. The enemy possibly thinks he is safe behind this great river obstacle. We all agree that is a great obstacle, but we will show the enemy that he is far from safe behind it. This great Allied fighting machine, composed of integrated land and air forces, will deal with the problem in no uncertain manner, and having crossed the Rhine, we will crack on in the plains of Northern Germany, chasing the enemy from pillar to post. The swifter and the more energetic our action, the sooner the war will be over, and that is what we all desire; to get on with the job and finish off the German war as soon as possible. Over the Rhine then let us go, and good hunting to you all on the other side. May 'the Lord mighty in battle' give us the victory in this, our latest undertaking, as He has done in all our battles since we landed in Normandy on D-Day."

The final decision that Operation Plunder was to take place was made by Commander-in-Chief 21st Army Group at 5pm (1700) on 23rd March.

The weather forecast was favourable for the launching of Varsity.

Prime Minister Winston Churchill had been prevented from going out to Normandy during the landings in June 1944, as it was felt he was too important a person to be in the danger area so soon, but he was determined to be at the crossing of the Rhine. He would be accompanied by Field Marshal Allenbrook, Chief of the Imperial General Staff. They left at 3.30pm on the 23rd and arrived at Montgomery's HQ near Venlo for tea. It had been he who had invited Churchill out adding a note, 'I shall ask you to write a Chapter for my book'. Churchill replied straight away, saying he would come in a Dakota as his Skymaster was taking 'Clemmie', his wife, to her mission in Russia.

From the airfield at Venlo they drove to Straelen, where they were met by Montgomery. Churchill sent a telegram back to Stalin.

'I am at Field Marshal Montgomery's HQ. He has given orders to launch the main battle to cross the Rhine on a broad front from a centre, about Wesel, supported by the landing of an Airborne Corps and about 2,000 guns. It is hoped to pass the river tonight and tomorrow and establish bridgeheads. A very large reserve of armour is available to exploit the assault once the river is crossed. I shall send you another message tomorrow. Field Marshal Montgomery asks me to present his respects to you.'

D-Day -24th March 1945

Codename	
Turnscrew	Assault by 30 Corps 2100 on the evening of the 23rd
Widgeon	Assault crossing No 1 Commando 2200
	Attack by Bomber Command on Wesel 2230
Torchlight	Assault Crossing by 15 (S) Div 0200am on the 24th
Flashlight	Assault crossing by the 9th US Army 0200
Varsity	Airborne assault 1000 D-Day

On 23rd March, troops were withdrawn just 1,000 yards from the river – a record for close-support bombing.

On 23rd March 1945, at 15.30 (3.30pm) 77 Lancasters of Bomber Command attacked and bombed the town Wesel, later to be the objective of the 1st Commando Brigade. As soon as this had taken place the order was sent to 21st Army Group that the crossing of the Rhine and the landing of troops near the Diersfordter Wald was to take place as planned.

At 22.35pm on the same evening 218 Lancasters and Mosquitoes again attacked Wesel, the main weight of the attack falling on the North West part of the town as planned. The intention was to destroy troops and defended positions. Photographs from the afternoon raid showed heavy damage throughout the town. Many streets were blocked by craters and debris.

Bert Allam had trained with No.1 BFTS and at the time of the Rhine Crossing was a pilot with 227 Squadron based at Balderton, Notts.

At the briefing for the second attack on Wesel the crews were surprised to learn that as moonlight conditions were expected the Pathfinders would not be using a flare force but marking the target 'by the light of the silvery moon', as someone commented at the time. It showed considerable faith in the 'met' forecast.

There was little defence over the target, only light flak and no fighters. The target was bombed from 10,000 feet and the bomb aimers told that accuracy was essential as the 2nd Army Group were waiting on the west bank of the Rhine only 1,600 yards from the bombers' aiming point. At one point during the raid the Master Bomber was very upset at seeing a stick of bombs end up in the river. The whole raid was over in ten minutes.

In Bert's words, as a bomber pilot who took part in this raid:

"The Airborne troops who went in next on Varsity have never been given proper recognition for their efforts and sacrifice. For my part I would not have liked to have been there, and had anyone suggested to me that I become a glider pilot I think I would have waked rapidly in the opposite direction. Gliders did not have enough engines for me and were an uncomfortable way of getting you to a place where nasty things could happen and with no hope of getting back."

The outstanding success of the raids on the 23rd was commended by Field Marshal Montgomery who said they were "a masterpiece and a decisive factor in allowing the army's entry into that city before midnight."

The taking of Wesel cost only 36 casualties.

War Correspondent Alan Moorehead was able to watch the bombing from a holiday villa on the west bank. He remarked in his book *Eclipse* that as he watched the Lancasters coming

A tank inside a Hamilcar glider. [Bob Randall]

in for the attack he realised that Wesel had just about ten minutes to live.

The afternoon air attack was followed by the guns of 12 Corps, 2nd Army and 9th US Army, who continued to pour shells into German positions until 9.45am on the morning of the 24th. The evening attack was followed by a barrage of two hours from 1,300 guns of eleven medium regiments, two heavy batteries and one super heavy battery of the 7th Armoured Divisional Artillery Group and one Horse Artillery Regiment, plus three US Field artillery battalions with 155 mm guns. Corps smoke screens to blind the high grounds east of the Rhine were arranged from first light on D-Day.

At 10pm (2200 hours) the town of Wesel was taken by the 1st Commando Brigade (46th Royal Marine Commando and 3rd and 6th Army Commandos) and the 51st Highland Brigade with the code name Operation 'Widgeon'. The 51st Highland Division went in on the left, around Rees and the 15th Scottish Division on the left near Xanten. Beyond them and close to Wesel the First Brigade of Commandos were entering the water. Intensive training had taken place in landing craft and storm-boats manned by Royal Marine engineer Commandos in a creek in the River Mass.

Brigadier Mills-Roberts plan was for 46th Royal Marine commandos to lead the assault by crossing with Brigade HQ and securing a bridgehead two miles downstream of Wesel, in an area known as Grav Insel. The remainder would follow and make their way cross-country to the town. The 46 RM Commando would follow behind since it was essential that the bridgehead was cleared by first light as it was dominated by high ground inland. As the last bomb dropped on Wesel 6th Army Commando moved into the town, followed by 45th Royal Marine Commando and 3rd Army Commando. They captured 850 prisoners and killed a number of the enemy.

The first messages came back from the Commando GHQ:

'First wave across without opposition'
'Second wave across, still no opposition'
'Forty prisoners gathered in'
'Third wave crossing river.... all first objectives taken'

They had been so close to the bombing that they only narrowly escaped being bombed themselves, but they were able to take advantage of this and capture the surviving defenders, who were still dazed after the bombardment. The Commandos soon set up HQ very near to where the German HQ had been established.

The Mosquitoes of No.2 Group were heavily involved against enemy transport deployed opposite the 2nd and 9th Army fronts, dropping, in all, 138 five hundred pound bombs on towns, villages and woods.

The morning of the 24th, as predicted by the weathermen, afforded unlimited visibility over the bases in the Eastern UK from where the main airborne force would take of, in the Paris area where the American fighters would be taking off and over the target area itself.

Reveille for the troops was between 2.45am and 4am.

The largest single airborne lift in history was about to begin – a force of 1,700 aircraft, 1,300 gliders and 21,000 troops would shortly be arriving on German soil.

There were various code names devised and to be remembered by the troops.

The code name for the main objective of Hamminkeln was 'Norfolk'. The code for the River Rhine was 'Prune' and the road and rail crossing at Hamminkeln was 'Horse'. The password challenges/responses were changed every 12 hours:

D–1 to D-Day	'Lighting' / 'Thunder'
D-Day to D+1	'Hither' / 'Thither'
D+1 to D+2	'Hundreds' / 'Thousands'
D+2 to D+3	'Please' / 'Thanks'

In the main briefing for 'B' Squadron before the operation the objectives were:

- to land 30 gliders on LZ 'P' and 30 on LZ 'R'
- to send out fighting patrols in the area west of the LZ to lay high tension cables and to clear the area of the enemy.
- on 'R' glider pilots would rendezvous at a Squadron HQ selected by Cpt Norton and take up positions for the local protection of Brigade HQ.

Lt-Col Murray's general military and personal briefing note instructed the gliders to fly in low

Unloading a tank from a Hamilcar glider.   [Bob Randall]

and remember to instruct passengers in ditching drill. On landing, if the nose of the glider was smashed they were to remember to carry out tail unloading. There was to be a supply drop by 240 Liberators two hours after landing. 'Don't listen to rumours once on the ground, hold your fire, and remember speed and offensive spirit the moment you land.'

Friday 23rd
1030 .... Special brief for tug crews
1400-1700 ... Tugs marshalled
1700 .... Gliders marshalled
1800 .... Main briefing 1st lift by 296 Squadron
1900 .... Main briefing 2nd lift 297 Squadron

Saturday 24th
0400 .... Reveille
0430 .... Breakfast
0515 .... Final brief
0615 .... At Aircraft
0715 .... Take off

Gliders No.400, 401 and 402 of 'G' Squadron to land with Devons and stay with loads and at Devons HQ under Pilot Officer Castle.

Glider No.364 to carry a 25-pounder gun to be marked with a yellow tailplane and to remain with his load until jeep arrives.

The gliders at Earls Colne near Colchester in Essex were loaded three days before the operation. The two tug squadrons at this station – 296 and 297 – had moved to Earls Colne from Brize Norton in September 1944, where they converted from Albemarles to Halifaxes. Excellent air photographs of the landing zone were shown at the briefings. At the final briefing on the evening of the 23rd, everybody was surprised but delighted and honoured to have Air Chief Marshal Sir Arthur Tedder attend. He told them that the majority of the enemy's aircraft were out of action but that, although the majority of enemy anti-aircraft guns were out of action or damaged they had not been entirely eliminated.

How right he proved to be…

As Lt-Col Ian Toler was having a last drink in the bar at the officers mess, Tedder came over and said. "My boy, you have work to do tomorrow. You had better go to bed." With reveille at 4.30am, he had a point.

The first off was the 6th British Airborne Division, taking off from 11 airfields in East Anglia at 6am. The entire British parachute lift was carried in 240 C-47s of 9th Troop Carrier Command under Maj-Gen Paul L. Williams.

The first glider force from 38 and 46 Groups despatched 440 gliders and tug aircraft combinations. They also started at 6am. Only one failed to take off, the undercarriage of the tug aircraft collapsing before it became airborne.

The 3rd Parachute Brigade had taken off at 7am and three hours later were arriving at the DZ. They found the enemy anti-aircraft moderate at first but becoming more intense as the operation progressed. The enemy at first were still recovering from the bombing and shelling, but some gun positions had not been overrun or destroyed. The task of the 8th Parachute Battalion was to clear the DZ.

The 5th Parachute Brigade began to drop on schedule at 10.15am but its drop was not as accurate as that made by 3rd Brigade despite accurate anti-aircraft fire, airburst shelling and mortar fire from the DZ. On the ground, bad visibility from smoke and dust made it difficult for troops to get their bearings and there was some delay in re-organising the three battalions.

While this was taking place the 8th US Air Force renewed its attacks on German airfields, with particular emphasis on the ME-262 jet-powered aircraft. The first attacks were carried out in the morning on 12 airfields and timed to catch as many enemy fighters as possible on the ground. In the afternoon four further airfields were attacked.

Under the Varsity plan the 9th US Air Force was committed to bombing flak positions prior to the airborne attack, particularly those beyond the range of the 21st Army Group's artillery. From first light, the medium and light bombers kept up a continuous pounding of all known flak positions within range of the drop and landing zones. A total of more than 400 effective sorties were flown against these guns and more than 700 tons of bombs were dropped. The results were gener-

Take-off. [Charles E. Brown]

ally good, despite the fact that the target areas were hazy with smoke from burning buildings and other targets.

These attacks on flak positions were supplemented by those of medium and light bombers of the 2nd TAF. During the morning more than 70 Mitchells and Bostons hit similar targets with good results and they were followed by further-bombers on the same mission. Fire was seen to be coming from five positions that had not been mentioned in the briefing.

On the 24th, 150 heavy bombers of the 15th US Air Force mounted a long-haul attack on Berlin with the intention of drawing enemy fighters to the east and away from the invasion area.

From 1000 hrs to 1304 hrs, six parachute serials and 15 British glider serials, together with seven US parachute serials and 15 US serials were accurately dropped in their designated four drop zones and six landing zones. They were followed by 240 heavy bomber aircraft of the 8th US Air Force in 10 serials, who dropped an initial re-supply drop of 582 tons. The 17th Division reported 100% recovery and the 6th Division reported 85% recovery of these supplies.

Mobile 20mm anti-aircraft batteries were quickly moved to the threatened area by the Germans. The incendiaries used by this lethal weapon accompanied by accurate small arms fire, began to take its toll on the low-flying parachute aircraft, flying at 600 feet and the glider and re-supply aircraft at 200 feet.

General Josiah T. Dalby of the Airborne Training Centre in North Carolina, and General Ridgeway M. Gaither of the Parachute School, Fort Benning were given permission to take part in the operation. They found themselves dropping on top of a battery of 20 mm guns, reinforced by machine guns and German infantry. Shortly after the gliders began to land, Dalby organised what he called 'Chattahoovhee Task Force'. The force consisted of US Artillery, British and US Glider pilots and any other soldier in the area. The force eliminated the German battery and all resistance in the area. The Dalby force was then, with the help of a number of glider pilots, able to guide 3,500 German prisoners to the rear.

The bombers of the RAF attacked the marshalling yards at Sterkrade. 155 Halifaxes, 16

Lancasteres and 6 Mosquitoes completely destroyed the well-packed yard.

The 6th Airborne Division column crossed the Channel at Folkestone and made landfall near Cape Griz Nez in the area of Calais, then flew south-east to Bethune to a point south of Brussels where it converged with the US 17th Airborne Division column at Wavre.

From this junction the route led straight northeast to Wesel, where the turn into the drop and landing zones was made on schedule, shortly before 10am. The northern column proceeded to the target area on the left and the southern on the right.

The northern column was escorted by 213 fighters of RAF Fighter Command as far as the Rhine. The southern column was escorted by 676 fighters of the 9th US Air Force. Over the target area 2nd British TAF had 900 fighters.

The US 17th Airborne Division, took off from Coulomnies, Bretigny, Melun, Chateandun, Bricy, St Andre, Chartres, and Poix, airfields near Paris and met up with the 6th Airborne at Wavre south east of Brussels.

At Chateaudun the combat crews of the 439th Troop Carrier Group of 50 Wing assembled in the town theatre. At the briefing the were told they would meet the other groups of the 50th Air Carrier Wing and would then fly directly by way of Saint-Quentin to Wavre where they would meet up with the British.

Take off from Earls Colne was at 7.35am. Ian Toler was flying with F/O Telfer as his co-pilot. The door of the glider was closed, the tug took up the slack and they were off. Forming up over the airfield Ian saw that all his gliders were safely airborne. Having crossed the Channel, Ian flew over the area of Dunkirk and looked down, remembering when he had been there before at the retreat in 1940. Visibility today was 5 to 8 miles.

There were aircraft in every direction with squadrons of fighters weaving about, above and below.

The first serial of gliders at Earls Colne under Wg/Cdr Musgrave, CO of 296 Squadron in Halifax NA-304 were airborne in 26 minutes. One glider, No.154, was re-marshalled owing to tug trouble, but managed to take off at the end of the serial. The take-off at 7am was witnessed by the Secretary of State for Air Sir Archibald Sinclair and Air Chief Marshal Lord Tedder.

Wing Commander Musgrave, CO of 296 Squadron. [Ian Toler]

All the gliders were off by 8.04am. Here at Earls Colne gliders were marshalled along the runway for approximately one third of its length. The remaining tugs and gliders were placed alongside on the perimeter each side of the main runway.

F/Lt Priest flying in Halifax NA-698 crashed in flames. He was killed and is buried in the Reichswald War Cemetery. Two of the crew who survived were taken to hospital.

The other squadron at Earls Colne was 297, commanded by Wg/Cdr R.G. Dean DFC. He led the take off at 0734 hrs in Halifax NA-297. They had three aircraft diverted to Gosfield on return with hydraulics trouble and one to Woodbridge with no brake pressure.

Take off at Birch by 233 Squadron under Wg/Cdr K.G. Mellor DFC* and 48 Squadron under Wg/Cdr Squires DFC, was at 6.18 am and all 60 aircraft were in the air by 7.34 am. Two gliders, Nos. 40 and 43, broke their tow ropes on take off, but were retrieved and remarshalled at the tail of the second serial.

Also at Birch, Wg/Cdr J.A. Sproule RCAF DFC in Dakota KG-600 led 437 (RCAF) Squadron and took off at 0702 am.

At Gosfield the take off time was 6am. Thirty gliders were led by Wg/Cdr R.G. Dutton DFC* of 512 Squadron, Lt-Col P.S. Joubert AFC of 271 Squadron and Wg/Cdr E.C. Deanesley DFC of 575 Squadron in Dakota KN-290, carrying the two 'Coup de Main' parties and elements of the 2nd Ox & Bucks. They took off in 30 minutes. This was followed almost immediately at 6.33am with a second serial of 30 gliders.

On 21st March, Jack Cottam of 575 Squadron took off from Down Ampney to RAF Gosfield on detachment for Operation Varsity. After a 7pm briefing on 23rd March they were given an early call at 4am and by 5.30am the engines were being warmed for take off. Jack remembers seeing Dakotas all around, all very close and moving forward to the take off area. At 6.32am in Dakota KN-296 the slack was taken up, the throttles opened and they were off down the runway. The glider felt heavy as they got into the air and left the green fields of the Essex countryside behind them.

The journey was uneventful until they got near the Rhine, where puffs of smoke were coming up and getting nearer and nearer, with the aircraft bucking from the explosions. "Any moment," Jack remembers thinking, "we shall get a direct hit." On the port wing were two American Typhoons who, after seeing the ground fire coming up, broke towards an area of poplar trees and a farm complex. Suddenly there was a big explosion and the shelling, as if by magic, stopped. The time had come for the glider to cast off, and once this was done they had to get out of the stream. The cable was dropped in a designated area before heading for Brussels (B56).

"The landing was hairy to say the least," remembers Jack, "because of recent enemy bombing of the runway."

On landing they were marshalled to the outer boundary, where they were refuelled and large panniers put inside ready to take off and return to the Rhine area for re-supply drops. However, as the American supply drops were successful, their services were not required.

They returned to RAF Broadwell on 26th March, thankful for safe return. The accommodation at B56 had been in tents.

Jack's glider pilot, who he describes as "a 21-year-old rugby-playing type" got down safely but "had a bad time on the ground – more shell shock than physical injury – from which, in time, he did recover."

Jack now lives just 600 metres from the site of the old airfield at Gosfield and so every day has a reminder of that day in March 1945. Today the only flying he does is by radio-controlled model aircraft. The control tower at Gosfield still stands today and was the last thing Jack remembers seeing as he took off for the Rhine.

The last combination took off from Gosfield at 6.57am.

At Great Dunmow it was time for take-off for 190 Squadron under Wg/Cdr R.H. Bunker in Stirling LJ-930-A carrying a Mr Singleton, an American War Correspondent, and 620 Squadron under Wg/Cdr T. Wynne-Powell DFC flying Stirling LK-123. The first serial of 24 gliders was fully airborne in 26 minutes. Two gliders, Nos. 187 and 205, carrying the 12th Devons, returned to base through tug failure, but later took off again. Another glider No.197 was unserviceable after the rope broke at take off time, but was later remarshalled at the tail of the second serial. The second serial took off at 7.07am and the last combination at 8.01am. One glider, No.406, carrying the AARR Mortars, was remarshalled owing to the tug aircraft LJ 826-J of 190 Squadron, flown by Flying Officer Weldon, developing a nasty swing on take off and writing off the undercarriage completely, obstructing the runway in use. The crew were shaken up, but only one, F/O Walden, sustained a slight cut.

Flying Officer Connell had an engine pack up on take off and had to cast his glider off, which landed as soon as possible. Connell later, after the last glider had taken off, took another glider, which was successful and landed in the LZ area.

The form up was at 120mph instead of the arranged 130mph. The journey to the Rhine was at 140mph – once again under the speed arranged – as most of the aircraft were finding it difficult to maintain even 140 mph let alone 145 when tugging fully laden gliders.

The Halifax stream ahead began to draw away, leaving an 8-mile gap. As it was essential to keep continuity, the squadron had to disregard the time briefed for Marfax and by cutting corners attempt to bridge the gap. The CO of 190 Squadron, Wg/Cdr Bunker in LJ 630-A was unable to do this and 190 arrived at the LZ almost as a single unit.

As they approached Marfax with the US Air Force coverage on them, soon the two streams were flying along in perfect harmony, Stirlings and Halifaxes with Horsa and Hamilcar gliders on the port side and Dakotas, each pulling two Waco gliders on the starboard side.

One Brigadier said, "I could see the Rhine, a silver streak, and beyond it a thick black haze for all the world like Manchester or Birmingham as seen from the air."

At each turning, Rebbeca and Eureka sets had been set up, but with extremely good visibility they were not needed. The only heavy flak encountered was coming from the direction of Rees. The artificial smoke envisaged in Monty's plan was seen to be covering the Landing Zones.

S/Ldr Robertson in LK 566-G saw a Halifax go down in flames in the Landing Zone area and three chutes appear. This would have been WO Symond's aircraft. F/O Fogarty in LJ 895-K saw a Halifax with the wing off go down in flames. F/O Hook in EF 242-Q saw a Horsa glider go down in flames. F/Lt Bliss USAF in LK 276-Y saw a Stirling with one port engine on fire in the Landing Zone area. F/O Whiteley in LJ 832-U saw a glider go down in flames.

At Matching, the twenty combinations were airborne in twenty one and half minutes. One glider (No.222) carrying men from the 12th

Australian Flying Officer Mason and crew of Stirling of 190 Squadron, based at Great Dunmow.

Devons, broke its rope three minutes after take-off and landed back at base with damage to the wings.

The tug and glider No.215 returned to base through engine failure and were too late to take off again.

At Woodbridge in Suffolk, the twelve Horsa combinations led by Wg/Cdr Law-Wright DSO, DFC in NA 282-8TU of 298 Squadron took off in seven minutes. The 48 Hamilcars led by Wg/Cdr Archer AFC of 644 Squadron were off the ground in 28 minutes. The rope of glider No.241, carrying an anti-tank battery of the Royal Artillery, broke its rope three minutes after take-off, the glider landing just outside the airfield.

F/O Griffiths RCAF, flying NA 658-8TE aborted and its glider cast off at Brussels. F/O Buchanan RCAF in NA 118-8TO had a War Correspondent in his crew, Wilmot Ragdale.

Warrant Officer Mackrill in NA 660-8TH had an engine abort on take off and the glider was cast off. The tug aircraft managed to land at Woodbridge; the glider landed at Manston and one of the crew was seriously injured.

The glider tugged by NA 289-8TM had the tail fall off and then blew up in the area of Goch. Tug NA 115-8TG aborted and the glider cast off. F/O Reid RAAF in NZ 983-8AF had the glider pull off and landed at Manston. F/O Watkins in NA 113-8AQ was hit by flak and the glider cast off.

F/O McGillivary in NA 311-8AK took off at 0743, and as only two free tugs were seen to be shot down, it was assumed that they had completed their duty. F/O Williams in NA 613-8AZ was hit by flak on the way out and trouble with the hydraulics caused them to land at Manston.

At Shepherds Grove, Wg/Cdr R.T. Turner of 196 Squadron, flying Stirling PW 392, and Wg/Cdr P.I.N. Jennings in Stirling HK 225, led the twenty eight gliders of the first serial. All successfully took off in 26 minutes. One glider No.309 was cast off near Kings Lynn as the tug aircraft flown by Warrant Officer Jury of 299 Squadron had engine trouble. F/O Curry of 299 did not get off because of engine trouble, and F/Sgt Cross had his glider cast off. F/Lt Brown of 196 Squadron had his glider break loose, F/Lt Spruell had his glider break off in a slipstream and F/Lt Vanrenen had to force land. One glider (No.136) towed by F/O Smith of 295 Squadron, carrying men of the 12th Devons, cast off because the rope was fraying; it was later towed off by Flt/Sgt Sabourine. The remaining 33 of the first serial took off at 7am and were all airborne in twenty five minutes. F/O Webster's glider cast off 40 miles from base at 8.15am during the form up. The 26 in the second serial, under Wg/Cdr T.C. Musgrave of 296 Squadron in Halifax NA 304, were off in 26 minutes.

One aircraft was lost. Warrant Officer Symmons' aircraft was seen to crash; five crew managed to bale out successfully but Symmons himself was killed in baling out. The aircraft had been hit by heavy flak at about 1033am and crashed in flames.

From Rivenhall, No.295 Squadron, commanded by Wg/Cdr Bill Angell was to lead all the 38 Group Squadrons. Bill took off at 0700 and landed at 1200 hrs. Also at Rivenhall were 570 Squadron, led by Wg/Cdr R.J.M. Bangay who led 26 aircraft off at 7.37am in Stirling LJ 640-U8B. Four of the 570 Squadron aircraft had been loaned to work with 295 Squadron.

At Broadwell Wg/Cdr Dutton DFC* in Dakota KG 590-AP led 512 Squadron off at 6am; they previously had taken part in the D-Day and Arnhem operations. S/Ldr Mostyn-Brown in KK 193-HK was the second off at 6.01am, his second pilot was no less than the AOC of 46 Group, Air Commodore L. Darvall MC.

'D' Squadron mascot at RAF Broadwell. [John Crane]

The number three aircraft of Sqn/Ldr Clarke, KG 641-AC, had some difficulty in formatting, despite identification and formation lights. The 21 aircraft turned at the estimated time of arrival (ETA) followed by the remainder which put the leader downstream and four minutes late at Gosfield but this was made up and Dutton took the lead at Cap Griz Nez. As the leading aircraft made its turn at Bethune the first wave of American paratroopers in Dakotas of US Troop Carrier Command appeared below and to port. They were seen dropping the paratroopers ten miles ahead.

From No.48 Squadron, F/Lt Whitfield DFM in KG 439 lost his glider over the Lille area and S/Ldr Harries lost his glider 12 miles from the landing zone. In each case the towing ropes were brought back for inspection.

The RAF ground staff on one station cheered the airborne troops as they drove into the gliders. In one of the gliders was L. Marsland Gander, Special Correspondent of the *Daily Telegraph*. A Lt-Col in the Royal Artillery was also in the glider along with the Rev A.P Cameron, a Divisional Senior chaplain.

The six Air landing Brigade landed about 1030am. Accurate tactical landings were not possible owing to bad visibility due to dust clouds caused by bombing and shelling, smoke from crashed and blazing aircraft and smoke put down by the enemy.

Parts of the 17th US Airborne Division were landed in error in the same area, but gave considerable help in clearing the early strong opposition on the landing zones during the first hour or so after landing.

Ian Toler remembers that on the landing zone there was a very prominent feature in the form of a small wood – codenamed 'Bunty'. This was completely obscure, but luckily the run in to the release point was clear and Ian blessed the pilot who had taken the oblique photographs which showed him where he was. Over the release point he said " Cheerio" to the tug pilot and hoped he would have good breakfast.

The tow-rope was released by Ian and he flew towards the railway, which he could just about see. By this time they were flying blind because of the smoke. Another glider came out of the smoke and Ian had to dive to 140mph to avoid it. At about 200 feet, he saw the tops of high tension power lines and this told him he was going in the right direction, but as he was about to land he ran into low tension and telephone cables, which slowed them down while they were still at 20 feet, so they landed heavily. The front of the glider was damaged but no one was hurt. He was relived to see 'Bunty' only 100 yards from where they had come down. Not bad considering he had been flying blind for 2,000 feet.

By 1100 am 402 British gliders were down. Of the 440 gliders, 35 had aborted for a number of reasons. The release height had been set for 2,500 feet but some were coming off at 3,500 feet, which made them more vulnerable to the guns. Moderate, medium and heavy flak were experienced over the landing zones, the rope dropping area and Viersfordterwald, but it was mostly inaccurate.

The train of gliders and tug aircraft from the UK was an hour long and when they met up with the US gliders it became two and half hours long.

Some gliders landed within 200 and others 50 yards of the objective, despite the smoke which limited the length of vision to less than a furlong. Other landings were more, or less, eventful.

CHAPTER 14

Personal Memories of Operation Varsity

On the night of the 23rd March, Sergeant Gerard Coughlan of 'A' Squadron, based at Rivenhall, had hoped to get to bed early with a 4 am call the next morning, but the Army made sure this did not happen.

He was required with his first pilot, F/O Edwin Cook, to report to the armoury at 8pm to pick up live ammunition. It was packed in heavy grease and had to be removed in slabs. They were handed a supply of ammunition and a piece of rag to clean off the grease so that the ammunition could be placed in their belts and pouches.

Earlier in the day they had packed everything they would need for the next two weeks behind enemy lines, by which time they hoped they would be relieved by the main allied land forces.

At 4am on 24th March 1945, Gerry was awakened with a cup of tea and a biscuit, brought to him by a WAAF who, it would appear, had taken a shine to him. After breakfast they arrived at the runway for 6am and deposited their heavy packs inside the glider. Their load was 16 men, led by a Major – and a jeep. F/O Edwin Cook, the first pilot, was newly married and his wife was expecting a baby in a few months time.

The flight was uneventful and the Rhine came up after three hours where small puffs of smoke were seen from bursting shells. When they hit the ground, the hinged cockpit broke away from the rest of the glider. Gerry remembers thinking "If this is dying then its not too bad…" When he regained consciousness he was looking up at a bright blue sky but could not work out where he was. When he finally came to, he found he was strapped to a piece of the glider – the cockpit having broken up on landing. He heard firing, so released his harness and rolled over onto his stomach. As he did, bullets hit the ground near him. He was in the open, more or less in the middle of a flat field. The Major he had carried was lying dead in a heap with one arm twisted above him. Blood was running down his sleeve and over his wrist. Not having been strapped in, he had been thrown out on impact without the cockpit to cushion his fall. Edwin Cook had been hit whilst in the air and died shortly after landing. Ahead was a wooded area which would give some cover from the German gunfire coming from a nearby farmhouse. The problem was cover or a distraction to enable him to get to the woods. It was now mid-morning and he saw German soldiers crossing from the barn to the farmhouse, and vice versa. To his amazement he found that he had dozed off – seemingly odd in the circumstances of such danger – but later he was told that in times of stress sleep is not uncommon. He then saw about a dozen Germ-

Troops in flight inside a glider.

ans, led by a revolver-waving officer. The majority of them were converging on the glider, but one was heading in his direction.

He decided that if he startled the German it may get him shot, so he rolled over, raised one arm in the air and called him over. The German stopped, sprang to attention and then approached cautiously with his rifle pointed at Gerry, who then got to his knees, raised both arms and stood up slowly. As he did so, two more Germans hurried over and started to disarm him. They threw the live grenades he was carrying on the ground and made him unbuckle his webbing, which dropped to the ground. The two soldiers then went to the deserted glider and started to go through the pockets of the dead men, turning over their bodies with their feet. One soldier in the glider was still alive, but only barely; his stomach had been torn open. As the Germans approached he offered them a cigarette, saying "Don't shoot. Don't shoot." This upset Gerry, seeing a dying man pleading for what little life he had left. He looked at the dead bodies and thought how only hours ago they had been fit, healthy young men. Now they were dead and their relatives in the UK would never know the circumstances of their deaths. They would shortly get that yellow telegram delivered by a telegram boy on a bike 'We regret to inform you … killed as a result of enemy action.' If he got home safely, he would be the one to have to tell Edwin Cook's wife how he died. The wounded soldier was picked up by four German soldiers and taken behind the farmhouse. Some hours later Gerry was told the man had died.

A German officer told Gerry that they had been waiting for the landings for 3 days – so much for the 'element of surprise'. He was taken to an area where prisoners had been assembled. This included some Dutch Underground resistance members. In groups of 50 they were locked in railway freight cars while the train shunted back and forth, day and night. Eventually they reached the village of Fallingbostel and Stalag IIb. The sight was foreboding – men with sunken eyes and cheeks, stripped to the waist, exposing sunken chests, pot bellies and skeletal frames. He had never seen such emaciated people. The only advantage they had was that, being long-term prisoners they had a bunk to sleep in, a knife, fork and spoon and the other everyday things, whereas Gerry, just arriving, had nothing. Every space, let alone bunk, was covered in sleeping bodies. He managed to get a space and after three days a blanket that had belonged to someone who had died.

"This was the only way to acquire anything in this camp," he remembers.

The diet was watery soup, which he missed on the first day because he did not have a container to collect it in.

Finally, he found a rusty can, which he managed to straighten out and then wash out the caked dirt and rust under a cold tap. He learned a hard lesson on his first night. His boots, which he removed to sleep, had vanished by the morning, in their place a warped and worn out pair, too small for Gerry, but he had nothing else so had to wear them. The Red Cross parcels, which came occasionally, enabled him to acquire cigarettes, which, being a non-smoker, he was able to trade with the German guards for bread.

With the end of the war in sight, they were forced by the guards to leave the camp, and the forced marches began, first going one way to avoid the advancing British and American forces and then in the other direction to avoid the Russians. As they passed through the camp gates, they were given a third of a loaf of bread and three inches of German sausage. This Gerry managed to make last for three days. Over the next four weeks they travelled some 700 miles, going nowhere in particular, but avoiding major roads and sleeping at the roadside or in barns. Another problem was being attacked and strafed from the air by Allied aircraft, who mistook the men on the march below for an enemy column. One day Gerry collapsed without any warning and was put on a horse drawn cart and taken to a barn, where he fell asleep and lost track of time. He awoke to a putrid smell and moaning.

When he looked around he saw bodies, some of whom seemed to be dead. He soon realised that he had been left here with the others to either recover or die. He knew that although he still felt weak he had to get out and asked the guard outside if he could re-join the column. It was still only a short distance away and en route the guard allowed him to pick some vegetables. As they passed through one village they saw buildings on fire. They had been set ablaze by retreating German soldiers in what was called the "scorched earth policy" – leaving nothing behind that could be of use to the advancing enemy.

They soon found themselves between the Allied armies in the west and the Russians in the east. The German guards realised that they themselves would soon be taken prisoner and marched back towards the Allies, not wanting to be taken by the Russians. The tired prisoners heard the rumble of tanks and at first thought they were German, but when they appeared it was realised that they were Allied tanks including those of the 6th Airborne. As one American tank passed, a large black face appeared from the turret and said, "We's comin' for ya boys, we's comin'!"

• • • • • • • • • •

Phil Johnson's glider carried troops of the 2nd Ox & Bucks, a jeep, a trailer with high explosives aboard and a 75mm Howitzer gun.

With an early take-off, they headed north in a loop to allow the rest of the formation to catch up before turning back on a course south. He was due to land in a field north west of Hamminkeln, but they had problems and were dropping back in the stream. It was thought that the Stirling tug had engine trouble, possibly overheating, and they were running to the north of the intended track. On crossing the Rhine, which was wide and muddy-looking, they got a green light, indicating they were in the area of the landing zone and so they cast off the tow-rope, intending to head south east and to the landing zone. Phil could not see the ground for smoke and so had no idea where he was. Suddenly he was forced to turn violently to port as they were on a collision course with a blazing Halifax tug aircraft.

A lot of small arms fire came up, putting holes in the woodwork but without doing any serious damage. A good landing was made in a field.

A damaged Horsa glider on the ground near Hamminkeln.

"There was no one else there except a few German parachute troops," remembers Phil, "who not surprisingly seemed to resent us being there."

Suddenly holes started to appear in the fuselage, and without thinking Phil opened the door and jumped out of the glider. He took hold of the Bren gun and ammunition with the intention of stopping the fire being aimed at them. However, he found it difficult to determine where the fire was coming from, as there were two groups of the enemy, one on line with the starboard wing at the edge of the field and the other in a group of trees behind the tail of the glider.

After a while, Joe, his second pilot, got out with his rifle, followed by a sergeant and one other. The third man stayed on board, removing the shackles from the jeep. Phil had already decided that unloading was not practical. The Horsa Mk 2 unloaded from the front and it would have taken five men standing up to unload the gun. This was not a healthy thing to contemplate under the circumstances. Phil had already been hit three times by the sniping and was more or less out of action, so Joe took over the Bren gun until it jammed on him. Phil thinks he could have fixed it, but he could not move to help. The sergeant decided to make a break for it, but was hit in the chest before he had got 50 yards and the second man was wounded in the hand by shrapnel from a German grenade. Within an hour of getting down, Phil and the others who survived were taken prisoner.

• • • • • • • • • • •

F/O Maurice Laing, serving with F Squadron, was one of six chosen for the 'Coup de Main' No.1, led by Cpt A.M.D Carr. They were the second glider over the Rhine and immediately behind Cpt Carr. As they approached the target area, a considerable amount of anti-aircraft fire was encountered and almost immediately Cpt Carr's glider was hit and exploded. Maurice always thought this was because he was carrying a jeep and trailer full of ammunition. Presumably the jeep's petrol tank was hit by tracer, which Maurice saw coming up. At the time they were about 150 feet above and 100 yards behind Carr's glider. They then became the primary target of the gunners below, so the only thing to do was to get down fast. Having identified the landing zone, they weaved and dived steeply under the heavy flak at what eventually became a very considerable speed – off the clock. At ground level, they were still being shot at, and with a row of very tall poplars ahead Maurice deployed the emergency parachute. He afterwards discovered that the tail had come off. They were fortunate enough to crash land in a shallow ditch in the middle of a small field in the landing zone. The ditch was not deep enough to protect the remains of the glider from coming under fire, so they evacuated the glider quickly.

• • • • • • • • • • •

Cy Henson of 'G' Squadron at Great Dunmow was up at 5.30am on the morning of the 24th, despite having been at a party in the airmen's

Using ramps to remove a jeep from a glider.

mess the night before. The party had got a little out of hand and when "a wingless wonder" (as Cy describes him) attempted to restore some order to the proceedings, somebody "modified his car with a grenade". At 7.30 Cy dressed in the standard Denison smock, which had been introduced for Airborne troops in 1942, with webbing equipment over that plus the glider pilot flying helmet with its incorporated ear phones and mouthpiece, which enabled the glider pilot to talk to the tug aircraft pilot. On the ground they wore an airborne pattern steel helmet designed for fighting as infantry once the glider had been safely landed.

In his Horsa II, Cy had seven men of the 12th Devons, a motorcycle, a jeep and a trailer full of ammunition. His tug pilot was F/Lt Croft. Take-off was smooth and without incident, the Horsa behaved itself and they reached the channel, crossing over Brighton and heading for Brussels. As they reached Waterloo, scene of a famous battle 130 years before, they could see the US aerial armada of tugs and gliders coming to join up with them and head for the Rhine. As they approached the river it at first appeared to be an easy task to locate their landing zone, but the situation soon got out of hand with so many aircraft in such a small area of sky.

Then the anti-aircraft guns started up.

A tug on the left was hit and left its glider on its own. Cy was soon o have his own problems. They were at about the correct height of 3,000 feet, although the briefing said it was to be 2,500 feet and the LZ had been established. The tug aircraft gave them the word that this was time to depart, goodbyes were said and they cast off. In those precious few seconds, everything changed. The flak became so intense that they could not see the ground. Rather than go on flying deeper into Germany, a quick prayer and a 360 degree descending turn seemed the order of the day, until through the haze some sort of position could be established.

Visibility improved and Cy, thinking that they had been hit, decided that the time had come to point the nose down, increase speed, reduce the time exposed to the gunners and get dwn to *terra firma*.

"The first part of the landing was bound to be alright," he recalls, "raise the nose and the speed would reduce, meanwhile a suitable landing site seemed to be available. However, on attempting to lower the flaps I discovered they were inoperable – so we were going to be one of the fastest low-flying Horsa gliders around!"

All they could do was wait for their airspeed to slow before they had any hope of landing.

"Directly above was a line of power cables," Cy continues, "we had two choices, go over or under. I chose to go over and managed it without stalling."

They then saw a large field ahead, with many grounded gliders on it. To the right and in the next field was a large farmhouse with a barn at the back and three or four big trees in the foreground.

"I thought a successful landing could be made here," Cy recalls, "but what about the enemy troops firing from the barn at the gliders as they landed?"

Cy chose to go to the right, clear of the other gliders, who were taking all of the enemy's attention.

"On touching down I braked to keep a distance from the buildings – only to find the brakes were not working [it turned out that the air bottle that controlled the flaps and brakes had been damaged]. We kept on going, getting nearer to the enemy all the time. The only way to stop was to go between the two trees."

The terrain was starting to slow them down and when they got there the glider was only doing about 5mph, but they were left exposed to the enemy buildings, now only 12 to 15 feet away. As Cy dived from the wheelhouse of the glider and into the back, there was a burst of gun fire and then silence, until some wit said, "Hadn't you better look outside, *Sir*."

Cy soon discovered that this was the negative side of being an officer! He opened the cockpit door, armed with a sten gun and saw a double-barrel machine gun facing him, fortunately unmanned. The airborne troops who had been pinned down were now starting to turn up in numbers and the Germans in the barn had surrendered.

"There were about 10 to 15 of them, and not one was under six feet tall," Cy remembers. "It was a great relief because for a while the situation looked grim."

One of the lads in the back of Cy's glider had been killed, but the remainder were unharmed and started to get their equipment out of the glider.

Near the German machine gun was a box of stick grenades.

"If just one had been thrown at us," Cy conjectures, "it would have wiped the lot of us out." Wounded were now being brought to the house, which became a first aid station. Serious medical attention was needed – a bit more than the average first aid that each man had learnt in training. An ambulance was seen coming down the road from Hamminkeln, so one of the soldiers ran down to stop it. Sadly, it was a German ambulance and, without stopping, it knocked the soldier down.

At that moment a message came from the within the house that a wounded lieutenant wanted to talk to the glider pilot who had just landed.

"As I fitted that description, in I went," Cy continues. "The officer was lying on the staircase, having been mortally wounded in the stomach. He desperately wanted me to know that if we had not turned up when we did, they would not have had a chance. Having said that, he died."

Cy was told that the owners of the house were in the cellar, the entrance to which was near the starboard wing of his glider. When he tentatively went down the steps, he found an elderly couple with their son, a wounded German soldier who had been sent home on medical grounds, having been a prisoner in a US prisoner of war camp. He spoke reasonable English but was not prepared to show them on a map where they were, however, having been told about the wounded in the house he did confirm the direction of Hamminkeln.

• • • • • • • • • • •

Sgt Alan Kingston and F/Sgt Jacks of 'A' Squadron left Rivenhall without incident. When they arrived in the area of the landing zone it was covered by smoke and a landing had to be made blind, using the spire of the church at Hamminkeln, which stuck up above the smoke and debris as a marker. Alan jumped out to look around and the glider was soon unloaded by the Royal Ulster Rifles who wanted to get away promptly to stop the Germans blowing up the bridges over the Rhine. Alan and F/Sgt Jacks then set off for their designated assembly point...

• • • • • • • • • • •

On 23rd March, Len Jordan was with 'D' Squadron at Shepherds Grove; his second pilot was to be Sgt Norman Cambridge from Kent. On this day they were allocated their cargo: a jeep and a trailer of ammunition. The weight was calculated, distributed around the glider and then chained in such a way as to ensure a balanced flight.

On the 24th, take-off was at 7am. They now carried an additional four Canadian paratroopers, who would take over the cargo on landing. Len's job was to get them there. They were, as Len describes it, "kitted out like pirates" with dirty faces, each armed with a sten gun, a 9mm pistol, four grenades, a dagger, binoculars and maps.

"It seemed like the whole camp had come out to see us off, wish us luck and hope we enjoyed the ' holiday'," remembers Len.

His take off, however, was a bad one. As they became airborne they came under sever buffeting and Len had great difficulty in controlling the glider. With all the weight on board, he could not seem to get above the Stirling tug's slipstream. At one time it became so bad that he wondered if he was going to have to cast off. But when they were clear of the runway things got better and they began to climb to join the rest of the armada.

"People in the UK later said that it was a magnificent sight," remembers Len, "the sky appeared to be full of aircraft and they wondered

A typical glider payload

what was afoot." Len, in turn, admits that he wished he was down there with them!

His radio link with F/O Thompson, the tug pilot, was soon lost – the cable in the tow-rope must have broken on take off. They settled down in formation at about 4,500 feet. There was no sign of enemy fighters, so they guessed the RAF were keeping them occupied or at bay. The fighter escort was above and below the stream.

When they arrived in the area of the Rhine they were amazed at its size.

"Even from that height it looked big," says Len. He has, since the war, been on the Rhine a number of times – but not in the same circumstances. As they neared the landing zone they found smoke was making identification of the landing area difficult.

As they had lost contact with the tug aircraft and not being sure of their landing zone, Len admits to being guilty of hanging on too long.

"The tail gunner in the Stirling must have been on the verge of a heart attack," he laughs, "as he kept flashing at us with a signal lamp to 'get lost'"

Taking the hint, they cast off, turned to starboard and headed for the open fields ahead of them, where they could already see gliders landing. They soon realised that in spite of lowering full flap they would overshoot, so with what height they had to spare Len made a looping 360 degree turn to admire the scenery, then back onto the original course to line up on the fields and to make what he thought was his best ever flapless landing.

They tore through the wire fencing and, avoiding the shell/bomb holes, came to stop two hundred yards from the woods Len had seen from the air. It could not have been a better spot; the journey had taken about 4 hours.

Now they were at war, but Len felt no sense of panic as there was plenty to do in getting the cargo out. The opening of the nose of the glider and the fitting up of the ramps went well and out rolled the jeep and trailer to set off for an unknown destination. One of the Canadian lads gave Ken his cap badge to show his thanks for a perfect delivery. He did not know how relieved Len felt at that moment. Len and Norman made for the woods as quickly as they could, their planned rendezvous as given out in the briefing.

His 360 degree loop had paid off, as other gliders had crashed into the woods. One of the first they confronted had overshot and smashed into the trees, with the jeep and trailer carrying on forward through the cockpit when the glider came to standstill. The result was devastation. On the side of the glider was chalked 'Hail Calidonian' – its number 416. It was F/O

Andrew McGregor's glider, one of Len's best pals. He and his passengers had suffered terrible injuries and Len identified the bodies with great sadness. The second pilot however, Sgt William McFadyen, although wounded, did survive and got back to the UK. Andrew came from Kirkcaldy in Fife. They spent some time at a temporary first aid post with the wounded then sorted themselves out into a section of a platoon and made their way through the woods towards the Rhine.

● ● ● ● ● ● ● ● ● ● ●

Tony Wadley awoke very early on the 24th, with tea brought to the Nissen hut by members of the WAAF cookhouse staff. Take-off was at 7.30am. His Horsa load consisted of five soldiers and a jeep and trailer loaded with radio equipment. The take-off came to an abrupt halt as the rope broke on glider No.177 and the tug aircraft flew off without them. A tractor was soon brought up and they were towed clear of the runway. There were spare tug aircraft waiting for this eventuality and they were soon attached and took off. The flight took three hours and thirty minutes. They saw one Horsa break away over the North Sea, but it was behind them and was soon lost to sight.

"As we reached the Rhine, smoke could be seen coming from the ruins of Wesel, which looked as if it had been flattened," remembers Tony. "The river passed beneath us and some sort of flak was coming up, but at the time it seemed quite unreal. After parting from the tug aircraft we headed for the landing zone and touched down quite smoothly, although – as it turned out – not quite early enough…"

A road ran across the far end of the field on a low embankment, the top of which was just below the level of the underside of the Horsa fuselage, as they were shortly to discover.

"Even with the Horsa's barn-door flaps down and the wheels locked with the brakes, we were going too fast for comfort and had no chance of stopping in time," Tony recalls. "We reached the embankment and with an almighty crash the glider's undercarriage was swiped off."

The Horsa ended up in a ditch on the other side of the embankment with the fuselage pointing to the sky and behind them at an angle of about twenty degrees to the horizontal.

Tony's immediate concern was how the men and the load behind them had fared, but he was relieved to see them all get out safely. A few yards away they saw a German army medical orderly, who was a prisoner of troops who had landed earlier.

"It still seemed unreal to have had breakfast in the UK and now at just 11 o'clock in the morning there we were on the other side of the Rhine in the middle of a war," Tony says.

"Unloading the glider was normally a simple operation – swing the nose section open, assemble the two ramps that were carried in the glider, and the jeep and trailer could drive out. But here we had a glider with its tail cocked up in the air and its nose buried firmly in a ditch."

The decision was taken to blow the nose off. Sgt Wilson, the first pilot, packed some Nobel 808 plastic explosive around the hinges of the nose section. He then fitted the detonators and retired behind the embankment with the rest of the men.

"After what seemed an age, nothing happened, so with what I thought was immense courage 'Tug' returned to the explosives," remembers Tony.

The second time it worked and the hinges were shattered.

"With some elbow grease we got the nose section clear and put the ramps in across the ditch. Somehow the jeep and trailer were driven out into the field and onto the road. The troops got aboard and headed off east. We never saw them again."

The next problem was to move the crashed glider out of the way, as it was forming an effective road block. The solution came in the form of a Bren gunner carrier that had been transported in Sgt Graham's glider of 'A' Squadron. With a tow-rope it pulled the glider off the road and back into the landing zone.

"In the process the glider came off badly when the whole tail unit came off," Tony recalls, "it ended up looking as if it had exploded."

Having landed, Tony and 'Tug' were among those tasked to defend Divisional HQ. Accordingly, each glider crew dug themselves into a foxhole in a small orchard by a farmhouse.

• • • • • • • • • •

Geoffrey Atkinson was summoned to Earls Colne on the 22nd March, for a briefing with the other intelligence officers on the operation. When he arrived back at his base at Broadwell, he was amazed to find that 'F' Squadron and the two tug squadrons had departed. All that was left was one solitary Dakota, which had stayed behind to convey him and his kit from Broadwell to Gosfield, Essex. When he had left in the morning for the briefing no one had known that the squadron was to be moved back, lock-stock-and-barrel from Oxfordshire to Essex.

Briefings were carried out on the 23rd and the airfield sealed. In the early hours of the 24th he met his 'passengers' – the OC Signal Platoon, seven soldiers of the 2nd Ox & Bucks Light Infantry, plus the inevitable jeep, trailer and three 350cc motorcycles.

Take-off was uneventful, as was the flight, except for a call from the tug pilot to say that his fuel reserves were low. Geoffrey assumed that this might mean they would not reach their objective and he was hit by a feeling of dejection that all that training and effort might be for nothing. He consoled himself with the thought that perhaps they were just afraid that they may not be able to get back to base before their fuel ran out. Like many gliders on the operation, Geoffrey's was loaded to maximum, which meant excessive fuel consumption for the tug.

They were the leading squadron of the 6th Airborne Division and the first 15 aircraft carried the 'coup de main' parties bound for the two river bridges.

"We were flying at 2,500 feet and like others, circled to lose height," he recalls. "This was the most hazardous part of the flight with a great risk of mid-air collision, due entirely to the conditions on the ground which, it seemed, had not been anticipated by anybody.

"The final approach was at high speed, probably about 15 to 20 knots above that recommended for a Horsa. We crashed through several posts and wire fences, with German troops being scattered left and right and came to rest in total silence. More by luck than good judgement we had reached the correct landing zone, near Hamminkeln railway station."

After getting out of the glider, Geoffrey has no memory of what happened next. When he regained consciousness he was on the ground with a soldier slapping a field dressing on his right calf and remarking that the wound was 'a nice clean hole'. In fact the soldier had seen the exit hole, which was much larger than the entry hole and for a few hours Geoffrey was hobbling about in the belief that that his calf muscle was harbouring a large piece of metal. The arm wound he had received turned out to be far more serious – it has severed the ulnar nerve.

• • • • • • • • • •

John Herold was at Tarrant Rushton when on 20th March, 'C' Squadron Hamilcars and Horsas and the two tug squadrons 296 and 644 flew to Woodbridge.

"It was," he remembers, "a fantastic sight to see some 60 tug/glider combinations formed up along the vast runway at Woodbridge."

His passengers were an artillery sergeant and three men, the crew of a 6lb anti-tank gun, a jeep and a motorcycle. One of the men was obviously a despatch rider. This crew had taken part in the Normandy operation, which made John and his second pilot Sgt Jones feel secure that they had men in the back who 'knew what it was all about'.

Shortly after taking off in Glider No.396 and climbing to 2,000 feet a VI flying-bomb came across their bows, slightly below them. After a flight of about 2 hours 50 minutes the Rhine loomed up out of the mist. The tug radioed through the tow-rope cable that the release point was dead ahead. John released and they were on their own.

Sgt Jones had a map and was scanning the area to the right of the glider, hoping to identify the landing field in Landing Zone 'B', but the whole area was covered in battle smoke, added to by the smoke drifting from Wesel from the bombing the night before.

In no time John realised he was flying towards the eastern perimeter of the battle area as he could see the vague outline of the autobahn running north to south. A quick 270 degree turn to port established a southerly heading back into the area in which he had been detailed to land. He applied full flap, reduced speed to just about stall speed and down he went. He could still see nothing ahead, but he estimated they were somewhere near the intended landing area.

"At about 700 feet Sgt Jones informed me that 'the bastards' were firing at us," John remembers. "We could see the slow approach of multiple red tracer coming towards us, getting faster until it zipped past on the starboard wing. Thankfully, they were lousy shots, as nothing hit us, despite us being a sitting duck. Then they seemed to give up, as no further shots were fired, although at the time my whole concentration was on landing the glider in one piece, and not that someone on the ground with a 20 mm anti-aircraft gun was using us for target practice."

John remembers that his second pilot was sitting there beside him "as cool as a cucumber", keeping a sharp look out.

"The map he had was useless but he did not want to distract me by talking to me. He was like a man sitting in the Grand Circle just keeping his mouth shut and watching the show.

"Other gliders were in the same predicament, wondering what the hell was going to happen next, then, at a height of about 500 feet or lower, the ground through the smoke began to take shape. A burning building to the left and under the port wing, a line of very tall trees in front and to the left and dead ahead, two small fields fringed at the far end by a line of very mature trees.

"The landing was slow and soft through a barbed wire fence and then finally coming to a halt. We were down! The unloading drill went like clockwork. John went forward of the glider to position the Bren gun, and as he put it on the ground all hell let loose. We had landed about 100 yards from the very guns who had been firing at us when in the air. They opened up and a short burst went through the middle of the men in the glider. Thankfully, no one was hit.

"Within seconds, the German gunners were coming out of their gun emplacements. Sgt Jones said, 'Look! The bastards are coming out!" It turned out that they had, had enough, and all eight of them came running towards us with their hands up, waving a variety of dirty handkerchiefs.

"They were soon covered and encouraged to run faster. When they arrived they were put in an adjacent ditch, searched and then sat down. They were a motley lot, all youngsters except for a nasty looking NCO whom we segregated and sat down on his own."

They later learned that the youngsters had persuaded the older man to surrender, he then telling them that if they did the English would kill them.

They had landed 100 yards from the Hamminkeln Railway Station and within a half a mile of Area 'B', their intended area of landing. The cargo carried in the glider was unloaded and they were both invited to join the gun crew, as they were two men short. They agreed, and received instructions as to what to do in action. They stayed with the gun team until they were away from the battlefield area but without even having fired a shot.

John had a look around the area of his landing zone and found a crashed Horsa only a few yards from the railway station at Hamminkeln, the aircraft of Sgt Grant, also of 'C' Squadron. John later came to the conclusion that the gun that had fired at them and whose crew they had captured had brought Grant's glider down.

"There was another glider a few yards from where we landed which didn't have a tail unit but seemed to have made a fairly safe landing. It had lost its tail on the adjacent railway line," John recalls.

It was while they were driving the jeep and gun combination that they saw an armada of

USAF Liberators flying in at only about 200 feet to re-supply the troops on the ground.

"They flew right over us and we could clearly see that one had been hit and was on fire. The crew were at the midship exit. Despite being hit, it kept in formation while dropping its containers. We didn't see its demise."

• • • • • • • • • • •

Gordon Procter, with 'A' Squadron, was towed by a Stirling to the Rhine. He remembers there was frustration and impatience in waiting for take-off, which was delayed. In glider No.342 with Sgt Reed as his co-pilot, he carried a jeep and trailer, a Cpt Bailey and eight men, either of the Royal Ulster Rifles or the 12th Devons. He had been told that they were overloaded and to watch his descent. The delay was because of fog, compounded by the smoke screen set up during the night previously.

They took off 40 minutes late and were told to fly at 2,500 feet. Nearing the target area Gordon remembers that the sky seemed to be full of anti-aircraft fire and the air full of cordite. The tension was built as they saw gliders on fire, and going down out of control. The second pilot, Sgt Reed, reminded Gordon that he was up to nearly 4,800 feet. Below them, the LZ was almost totally obliterated by smoke and the ant-aircraft fire intensified.

Gordon decided that as they had so far to come down, he would attempt a landing without flaps until the very last minute. He received the instruction 'matchbox' from the tug – codeword for a glider to pull off. They did, and followed a number of other gliders to the same landing zone.

"Three of the gliders ahead were hit," remembers Gordon, so I adopted the flapless descent. With the heavy overload, our speed built up and I knew we were over the red line as I struggled to pull the Horsa out of its dive. I succeeded, but Cpt Bailey told me later that his men had blacked out. We landed safely despite all the fire around us – one of the few undamaged Horsas on the ground."

A Horsa glider in flight as seen from the tug aircraft. [Cy Henson]

The flight from Rivenhall had taken 2 hours and 45 minutes. They landed close to a farm, a couple of miles from the village which was to become Divisional HQ.

• • • • • • • • • • •

Jim Rudkin was at Great Dunmow and remembers: "It was great living in an operational environment and still being able to go up to London most weeks. It was obvious that a big operation was imminent and everyone assumed that it would be the Rhine crossing or something of that nature."

For three days before the operation, everyone was confined to camp. On the evening of the 23rd, his glider No.396 was loaded with a jeep and trailer – which contained ammunition – two motorcycles and six men of the 53rd Light Regiment, Royal Artillery.

On the morning of the 24th, a beautiful day, nearly all the station came out to line the runway and wave them off. Take off was without incident and Jim could see people in the streets as they passed over, waving to them. Jim and his co-pilot Sgt Smith shared the controls throughout the journey.

"During the journey I asked the troops in the back if they were all right and they said they were, but I was sure that it must have been uncomfortable at times for them," he recalls. "We reached the target and saw the Rhine for the first time … how muddy it looked. Then the flak came up and it was quite heavy.

"I released the rope and followed other Horsas down. Everything was going quite well until we came under heavy fire. This made the glider become uncontrollable to such an extent that, as the ground got nearer I thought we were done for. It was at this time that Sgt Smith must have been hit, because he never said anything to me as we got near the ground. How we actually got on the ground I don't know because I came to lying outside the glider, to see the bones of my right ankle protruding through the skin…"

On hearing a call from amongst the wreckage, he tried to stand on his left leg, thinking that he could hop across and help in some way, but when he stood up, his left ankle would not take his weight (he later learned that this too was broken).

"During the short time I was standing up, I was fired upon, so after collapsing for a second time I lay behind a piece of wreckage, hoping that no one would open fire again. Two German soldiers walked across the field in which I lay, but paid no attention to me at all, they were only intent on surrender."

He was found by an American first aid-team, who patched him up and got him to a field hospital where there were British and American casualties. Jim remembers talking to an airborne padre. "What wonderful special people they were."

As well a two broken legs Jim's face was badly cut after his being thrown through the windscreen of the cockpit.

"Although I was badly hurt, it probably saved my life…" he says, philosophically.

• • • • • • • • • • •

Sgt Hudspith was with 'D' Squadron at Shepherds Grove, his second pilot was F/Sgt Richard Taylor, who not only outranked him but also had more flying hours. His flight commander was an army Cpt, Jock Strathen, who was, sadly, to be killed landing his glider during 'Varsity'.

"Most of the RAF pilots," he remembers, "disliked flying gliders and thought it beneath them, including my second pilot, but I enjoyed it very much."

On operation Varsity he carried a 75mm gun, one of 12 carried by 'D' squadron to the Rhine, plus a jeep, trailer and gun crew. Many of the other gliders carried men of the Ox & Bucks Light Infantry.

"On landing we hit a sawn off telegraph pole, which pushed the glider off course and it ended up with the pilots in one field and the gun crew in another. Wire cutters soon resolved the problem," he recalls.

• • • • • • • • • • •

Ivan Lancaster was with 'B' Squadron at Earls Colne.

"The day came when we were confined to camp. It was obvious to everyone concerned that this was it – we were in business."

Ivan's Horsa was to carry a jeep, trailer, 17-pounder gun and six men. The troops planned to sit at the rear of the glider, a position Ivan objected to, so after a quick recalculation of the loading plan, the load was repositioned so the troops sat as far forward as possible.

After an uneventful take-off they flew north towards the Wash before turning south and en route for the Rhine. Ivan remembers it being a great sight.

"As far as the eye could see there were aircraft towing gliders, whilst overhead fighter escorts were patrolling."

Five minutes before the Rhine came up, F/O Ted Barton, the first pilot (Ivan was co-pilot) called Ivan to look out to the left, where there was a combination of a Halifax towing a Hamilcar glider.

"At that moment I saw the tank on board the Hamilcar break out of the rear of the glider and fall to the ground," Ivan remembers. "It bounced 50 to 100 feet in the air, then I lost sight of it. The Hamilcar was by now causing too much drag on the Halifax for it to continue towing, so the tow-rope was released and the Hamilcar crashed."

The consensus of opinion was that the tank driver must have left his vehicle in gear and when he started the engine in readiness for landing it fired first time with catastrophic results. [It was normal practise for tank drivers to start up the engines five minutes from the landing zone. The idea, in theory, was that the tank could be driven straight through the doors ready for action as soon as they were on the ground.]

"At a height of about 1,500 feet we looked down and saw the whole area was covered by dense smoke through which flashes from anti-aircraft fire could be seen. A call was received from the tug aircraft to say that we were in the right position so we released, turned right, steadied the glider and descended on full flap into the smoke. It was so thick that we could not see any other gliders and only saw the ground when we were 100 feet from it. The landing went well, although we went through two or three wire fences before coming to a halt about 15 feet from a ditch which contained several American paratroopers who were firing at the enemy."

With some difficulty the nose was opened and the troops and their equipment unloaded to head off to their RV point. Ted and Ivan picked up their gear and weapons and set off across a field to their rendezvous area…

● ● ● ● ● ● ● ● ● ● ●

Peter Davies was posted to 'C' Squadron, flying Hamilcars at Tarrant Rushton. In training for Varsity they practised 'circuits and bumps' almost daily carrying heavy concrete ballast weighing approx 9-10 thousand pounds. On 20th March they flew up to Woodbridge where the glider was loaded by civilians. Peter was co-pilot in glider LA 715 to St/Sgt Bert Bowman of the Glider Pilot Regiment, their load was a 17-pound gun, a Dodge towing vehicle and eight Royal Artillery gunners.

The briefing took place on the 23rd during which they were assured the operation would not be another Arnhem and that the flak would be 'dealt with' prior to the operation. They were third in the Hamilcar stream. They were towed by a Halifax at the briefing height of 3,000 feet; the journey time 3 hours and 30 minutes.

As they neared the target area they saw two aircraft hit by anti-aircraft fire. Peter also saw the tank fall out of the Hamilcar.

"As the tank fell out we saw troops sitting on the hull. The tank turned over in the air and they all fell off. Then the front end of the glider disintegrated at the end of the tow-rope…"

"We flew on until we reached our own release point, thanked the tug crew and pulled off. The ground below was obscured by smoke. At 1,000 feet we were hit twice, losing 10 to 12 feet of the port wing half way along and then in the fuselage, which resulted in us losing all flying controls except the tail trimmer. Luckily we were at the optimum gliding speed and altitude, but having no directional control we quietly drifted to port."

Peter's memory of the landing is vague, but he does remember they ended up with the tail at an angle of ninety degrees and that he was flung through the cockpit canopy.

"As it was, none of the troops in the back were hurt and they spent the next half an hour running around getting the load off the glider and away they went…"

The rest of the operation was uneventful for Peter and he arrived back in the UK from Eindhoven on 30th March, just six days later. His first pilot, St/Sgt Bowman, was awarded the DFM. The recommendation mentioned that:

"…while flying a Hamilcar, his elevator controls were shot away by flak, the flaps became unserviceable, and the undercarriage badly damaged. St/Sgt Bowman with great presence of mind decided to land his glider, loaded with a tank, by using the elevator trimming device, and in the circumstances made an exceptionally good landing despite the glider's damage. The load was not damaged and was used with great effect against the enemy."

The recommendation was approved at the highest level – by Field Marshal Bernard Montgomery, C-in-C 21st Army Group, on 18th May 1945.

• • • • • • • • • • •

Alan Head was with 'G' Squadron at Great Dunmow. For Operation Varsity he was co-pilot to St/Sgt P. Young. They made two attempts at getting to the Rhine. On the first occasion the starboard inner engine of the Stirling tug aircraft packed up, take-off was aborted and they returned to base. This was probably the Stirling flown by F/O Connell of 190 Squadron. They were then hooked up to another aircraft, probably belonging to 620 Squadron, and told to catch up with the stream. By this time they were over an hour late and apart from one other combination were on their own in the sky. It was, as Alan remembers, a rough ride.

When they reached Holland the tug captain decided not to go on and they started the long haul back. However, about 20 miles from Calais, at St Omer, the rope broke so they force landed in a ploughed field between two woods. No one was injured in the landing. They spent the night in St Omer and were then ordered to go by road in a jeep to Holland. Also in the jeep were the pilots of another Hamilcar which had come down in the Calais area. They arrived at Eindhoven, soaked to the skin, to find that Varsity had just finished.

• • • • • • • • • • •

Rick Brown flew a Horsa glider from Rivenhall, Essex, carrying a signals unit who were part of the Divisional HQ of the 12th Devons.

He remembers that only minutes from take off a jeep raced around the assembled serials of gliders handing out, as an afterthought, airborne-type helmets to the pilots.

The crewing up of pilots was, in Rick's memory, a chance affair so he had no objection when a fellow officer asked him if he would swap second pilots with him. At the time Rick had no idea that this friendly exchange would prove vital to his chances of survival. Just before Varsity his second pilot fell ill and Rick was posted to another squadron and thus as history tells missed the bloody action in which his previous squadron was involved in.

"As we flew towards the Rhine, instead of the familiar shimmer of propellers we saw the gentle curve of the slim tow-rope to the tug aircraft. My second pilot and I took turns to rest from the constant strain of keeping the glider in position above the tug aircraft. The slipstreams of the aircraft ahead, which included the squadron I would have been with, made the air extremely turbulent and the gliders dipped and tugged on their tow ropes like frisky dogs on a leash."

This problem caused one of the first casualties in the operation when a Hamilcar ahead of them got into difficulties.

"It was swinging from side to side in gigantic sweeps which in itself did not effect the glider too much but endangered others, in as much as it could go out of control or collide with another combination in the stream. It was soon obvious that the glider pilot could not regain control and eventually he dropped the tow-rope and glided away down and out of sight, with much cursing going on in the cockpit. As it dropped from sight I hoped the Air Sea Rescue boys were on the ball, as the weight of the Hamilcar – about 8 tons and a similar cargo – meant it would not float for long, if at all."

During one of his rest period Rick climbed into the back and chatted with the troops who, having seen what happened to the glider in front of them, were understandably shaken.

"I tried to reassure them that all was well with the glider they were flying in. I checked the lashings on the radio jeep and with the 12th Devons officer plotted their rendezvous point on the map, promising him we would land them as near as possible."

He was then recalled to the cockpit by his second pilot. The tug aircraft was calling them to say that they were crossing the Dutch coast.

"I looked down and thought that if we were successful those beaches below could soon be filled with holidaymakers," he remembers.

"We crossed the Rhine and the formations broke up. Stirlings and Dakotas banked away to starboard, now free of their burdens with their towropes streaming behind them. As we flew on, the sky became full of black cloudbursts, proving the Germans were awake and alert. A Dakota lurched away with its port engine ablaze. To the right a Horsa burst into flames and broke up. I took over the controls and waited for the green light. For what seemed a lifetime we waited, then it came – I pulled the lever and we were away – all that training would now come into use.

"The speed decreased and the noise dropped to a whisper as the tug aircraft dropped away with a final flicker of light. I dropped te nose and we soon lost several hundred feet in a steep dive. As we levelled out we could smell the smoke as well as see it. My second pilot was desperately trying to find a landmark, but it was impossible to see anything. Lower and lower we dropped but still nothing.

"Suddenly the second pilot pounded on my shoulder, pointing to starboard. Through the smoke I saw a narrow wood which marked the edge of our landing zone. I quickly checked our direction and found to my horror that we were going the wrong way. As I wrestled the glider over and around, my mind turned to my passengers and the rough ride they were being given. We levelled out through the smoke, hoping to find a landmark that would tell us where we were.

"Suddenly, in front of us we saw trees and banked hard. There was a rendering crash as the port wingtip hit the ground. The control stick went slack in my hands – we were now out of control. The ground came up and we hit it hard and slid to a halt. The cockpit was full of earth but at least we were the right way up. The next thing was to get out fast, off with the harness, pick up our weapons and get out. There was firing in the distance but in the immediate vicinity it was quiet.

"We were down and everyone was in one piece – in fact the troops congratulated me on my landing! The glider was in a bit of a state. The port wing was a just a splintered stump and the undercarriage smashed. The nose was the problem. It was buried in the earth, so how would we get the equipment out? We tried to dig it out with trenching tools without success but finally, by getting the troops to swing on the tailplane, we were able to ease the nose open. Out came the jeep – with much cursing and sweating!

"The signals officer examined his map and then gave me the thumbs up. Somehow, we had landed near their designated area."

Only Rick and his co-pilot knew how lucky they had been.

● ● ● ● ● ● ● ● ● ●

Alan Stredwick teamed up with F/O 'Tiny' Ledbrook as soon he arrived at Great Dunmow.

He remembers that each man was issued with a huge 'Commando' haversack which contained extra rations and clothing plus many other things, and was so heavy they needed assistance to get it on their backs to walk to the glider. Inside the glider, boxes of extra 9mm ammunition and a butted and handled sten gun (an up-market version) were stored by the side of each pilot. Also steel helmets, to be worn once on the ground – in Alan's case the most important part of the equipment…

The flight in a Horsa Mk I – No RN 923 – across the Channel took them over Cap Gris Nez, where they could clearly see the very heavy cratering around the gun emplacements. They were leading the stream and after release from the tug Stirling they came under anti-aircraft fire of all types, even at some distance from the landing zone. The heavy smoke screen was much in evidence but it was not obscuring the area of their own landing zone and Alan was able, with the help of the detailed photographs with which had been provided, to shout directions to 'Tiny' Ledbrook as they descended.

However, as they did so Alan was hit, and by the time they had reached the ground he had passed out.

"I woke up under the wing, where someone had placed me for shelter. When I tried to move, an Airborne medic quickly came over. He cut my clothing away where it was necessary and gave me a shot of morphine. The medics were very caring and had great respect for those taking part in the operation. I was taken across the fields on the bonnet of a jeep and then spent some time in a cowshed, which was being used as an aid station for both German and British wounded.

"By now I was very woozy with the morphine I had been given. I was then taken in a DUKW which made several stops including one for treatment in a tented field hospital and from there flown en route to the UK, but only as far as Brussels because of bad weather. Eventually the weather improved and I was flown to RAF Lyneham and then RAF Wroughton Hospital where I arrived on 29th March 1945, naked apart from the blankets covering me."

In his personal effects bag, which accompanied each stretcher, were odd coins, a pen knife etc and a piece of khaki cloth which someone had cut from his battledress blouse upon which were his RAF pilot's wings. He still has that small but important piece of cloth to this day.

"It was then that I heard the sad news that Tiny Ledbrook had been killed in the landing," he remembers.

•••••••••••

Maurice Thirkettle remembers his take-off for Varsity being "very routine" – but when he joined the main stream and set course across the Channel "the whole affair became very real."

The sky around was a mass of tugs and their gliders and they proceeded towards the Rhine with an air of anticipation and apprehension.

"As we came close to the Rhine we could see the flak coming up and identified our landing zone. After a quick consultation with the tug pilot we released bang on target and were on our way down. The landings were what one would expect in the circumstances, with gliders coming in at all angles.

Maurice's glider suffered a direct hit from a mortar shell, injuring one of the 26 men of the 12th Devonshire Regiment they were carrying.

"As soon as we came to a halt we leapt out and took cover behind the wheels of the glider, with the Devons making a protective circle. All hell let loose, but luckily some of the American paratroopers, who had been forced to jump at 2,500 feet instead of 800 feet, had drifted northwards onto our landing zone. They soon forced the Germans back and formed a wall around the perimeter of the landing zone which enabled an HQ to be set up in a farmhouse.

•••••••••••

Ron Watson flew from Shepherds Grove as second pilot to Pilot Officer Bob Dodsworth. Ron flew the glider as far as Liege, and apart from some severe turbulence over the Channel everything went okay. From there, Bob took over the controls for the final leg.

"A dark moving cloud to the south turned out to be the USAF in their Waco gliders," Ron remembers. "but there was no sign of the escort of Thunderbolts and Mustangs at that stage."

The armada of aircraft and gliders took two and half hours to pass a given point.

"We cast off as soon as the Rhine was visible through the murk. Our landing zone was a group of farm estate buildings near Hamminkeln. A limestone quarry near to the farm was a good navigational pinpoint. With about 2,000 feet to go, I saw the quarry disappearing behind us. I mentioned this to Bob, who made an immediate 180-degree turn and proceeded to make a spot-on landing alongside one of the farm buildings."

They were carrying a jeep and 25 pound gun and 6 men.

"With steel helmets on and carrying sten guns and grenades Bob and I jumped out and lay flat, keeping our heads down as a shell exploded in the next field, all thoughts of being heroic soldiers soon vanishing. Eventually we unloaded the glider and headed for the farm buildings. When we got there we were relieved to find the place deserted.

• • • • • • • • • • •

Eric Wiggan was with 'E' Squadron flying as second pilot to F/O Roger Topp. On 24th March they took off from RAF Birch, carrying three soldiers of the 2nd Ox & Bucks, a jeep and a 6-pound anti-tank gun. Their landing at Hamminkeln was not too successful – they hit a large dyke having had too much speed to miss it and not enough to lift over it. It was assumed that they had been hit and lost the use of the flaps.

• • • • • • • • • • •

Sgt Billingham flew as second pilot to Pilot Officer Trantor.

"It was," he remembers, "a long haul to the Rhine, pulled by a Stirling bomber and landing in smoke and confusion. In the back of the glider we had 20 soldiers from the 12th Devons. One, a medical orderly, was killed on the way down to the landing zone when a bullet entered the Perspex cabin. The landing ended in a confrontation with a hedge…"

• • • • • • • • • • •

Tony Spicer was also with 'E' Squadron at Birch, in Essex. On the 23rd he went to bed early and woke at 3am to a find it was black and cold – but he did have an egg for breakfast…

In his glider, he and his co-pilot carried a sergeant and two gunners, a jeep and a 6-pound anti-tank gun. They were in an early stream and take off was at 5.30am.

"As a consequence had to stooge around for an hour while the rest got off and formed up. As we set off, the sun rose and we flew into its rays for most of the way. Over the Rhine, map-reading proved difficult due to the common enemy of all glider pilots that day – smoke. The orders were not just to get down, but at a precise spot, easier said than done. The tug told us we were at the right spot and we cast off. More by luck than good judgement I saw a familiar landmark and turned towards our objective.

"Things by now were very confusing with the air full of tugs, gliders and tow ropes all milling around. A glider straight in front of us dived into the ground and we saw a Dakota making its way home with both engines on fire."

This could have been F/Lt Vanrenen DFC, from Logan, Australia. He was flying in 196 Squadron. His aircraft was hit over the landing zone and he, his navigator and wireless operator were all wounded. He managed to get the aircraft back to land in friendly territory, made a successful forced landing and refused any medical assistance until the other two members of his crew had been attended to first.

Coming in to land, Tom saw a series of small wire fences some 80 to 100 yards apart that had not shown up on the aerial photographs but these were not a serious problem.

"When we stopped we had several fences wrapped around the undercarriage and the port side had collapsed. We had landed 100 yards from the nearest German weapon pit and unloading was comparatively undisturbed."

The broken undercarriage did however cause problems with unloading.

"The front exit was open and the ramps in place, but when the gun was released from its lashings it slid sideways and caught against the inside bulkheads of the glider. It became impossible to drive it out so eventually they had to remove the tail and lever it out of the way."

With the load removed they examined the possibilities of reaching the GP rendezvous which was a farmhouse some 1-2 miles north of Hamminkeln.

"We were not sure if it had been cleared, but as we approached we saw a number of Red Berets, so all seemed well. On arrival we found the Flight Commander, Cpt Graham, whose controls had been shot away. The platoon he was carrying had suffered greatly. He was looking after the wounded in the farmhouse.

• • • • • • • • • • •

F/Lt Ken Scolding was a member of 2 Flight of 'A' Squadron at Rivenhall under the command of Cpt Tony Turner, who had the reputation of being 'fireproof'.

The time for Varsity came. Ken was allocated chalk mark No.140 on his glider. They met for the first and last time their Stirling tug crew. His orders were to land his glider virtually in the village of Hamminkeln. He was to carry three men of the 12th Devons, a 6-pound anti-tank gun, a jeep and ammunition.

"To me, the whole set up seemed fraught with danger and on the night of the 23rd I didn't sleep very well. We were told to pack all our kit as we would not be returning to Rivenhall, which made us feel even more depressed and did not help in anyway to raise our spirits.

Ken describes the organisation and effort of the ground crews to get the armada off the ground as "truly amazing".

"With our full load we had a total all-up weight of 6,000lbs whereas in training the heaviest we had carried was 3,000lbs. We had only the length of the runway to decide if the glider would get off or not. Would it need correction? When would it start to fly? If I were to overcorrect and pull the tugs tail up, he would be prevented from getting off the ground. The take off was in the lap of the Gods…

"My mind went back to the amount of time I had spent studying the combustion engine and here I was flying an amalgam of glue and plywood with not one engine between 1300 gliders. Neither did I have a parachute to sit on. It had been decided that glider-borne troops could not be restricted by a parachute and the pilot could not jump out and leave them so he shouldn't have one either. It was a case of 'stick to the job' – even if the aircraft was breaking up around you."

His second pilot was an RAF sergeant from Lancashire, Nick Nicholson, who Ken remembers as being "of infinite humour". He and Ken took it in turns of about 15 minutes to fly the glider.

"All you could see," Ken remembers, "was a stream of aircraft that never seem to end. The pull and swing of the glider was as if the tow-rope was made of elastic. The sten gun magazines I had stowed in improvised pockets in my Dennison jacket were digging into my back making it impossible to relax. I felt I must look like a badly wrapped parcel – that's how I felt.

"The coast of France came and went, so at least if we came down now we would not get wet. I turned to look at my three passengers – one was sleeping peacefully, another grinned at me and the third gave the thumbs up. 'My God!' I thought, 'if only you knew…' How I envied the man sleeping, he either had nerves like steel or felt his faith in the Almighty would carry him through.

"We had fighter cover on the flanks, which was reassuring but I was thinking about the German Panzer Division known to be in the area of the landing zone. It was 9am and the Americans should have joined them by now in their notorious Waco gliders. They were notorious because of their reluctance to land. The Horsa was ugly but it had an ability to get down quickly. A voice came over the intercom 'Ack Ack activity ahead.'

"The horizon up ahead seemed as if it had an industrial haze over it with shell bursts among the gliders and tugs. There was no question of evasive action – only Lady Luck could help now. I was looking for a tall-spired Protestant church in the middle of the village of Hamminkeln… There was the church – but where had all that smoke come from? There had been no smoke in the aerial photographs were shown…

"A voice came over the intercom again, 'Ten seconds to release Matchbox'. So this was it … I pulled the release lever we were now free of the tug but too high, so down we went. Being too high was a problem, we could maybe go around again to lose height but that would risk a collision with another glider... A bullet came up through the floor, puncturing the front nearside tyre of the jeep and an other hit the air cylinder and ricocheted around the adjacent ironmongery like an angry bee looking for a target.

"Then suddenly we were nearly down, and ahead a trench full of German soldiers. Then we came to a halt. One wheel had been torn off when we went into a trench, the glider was at an astonishing angle, on one wing tip. The next thing bullets were coming through the windscreen, the Germans had recovered and were firing. The Devon Regiment sergeant was hacking away at the fuselage from the outside with an axe. The gunner had dug himself a hole.

"I started to rip panels off the glider with the idea that once inside we could release the lashings around the jeep and gun, shielded from the enemy fire. This we did, all it needed now was to get the front of the glider open, but with the glider at such an angle it was not going to be easy. I snapped a magazine in my Sten gun and attempted to give covering fire, but when I pulled the trigger nothing happened, the gun remained cocked. On examination I found the firing pin block and recall spring to be full of sand, as was the magazine. Oh now how I wished he had a .303 rifle!

"At this moment a jeep crossed the field of fire, but without realising the danger he was in, and despite our shouts he carried on. One man on the jeep was hit and fell off but it kept going. Back inside the glider we managed to get the front open and push the jeep through the opening and it tumbled to the ground. Now for the 6-pounder gun, but that was not as easy. As we attempted this, a jeep turned up driven by a Major who cursed at us for not getting the gun into position. Urged on by his ranting we coupled the gun up to the jeep with a tow-rope and pulled it out without too much effort.

"As the Major drove off I was thinking 'I bet he thinks RAF pilots are a right shower'. The three army men climbed in the jeep and set off in the same direction as the Major. We decided to make for the trench recently vacated by the Germans. As we crossed the open ground where the jeep had come under fire we found the soldier who had been hit. He had died instantly, never knowing what had hit him. I was still carrying the now-useless Sten gun, mistakenly chosen by me as the best weapon to have. We jumped into the now vacant trench – there was nobody about, the enemy had fled.

We had been told that the smoke was from the bombing of Wesel by Bomber Command, but we later found out that it in fact came from smoke canisters that were used to provide cover for the river crossing by No.6 Commando and No.46 Royal Marine Commando. For them it must have been a useful element to cover their hazardous river crossing, but for those arriving by air it was a different story.

• • • • • • • • • • •

BBC Radio correspondent Richard Dimbleby was heard speaking from one of the tug aircraft:

"Down there is the smoke of battle. There is the smoke screen laid by the army lying across the far bank of the river. Dense clouds of brown and grey coming up."

Dimbleby flew in one of the tug aircraft and Stanley Maxted, another well-known war correspondent, flew in one of the gliders. As they roared down the runway Dimbleby was heard on his microphone:

"We are off, full boost now, flat out, as fast as we can go, we are climbing gently into the air and on our way."

As they got near the Rhine, Maxted took up the microphone:

"It must soon be time to cast off, so Richard Dimbleby, tell them when you get back about these guys and how they went into battle. Tell Britain, Richard. Tell the world. There is not much time now..."

As he cast off, Dimbleby reported seeing a glider going down, hit by German flak, then paused and said:

"There are no parachutes in gliders... A British Stirling is going down with flames coming out from under its belly –parachutes are coming

BBC correspondent Richard Dimbleby in flight during Operation Varsity.

out – one – two – three – four have come out. Now the glider has gone – we've cast off our glider – we've let her go – there shegoes down behind us. We've turned hard away, hard away in a tight circle to port to get out of this area. I'm sorry if I'm shouting – it is a very tremendous sight."

This was Richard Dimbleby's last operational flight.

• • • • • • • • • • •

L. Marsland Gander, *Daily Telegraph* Special Correspondent, travelled in glider No.277, towed by S/Ldr Scott of 644 Squadron in a Stirling. With him was a lieutenant colonel of the Royal Artillery and opposite him was the senior chaplain to the Division, Rev A.P. Cameron. Over the landing zone the pilot said, " Strap in, we've cast off and are going down."

Gander saw another glider hit squarely and go down in flames and then a Halifax bomber plunged down on fire.

The landing broke the gliders back. Two or three of the men had broken bones but most were unhurt. Marsland was hurt in the landing but carried on.

• • • • • • • • • • •

The day before Operation Varsity, Flt/Sgt John Crane remembers that he and others were advised to load their rifles and 'put a round up the spout'.

"The chap who was in the bottom half of his bunk forgot he had done so and pulled the trigger of his rifle. The bullet he had up the spout passed through the Nissen huts and lodged in the fourth bed along, fortunately missing everyone on route."

They were bussed from Gosfield to Earls Colne, arriving at about 5am. The tug and glider got off at 6am, flew up beyond Cambridge then turned to take their place in the air armada. As they crossed the Channel, they saw a few gliders ditching into the water. They crossed the Rhine at about 10am. The landing area was covered in smoke and fog and they did not have any communication with the tug, having lost the link that came down the tow-rope just after take-off.

"We just pulled the lever and cast off – much, one would imagine – to the surprise of the tug crew," John remembers.

They came down without much trouble and landed with the nose of the glider in a small wood. The soldiers of the 1st Royal Ulster Rifles soon got their jeep and trailer out and were away.

• • • • • • • • • •

For Ken Ross, reveille was 2.45am, and two hours later he was aboard a lorry bound for Earls Colne. At the briefing he was designated to land on LZ 'A'. When the briefing was over he hung back and removed the low-level aerial photographs showing LZ 'A'.

In the glider, Ken and F/Lt Halley, the first pilot, carried an HQ Signals vehicle and specialist staff. As they approached the landing area, the clarity of the photograph was not in evidence. Despite the clear sky, a pall of smoke hung over the West bank of the Rhine. They cast off around 3,000 feet and started to descend. The next few minutes, he remembers, were the most hair-raising of his life. To their right, a tug aircraft with smoke pouring from it rolled over slowly as it arced earthwards. This was probably one of two Halifax's shot down over the landing zone. All around, gliders were going down, but because of the difficulty of trying to find their own landing zone Ken remembers no sense of fear.

"Suddenly there it was, directly ahead," Ken remembers, "a corner of a field with a forest on two sides."

They were, however, far to high to land and the airspeed indicator showed them to be flying far to fast for landing. Then Halley said, "I'll land on top of the trees…"

Ken could not believe what he had said.

" No!" Ken shouted, "We'll all be killed," at the same time grabbing the stick as he strove to put the glider into a steep bank.

"What the soldiers behind must have though as they saw a F/Sgt and flight lieutenant arguing and appearing to struggle with the controls is beyond me," says Ken.

Halley then let go and Ken was able to bank steeply and make a 360-degree turn so they could approach the forest again but at a much lower altitude.

The touchdown was still too fast, but if he had held off a second longer they would have gone into the forest, as the glider before them had done, killing everyone aboard.

"As we went across the field the cabin disintegrated and Halley screamed as his feet were torn backwards. We came to halt a few metres from the trees of the forest. This was ideal for the men in the back, as further back in the field gliders were under fire from snipers. Within minutes the jeep was out and away taking the injured Halley with them.

• • • • • • • • • •

Sydney Grieve remembers crossing France in bright sunshine.

"Sitting in our Perspex canopy, much like a greenhouse, it was remarkably hot and becoming even hotter when an army sergeant came from the back and gave us a swig from his bottle of scotch. Very acceptable in the circumstances."

They flew south of Paris and NNW to Wesel on the Rhine. The landing area, as everybody else had found, was covered in smoke. The tug aircraft, a Stirling waggled its wings and they knew they had arrived. Sydney pulled the lever and down they went.

"As we came out of the smoke we found ourselves only a few hundred feet off the ground. Gliders were milling about all over the place, some on fire. As we approached some farm buildings, bullets began to come up, passing through the Perspex between me and Sgt Harrop, the second pilot."

Sydney made a 270-degree turn and put full flaps down, which brought them down quite quickly to land in a ploughed field.

"As we landed, ahead of us was a small terrier dog going like the clappers across the field to get away from the giant glider. We got down with bullet holes in the fuselage, but no one was injured. Having landed we swung open the nose of the glider, the ramp was put in place, the jeep started and out it came. The anti-tank gun was then pulled out and all the bits to go with it and everyone, including me and Sgt Harrop jumped aboard and sped off towards some trees for cover," remembers Sydney. "We were met by the sad sight of parachutists hanging dead in their harnesses, turning slowly in the breeze."

● ● ● ● ● ● ● ● ● ●

On 24th March 1945, John Perry entered the briefing room at Earls Colne, where he found the walls were covered in photographs depicting roads, bridges and farm buildings. They had been taken a few days prior by a Mosquito reconnaissance aircraft.

"Brigadier George Chatterton opened the proceedings with 'now this operation etc…' This was the first indication that something was on. Each glider had been designated its own particular target for landing and the location had to be memorised, although, in hindsight, this was a total waste of time."

Two days prior to this John had loaded up his Horsa II glider with a jeep and trailer loaded with medical supplies, along with a small field hospital unit commanded by a young army captain. After he had checked the even distribution of the load in the glider he was offered a spare set of chains for securing the jeep, which he gladly accepted and which proved to be most fortunate.

On the 22nd the weather forecast came in for the 24th. It was good, and as they all sat around in the late March sunshine discussing things, Cpt Harold Norton – who was sadly to be killed on Operation Varsity and is now buried in the Reichswald War Cemetery – quietly suggested that they all shook hands, as some of them might not be around the next day.

"He was one of the first killed by enemy action after the Rhine Crossing," John remembers sadly. "In my opinion he was a fine example of what a good leader should be."

At 4am on the 24th came a loud 'Wakey Wakey' call, then a breakfast of bacon and egg. He also remembered Lord Tedder attending and speaking at the Earls Colne briefing.

It was a quick drive to the runway where an impressive sight met them.

"The Halifaxes and gliders were lined up ready for take off, spaced with pin-point accuracy and a credit to the ground crews who had been working all night for this moment. Take off was at 6am as the dawn was breaking on a fine day and we set a course north to assemble with the other glider squadrons over Earls Colne into one Armada with fighter escorts and then head off on course for the Rhine. As I looked down I imagined all my friends and the people in the little village of Coggeshall looking up and wishing us well."

The three and half hour trip was so uneventful that Peter Read, John's co-pilot, dropped off to sleep and John had to give him a nudge as the tug pilot advised them they were approaching the Rhine. Here they saw the thick haze covering the landing zones.

The tug pilot said on the intercom: "Hello Matchbox – can't see the ground. Pull off when I give you the shout – the navigator will give you a plot location. Good Luck!"

John pulled away just as the flak started.

He was now dodging other gliders coming through the smoke until he was about 600 feet off the ground when he was able to make out fields and wooded areas.

"As we set course for a decent landing area we felt the 'crump, crump' of flak under the fuselage and flew through a fair bit of tracer, so I guessed something was up. Then suddenly we saw something that had not shown up on the recce photographs – high-tension wires. I tried to lift the nose but discovered that my elevators and ailerons were not working. We he hit the high-tension power cables, but only with the wheels of the glider. The wires broke at the supporting pylon to the left of us and set off a firework display. I called Peter for flaps, we were going into a shallow dive at the time, but to no avail. At least the rudder was working, so I kicked hard to avoid some buildings ahead. Just before we hit the ground we passed over a blazing Hamilcar, but with no sign of the occupants."

In the crash that followed, John remembers vividly his good fortune.

"The landing gear came up through the floor to meet us and Peter and I parted company with the rest of the glider. Our crash helmets saved our heads, which were thrust partly through the nose of the glider. Thankfully, the jeep stowed in the glider just behind us, remained in position throughout the crash, due, I am sure, to the extra chains that I had been offered, accepted and put to good use."

They both crawled back to the main fuselage, which had broken its back. As they did, they came under fire from mortar and Spandau machine gun fire.

"One chap they called 'Taffy' had been hit by bullets on the way down and was dead and another chap was wounded. In the landing no one was hurt. I tried to explain to my 'passengers' that I didn't normally land that way.

"We were pinned down in a ploughed field to which we had added our own furrow. We had an unarmed unit aboard and my .303 rifle, along with Peter's, was somewhere under the wreckage. I remember Peter muttering that we looked like missing the christening [John was to become godfather to Peter's son during their next spot of leave].

"The medical captain of the unit retrieved a flag from the jeep that showed a red cross on a white background. He stuck it in the ground and after a short period of covering fire two groups of Germans approached each side of us along the edges of the field. The firing stopped and we were all taken prisoner."

• • • • • • • • • • •

At RAF Birch, William Davies remembers that in the run-up to Varsity the camp was sealed off from the outside world – no mail could leave the camp at that time.

"We were given photographs of the area that we had to land on, rather like parking cars in a car park," Bill describes it. "Upon landing we were to report to a farmhouse which was the assembly point for 'E' Squadron GPR. My co-pilot Wally and I were each armed with a rifle, hand grenades and something I had not had before – an entrenching tool. It had a small square blade which fitted into a short handle and looked like a pick axe.

"At about 3am on the 24th, after an egg and bacon breakfast, we were taken down to the runways in trucks. Here we saw a line of Dakotas down one side and on the other the Horsa gliders. The tug aircraft would pull out onto the runway and a small tractor would pull out the glider behind it, then the tow-rope was fixed on. If they had a rope break or the tug had engine failure they were then taken to the end of the line for another try.

"This was the first time we were to fly a loaded glider, on board we had a jeep, a six-pounder anti-tank gun and six men of the Royal Ulster Rifles. The crew of the Dakota were Canadians. They gave each of the glider crew and passengers a packet of Sweet Caporal cigarettes.

"The take off went without a hitch. The first glider off went North for a given time, and one after another the rest followed, circling round in such a way that when the first combination reached the airfield again the last was just airborne and tagged onto the end of the line."

A journey of three hours and 45 minutes followed.

"On reaching the Rhine, the air ahead was black, just as if a storm had broken out. When near, the flashes of the German flak came up. Some of the tug aircraft were trailing smoke and one exploded in a cloud of smoke and fire. As soon as the rope was cast off we headed down. When we came out of the murk we saw the town of Hamminkeln, turned right and flew over the roofs of the houses. We were now flying down a narrow lane, desperately looking for a place to land, but we were still going too fast – something like 100mph. On the left we saw a good fied and turned and landed.

"After we had landed I noticed a small hole appear in the cabin just in front of me. 'There is only one life Taffy,' said Wally. Someone was certainly shooting at us, so we got back into the glider and lay on the floor as the glider was peppered with bullets. The sergeant in charge of the troops soon realised the need to get out of the glider. If the petrol tank of the jeep was hit by one of the shells we would all go up in smoke. We all got out and made for a hole in which the sergeant and one of his men had already arrived. Some 200 yards away we saw a farmhouse from which the Germans were firing and to which we returned fire.

"When the firing stopped we went back to the glider and unloaded the jeep and gun. It was time for the troops to depart, but before they made their departure, a small German came to them with his hands held up high. He looked frightened to death. He showed them a photograph of his family and to quieten him down Bill gave him a cigarette. We could see airborne troops at the farm. It had obviously been captured. By now the field was filling up with gliders and the farmhouse turned out to be exactly the spot we had been looking for, as our CO, Major Jackson and other pilots from 'E' Squadron were already there."

A decision was made by Major Jackson to make for the areas they were allotted to defend until the 2nd Army arrived.

"As we moved off, Liberators of the US Army Air Force flew overhead. We were told later that they were dropping supplies, but they must have thought they were well past the allied lines as they opened fire on us with .5 Browning machine guns. We took cover behind trees, but as each wave came over the gunners opened fire so we had to move around to the other side of the tree."

• • • • • • • • • • •

Frank Hendry also took members of the Royal Ulster Rifles, including the headquarters platoon, the Adjutant, RSM and 8 other ranks. It was thought at one point that the commanding officer of the 1st Royal Ulster Rifles had been killed and the Adjutant had taken over command. The Commanding Officer, Lt-Col Carson, had in fact survived, but one of the senior officers in the 1st Royal Ulster Rifles, Major Charles Vicary, was killed in landing.

In order to give the troops at the back of the glider a break from being cooped up, Frank and the first pilot Mike Odlum took turns to fly the glider and let each of the troops sit in the vacant pilot's seat while each of the two pilots sat in the back with the troops. A little rum was shared around with great relish.

Over the Rhine, Mike pulled the lever and they cast off. Suddenly the flak came up and shells were bursting below them.

"As we came in to land, we both gripped the controls, but the brakes did not respond. We were going too fast and dead ahead on Frank's side was the wide trunk of a tree. I forced my left foot hard on the rudder but nothing happened. We were only 60 to 70 yards from an impact, when suddenly the glider's direction changed slightly to port. We struck the tree, which began to scythe into us, only feet from Frank's shoulder and deep on to the starboard wing. We crashed into the foliage and then partly rolled over, with the wings taking most of the damage and the cabin staying in one piece. Some bullet holes appeared in the wood just in front of my head. For a moment we seemed trapped until the RSM from the Ulsters took hold of the escape axe and hacked a hole in the lower side of the glider and we all got out safely and below the line of the enemy's fire.

"While the Ulsters got away they asked me to cover them with a Bren gun, but because of the smoke this was not possible in case I hit them instead. While we were in the air I had felt a sting in my bum and asked Frank to take a look. He found a large fragment of ack-ack shell embedded in the middle of my right buttock. Frank put a shell dressing on it. The Ulsters returned, having silenced the enemy fire, but said that a German armoured car was in the area."

It was then that Mike got up and ran 100 yards to the glider to see if it was possible to get the jeep and trailer out of it.

Frank also ran over to find the back of the glider intact and Mike trying to get the safety chains off, but it was impossible, both jeep and trailer were jammed in the chains. There was nothing left to do but to make for the rendezvous area.

• • • • • • • • • •

John Barnsley, along with other aircrew, was called by the Tannoy to the briefing room at 2pm on the 22nd. The briefing took about three quarters of an hour. The following day was busy and yet frustrating.

John's squadron was designated to carry the Royal Artillery units, who duly turned up with their equipment throughout the day. John's glider was to carry three men, a 75 mm Howitzer gun, a jeep and a trailer loaded with ammunition.

Loading itself was supervised by representatives of the glider manufacturers. The loading of the Mk II Horsa was much easier that the Mk I. The nose of the Mk II, including the cockpit, was hinged and opened to the right, allowing easy access.

"The Howitzer and trailer went in quite smoothly," recalls John, "but the jeep would not go in without the steering wheel being removed. Another crew had to carry a 25 pounder, but to get it into the glider, the tyres had to be let down. The tail of the glider was painted yellow, as was that of another glider that carried a jeep that was to pull the gun. In theory they were supposed to meet on the landing ground."

At 4am on the 24th, after the final briefing, the weather was clear and the wind from the south was light.

"As we approached the landing zone there were three checkpoints – the first at 15 miles, the second at ten miles and the third 'cast off and descend in a right hand turn'. Any changes of wind speed or direction would be given to us on the radio. We set off towards Ipswich, back over Earls Colne and then on a course for Hawkinge, Kent. After crossing the Channel we went east of Dunkirk and then on with a minor change of course to avoid going over Brussels.

"The orders for landing were to fly on course for 2 minutes after release, then turn right and land. We were hit by flak on release, according to the Tug crew, and were hit again on the way down. The total weight of the loaded glider was 8 tons and we were coming down at about 120 knots. We came out of the cloud at about 200 feet and made immediate plans to land straight ahead, crossing a road lined with trees with a ditch on our side. We crashed through the trees and in crossing the ditch lost the nose-wheel, which tended to slow us down… As we came to a bumpy halt we came under fire from about 2 or 3 rifles. The gun crew evacuated first and made for the ditch. Danny Bruce [the other glider pilot] and I followed. The Battery sergeant-major was hit and fell, the Bombardier was wounded in the arm but the third man made it without being wounded."

The sergeant-major did not get up so John and Danny went out and got him back to safety. He was injected with morphine and made as comfortable as possible.

"A Hamilcar glider crashed landed near us. It was on fire, but the men were able to get the Bren Gun carrier out before it blew up. They offered to take us with them but we declined, not wanting to leave the wounded. Just after they left we heard an explosion and it would appear they suffered a direct hit."

• • • • • • • • • •

Johnny (Titch) Rayson and his co-pilot Sgt Priddin were briefed that they had to land their glider by a certain farmhouse shown on a sand table model which they had been studying for three or four days. They would carry six troops and a jeep and a trailer loaded with radio equipment to be used as a forward observation unit for the artillery. During the briefing they were told that the codename for the gliders was "Matchbox". Apart from the standard .303 rifle and ammunition and hand grenades they were given a 2-inch mortar and bombs.

The take off on the 24th was 6am. John clearly remembers knocking the cork out of his water bottle when he arrived at his glider and losing all his water over his trousers.

"This worried me," he says, "being without water and not knowing if the water in Germany had been poisoned or contaminated."

The take off and journey went without a hitch, although they did notice a glider that had cast off over the Channel and was circling down and about to ditch in the sea. They met up with the Americans en route, who were scheduled to land about a mile south of the British and towards Wesel.

After release over the target area, John followed the glider ahead of him.

"He did a turn to port of 360 degrees and while he did, a certain amount of flak came up. I started to follow him in the turn but he appeared to be flying straight into a stream of tracer bullets, so I declined to follow him. I got down to 250 feet and then saw the ground and recognised on the port side the village of Hamminkeln so we continued south, looking for a field in which to land. The captain in charge of the troops in the glider was standing between me and Sgt Priddin, holding a Bren gun. We crossed the road leading to Hamminkeln, upon which was a convoy of lorries carrying German troops. As we dived down, they put their hands in the air in surrender, not that we could do anything about taking them prisoner, but the captain said he was tempted to give them a burst with his Bren gun.

"A field was spotted which we hoped was near our target farmhouse, but as I pushed the nose down, to my horror the speed of the glider went up to 120mph. It was obvious the flaps had not gone down. It would appear that a bullet had pierced the compressed air bottle which powered the flaps. It was going to be impossible to land without crashing so I decided to do a shallow dive into the field and aim between two trees at the far end, hoping the wings would be broken off by the trees and bring the glider to a halt.

"But this did not happen. We hit the ground and broke the nose wheel, so the cockpit started digging into the ground. At this time a mortar bomb exploded under the starboard wing, which turned the glider upside down. The nose broke away from the glider and rolled over and over like a ball until it eventually came to a halt. I pulled the release of my safety harness but did not realise I was upside down until I fell on my head, Sgt Priddin and I were both unhurt and crawled out and ran towards what was left of the glider.

We came under fire from two Spandau machine guns situated near the trees, the very trees we had been aiming for. We kept very near the wreckage of the glider and the firing stopped, it would appear the Germans thought we were all dead. The captain then took charge and asked 'Where is the farmhouse?'

"I thought I had spotted it two fields away in a westerly direction and he agreed that this was the farmhouse we were meant to land near. The captain said, 'Let's get the jeep and trailer out and drive there.' Normally one had to get ramps down to unload a glider, but as the fuselage was lying on the ground it was easy to drive the jeep and trailer out and we all jumped aboard. The Germans opened fire again, but were not very good shots, and missed."

● ● ● ● ● ● ● ● ● ●

The 24th March 1945 is a day Bleddwyn Williams will never forget. His task was to deliver a signals unit to service the Airborne Division.

"The take-off and the trip across the Channel were uneventful, except for the extreme turbulence caused by the vast numbers of aircraft in such close proximity," he remembers. "Controlling the glider taxed the pilot's muscles to the full. Our designated landing zone was between the towns of Reca and Wesel, but it was covered in a smoke haze much like fog-bound Essex back in the UK. My co-pilot Graham Richmond was second to none – he was as cool as a cucumber – and it was as a result of his meticulous instructions in the most difficult conditions that we arrived at our specified destination with the nose of the glider protruding through a farm orchard fence. This came about because of brake failure on landing. The only reason we came to a halt was because the nose wheel snapped off as we ploughed through a deep ditch. In the event, this saved the signals unit having to set up the ramps to offload the vehicles and equipment. All that was required was that Graham Richmond and I unlatch the swivelled nose section of the Horsa II, upon which the army signallers drove out and only a hundred yards to their designated HQ!"

• • • • • • • • •

Eric Ayliffe was co-pilot to F/Lt Peter Ince. On the 24th he took off from RAF Gosfield for a 4½ hour trip to Germany. Sixteen 'coup de main' gliders from 'F' Squadron led the armada. The first eight were led by Cpn Carr, second-in-command of the squadron. The second eight were led by F/Lt Ince and Sgt Ayliffe. The first eight made for the Northern Bridge over the Issel and the second the Southern Bridge.

"Because of the glare of the sun, we flew ten minute stints," remembers Eric. "It was so hot that I undid my safety strap and forgot to do it up again. We carried a jeep and a trailer full of ammunition and explosives. The men in the back were from the Royal Ulster Rifles. We saw the leading glider in front, flown by Cpn Carr, break up in the air and the occupants fall out. Other gliders in the Northern Bridge party were also hit. A shell exploded under our glider as we saw the field we were to land in, and when I pulled the flap lever nothing happened – the air supply had been cut. As we gained speed the airspeed indicator went off the clock. We hit the ground hard and sped along at zero feet. The German gunners had to duck to avoid being decapitated. The excess speed caused us to climb away, but as we tried to turn back we hit the tops of some trees, which helped to save us. As the port wing touched the ground we came to an abrupt halt."

Those who had survived were pinned down by machine gun fire and soon the glider was ablaze and the flames getting ever nearer their cargo of explosives. They had little option but to make for a ditch in the distance.

"It was then and only then that I realised the two soldiers lying next to us had been killed by the machine gun fire," recalls Eric. "The so-called ditch was in fact a sewer, into which we sank up to our waists. But for once in our lives we were glad to have landed in the shit," he laughs.

• • • • • • • • •

Ken Ashurst served as a flight commander and later second in command to Major Toler with 'B' Squadron.

"When we arrived over the Rhine we found smoke from the bombing in Wesel and from what we understood to be German Army smoke canisters making visibility impossible until we got down to 800 feet."

His glider landed in a ploughed field with part of its starboard wing shot off and they were unable to off load their cargo because the glider nose was half buried in the soil.

"The problem was solved by blowing off the tail and then extracting the jeep, trailer and motorbike," he remembers.

• • • • • • • • •

John Codd, also with 'B' Squadron, crash landed on the roof of a farmhouse at the edge of a wood.

"Both the farmhouse and the wood were still heavily occupied by the Germans," he recalls. "One of the troops I was carrying had been critically wounded in the air by a German bullet and died shortly after we crash landed. I had got him out of the glider and dressed his wound, but to no avail. After we shot dead a German officer who tried to lead an attack on us there came a short respite and we tried to gain cover across the field, but the Germans opened up again with a machine gun, killing three of the troops and one officer.

"I had a bullet through my trouser leg, behind the knee, and another knocked my steel helmet off. After more close shaves we attempted to return to the glider to rescue the wounded men and to salvage anything that was available and useable. The glider still had a jeep and a trailer full of demolition charges. The Germans still occupied the wood but they had made no attempt to attack the glider.

"This soon changed, however, when they brought a mortar up and started to shell it. They quickly hit the glider and the demolition charges and everything else went up with a bang."

During the run-up to Operation Varsity, Frank Haddock had heard a rumour that they would be landing 'in the Arnhem area' and was relieved to learn that they were going straight into Germany, "although the mention of towns like Wesel and Hamminkeln did not mean much at the time."

The briefing had stated that any anti-aircraft guns in the area would be dealt with by the planes of the 9th US Air Force and 2nd TAF. However, post-war records show that there were 712 light guns and 103 heavy guns located in the landing areas. In addition to this, the German 6th, 7th and 8th Parachute Divisions, and the 47th Panzer division were there to defend the area.

"One of the Hamilcar pilots enquired about parachutes, but his request was soon turned down on the basis that they were carrying passengers. The enquirer added to the embarrassment by pointing out that he would not be carrying passengers but 10 tons of petrol and ammunition. Furthermore, the tailplanes of gliders carrying such loads were to be painted bright yellow for identification purposes. This caused a bit of a flap and the Commanding Officer Major Alec 'Dicky' Dale DFC sent someone out to make further enquiries. Back came the answer that parachutes *would* be available providing a deposit of £30 was paid to ensure that they were returned undamaged. As this was equal to 5 weeks pay at that time, it was obvious no one was going to take up the offer! There was a strict security clamp-down, no telephone calls were allowed, so after a few drinks in the mess we retired early, as reveille was at 4.30am. After a hearty breakfast we collected our rucksacks, weapons and pouches containing two No.36 hand grenades and ammunition before being taken out to the runway, where the tugs and gliders were ready for take off."

The Horsa glider had been loaded on the 23rd with a jeep loaded with ammunition, a 6-pounder anti-tank gun and a motorcycle. The five men in the back were from the Air Landing Brigades, Anti-Tank Battery Royal Artillery. They, under a staff sergeant, were already at the glider when the two pilots arrived.

"As we stood chatting there came the sound of a two-stroke motor cycle from the east. It turned out not to be a motor cycle but a doodle-bug – a German V1 flying bomb – on its way to London, followed by another within the space of two minutes."

At about 7.15am the Hamilcars started to move out, followed by the Horsas 30 minutes later and by 8am the whole squadron was airborne and in two streams line astern. Below in the streets of Herne Bay people were waving as the great armada moved across Kent towards the English Channel.

"As we approached Germany, via Belgium, a Stirling bomber came across the formation in a shallow dive with its starboard engines on fire from which five parachutes were seen to blossom in the air. A call came from the tug pilot 'Good luck, and come back safely lads,' followed by 'Flapjack, Flapjack' – the call-sign to cast off when ready. In free flight the glider became very quiet and even at 2,500 feet we were acutely conscious of the fierce battle raging below. It was necessary to take violent evasive action to port to avoid another Horsa diving from above, immediately followed by finding ourselves heading into our own squadron aircraft from behind.

"For a few minutes it was like a Biggles dog fight, with aircraft ducking and weaving all over the sky, with the difference that gliders cannot gain height and that seven and half tons all-up weight did not aid manoeuvrability. By the time we had completed a weaving 360 degree turn, any sense of formation had gone, and with it Plan 1 – to follow the flight commander in line into the Landing Zone.

"Cecil Law, the first pilot, said 'I've got it [meaning control of the glider]. You look out for a space to land.' Peering through the smoke and murk I spotted a clear field about 90 degrees to port. As Cecil started to turn a constant stream of pink 20 mm tracer shells came towards us from the ground. For a moment it was still, then it slowly followed us until it was within a yard of the cockpit. We waited for our fate, but the stream of tracer suddenly stopped. Perhaps the

German AA unit was overrun by paratroopers or just ran out of ammo – one will never know…

"We landed in a ploughed field and came to a halt. The pre-arrangements were that as soon as we had landed, I would jump out with the Bren gun, which came off the jeep, and defend the position while the gun crew unloaded. Cecil would stay inside assisting. Having settled myself in a defensive position outside the glider I suddenly heard Cecil say to the St/Sgt "What? Are you telling me you don't know how to get the bloody gun out?!" Here we were in a battle zone and the gun crew had not been shown how to unload the glider! Both pilots knew *how* it was done but had not actually *done* it. It wasn't part of our training. We flew the gliders and the passengers unloaded –that was the way the script went. In the circumstances, Cecil took charge and with the nose open and the ramp channels locked in position everything was unloaded in 15 minutes.

"As I lay there I saw another glider crew and its passengers being taken prisoner by the Germans just 250 yards away. Once the load was out, we made for a wedge-shaped depression in the ground about 30 yards away to take cover and decide on a plan of action. In the distance was a farmhouse, which we felt would afford better protection and once inside would be easier to defend. We went across the field in the jeep, towing the gun and hoping to find a friendly reception. All we found was a pool of blood in the hall, and wounded German troops in the cellar. The family who owned it were outside, hidden in a bunker.

"Suddenly I heard movement on the other side of the door behind me which I thought had been checked. Releasing the catch on his Sten gun I lunged at the door with the sole of my size ten boot and burst through, preparing to open fire. The door led to a lean-to stable where the 'enemy' turned out to be a sheep with two small lambs, all looking up appealingly for food.

"The lady of the house came in carrying a loaf of bread. She demanded a knife to cut it. When permission was given to get a knife, she opened a draw and pulled out a vicious looking knife, which I took off her and made her use a table knife. She was not pleased by this and came out with a burst of abuse and it was only when I pointed the Sten gun at her that she made a hasty retreat to the garden whence she had come.

"An army glider pilot, St/Sgt Andy Kerr, turned up and told us we were outside the main perimeter and in an exposed position if the Germans should decide to return. He suggested that we join a bunch of paratroopers who were well dug in around a large farm complex about a half a mile south towards Hamminkeln.

"A US Army paratrooper then turned up with a badly wounded jaw, so we used a field dressing to patch up his face, loaded him on the jeep and with the gun crew followed Andy across the field, which was now scattered with dead bodies and burnt out Dakotas…"

• • • • • • • • • •

'Passengers' in the glider that Stan Jarvis flew on Operation Varsity included Wally Parr and Harry Clark of the 2nd Ox & Bucks Infantry, who had both been part of the 'coup de main' party who took Pegasus Bridge in June 1944.

At 7.25am on the 24th March, Stan and his co-plot Peter Geddes, along with the other glider pilots at RAF Birch and their passengers lined up in their gliders and take-off commenced. Stan was No 5 in line and towed by S/Ldr (later group captain) Alex Blythe DFC of 233 Squadron, normally based at Down Ampney. As they sped down the runway the tow-rope broke. Stan steered into the perimeter track as the others behind roared past. Alex Blythe managed to stop his Dakota before running out of runway.

Alex Blythe and his crew had been together since June 1945, much of their time together spent in the Far East, but individually a number of the crew had been flying since 1940. Alex himself began flying in 1941.

He had taken part in the D-Day landings from Down Ampney, dropping Royal Engineer paratroopers south of the road to Caen, and also had been involved in the Arnhem operation in September.

Alex Blythe (2nd from right) and crew. [Alex Blythe]

"When the tow-rope broke it meant we were 50 tug/glider combinations behind our original position on the starting grid. The main problem was that each group of gliders had a specific target to aim for," Alex recalls. "Stan had been detailed to land beside the railway line at Hamminkeln. The original route would have meant them arriving over there on their own, and being sitting ducks for the enemy gun positions. I decided that instead of following the glider stream in a south easterly direction I would go direct, with the hope of catching up."

This meant a lonely and lengthy sea crossing via the coast north of Dunkirk which was still in German hands.

"I told Stan over the intercom of my intentions, although he had no alternative but to go where the tug aircraft took him. Stan was only 19 and this was his first operation."

The crossing went well and they caught up the stream of tugs and gliders, as it turned out they were only five to six places behind their original position. Alex gave Stan the sign that this was the point where he should cast off, though when he did it was entirely up to him. Once Stan had released, Alex turned westbound, opened up the throttles and got clear of the area as fast as possible.

Stan could see the autobahn from about 1500 feet and an area of trees that they had seen in the briefing photographs. All around them gliders were going down in flames or breaking up in the air.

"We managed to land near the landing ground and the troops, including Harry Clark, got out of the broken tail unit quickly and into a ditch, remembers Stan. "There was a lot of gunfire, but in the heat of the battle I heard a voice. It was one of the men I had carried. 'When we were back at Birch we asked you to land as near the station as possible,' he said. 'If you had got any closer we would be in the booking office!" I just replied, 'complements of the RAF!'

"A lonely figure came across the field, dressed in a brown jacket. He thought we were Germans and put his hands up to surrender. He was an American War Correspondent who had baled out of his Dakota, which, after dropping its load of paratroopers, had been badly hit. All he had with him was a pencil and notepad."

• • • • • • • • • • •

On the 23rd, D Company of the 2nd Ox & Bucks left Wing Barracks, Bulford, Wiltshire in a large convoy of lorries heading in the direction of North Essex. Only weeks before Harry Clark had taken part in an exercise in that area. On that occasion they had to make an emergency landing in a local recreation ground in March, Cambridgeshire. At the time he was member of 25 platoon, consisting of 28 infantry soldiers of which 50% had taken part in the Pegasus Bridge operation some nine months previously.

Some had taken part in other operations in the Ardennes and Holland. For others the Rhine Crossing was to be their first baptism of fire.

Their camp was a number of Nissen huts set in a wooded area somewhere in Essex. They quickly unloaded their kit, had a hurried lunch and then set down to prepare for the next day. The atmosphere in the hut was tense. The veterans sat in groups chatting. The platoons were woken at 3.30am for a quick, cold wash followed by a hurried breakfast, after which they checked and loaded their weapons and made sure the pins on the Mills 36 grenades were safe. They then fell in outside the hut for a final check over by the platoon commander. The transport left at 4.45am from Birch airfield.

They arrived at 6.15am and through the crisp clear light of dawn they saw a large number of Horsa gliders and Dakota tug aircraft lined up on the runway. Harry chose a seat on the starboard side of the glider. In June 1944 he had flown in glider No.2 with sergeant pilots Boland and Hobbs and had chosen the port side. Having been ejected through the side of the glider on landing on that occasion, he chose the opposite side this time.

They began to move down the runway and expected to be airborne at any time when suddenly the glider appeared to veer off the runway and come to a halt. The tow-rope had broken . After his previous experiences and his recent crash landing, Harry hoped that 'third time lucky' would work in his favour. The glider was towed by a tractor to the end of the line. This time the take off was OK and they were soon off the ground and on their way.

"We reached the Rhine and found ourselves back in the main stream of aircraft. I saw a Horsa blown part and vanish into the smoke. A second glider was seen plunging to the earth, trailing a stream of smoke. Suddenly we went into a dive too – but a controlled dive. When the Horsa levelled out we hit the ground with a thud and passed through a number of what sounded like hedges, then slowed, slewed around and stopped.

"The drill was to exit the glider as quickly as possible and take up a position of all-round defence. As I moved towards the forward exit, I saw the two pilots leave the cockpit and crouch down by the door. One of them looked at me and said 'Sorry about the rough landing.'

'I thought it was a bloody good landing!' I said. Within seconds two Horsas appeared out of the smoke and crashed in the area of the railway line. I have since discovered that everyone on board was killed."

• • • • • • • • • •

Major John Tillett was 'D' Company Commander of the 2nd Ox & Bucks. He had taken over the Company from Major John Howard (a platoon commander at the time) who had taken Pegasus Bridge at Normandy. Tillet had quite a pedigree, being a qualified parachutist and having also flown on leaflet raids in a Whitley of Bomber Command in order to gain experience of operational flying.

On the 23rd March, John Tillet spoke to Major Heath-Smith, who commanded the Heavy Weapons Company, about anti-aircraft defences in the landing area. Heath-Smith thought they would meet with stiff opposition. He was not wrong: Major Heath-Smith, aged 26, was killed on the morning of the 24th when his glider was destroyed in mid air by the very guns he and John had spoken about just 24 hours earlier. He came from the Oxford area and is now buried in the Reichswald War Cemetery.

"As we came in to land I heard one of the pilots shout 'Cables!'," John remembers, "and we jumped over some high-tension electric cables. This cost us flying speed and the only way now was down. The glider was hit in the tail, but nothing vital damaged. We hit the ground hard and tore through a couple of fences. Although parts of the glider broke off, we managed to finish in one piece. We had landed in an open field and there was no sign of the buildings that were to be the 'D' company objective. From the ground we saw one glider hit and its load fell out also a tug aircraft on fire..."

He was ordered by the CO to send one platoon to help 'B' Company at the Road Bridge over the River Issel and to move with his other two platoons to assist 'C' company at the Railway Bridge, and if possible attack Ringenberg. This was beyond the river and would help relieve the pressure on 'B' Company.

This was, for him, the start of a long trek…

• • • • • • • • • •

Lance Corporal Richard Dunkley had joined REME in 1943 when he was 18 years of age but was soon transferred to the newly formed 12th

Battalion of the Devonshire Regiment, which had just been designated as the third battalion making up the 6th Air Landing Brigade at Bulford Camp, Wilts.

On 20th March 1945 they were told to make sure their wills were in order and bed rolls and all personal belongings deposited in the Company store. They then drew ammunition and after a meal set off in three ton lorries for a tented camp in Essex.

"The weather was beautiful," he remembers, "with blue skies, bright sun and not too hot. On the 22nd we were briefed about our landing zone and what to expect after landing. We were to fight our way to the church in Hamminkeln, set up mortars and help with a defensive position to the north east of the church.

"On the 23rd we were issued with army 'funny money', given a lecture on non-fraternisation and issued with grenades. I was very wary of grenades and I reckon the top brass felt the same, as they always left the grenade issue to last to avoid the possibility of accidents. The phosphorous/smoke grenade (No 77) was a real 'nasty'"

"In the late afternoon of the 23rd we were given a meal with lots of tea and cheese and corned beef sandwiches, then off to bed for an early call at 2am.

"We were about number six or seven of the twenty lined up to take off. On board were 23 men and two hand carts of mortar equipment. Up front was the battalion padre, Cpn J.W. Hall. who was later awarded a C-in-C's Certificate. I was sitting on the port side and under the wing.

"At 0630 the co-pilot shouted back 'Hold tight' and slowly we rumbled down the runway. Even more so than on the Normandy landings, I feared that my life was about to come to an end. The noise inside the glider was more a drone than a roar and felt quite smooth. Inside it was quite crowded and we were not allowed to walk in the aisles – you just sat there with your small pack and rifle. The co-pilot shouted 'you will never see so many aircraft in flight again, so just look out of your windows.' I managed to do this with the help of my friend Jimmy Bick from Gloucester. When the warning came from the front to be ready for landing, the Padre suddenly decided to offer up a prayer on our behalf. I thought he meant well, but it had the effect of making us feel nervous and how fragile life was. We were well and truly in the hands of God at this time.

"We were told to take up landing positions and then felt the familiar sharp turn and dip of the wing. Suddenly it became dark inside the glider due to be the artificial smoke – known as 'Monty's Fog'. There was a distinct chemical smell from explosions. We then went into a steep dive and all the men on board slid against each other. As we pulled up to level flight someone shouted 'I've been shot!' It was a soldier three down from me; he had been hit in the upper thigh and nothing else was heard from him.

"The pilot made a beautiful landing and the glider stopped 50 feet from a hedge on the port side and just in front and little to the left of a large farmhouse. As we left the glider someone shouted that the co-pilot had been shot through the neck and two or three men were struggling to help him out on a stretcher."

• • • • • • • • • • •

John Love carried a Tetrarch tank and a detachment of soldiers under a Lieutenant Starkey. They flew on a northerly course from RAF Woodbridge up to Norwich then turned 180 degrees and flew south to the Thames. His second pilot was F/Sgt 'Mac' McEwan. They were towed by W/O Jacques of 644 Squadron at Woodbridge.

"As the Rhine loomed ahead so did the ack-ack," he remembers. "We received a direct hit. The explosion blew a hole in the side of the glider and hit me in the side of the hip and left leg. It also damaged the hydraulics and they had no flaps or brakes to reduce speed. They touched down at a great rate of knots and careered between two trees, which to some extent slowed them down and they finished up in a small river or stream. The tank broke its moorings and shot through the front of the glider. The only casualty was Lieutenant Starkey, who had his earphones on, listening to what was going on. They were

Taking cover behind a crashed glider.

torn from his head and with it his ear – although it was not completely severed. One of the soldiers put a field dressing on it and bandaged him up. Every one apart from me took cover in the bank of the stream. I was trapped by my legs and said I would stay put.

• • • • • • • • • • •

Sgt Cyril (Cy) Hargraves describes his second pilot, Sgt Jock Cooper, a Scot, as "the salt of the earth". They had often practised in training for the event of one of them being hit in the air by suddenly saying "You have control" – even on the final approach and as low as 10 feet from the ground. Their flight was uneventful except somewhere on track just north of Venlo they saw a V2 climb into the sky.

In the briefing they had been shown photographs of various landing zones. He and Jock had picked out an arm of the woods on their LZ near Bielfeld, north of Wesel. They decided to try and roll into that corner, which would give them protection from view from both sides. The photograph also showed it to be free of fences.

"When we arrived at the 'pull-off' point we said our goodbyes to the tug crew and dropped the tow line. Cyril eased up the nose and at 65mph lowered full flap, dropped the nose and turned into a descending spiral to his left, however as he completed his first full turn he saw on his left a Horsa was also spiralling left, so we were meeting each time round with no more than 20 feet separating us. On his right, to make matters worse, a Horsa was spiralling right, so we were both going the same way, but overlapping."

As he turned on his final approach, Cyril could see that the area was covered in wire fences, through which they ploughed, rolling towards the spot they had chosen.

"The wire fences appeared to have cut the brake airlines and we were approaching the trees a lot faster than we should have been. A large tree, about 3 feet in diameter was straight ahead and as I had no wish to hit it, I applied full left rudder. I had just enough response to avoid it, but still managed to run into lesser trees surrounding it at about 25mph.

"The front of the Horsa disintegrated and a tree about 8 inches in diameter pinned Jock to his seat, with his legs each side of it. It had dented the front of the seat by about 3 inches so that he could not move. The control column on his side was completely gone and I was able to tear out the central control column pillar with little trouble so that with help, Jock was heaved out sideways and unhurt.

"The next problem was unloading, with the front stuck in the trees. We made our way back to the tail mounting bolts, four of them with the nuts split and held in place by a box spanner over each nut. In theory all one had to do was cut the control wires with a bolt cutter (provided), take off the four box spanners from the split collets and jump down – the tail would then fall off… That is what *should* have happened – but did not. So with the axe (provided), the skin of the glider was partially torn off so that with the saw (also provided), the longerons and skin could be cut through and then the tail would fall off. We all took turns to saw away at the longerons and skin and then Jock pointed out that little holes were appearing near to where we were sawing. It dawned on us that if someone – particularly the Germans – could see our legs under the glider, they would shoot through the glider at where they thought the rest of us would be! We soon got the job finished and the troops were on their way."

• • • • • • • • • •

Denis Mills with Art Pogson as his second pilot were towed from Tarrant Rushton to Woodbridge a few days before Varsity. On the day of the operation they were carrying Lieutenant Robinson and men of the Anti-tank Regiment, Royal Artillery. Their journey was uneventful and the landing, apart from a few hedges and fences, was smooth, ending up against a grassy ramp adjacent to a farmhouse. After unloading, they travelled with their passengers in a jeep for about a mile and then went their separate ways…

• • • • • • • • • •

S/Ldr Reynolds, the Commanding Officer of 'F' Squadron, carried Lt-Col Darrell-Brown, the Commanding Officer of the 2nd (Airborne) Ox & Bucks. He had requested being put down near the railway station at Hamminkeln. As they came in, they found they were near a flak battery and the station itself, and after landing took part in the capture of the enemy battery. It was Reynolds, with a PIAT gun, who put the enemy guns out of action. As they landed the port wing was blown off by enemy fire – meanwhile the second-pilot was firing with his sten-gun at the enemy gun battery.

• • • • • • • • • •

F/O Colin Miller was at Blake Hill Farm, Cricklade in March 1945. He was ordered to ferry three gliders to Colchester just before Varsity. 'E' Squadron moved over there on the 23rd and took off on the 24th at 8am. Colin's glider had been loaded the day before with a jeep and trailer. His second pilot was Sgt Ted Obbe and he carried nine soldiers, including an army padre. He saw the ground at 200 feet and landed near a farmhouse and a group of trees. They immediately came under small arms fire and the soldiers in the glider exchanged fire with 3 or 4 small groups of very young German troops, during which the glider was set on fire by a mortar bomb.

• • • • • • • • • •

Percy M. Edwards was with 'G' Squadron at Great Dunmow. His second pilot was Bill Fleming whom he had trained with at No.3 BFTS at Miami, USA. His glider like many others was loaded with a jeep, a fully loaded trailer, a motorcycle, ammunition and six soldiers, including a Lieutenant from Wrexham, the home of Percy's wife. This, it would appear, was Lieutenant Ash's mortar platoon.

The take-off, in glider RAX 754, Percy describes as being 'dicey'. The tug pilot, F/Sgt Webb in Stirling LK 331, seemed in a hurry to climb as soon as he had reached flying speed, although the glider, fully-loaded, had hardly reached stalling speed.

The rest of the journey was not easy, with Percy fighting with the sluggish controls as they hit the slipstream created by the aircraft up ahead. Percy describes it as like 'a puppet on a string'. They were about half way across the Channel and were again subjected to slipstream problems with the glider being thrown to the left and right when suddenly the tow-rope snapped. A ditching lay ahead. Bill Fleming gave the men in the back the pre-ditching instructions such as cutting an emergency exit in the roof of the plywood fuselage. To Bill's horror, a tough 'Geordie' was seen wielding an axe towards the elevator controls and was quickly told that the controls were needed at this time!

"We decided to ditch without using flaps. We had heard of bad experiences when the barn door size flaps were used, which caused the aircraft to plough in. We therefore descended to sea-level and could feel the undercarriage rippling on the surface of the water. I stalled us in and although part of the cockpit caved in, we were wet but unhurt."

They climbed out onto the roof of the glider, by which time Air Sea Rescue High Speed launch No.190 from Newhaven was alongside, skippered by F/O Davies. A 67 Thorneycroft launch from No.27 ASR/MCU Ramsgate, under F/O Milton, also turned up, but HSL 190 beat him to it. They were picked up at 9am, 8 miles off Cap Gris Nez and instructed to take them back to Dover, where they arrived at 9.55am and were taken straight to Dover Castle and handed over to the Army Medical Corps.

Another glider also had to ditch. The crew were picked up by HSL 145, skipped by F/Lt Ferguson from Newhaven at 10.25am. Seven of the men in the glider were on the starboard wing and one in the water in a Mae West about half a mile from the glider.

• • • • • • • • • •

When Bill Sampson touched down at 140 mph he fully expected his glider to break up, but instead it just ran across several fields before ending up with the cockpit overhanging a road.

"This would have been perfect," Bill remembers, "if I had been flying a Horsa Mk II with a nose-opening, but unfortunately I was flying a Mk I, which required the removal of the rear fuselage tail. I was carrying a jeep and trailer and a sergeant and six men. My admiration for this sergeant increased minute by minute as, for a period of one and half hours, he and his men battled to swing the tail round in a muddy field, all the while being shot at by the Germans. When they finally succeeded, they mounted up and disappeared in their jeep."

While they toiled at the task, Bill and his co-pilot gave covering fire and a warning of any mortar bombs coming their way.

• • • • • • • • • •

Ken Scolding came over the village with his load of 6-pounder anti-tank gun, a jeep and three members of the 12th Devon Regiment at a height of 500 feet instead of the intended 150 feet. The heaviest load he had carried in training was concrete blocks weighing 3,000lbs – his load on Varsity weighed twice that amount. He recalls:

"When I said to my co-pilot Nick Nicolson 'I am going around again' his reply was 'For what we are about to receive…' as we crossed the road for the second time."

On this occasion, despite tearing through telephone and power cables, they made a safe landing.

• • • • • • • • • •

When Leslie Norris arrived over the Rhine and his tug pilot, from 437 RCAF Squadron said it was time to release, Leslie remembers saying, "Have a beer on me."

The reply, "Yes, I will be at the bar in three hours."

"The area was covered in smog – or as someone called it 'Monty's fog' and instead of the release height being 1,600 feet it was 2,600 feet. As we came in to land we found ourselves heading for a big area of woodland, so I took a southerly course, parallel to the woods, road and canal to get us all down safely in an open field. The American GIs on the ground rolled over to let us pass. Having been hit by small arms from the ground, the air compressor was punctured and as a result we had no flaps and no brakes. Despite this, the glider came to halt without too much damage and one of the soldiers got in the jeep and started it up, while I pulled the twin levers to unlocked the fuselage down and opened it. Another soldier came up to get the ramps for the jeep to drive down. On the ground we saw a long column of German prisoners being escorted away by an American soldier.

"An American came over to the glider and proceeded to, with an axe, cut the compass out of the glider to keep as a souvenir."

There were other landings that Leslie has memories of.

"Bunny Austin was killed by friendly fire. He had fired upon what he thought was the enemy and when it was returned he was hit in the back by two bullets. His mother sent a scathing letter to the Air Ministry because of the manner in which he had been killed. He was, in her opinion, a pilot, not an infantryman, and should not have been killed in that role. One soldier who came in by glider was crushed inside the glider when a gun fell on him as they landed. F/O Bill Hamilton received a bullet in the thigh and was taken to hospital on a jeep and trailer."

• • • • • • • • • • •

On 18th March 1945, Len Macdonald was detached to 'G' Squadron at Great Dunmow. For Operation Varsity he was crewed with a St/Sgt Penketh.

"The main problem," remembers Len, "is that nobody knew where he was!"

On the 20th, Len discovered he was in the sick bay and paid him a visit.

"He was recovering from a minor complaint and but medical officer said it was up to him – he could stay in the sick bay or be released for the operation. He chose the latter, but decided to stay off sick as long as he could…"

On the 22nd, Len's glider chalk marked No.397 was loaded with a jeep, a trailer and two motorcycles of a signals unit of the 53rd Light Regiment Royal Artillery. He then went to the sick bay to obtain a progress report on his pilot. He found him much better and it was agreed that he would report to the glider at 7.15am, which he did. As they walked out to the glider he told Len that he had not flown for about nine months and that it would be better if Len took over on the take off. The tug skipper was a New Zealander, S/Ldr W.A. Jack, in Stirling LJ 983 of 620 Squadron, (although Len is certain it was a Halifax).

"After we had been flying for about five minutes, St/Sgt Penketh asked me if he minded if he 'had a kip'." Len recalls. "I just said 'go ahead.'

Gosfield 1945.

[Ted Giles]

He then pulled a blanket out of his knapsack, placed it over his head and promptly went off to sleep!"

"The senior NCO in the back of the glider was not too happy about this and said to me that he would soon wake up the sleeping pilot if the need arose. As it turned out, it was a very smooth flight, with practically 'hands off' for most of the journey."

With the Rhine in sight, Len asked the NCO to wake up his sleeping partner.

"He awoke and the signal was given to cast off by means of a Aldis lamp – a steady green signal – and with the help of Penketh we made an excellent landing, only a couple of fields away from our designated landing spot," Len continues. "I hopped out to open the nose and commence the unloading, but as I did we came under heavy fire. It was then that Penketh showed what a fine soldier he was. He went into action straight away with a Bren Gun and the unloading went on in relative comfort."

A senior officer was looking for the unit Len was carrying – they were the communications unit – Le remembers that he looked at his watch, looked at them and said with a twinkle in his eye…

"You're late – what kept you?"

• • • • • • • • • •

Ted Giles was towed from Gosfield by a Dakota of 512 Squadron. His load was jeep and trailer with Lieutenant Rice and five men of the Ox & Bucks Regiment.

"The take off was like an exercise," remembers Ted, "but I had two things on my mind as we made our way towards Dungeness and the Channel – 'Don't cross the autobahn' and 'Land near the L-shaped wood'. During the journey I talked to Lieutenant Rice and told him that on the 25th I would be 21 years old."

As they were being towed by Dakotas, they had to lead the stream. The tug pilot helped Ted with the map reading.

"In a few minutes you will see the Rhine," he said over the intercom, and they both set out to identify the L-shaped wood.

"There it is…" the tug pilot said, "There it is!" at the very same moment that Ted was about to say "I've got it!"

"We were much higher than I wanted to be but I still said 'I'm pulling off'" recalls Ted. "The tug pilot said 'Good luck' and with the usual bump, tugging became gliding. I was lucky in as much that we never lost sight of the wood, despite the smoke. We went over a low fence and into the field as briefed – nobody had said anything about the field being a ploughed field however… Having landed we all set about unloading. The sergeant came over and said, "Thank you sir, a very nice ride."

Ted had a 'near miss' later when a discarded tow-rope dropped just a few feet from him.

• • • • • • • • • •

Geoff Dines was with 'D' Squadron at Shepherds Grove and his second pilot was George Irons. When he arrived over the landing zone in Glider RX 300, he remembers it was "complete chaos: smoke, burning gliders and aircraft."

• • • • • • • • • •

Sid Edwards flew as second pilot to St/Sgt Edgar (Eddie) Raspison who had taken part in the Arnhem operation as a second pilot and before that D-Day, so Sid knew he was flying with a very experienced glider pilot.

"On the 24th we were transported from the sergeant's mess at Earls Colne to the airfield. The glider was loaded with a jeep and trailer, a bren gun and six men from the Royal Artillery. Before taking off, a captain in the Artillery came up into the cockpit with a bottle of whisky and said 'This will fortify you during the operation.' Eddie and I both took a good swig from the bottle and the captain returned to the back to fortify his men in the same way. They were to set up an Artillery Observation Post after landing and the trailer carried vital radio equipment and reserve ammunition."

After crossing the Rhine they were advised that it was '10 minutes to cast off'. As soon as they could pinpoint their designated landing area they parted company with the tug aircraft.

Eddie had to turn to port to bring them into line with their approach and straighten out before applying full flaps. As they glided in, Eddie felt two impacts on the glider, but everything seemed to be okay, so he presumed the glider had not been badly hit or damaged. However, Sid was not only slumped in his seat but smoke was coming from one of his ammunition pouches, one of which Eddie knew contained two phosphorous grenades. At that time all Eddie could do was land the glider.

On landing the glider did not behave as normal, and Eddie assumed the undercarriage must have been shattered by one of the hits – he was right, it had been.

"I unstrapped Sid as carefully as possible, but with some urgency, and got him into the fuselage, where all was in disarray. Where once the entrance door had been was now a great big hole."

The driver of the jeep helped Eddie get Sid through the hole and into a shelter created by the glider 'ploughing' a deep furrow in the earth.

"The glider was wrecked and sloping to the left, the port wing just about smashed off. Behind the jeep we heard the sound of machine gun fire and there was a strong smell of smoke."

When Eddie and the jeep driver returned to the glider they found all the rest had been injured, although not critically.

"We got them all out and into the shelter and then took stock of the situation, remembers Eddie. "Sid still had his smouldering webbing on, so I got it off and threw it away as far as possible, just in case the phosphorous bombs had been triggered. The jeep driver and I managed to get the jeep out and I told him to load all the wounded into it and make for the main force, where they could be given proper medical attention."

• • • • • • • • • • •

On 24th March F/Lt Howard Curry took off with 'A' Squadron flying a Horsa Mk II – it was the first time he had flown one. After an uneventful take-off and flight, they found themselves over the target zone…

"At about 1000 feet there was a loud bang and a lot of shaking and shouts from the back of the glider. Looking behind I saw a bunch of gesticulating soldiers and a lot of open sky where the tail should have been. My second pilot, Sgt Graham, was pointing to the rapidly increasing reading on the Air Speed Indicator…

The next memory I have is of regaining consciousness in a mass of wreckage. I was tangled up with the front offside wheel of the jeep we were carrying. Some time later I heard a voice say, 'Drive it out, he's dead'. I can still remember that voice to this day – the owner had a Yorkshire accent."

Howard soon indicated that the Yorkshireman was wrong in his diagnosis. Sgt Graham, however, was dead.

"They had to take the wheel off the jeep to get me out," Howard remembers, "But I've always believed that they wouldn't have bothered if an Army padre had not turned up…"

• • • • • • • • • • •

John Fretwell was an Army glider pilot with 'D' Squadron. One of his colleagues there was RAF glider pilot F/Lt John Nash, who Fretwell remembers as having "a crisp clear voice". Nash came from North Wales and Fretwell from London.

John Fretwell takes up the story:

"As we crossed the Dutch coast the gun emplacements opened up and within minutes we were in the middle of hell. It was sheer carnage. I saw F/Lt Nash's glider [Horsa 431] go up in smoke after being hit by tracer shells. The towing aircraft was also hit.

Nash, known as 'Jack', was near the nose of the arrow formation, three ahead of Fretwell's glider on the right hand side.

"The entire front of the formation was destroyed. It was like being in the middle of a swarm of bees, with tracer bullets and shells everywhere. Out of the first 40 gliders only seven survived."

Glider No 431, piloted by F/Lt Nash was seen to be fiercely burning – no one could have got out alive.

At the same time Fretwell's own first pilot was killed as he wrestled to control Horsa No 544.

Fretwell managed to land, but only two of those on board, including himself, came out alive. Fretwell was peppered with shrapnel.

"I got out of the glider and turned over my comrades to see if any were still alive. When I found they were not I just went berserk with a machine-gun, firing it until it was too hot to hold any more."

• • • • • • • • • •

Sgt Worrall arrived at Woodbridge from Tarrant Rushton on 22nd March. He was issued with a gun covered in grease and the spent the entire evening prior to moving to Woodbridge cleaning it with rags and cold water.

"After the briefing, an army friend who had taken part in the Normandy landings said, 'I shouldn't take too much notice what they said in there. They made the airborne landing in Normandy sound as if it would be a picnic … and it wasn't!'"

Worrall's landing on the 24th was: "not too bad… although we did loose the undercarriage after it became embedded in loose shale. But before we could leave the glider we came under fire from a machine gun. As we lay on the floor of the glider, a row of small bullet holes appeared in the plywood bodywork. Happily, no one was hit, although the bullets were only inches above our heads. The soldiers in the back were the first out and soon came under fire. One was struck by a bullet, which cut through the zip of his smock and buckled the cigarette case he was carrying in his breast pocket. He later was able to retrieve the bullet as a souvenir. As we were pinned down and surrounded, after a while there seemed no alternative, but to surrender – which we did. We were disarmed and taken at gunpoint to a nearby farmhouse, where other prisoners were being kept. There was a pile of kit, for which there seemed to be no owners. On glancing at this, I noticed the names 'Stevens' and 'Hayman', who were obviously casualties."

• • • • • • • • • •

RAF pilot Alan Head met his second pilot, St/Sgt Young, at Great Dunmow in March 1945. Flying with such an experienced glider pilot, who also had ground combat experience, reassured Alan.

"Young asked me if I minded him becoming first pilot," remembers Alan. "Although I had more flying hours than him, it was not on gliders. I assured him that I had no objection and that I was happy with such an arrangement. I also secretly agreed that I would stick to Young like a long lost son once we were on the ground. I never regretted it. All went well, and thanks to Sgt Young, I survived unscathed."

• • • • • • • • • •

Jimmie Stark was one of the pilots who towed a glider on Operation Varsity.

"On Wednesday 21st March, 298 and 644 Squadrons flew from Tarrant Rushton to Woodbridge, towing empty gliders – that is, apart from a pilot! On the 22nd and 23rd we had nothing to do but wait for the gliders to be loaded and towed by tractor into position on the runway. During this time we did spend a lot of time in the briefing room. On Saturday 24th we went out to the aircraft and the formation started to take off at 6am. On my way to the aircraft I noticed that the Hamilcar glider I was to tow had the tail fin painted bright yellow. On enquiring why, I was told that the gliders marked in this way were being loaded 35,000lbs of ammunition – a pleasant thought when you are only 100 yards ahead in the tug aircraft!

"The flight was uneventful, apart from the occasional wing stall that one gets when flying in line formation. In the landing zone area the glider released and the tail gunner said 'Glider Away'. With that, I felt the aircraft surge forward. I flew a short distance to the east and circled the battle area. As I banked to the left I saw a Stirling going down with a wing missing. I then said to my crew "If you have seen enough of this bloody battle we're going home." I headed west and the navigator gave me a course for home. We flew straight to Tarrant Rushton, which meant that we had all our overnight kit with us."

As well as glider operations, between April 1944 to February 1945, Jimmie took part in 30 SOE operations to France, Holland and Norway. He also participated in the D-Day operations and five days after the landings dropped a 25 pounder gun and jeep by parachute to the beachhead. In September 1944 he took part in the Arnhem operations.

• • • • • • • • • •

Doug Coxell was airborne in Halifax NA 688-N of 297 Squadron at 7.56am from Earls Colne.

"We saw a Hamilcar being towed by a Halifax break up, and nose the open and a tank and crew plunge earthwards, followed by the remains of the Hamilcar. Having cast off our glider successfully we were on our way home when we suddenly heard a loud bang. This was followed within microseconds by my wireless operator passing rapidly to my right in the direction of the forward hatch, parachute already clipped onto his chest harness. Happily, he was within reach, and my right hand dropped onto his collar to stop him from going any further. (I had served in the police force before joining the RAF so I knew how to 'collar' someone!")

"We had lost all pneumatic pressure and were without flaps or brakes the loud bang had been a burst pneumatic pipeline, which was routed along the bulkhead behind the pilot's seat and close to the right ear of the wireless operator – hence his rapid departure towards the exit door when it blew. The pressure relief valve had failed and the pressure built up until something had to give.

"We were ordered toland at Woodbridge, an emergency landing strip. After landing on the 9,000ft by 200ft runway, the order was given to shut down the engines, but because of a strong wind, the aircraft started to weathercock into the wind and towards the fir trees which lined each side of the runway. The order was given to start the starboard engine, which burst into life and provided thrust in the opposite direction to correct our drift. The order was then given to start the port outer with much the same result. After much juggling, the aircraft was eventually brought to a standstill.

On reporting to Air Traffic Control they were greeted by Control staff with broad grins. The Senior Air Traffic Control Officer remarked: "We knew we had an unusually long and wide runway but this is the first time we have seen anyone make use of it!"

• • • • • • • • • •

Dick Wynne was a pilot with 437 (RCAF) Squadron, flying Dakota KG 577-DS out of Blakehill. He was carrying nine men of the 1st Ulster Rifles, a jeep, trailer and two motorcycles.

"The take off at 0710 hrs was controlled by a Tugmaster, using a flag to tell the pilot what to do. A flag waving rapidly from side to side at waist level meant 'fast taxiing'; the Tugmaster would watch the tow-rope while doing this until the slack was taken up, then would follow the signal to 'taxi slowly' (arm out straight and waving from side to side in front of his legs). When tug and glider were moving together he signalled to 'open up and get rolling down the runway for take off' – this he did by waving the flag over his head. I had developed my own technique of using the brakes to control the taxiing speed while at the same time continuing to open the throttles, so that by the time I got the signal to go I had practically full power on. I would then hand the throttles over to my co-pilot to get them up to 48 inches of boost while I gradually eased off the pressure on the brakes. Meanwhile I would try to get the tail of the aircraft up as soon as possible – usually within a very short distance.

"Another thing I did as a double check was to have the wireless operator stand and look out of the astrodome and give a running commentary on how the rope was doing and when the glider was moving with them. He did this until the glider became airborne and then I knew I could lift off when I had sufficient airspeed, and this was usually well before the end of the runway.

On the 24th, Dick towed a glider bearing the number 99 –its pilot was RAF F/O Geoffrey Atkinson and its second pilot was from the Army Glider Pilot Regiment.

"We got airborne quite easily, but just as I was taking up the slack in the tow-rope my navigator, Flying Officer Simpson, told me that he had dropped a lighted cigarette down a hole in the floor just behind the pilot's seat, in the centre of the aircraft. Now was not the time to bother about it, I told him, and instructed both him and the wireless operator to pee down the hole and not use the fire extinguisher, as we might need it later. All was well, as nothing happened. The Dakota KG 577 was a Mk III, which I liked. I did not care for the new Mk Ivs – the engines tended to overheat when they climbed.

It took them a long time to reach the briefed altitude. The aircraft had steel plates beneath and behind the pilot to protect him from flak, and all the crew wore flak suits and helmets, which were put on when they got near the Rhine. They also wore Mae Wests for the Channel crossing.

"After casting off we did a 180-degree turn and dropped the tow-rope on the way back across the Rhine. The wireless operator had seen tracer coming up over the tail of the aircraft shortly before cast-off time. We landed at B 75 at Nivelles in France where we discovered that we had been hit – a lone bullet had damaged a main hydraulic line, which had been leaking fluid. We flew back to Blakehill Farm on the 26th."

• • • • • • • • • • •

John Gray was a flight engineer with 644 Squadron on Operation Varsity, flying out of Woodbridge.

"We flew from our normal base at Tarrant Rushton on the 20th and slept inhangers at Woodbridge, being fed from field kitchens. The briefing was attended by Major-General Richard Gale, Commander of 6th Airborne. Our take-off was at 7.50am. The crossing went smoothly but as we released the Hamilcar we were towing over the landing area everything and everyone seemed to be firing at us. The tow-rope was dropped on a railway building, which was destroyed."

• • • • • • • • • • •

Flight Officer Rosemary Britten was an intelligence officer at RAF Earls Colne. All the intelligence officers were keen to go on the operation and it was decided to hold a draw to select who should go. Rosemary was as keen to go as the rest, but being a woman she was told that she was to be excluded from the draw. S/Ldr Mayer, the Senior Intelligence Officer, thought this unfair, and went to see the Station Commander, Gr/Cpt Bertram about it. He later relented and said she could be included. When she actually won the draw, Mayer went off to get the CO of 296 Squadron's permission for her to go on the operation. There were a few problems to her going, one being that the AOC was flying in the 5th aircraft. She was eventually put in the 17th aircraft off, piloted by F/O Ron Lamshed flying Halifax NA 698-D 'Dog'.

Throughout the briefing Rosemary avoided the group captain like the plague in case he asked her who had won the draw. She remembers Air Chief Marshal Tedder saying a few words and delivering a message from General Eisenhower. Then Sir Archibald Sinclair, Under Secretary for State for Air, made a speech about 'the brave boys of the Glider Pilot Regiment'.

"Suddenly, half way through, he remembered he was talking to the men of the RAF who would *pull* the gliders and proceeded to give them a colossal build-up too. The most astonishing thing I recall was that Sir Archibald had a very noticeable speech impediment, a considerable handi-

Rosemary Britten. [Cy Henson]

cap for a man in his position, and I remember thinking that he must be extremely clever to have got over such a handicap."

It was suggested to her that perhaps she should let one of the men go in her place, but, she remembers, "so many people already knew that I had won the draw that I couldn't decently back out, even if I had tried."

She went to breakfast at 4.15am having got a call for 3.45am. She had already emptied her pockets in the approved aircrew style. All she took was a comb, escape kit and powder and lipstick, even though she did not use makeup all the time – she wanted to look like a German girl if she had to bale out. She wore slacks, her oldest tunic, a German scarf and was carrying 'Ebenezer' the mascot of F/C O'Donnell.

"I kept well out of the way of the senior officers present and the aircrew carried my Mae West and parachute so that I would just look like a love-sick WAAF officer seeing off her boyfriend. An awkward moment arrived when my uncle, Major Ian Toler, came up to say goodbye and asked me to come and see the take off. He was flying one of the gliders. Things got worse when as I got into the crew bus. I found a Canadian War Correspondent already sitting in the bus. When he saw me, his eyes lit up at the thought of a 'scoop' but somehow I talked him out of using the story – until the end of the war at least…

From then on, everything went smoothly and she was soon to find herself looking down at the landing zone.

"I was surprised to find that I recognised the countryside from the briefing photographs and the wood near Hamminkeln, although the actual landing zone was out of sight, covered by a very effective smoke screen – for the ground troops but not the aircrews. I was told that a Halifax had gone down in flames and that only three parachutes had come out, one floating down into the site of the crash. I was also told that a Hamilcar had disintegrated, spilling out a tank and its crew. I did not see either incident myself as I was in the second pilot's seat on the starboard side and they occurred on the port side.

"The flak was coming up and seemed to be homing in on us so Ron took violent evasive action – but not violent enough, as D-Dog suffered a massive hit and shook all over. Things did not look good and thoughts of baling out were on our minds. The pilot was hanging on to the stick for dear life. The inter-com then went, upon which the wireless operator, Warrant Officer Stewart, did something to Ron's helmet, which for a while improved the situation. Getting the helmet back on his head was Ron's big problem, not having his hands free. For a while I passed messages back and forth, but this proved to be rather hopeless as the noise was deafening. The control column was held together by a quarter inch of metal, everything depended upon whether it snapped or whether it didn't.

"Sgt Fred Hambly tied a hammer onto it to act as a splint, which saved the situation. Luckily, I didn't see this, but I could tell by the amount of frantic pushing and pulling of knobs and wheels that things were not working properly. When we boarded the aircraft the crew said they did not bother doing up their parachutes properly, so I had followed suit – this meant a few minutes fumbling to get my chute done up. McGhan opened the escape hatch and told me what to do.

"Harry Rostron, the navigator, worked out the distance home. As it was a distance of 200 miles with a stretch over the sea, it was unanimous that we would not make it, as any minute the control column might break. The rear gunner, Pilot Officer George Wright, was going to shoot the tow-rope, which had got jammed over the sea, but it suddenly came away over a village – not intended and most unfortunate for the villagers.

"The compass was u/s and so were the hydraulics, so it was a question of a crash landing or baling out. I would rather have baled out as I did not relish a crash landing and rather liked the thought of having a Caterpillar Club badge. But having found a suitable airfield, Ron decided to land. He asked me what would happen if I turned up on the Continent, I thought this was most considerate of him. George Wright, Harry Rostron and I all sat on the floor in the rest bay in the crash position. The escape hatches were open above and below and the wind was blowing through the area that had once been the door. George went back to the rear turret to get his hat, then sent me to get mine – if we survived we may as well look our best... Somehow Fred Hambly was able to manually get the undercarriage down, he said afterwards that it had never been done before.

"Somehow or other Ron made a perfect landing – to the extent that the crew said he had never done a better one.

When I saw the control column I felt sick..."

A direct hit had burst inside the fuselage, blowing the door away and peppering the aircraft all around, cutting a lot of the vital parts but missing the petrol tanks and the crew. They had landed at Strip B 53 at Merville, near Lille in France.

"It was an American landing strip and soon a circle of Yanks and French were all around the aircraft. They asked where was the guy who was hurt. We all looked at each other and then George, who had scratched his hand, had it bandaged up with great pomp and ceremony. Ron went to flying control to signal back that we were safe and down. He was worried because he had put my name down as part of the crew, but, as it happens, the signal came over at the other end as "F/O Lamshed and Crew have arrived..." so my name was not mentioned. There were questions and funny looks at a woman being in the crew, but it was passed off by saying I was an Intelligence Officer, implying that all crews carried a WAAF in the crew.

"One officer was not at all impressed or pleased and it looked like a report was going to the Supreme Commander, Eisenhower but with some swift thinking and talking Ron got the same man to help us get back to the UK in a Flying Fortress or Liberator. Ron also shot a horrible line about us being a special duties squadron and being needed urgently. We then got the 'secret' equipment out of the aircraft and onto the grass, where we sat drinking the tea left in our flasks and waited. Eventually a truck turned up to take us to the officers mess, which was in the village.

"I sat in the front with the driver and asked him if there were any WAACs (US Servicewomen) there. He replied "Sure Honey," and gave me a stick of chewing gum. After a meal we were asked to return to the airfield. We sat there waching aircraft taking off. A Dakota landed and we were told it would be taking us back to the UK. We were going to go to RAF Honington, but persuaded the pilot to drop us at Earls olne. The journey over was very bumpy and I was very nearly sick. When we got back a rumour was all around the airfield that I had been killed..."

● ● ● ● ● ● ● ● ● ●

Cpt Michael Graham was Flight Commander of 21 Flight with 'E' Squadron. For Operation Varsity the squadron was split into two and Michael was given two flights to command at Birch. His second pilot was Dennis Hardy.

"We were carrying a platoon of the Ox & Bucks and so much equipment that we only just managed to clear the boundary fence at Birch," remembers Michael. "The air over the Rhine was full of gliders, like a flock of seagulls. In the final crosswind approach, nicely placed, we met another Horsa head on. Both of us turned violently to port and the starboard wing tips missed by a matter of feet. The loss of height and distance meant we could not reach the landing zone we had been heading for, so we turned into land on the west bank of the road running straight out of Hamminkeln to the north. It was a large open field where other Horsas were landing, but we were still under full flap, and due to the low height and heavy load the Horsa would not level off in time..."

The undercarriage collapsed, the nose hit the ground and the two pilots went out through the Perspex. Dennis suffered a deep cut on his forehead and bad concussion. The platoon commander in the back of the glider had unstrapped himself for the landing and was killed. Six men were wounded, two or three of them seriously."

• • • • • • • • • • •

Roy Howard was a veteran of D-Day, in which he flew glider No.6 – the last of three targeting the Orne River Bridge. For that operation he was awarded the DFM. His next operation was Arnhem, but when on the way the tug aircraft towing his glider had engine trouble and turned back. On Operation Varsity his second pilot was F/O Daniels. They were able to get down without damage or casualties.

• • • • • • • • • • •

The main thing remembered by St/Sgt Dennis Fitzgerald – who flew with 'D' Squadron from Shepherds Grove – was the bravery of his tug pilot, who, it would appear, was F/Lt H.P. Vanrenen DFC, flying Stirling LJ 979 of 196 Squadron.

Dennis tells the story as follows:

"While we were at Shepherds Grove and waiting for Operation Varsity, as we lay in our billets at night we would hear the Stirlings returning from operations. On one occasion, the approach of a Stirling we accompanied by the sound of another aircraft engine, followed by a burst of machine gun fire. A German aircraft had followed the Stirling back, the pilot was Vanrenen. We then heard the German aircraft make another run, shooting up the billets, which still had their lights on at the time. All the men in the hut, including me, pulled their blankets over their heads – as if that was going to help! – but luckily no one was hit and the German aircraft flew off. The next day we heard that the Stirling had been hit and came in to land with smoke coming from it. In order to land, Vanrenen had put his head out of the roof of the Stirling to see the ground ahead. He was a very tall man of about six foot two or three. Two days later and after the briefing for Varsity, I was asked to have a word with Vanrenen and found him to be a very smart and friendly person. I was pleased that he was to be my tug pilot.

Dennis's second pilot was called Shipway. They carried a captain in the Royal Artillery, five men, a jeep, a Howitzer gun and a trailer full of ammunition.

"Take-off was good and we levelled out at about 1,500 feet. After about five minutes the port outer-engine on the Stirling stopped, but Vanrenen came over the intercom and told me not to pull off and he would take a different course that his navigator was working out. Ten minutes later one of the starboard engines failed…

"Any moment I was waiting for the message that we would be landing at the nearest aerodrome but not Vanrenen. Once again he said 'don't pull off' as his navigator was again making adjustments to the course. We would now be making a straight course over France. The short cut took us over the North Sea instead of the Channel. Near Hamminkeln we cast off and I slowed down the speed of the glider by climbing. In the meantime th Stirling made a steep turn and came back close to us, waggling its wings in a farewell salute, which at the time I thought was cheeky. I later learned that the Stirling was hit over the landing zone and force-landed at Overloon; Vanrenen and two of his crew having been wounded. He refused any help for himself until the other two had been attended to."

The men that Dennis carried were wounded, soon after landing, by a German mortar.

• • • • • • • • • • •

F/O Stephane Mansell was taken prisoner but later escaped only to be re-captured again on the 29th. He was re-captured by two members of the German Police Battalion and his body was later found in a village by his brother, Major Gerald Mansell, who was serving with an Armoured Reconnaissance Unit. He had been shot and was originally buried in Venlo but is now buried in the Reichswald War Cemetery.

• • • • • • • • • • •

Jack Newton was serving with 'B' Squadron as a second pilot to F/Lt Mike Stringer.

"We landed very heavily, having descended through flak. I must have been knocked out. When I regained consciousness I had a label pinned on my jacket – it was a German one, with my name, rank and serial number on it. I was taken across the river where I was told by a medic that the Germans normally labelled corpses with this type of label. So the Germans had thought I was dead!"

• • • • • • • • • • •

David Richards trained in Miami, Oklahoma with No.3 BFTS and joined 'F' Squadron at RAF Broadwell, Oxfordshire in January 1945. On 14th March 1945 they had a full scale rehearsal called exercise 'Vulture 4' in which he carried the Air Landing Brigade, part of the Battalion HQ of the Royal Ulster Rifles, including the Commanding fficer Lt-Col Jack Carson. Two days later they moved to Gosfield, Essex to prepare for Operation Varsity. 'F' Squadron were to be tugged by 512 and 575 Dakota Squadrons of 46 Group, already based at Broadwell.

David's glider was Horsa RZ 227, chalk mark No.26. He carried a 6-pounder anti-tank gun of HQ Company of the 2nd Ox & Bucks Light Infantry, plus a jeep and a crew of three. Their objective was a garden in a particular house on a secondary road running north from the village of Hamminkeln, landing zone 'O'. This was the northern part of the perimeter around Hamminkeln, which was to be occupied by the Air Landing Brigade. His second pilot was Sgt Jeff Cohen, who had been trained in Florida, USA. On the 23rd, an intelligence report came back with the information that a Panzer Grenadier Unit had occupied the farm around the landing zone. Because of the Dakota's slow towing speed the 46 Group Squadron had to be airborne before the 38 Group Stirlings and Halifaxes.

"For some reason – probably," David thinks, "the very go-ahead manner of S/Ldr Reynolds – we provided the two coup-de-main parties assigned to the bridges over the Issel Canal, but were also at the head of the stream."

His low chalk mark meant in theory David would be among the first to land, but this it reality was not the case.

"I was awoken at 2.30am for breakfast at 3am. The take off was at 6am in semi-darkness with a 16,000lb loaded glider. Contrary to the normal practise, the Dakota became airborne before the glider, upon which I had to struggle to avoid the slipstream in the low-tow position, which was normally only adopted above 500 feet. I had only experienced this once before and was not keen to repeat it. But all was well and the form-up across East Anglia went according to plan. At one point I saw a V1 bomb launched, presumably from an aircraft over the North Sea.

"One of the 'F' Squadron Flight Commanders, Cpt Roger Ford, had a tow-rope break soon after crossing the Belgian frontier, but managed to make a successful landing with his load of a jeep and trailer and rejoin his squadron in Germany within 24 hours. After the pull-off I saw the line of trees where w were detailed to land directly below but at that time we were still only just below 3,000 feet. I promptly made a 90-degree turn to starboard, with full flap, but even with this action it did not appear as if we would make it – then, directly ahead came the village of Hamminkeln. There was nothing else to do but repeat the exercise. By now we were down to 1000 feet and we came under machine-gun fire and were hit a number of times. The jeep, having been hit, began to leak petrol and then a few tracer bullets came through the cockpit and the constant chatter that had been coming from Jeff about the flak stopped abruptly.

"After touching down we ran across the field at a considerable speed and would have probably scored a direct hit on the target if we had not, at a speed of about 40mph, hit a slit trench which had been dug by some methodical Germans. I could not avoid it and went straight through it – in the process taking off the starboard undercarriage leg and the nose wheel. When we came to an abrupt halt, the 200lb steel ramps, down which the jeep and gun were supposed to run, lurched into the cockpit doorway.

"In the confusion, Jeff forgot to remove his regular glider pilots crash helmet (I tink he was the only RAF glider pilot who wore one). This caused him to nearly break his neck, and also to get in my way. The delay caused a corporal in the back of the glider to grab my Bren gun before we all dropped into the convenient slit trench over which RZ 227 had come to rest. The loss of the

Bren gun reduced my personal arms to a single '36' grenade and a bayonet on the end of an entrenching tool handle…"

"Two members of the gun crew we had been carrying had been hit by machine gun fire, one in the buttocks and the other in the foot. In the fields on each side of us were a cluster of gun pits containing a battery of light ack-ack, each having three quadruple 20 mm guns which were happily firing up at the gliders as they came in.

After seeing two gliders hit we decided to do something about it by using a two inch mortar to create a smokescreen. The first round, however, hit the wing of RX 227 and stayed there smoking heavily. As the fuselage from the leaking jeep was now covered in petrol this started a fire. We tried to put the fire out with a hand extinguisher but in the end it went out on its own.

"The next problem was getting the jeep and gun out – not easy as the nose was well dug into the ground. Being a Horsa Mk 2 with a swinging nose section, there was no side door. The only alternative was to remove the tail, but as this was stuck up in the air, even when the eight securing bolts were removed and the control cables cut with an axe the tail stayed in place. By this time an Ox & Bucks officer had turned up to find out what the problem was. He was shocked to see the state of the glider as his had come in unscathed.

• • • • • • • • • •

On the ground John Mansell was serving with the 5/7th Gordon Highlanders. They crossed the Rhine late on the evening of the 23rd March 1945. Early on Saturday morning – the 24th – he witnessed the parachute drop just south of Rees, Northern Germany.

• • • • • • • • • •

St/Sgt Jack Harris was serving with REME, attached to the 158th Infantry Brigade. Prior to the Rhine Crossing my unit had had a very autocratic officer who came into the unit and wanted everything done by the book – so much so that the sergeants got together and en mass asked for a transfer to the Glider Pilot Regiment. However, this transfer request was later withdrawn.

When they crossed the Rhine in March 1945, they were astonished to find many crashed and burnt out gliders and crews. He suddenly thought "there but for the grace of God go I."

• • • • • • • • • •

Pte Lee was in the Royal Artillery and remembers that many of the gliders and soldiers had landed practically on top of a German gun emplacement.

CHAPTER 15

The Men The Gliders Carried

One of three regiments carried in the gliders was the 1st Royal Ulster Rifles. All three were at Bulford Camp before Operation Varsity. The Ulsters were assigned to land on landing zone 'U', south of the village of Hamminkeln. The task of Major Tony Dyball, commanding 'D' Company, was to take the bridge over the Issel River. At 10.25am his glider landed 150 yards from the bridge.

His glider was the first to hit the deck, followed in a matter of seconds by two further gliders. However, they were not part of his party. Those at the front of the glider were thrown out and those at the back were able to get out via the door. During this time the glider was being riddled by machine gun bullets from a range of 75 yards. Fortunately, only one man was killed and two wounded.

The man killed was the wireless operator so Tony was unable to get in touch with any other units as the set itself had been damaged by machine gun fire. In a matter of seconds they were in a trench created by one of the gliders wings and set a up a Bren gun to reply to the enemy fire This silenced the machine gun but another opened up from 30 yards to its left. Eventually the bridge was taken and 50 Germans taken prisoner.

• • • • • • • • • • •

The Support Company HQ of the 1st Royal Ulster Rifles was flown in by F/O Rushworth and F/Sgt Gillets of the RAF. A Landing was made in a small field beside the level crossing in the 2/Ox & Bucks area. The glider lost one wing and the starboard landing wheel in the landing. It was lying on its side when it came to rest but no one was injured in the crash.

The unloading took twenty five minutes owing to the angle at which the glider was lying. This was hindered by fire from a 20mm Anti-Aircraft gun situated in a field on the other side of the railway. No one was hurt, but the glider and jeep were hit.

The railway line was cleared by the 12th (Airborne) Battalion, the Devonshire Regiment, who were under fire from another 20 mm gun position. F/O Rushworth and the Adjutant, Cpt Robin Rigby proceeded down the railway line and eventually made contact on the level crossing with a Lt Laird who had organised the defence of the crossing. Major Charles Vickery, officer commanding 'A' Company, was killed early in the action and the Commanding Officer, Lt-Col Jack Carson was injured when his glider broke in half on landing. On the 24th, they suffered 259 casualties, 16 officers and 243 other ranks.

• • • • • • • • • • •

The landing zone allocated to the 12th (Airborne) Battalion Devonshire Regiment was 'R', to the south west of the village. Their task was to hold the village of Hamminkeln, preventing any enemy movement in or out from the west of the main road and running north and south. The Commanding Officer, Lt-Col Paul Gleadell, was flown in by Major Maurice Priest with an RAF sergeant as second pilot in Horsa 188. Priest was later awarded the DFC.

• • • • • • • • • •

Major Walli Barrow commanding 'B' Company was the only survivor when his glider was hit by anti-aircraft fire as it was about to land. Despite being wounded, he held out for 20 minutes before being captured. With them they had the 3rd Air landing Anti-Tank Battery, Royal Artillery.

• • • • • • • • • •

The task of 'B' company was helped by the Americans of the 17th Airborne Division who had cleared the Landing Zone area of the enemy. On the 24th, they lost 110 killed and 30 wounded.

• • • • • • • • • •

Before they left Bulford Camp in the UK the men of the 12th Devons had been issued with the maroon badge with the winged horse Pegasus. After 8 hours flying in gliders, they were entitled to wear a small sleeve badge depicting a glider.

• • • • • • • • • •

Lieutenant Allanson of 'B' Company saw a glider go down in flames and a tug aircraft crash on top of another glider and its tug – all three going down together.

• • • • • • • • • •

Lieutenant Slade of 'C' Company saw a glider blown to pieces by a direct hit after casting off.

• • • • • • • • • •

Major Palmer of ' D' Company had the nose Perspex of his glider blown in by a burst of fire from a Halifax tail gunner testing his guns. He went on, despite this, to the DZ. As he cast off, the glider/tug combination in front of theirs was shot down by an ME-109 fighter.

• • • • • • • • • •

The Commanding Officer of the 2nd (Airborne) Ox & Bucks Lt-Col Mark Darell-Brown DSO was flown in by S/Ldr V.H. Reynolds who was Commanding 'F' Squadron of the Glider Pilot Regiment. As they came in to land, the co-pilot opened up with a sten gun through the cockpit windshield. They landed near a German gun emplacement and were quickly out of the glider and overpowered the gunners. Over 100 men of 2nd Airborne Ox & Bucks were killed in a short time, mainly in their gliders.

• • • • • • • • • •

Quartermaster Lieutenant Bill Aldworth, had been in the army since 1929 and was a very experienced soldier. He had very little flying experience, however, but nevertheless, when both pilots in his glider were killed at the controls he managed to pull one of them clear and land the glider safely himself, without flaps and at great speed. He was later put up for the DFC by his CO but it was not approved. After the war he rarely talked about it – but on one occasion he did reveal to his sister Majorie that he had felt he 'had to do something' to save the other men on board his glider.

• • • • • • • • • •

Colonel John Tillet, 'D' Company Commander at the time, wrote after the war about the flying of Bill Aldworth.

"As load commanders we officers and senior NCOs had accepted that this might happen. To this end a number of us had some flying experience in our earlier airborne days … some instruction in Tiger Moths, in level flying and landing drill, just in case what did happen to Bill Aldworth should happen in battle to us."

Bill died in 1981, aged 73. He never did know the names of the two pilots who had been killed but it is likely that they were from 'F' Squadron flying out of RAF Gosfield. On Varsity 'F' Squadron had 11 Army and 12 RAF Glider Pilots killed.

• • • • • • • • • •

Major Tod Sweeney was flown in by Cpt McMillen whose second pilot was a Sgt Stevens of the RAF. Their glider was towed by Wg/Cdr Deansley in a Stirling. Cpt McMillen built up quite a bit of speed in order to get below the flak when a very near burst went off under the starboard wing. He called for full flap when they were in position to land but nothing happened.

Sgt Steven's reported that the starboard undercarriage had been hit and the compressed air required for the flap operation had leaked out. This left him flying at 90mph and no means of slowing down. After flying over a large wood between the railway line and the autobahn they found a clearing. He put the glider down hard and dug in the starboard wing to slew him around, and slow the glider down and they stopped without any casualties.

• • • • • • • • • •

Charles Stewart was a member of the 6th Air Landing Brigade HQ. He saw a glider carrying engineers and explosives intended to blow up a roadblock, blow up in a vivid blue flash and fall to the ground in small pieces. Later as his own glider came in to land it was bouncing across a field when his safety belt broke and he crashed head first into the rib of the glider and was knocked unconscious. He came around with a lump behind his ear. It was then that he realised his good luck. A German half-track had blazed away at the glider's crew after they landed with heavy machine gun fire. He was the only one safe in the glider. He slid out and rolled to the far side of the field where he placed a field dressing on his head, which was bleeding.

• • • • • • • • • •

Harry Oakes was a cameraman with the Army Film Unit. He and colleague John Christie were sent from Pinewood Studios only two or three days before the operation. Harry was a cine cameraman and John a stills cameraman. They between them covered the loading sequence and the briefings. Both were parachutists, but when the War Office public relations department insisted that the 6th Air Landing Brigade be covered on Varsity, Harry and John had drawn the short straws. They went in a glider with the HQ of the 12th Devon's from Great Dunmow. Both the glider pilots were from the RAF. They crash landed on the landing zone just outside Hamminkeln in a lot of smoke and light flak. The pilot was unable to pull out of a landing dive. Both pilots, Harry believes, were killed in the crash. A battalion of American paratroopers was passing through the landing zone at the time. As they did, the glider came under sniper fire and casualties were suffered. The Americans soon dealt with the sniper and then pushed on to Hamminkeln.

• • • • • • • • • •

One casualty on landing was the Canadian Broadcasting Correspondent Stanley Maxted, who had already been through the Arnhem experience. His glider suffered a flak hit on the way into the landing zone and he was hit and cut in the head.

• • • • • • • • • •

At the casualty dressing station, Colonel Watts, one of the doctors, describes what he saw that day as "the worst of war… the slaughter and everywhere one looked crashed and burning gliders, and in one, charred bodies. Men were coming from all over in ll manner of transport, even wheelbarrows."

Charles Stewart. [Charles Stewart]

•••••••••••

Often the unsung heroes in battle are the medical orderlies. One such man was Corpral Frederick Topham, serving with the 1st Canadian Parachute Battalion.

At about 1100 hours he answered a cry for help from a wounded man in the open. Two medical orderlies from a field ambulance went out to this man, but both were killed by sniper fire as they knelt beside him.

Despite having witnessed the deaths of these two orderlies, Corporal Topham, regardless of his own safety, advanced through intense fire to attend to the wounded man. As he did so, he was himself shot through the nose. In spite of severe bleeding and intense pain, he completed immediate first aid and carried the wounded man steadily and slowly back through continuous fire to the shelter of a wood.

During the next two hours Corporal Topham refused all offers of medical help for his own wound and continued to work devotedly to bring in the wounded, showing complete disregard for the heavy and accurate enemy fire. It was only when all casualties had been cleared that he consented to his own wound being treated.

His immediate evacuation was ordered, but he objected to this so strongly that he was eventually allowed to return to duty.

On his way back to his company he came across a carrier, which had received a direct hit. Enemy mortar bombs were still dropping around, the carrier itself was burning fiercely and its own mortar ammunition was exploding. An experienced officer on the spot had warned that no one should approach the carrier.

Corporal Topham, however, immediately went out alone in spite of the exploding ammunition and enemy fire and rescued the three occupants of the carrier. He brought these men back across the open field and although one died almost immediately, he arranged for the evacuation of the other two, who undoubtedly owed their lives to his actions.

For his outstanding bravery and devotion to duty during a six-hour period, Topham was later awarded the Victoria Cross.

•••••••••••

Padre Jimmy Mack was a Methodist Minister and joined the Army Padre service in 1944. After training he was posted in 1945 to No 1 Wing of the Glider Pilot Regiment at HQ Gaston Manor, near Watford. He was told that the previous padre, George Pare was still missing from the Arnhem operation in September 1944. To get to know the tug pilots Jimmy would sit between them as they did their 'circuits and bumps'.

"My first experience of gliding was on a miserable winter day, the rain was beating down and bouncing off the runway and the cloud cover total. The pilot went up through the clouds and emerged into blazing sunshine with a blue sky from horizon to horizon and a carpet beneath of blue and silence. Incredible! When we landed the rain was still beating down."

"I had one or two trips with the pilots, testing my stamina and stomach. One army glider pilot seemed over interested in me and kept on asking where I came from and what squadrons I had visited. I suddenly thought there must be a reason for this, as he kept on pumping me for information that he thought I might have, but didn't. It was February 1945, and he wanted to know the timing of the next operation, but he probably knew more than I did."

On the 24th March at Earls Colne the final briefing took place in a huge hangar filled with khaki and blue uniforms.

"The actual flight was dull because I was not in my usual spot between the two pilots. The landing however was something else. There was a lot of noise and the sensation of gathering speed, then we crashed and the floor of the glider seemed to be split as if with a knife. I got out of the glider and the sky was fullof wheeling and diving aircraft. Some had already crash landed. As I stood there, stunned, a glider came in and landed just yards from me, then a voice said 'There's one for you, Padre.' I ran over to see what I could do…

"The rest of the day seemed to consist of gun fire, and I was getting angry because I could not see who was shooting at us. I helped the wounded under cover and into a safe place. I then asked the way to Glider Pilot HQ and in particular to Colonel Murray. I soon found them both. As I sat on the concrete floor we were mortared and I kept thinking what I would do if I got out of this situation. I had wondered what my role was to be behind enemy lines. The best thing I came up with was to attempt to keep the wounded clean. My brother was a doctor in the Royal Army Medical Corps so I had learned from him that the latest antiseptic was acriflavine and I got as many bottles of it in my pack as I could carry, but when the glider crashed so did the bottles. I later learned I could have had this antiseptic in powder form!"

"My transport became a motorbike driven by an RAF glider pilot. This unusual twosome caused much amusement among the Americans in particular, who were lined up before advancing. At times we came under fire from the Germans and had to make emergency stops and undignified dives into holes in the ground by the roadside."

The Royal Ulster Rifles padre had been shot in the eye, so Jimmy took on some of his duties. One of these was to bury members of the Royal Ulster Rifles who were Roman Catholics. The sergeant major in charge was not at all happy about a Protestant Padre conducting the service and forcibly said so.

"I said to him, 'Share the service with me,' recalls Jimmy. 'Take a couple of handfuls of earth and when I come to the bit "Earth to Earth, Ashes to Ashes, Dust to Dust," sprinkle it over all the bodies, Catholic and Protestant alike.'

This he did and seemed satisfied."

Having helped the wounded and buried the dead, Jimmy then found himself in a little church in the village of Hamminkeln.

"The church had three military cemeteries, the dead from the war of 1870, the Great War of 1914/18 and the early part of WWII in 1939. I had buried men from my division the previous day in a field not far from the village. Inside the church I picked up a hymn book and could tell although it was in German by the music that it was Lutheran Church, and found the famous hymn "A safe stronghold our God is still" with words and music by Martin Luther, the first man, since the early church, to teach Christians to sing in their own language. Later, at Twisteden, a collection camp for glider pilots, I used this hymn book, and music was supplied by one of the lads on an accordio that he had won in a card game."

Afteer returning to the UK on 8th May 1945, Jimmy tried to visit, if possible, the homes of the glider pilots he had buried in Hamminkeln. One was in Huddersfield.

"When the lady opened the door and saw me in the uniform of a padre, she could not speak, she was so overcome with grief, knowing why I had come. She said that for the rest of her life she would have an emptiness – nothing could compensate her for the loss of her son."

The only RAF glider pilot who came from Huddersfield was Sgt Tom Whiteley, who served with 'C' Squadron and is now buried in the Reichswald War Cemetery, Germany.

Padre George Pare later turned up, having been safely hidden by the Dutch ever since the Arnhem operation.

Padre Jimmy Mack of the Glider Pilot Regiment. [J. Mack]

Glider pilot John Crane stands next to the village signpost after liberation. [John Crane]

CHAPTER 16

Aftermath

Frank Haddock was relived to find himself in good company again, even though they were a motley group of about 60 British and US Paratroopers, Air Landing Brigade and Glider pilots, including several from 'D' Squadron, his own squadron. Two anti-tank guns were already in place this added to the one they had brought to the farm. As slit trenches were needed, 100 German prisoners of war being held in a barn were brought out to use their expertise.

"They were only too keen to help," remembers Frank. "Four prisoners dug a very neat line of defence trenches in double quick time while I and the others managed to scrounge some hot tea and nibbled away at our emergency rations of hard chocolate and biscuits. The bottoms of the trenches were lined with logs, which were then covered with a thick layer of straw. Even so, it was going to be a long cold night, but spirits were high."

"Just after midnight, two figures were seen creeping up the road which ran east-west past the side of the farm. The challenge was called out 'Hither' and repeated, but no password 'Thither' was received in return. The two figures halted about 70 yards away and turned in their tracks. Immediately, one of the paratroopers to our left opened up with a Bren gun and both fell.

"I awoke to find I was lying in several inches of water which had seeped into the trench. This did nothing to improve my spirits, but all my cursing and moaning only brought the remark 'If you can't take a joke you shouldn't have joined!'

"The area of the landings had been sown with anti-glider poles and wires. The woods alongside concealed an 88mm SP gun and other lighter weapons which had been waiting for us. In the centre of the field, in total isolation, was what at first glance appeared to be an undamaged Horsa. Closer examination revealed it to be the glider flown by Johnny O'Sullivan, a good friend, also from 'D' Squadron. John was a blond-headed lad from Cardiff; he had a brilliant mind and a wonderful wit and had provided much humour during training in 1944. He was still strapped in his seat, where he had died from a burst of machine gun fire that had struck him in the back. Over the road nearby we found two German paratroopers shot while trying to infiltrate allied lines, but seeing their grey faces I could not generate the hatred I thought I would feel, only a sense of futility of war and thoughts of the loss to their families back home. It seemed a strange way to feel with Johnny only yards away.

"Further down the road a Horsa had hit the roof of a farm cottage and somersaulted on to its back. One of the pilots was Sgt Grant, who I had travelled up to London with just a few weeks before...

"The next day tank engines were heard, and within minutes two very large tanks were rumbling up the road towards us, upon which we froze. When they arrived at the road junction opposite the farm entrance they stopped and the crews, adorned in black berets, emerged from the turrets. They were Canadians and they calmly strolled into the farmhouse asking who was brewing coffee...

"After three days, the order came for Glider pilots to withdraw; a tented camp had been set up t Xanten. From there we moved on to Helmont, Holland, where we stayed in a school. At the end of the week we returned to the UK, via Eindhoven in a Dakota, landing at Down Ampney. Here we waited for aircraft to take us to Tarrant Rushton. Then came an order that all our kit had to be cleared by HM Customs. The air became electric and the language strong, the bearer of the message was soon told where to go and what to say. He came back to say that Customs had decided to let us proceed on this occasion without inspection…

"The following day we were debriefed by the Squadron Adjutant and I was asked if I had lost any kit. When I said I had used my field dressing on a casualty he said, 'In that case you will need to submit a written report detailing how you came to dispose of it.' In utter disbelief I stared at him. He seemed not to sense my disgust until I gave him a blank refusal. At this the officer reluctantly said it could be 'overlooked in the circumstances…'"

• • • • • • • • • •

Dennis Mills and Arthur Pogson also reached the farm. During the afternoon while Frank and the others had been preparing defensive positions, Arthur had been wandering around the farm. When someone asked him if he could give a hand with guarding the 100-odd prisoners who had been crowded into the barn, being a streetwise lad from Leeds he was quick to realise that a large number of bodies under cover in a confined space would produce heat – heat that would not be available to the men in the slit trenches, so he happily volunteered. However, the best laid plans…

"The prisoners only had enough space to stand or sit but not to lie down. This gave rise to arguments on and off all night. It came to a head when one particularly obnoxious character started to kick out wildly at those around him. Soon there was the danger of a riot. Nowhere in the training for this operation had it covered the handling of prisoners of war."

Arthur sought the help of S/Sgt Andy Kerr, and drew on his vast experience as a glider pilot and in other military matters.

"We both stepped back into the barn and the German causing all the trouble was told to stand to attention with his back to the wall 'schnell' if not sooner. He soon got the message after seeing a wild-eyed Scot, complete with a ginger moustache and two guns staring at him. Andy knew that many Germans had a smattering of English so he turned to me and said, 'If he gives you any more trouble, shoot him.' As he left, he turned and said, "and if you do not want to shoot him call me and I will…" Not a sound was heard for the rest of the night!"

The troublesome man turned out to be an arrogant Major who felt that his rank entitled him to more space.

• • • • • • • • • •

John Stone and Jack Radcliffe had nothing to do but stay out of trouble. Their glider, which had landed intact, was being used as a temporary holding pen for prisoners.

• • • • • • • • • •

William Davies and Wally Martin were in a small orchard on the right hand side of the road from Hamminkeln into Germany. Across their front was a railway line, which ran along flat ground with no embankment. There was a small railway station. In front of the line was a canal with a bridge over it where the road on their right crossed. The holding of this bridge was the role of the Royal Ulsters, the men they had carried. William takes up the story:

"We set about digging a slit trench about 4 feet by 2 feet and 4 feet deep. As we dug this trench with our entrenching tools, a group of soldiers came up and started to dig four fairly large square holes into which they put a mortar, probably a 3-inch. The officer in charge came up to us and suggested we move away, saying, 'When we start firing the mortars at Gerry, he will more then likely fire back at us.' We needed no further encouragement and left! We moved about 50 yards across the orchard and began to dig another trench.

"After this we decided to have a snack. We found the tea in the ration packs awful. It was made by putting a cube, like an oxo cube, into boiling water, which had been boiled on a small methylated spirit stove. The cube consisted of tea, sugar and powdered milk. The tea came up with a yellow froth on top and it looked gritty, but at least it was hot and sweet.

"One thing that disturbed me was that no more then 20 yards away lay the body of an army glider pilot – a friend of mine. He was a friendly man from Yorkshire. He was unmarked and looked as if he was sleeping. A badly smashed glider lay nearby and it would appear that he had been thrown through the plastic nose of the cockpit when it hit the ground.

"The medical orderlies came out to collect him and as they looked at his identify discs I went over and told them who he was. This was something you didn't learn in training – seeing men killed for real.

"Then some big guns opened up and the explosions came near, this was the Germans responding to the mortars. Wally and I began to dig all the way to Australia…

"The next day we heard that the Germans were setting fire to the gliders. An Auster plane was flying around all the time spotting for the artillery. If they saw anything on the ground they reported it and the guns did their job. As it was flying nearby, there was a sharp crack of a light flak gun and a large chunk of the Auster's wing came fluttering down. The pilot was able to land some distance away from us. He was soon replaced by another plane…

"Near the orchard was a large house. As we looked around the area Wally found a black holster with a pistol, and as I looked around I found another holster, this time in brown leather. Having checked they were not booby-trapped we picked them up. The pistol was a 9mm Luger, which could use Sten gun ammunition. I pointed into the air and pulled the trigger upon which it fired. We quickly removed the ammunition and put the safety catch on…

"The CO said we had to move back towards the Rhine, as German tanks could be heard coming. The CO's batman turned up in a long flat cart pulled by a horse. All the kit was loaded on to the cart and the men marched alongside. We went through the village of Hamminkeln, through which British troops were pouring towards Germany. Later that day we stopped at a farm and took up a defensive position. One of the flight CO's got some German prisoners to dig a slit trench for him. When they got down to 3 feet they stopped, but were told to dig deeper. They made signs that if they dug any deeper they would hit water, but were told to continue. Sure enough, as the Germans dug deeper, up came the water…

"The next day we boarded trucks and crossed the Rhine. We were surprised at the width of the river – it certainly looked a long way from bank to bank and was flowing quite swiftly. It had been on our minds, with thoughts of Arnhem, that we may have had to swim for it if the operation went wrong. We had been issued with blow-up life jackets like a long straight sausage about 3 feet long. Seeing how big the river was, we were glad that we didn't have to use them…

"We crossed over a pontoon bridge near Xanten. It was here that Winston Churchill had been based, watching the battle develop. Here we were put in a tented camp.

The 28th March was my 22nd birthday. We again boarded trucks and set off for Helmond in Holland, where we were billeted in a school. On Good Friday 1945, we were taken to an airfield at Eindhoven and then to the UK in a Dakota, landing at RAF Fairford, Gloucestershire.

"On landing, HM Customs promptly boarded the aircraft. Considering that we had left the UK without any money and that we had not been anywhere to have spent it, the customs officers were given plenty of looks that would have killed. We were then taken by truck to RAF Shobdon, Herefordshire.

● ● ● ● ● ● ● ● ● ●

After landing and getting clear of their glider, Frank Hendry and Mike Odlum heard troops in a jeep hailing them, saying that they were in a minefield.

"We ran clear of it, thrusting our bodies forward to minimise the risk of injury should there be an explosion," remembers Frank. "As we did, a Liberator on a re-supply run was hit and on fire as it zoomed low overhead on its way to destruction. We made it out of the minefield safely and on arrival at our rendezvous area dug a trench to hold both of us.

"We were last to arrive so Mike and I were nearer any possible enemy attack than the rest. Mike had reported his wound and was sent to see the medics. At the time they were only dealing with seriously wounded men and, as he was not losing blood, he had to wait for another day or two. Near to the position a train had been derailed. The train driver was standing near the engine, bleeding quite profusely and being attended to by one or two others. Later we moved to a safer position on the perimeter, facing the territory between us and the American landings to the south. I never even saw Hamminkeln, the town at the centre of our landing.

"We had been warned that we must be prepared for attacks by upwards of 60 German tanks. The password for the first day of the operation was 'Oranges', the response 'Lemons'. During the early hours of the following morning, while it was still dark, it was my turn to report our position at Squadron headquarters. It was moonlight and with the possibility of infiltration by German troops and not knowing the route other than by vague directions, I set off alone. I decided to keep in the moonlight, as the balance was clearly in favour of showing myself to what must have been a majority of 'friendly' forces. As quick as a flash, two British soldiers jumped out from some thickets and held a bayonet to my stomach. One of them said the password to Frank, but it was the one for the following day. This was 'Hundreds' and the reply should be 'Thousands' but all I could utter was 'Lemons'. This convinced them that I was a German infiltrator, upon which one slipped a bullet into the breech of his rifle ready to kill me. They were Geordies, so would not suffer an nonsense. I started to talk about football and in particular one or two of the great games of recent years and players of note. Fortunately, this convinced them.

"The next day at Squadron HQ we had 'compo ration porridge' – a horrible mixture of porridge, dry milk and sugar. As I sat eating it, the word went up that a German attack was coming, and everyone rushed towards their positions, reaching for guns and grenades. The 'attack' turned out to be a herd of cows, who were mooing to be milked. As there was no threat from the enemy, we pilots began to learn how to milk the cows, squirting milk direct from our udders into our compo porridge!

"The weather was the best that I can ever remember for March and enabled the air support to drop supplies and contain the German armour whose forces threatened us for some days. An Auster spotter plane would take up a position about a mile from the allied positions, and above the enemy lines. Shortly afterwards, five Typhoons would circle. Each would peel off and hurl rockets into any German armour that showed itself. The Auster would have intelligence of any tanks and armoured vehicles hidden in the many wooded areas in the region, so the Typhoons could harass and destroy the enemy, depriving them of a safe place to hide. As each wave of five Typhoons left, another arrived. This went on to dusk each day.

"After about four days I awoke to see two German Tiger tanks – the most formidable tank of all time – that had penetrated our positions. One was in a duel with an anti-tank crew and the other was looking for targets…

"We were ordered to take out our yellow identity cloths and lie down in their dugouts with the yellow showing clearly to the sky to enable the Typhoons to establish the British positions on the ground. Suddenly, in addition to the normal five Typhoons, a further five turned up. They came screaming down, one by one. The earth shook around us and we were covered in debris. After the attack both tanks were engulfed in flames and utterly destroyed…

"On the eighth day the distant rumble of tanks was heard. This time they were allied tanks on their way into Germany accompanied by troops of the Welsh Division.

"Two days later we pulled out still with our horse and cart and carrying our kit. Then on to Helmond and then Eindhoven, from where we flew home. It was August 1945, before we left our army friends and returned to the RAF."

• • • • • • • • • • •

John Barnsley was soon captured by the Germans. He and others were taken to a house, still occupied by the owners, who provided blankets for the injured men.

"After a short while we were marched away, and as we went on more allied personnel were picked up as prisoners. There were bodies of airborne troops lying all over the place, waiting for collection. As we went through what I think was Wesel we saw only two buildings still standing amongst the rubble.

"As we marched on and the numbers increased we were provided with a lorry to take us on further. The sounds of gunfire could be heard and we soon found ourselves in the middle of an artillery bombardment. We had heard of Montgomery's 'artificial moonlight' and now we found ourselves under it. However, it soon stopped and we were on our way. After travelling all night we found ourselves in a farmyard where we were interrogated by a German officer. He spoke fluent English but, to his credit, he only expected number, rank and name from us.

"We were then put on a train in a wagon marked (in German) '40 men or 8 horses' – but it turned out to be about 100 men and no horses in our wagon! Here we stayed for six to seven days. We took it in turns to stand up and lie down. Exercise periods were once or twice a day and food an occasional luxury. This turned out to be black bread and a white grease the Germans called margarine. Eventually we arrived at Stalag IIB, Fallingbostel, Germany. When we arrived, it was already very overcrowded, as there had been an influx of RAF prisoners from Stalag Luft III, at Sagan & Belaria, Near Berlin. The huts were overcrowded and the bunk beds had long since been burnt for firewood. The previous winter, latrines had been dug at several points around the compound and were in full view of local people passing by.

"By this time, with the end of the war in sight, the guards were becoming edgy and one had to be very careful not to go over the inner wire. The meals consisted of a slice of black bread again with the white margarine and a cup or bowl of a watery substance with some 'floating bits'. I felt that even pigs would have turned their noses up at it.

"While in the camp it was common practise to 'swap identities' with other POWs. A friend of my mate Danny Bruce, an RAF F/Lt, swapped with an army private, which meant he could get an early release – which he did. When he got back to the UK he contacted Danny's parents to say that he was OK and they in turn got in touch with my parents to let them know I was OK.

They soon left Fallingbostel on one of the infamous forced marches that took place as the war came to an end. The German guards were ordered to march their prisoners away from the advancing Allied armies so prevent them from being liberated. Meanwhile the Russians were fast closing in from the opposite direction.

"When the sound of Russian guns faded we began to wonder what had happened to the war. For days we marched, about 150 prisoners with five guards who were all of pensionable age. We ate where we could, mainly in fields, eating root crops, sleeping out in the open or in farmyards. By this time we had met up with a Sgt Hughes, a wireless-operator who had been shot down while flying in a Dakota, one of the tug aircraft of 512 Squadron.

"When we arrived at the River Elbe we found a barge loaded with Red Cross parcels. It worked out at one parcel per man, so our meal that night was better than it had been for some time. The parcels soon went and our next meal was in a field, eating Swede peelings… In one village we came across a very thin, bony horse – it became our supper that night…

"We had been marching 20 to 25 miles per day and had now marched about 200 to 250 miles. We had not had a wash since the 24th March. In the Red Cross parcels there were bars of soap especially designed for prisoners of war. It was floating soap, so you wouldn't lose it if bathing in a river or lake and to prevent it getting soft. The Elbe was soon full of naked prisoners trying to wash. The problem was that it wouldn't lather – it was rather like trying to wash with a piece of plastic. While this was going on, two RAF Typhoons appeared. They were after a nearby Luftwaffe aerodrome which they started to shoot up…

"The weather turned cold and it began to rain and then to snow. We came upon a farm and settled down in the barn for the night. During the night, a Mosquito attacked the barn and within a few minutes it was on fire. Seven men were killed. The rest of the night was spent in a ploughed field…

"The next day we came upon some Allied airborne troops, but they did not stop to chat, not quite knowing who we were. Further on, in the direction they had come from, we came upon a German convoy which had surrendered. Their jeep-type vehicles were commandeered and we headed for home… An Ordnance unit gave us food and petrol. When we arrived at a town called Celle we found a barracks guarded by a Scot who refused us entry and suggested we find the Town Marshal. He was not interested in helping us and suggested we find the airfield, which we duly did, but here, as before, the RAF Police refused us entry. By now they we had been joined by others who had commandeered a bus and between us we made it clear to the police that we were going through whether they lifted the barrier or not. They soon relented and let us in…

"The next morning we boarded the first Dakota out which took us to Brussels and 48 hours later we landed at RAF Cosford, which had been set up as a reception centre for prisoners of war. Here they did a magnificent job in providing for our every need and got us on leave as soon as possible…"

● ● ● ● ● ● ● ● ● ● ●

In the aftermath of the Varsity landings, the task given to Bleddwyn Williams and the other glider pilots in his squadron, was to search for glider crews who had not reported in after landing.

"It turned out to be a heart-rending task as we came across glider after glider with the crew still on board, either dead or fatally injured. The German 88mm guns had taken a terrible toll and had caused a number of gliders to crash in areas far away from their designated landing zones. It was our belief that the enemy knew the date and time of Operation Varsity and were well prepared. I knew for certain that there had been a breach of security at our own airfield. The weekend before Varsity, my wife (who I had married in September 1944 and who lived near the airfield at RAF Rivenhall) questioned me as to whether or not the operation was to take place on the following Saturday the 24th. I was astonished and asked her where the information had come from, because at the time I knew nothing of the date or the destination of the operation. It transpired that the wives of some of the RAF

Welsh rugby star and glider pilot, Bleddwyn Williams. [Bleddwyn Williams]

ground crew, who worked with her at the local factory, had made it known that they had been warned by their husbands that they were not to make any arrangements for the following week as they would be involved in preparations for an airborne invasion of Germany... I reported this back to Major Bartlett, the 'A' Squadron Commanding Officer, who was completely shocked by the revelation and quickly issued instructions to that all personnel were to be 'confined to camp'...

"Before Operation Varsity I had been selected to play rugby for the British Combined Services XV against a Dominion XV, due to take place at Leicester on 30th March 1945. I was resigned to the fact that I would miss the match, but as it happened, the 53rd Welsh Division relieved our position in the field on 29th March, only 24 hours before the match was due to be played. I arrived in Leicester via Rivenhall, where I collected my rugby kit and my wife two hours before the kick off. It turned out to be a splendid game – and I was delighted to contribute by scoring two tries..."

• • • • • • • • • •

Eric Ayliffe continued towards the bridge and ducked for cover as a German tank rolled past them.

"We had nothing at the time to fire at it," I recalls. Peter Ince and I had parted company with our passengers from the Royal Ulster Rifles and made our way to our designated rendezvous area. There we helped stretcher bearers carry the wounded to a Field Dressing Station, where we found a young doctor busy operating. Only days before, the same doctor had delivered a lecture to us back in England."

Eric and 'Jock' Davies looked for arms and found a Piat gun, which they were told to fire towards an enemy gun emplacement.

"We put a projectile each side of the enemy and they promptly surrendered. Little did they know that the recoil from the second shot had bowled us over and down a sandy bank! After a German Home Guard and an SS Officer had surrendered I found myself, along with a paratrooper, in charge of them. As I marched them off I could not resist ordering them to give an 'eyes right' to an Airborne Colonel. On seeing my pilot's wings he was kind enough to congratulate the RAF pilots on their showing...

"The first few days after the landings were difficult. Casualties were piling up and dead cattle were everywhere. We found a horse, petrified with fright, stood like a statue and still harnessed to a cart. One glider had crashed into a fence surrounding a camp of 'slave' labourers. These pitiful creatures had to be rounded up at bayonet point for their own safety...

"Typhoons were flying around the area constantly. One knocked out an 88mm gun which had been firing over our heads only 100 yards away. A short while after this we called up the fighters to silence an enemy loudspeaker which kept playing 'Lilly Marlene' over and over again. They were only happy to oblige...

"My Sten gun had jammed, so I swapped it for a German MP40 automatic pistol, this however had a downside. After I had fired a few bursts at an enemy motorcyclist, which caused some traffic chaos, I came under 'friendly fire' which was distinctly unfriendly! Some of our troops had recognised the sound of an enemy weapon and returned fire. After that I felt safer with a British rifle...

"When we were flown back to RAF Down Apney on 30th March we were met by HM Customs, who wanted to know where we had spent the last few days! The answers we gave us are unprintable, but totally appropriate considering the circumstances. When tempers began to rise they diplomatically ran out of declaration forms...

"Those of us that returned from 'F' Squadron went back to RAF Fairford. Our kit had been laid out for us, but the empty beds brought home the reality that we had been to war – 11 RAF glider pilots and 14 Army glider pilots had failed to return..."

• • • • • • • • • •

"John Rayson was aboard a jeep crossing a field when another jeep was seen coming the other way…

"We stopped and asked them about the farmhouse ahead. They said it was occupied by Germans. The captain who was with us said, 'We were told that we had to go to this farmhouse and we are going in…' So in we went and pulled up at the front door. Opening the door was nerve racking, to say the least, but when we got inside the only occupiers were the farmer and his wife, who were equally frightened.

"We eventually reached a grassy bank, above which was a spinney. We came under fire but were saved by the cover of the bank. After about half an hour the Americans started to land in a field between the spinney and another farm. They should, in fact, have landed a mile to the south, but were very welcome as there was some concern about Germans in the next farmhouse. There was a glider quite near the spinney and the Americans wished to unload it, but every time they tried to lift the nose off, the Germans opened fire and they had to take cover. Eventually an American approached us and asked for assistance. Later, a fighting patrol was arranged to clear the Germans out of the farmhouse. The American who passed this message on to us was killed as he tried to get back to his glider. Soon the Germans were driven off and the Americans continued to unload. By this time, several more gliders had landed, which may have had some bearing on the German retreat…

"Although I saw a number of dead Germans, dead horses and cows and several dead Americans, I did not see one British casualty. We set about forming a perimeter defence and decided we ought to dig slit trenches. As there were many German prisoners around I suggested we get them to dig the trenches. F/Lt Ken Ashurst, my flight commander asked me to investigate this. When I went into the farmyard I was amazed to find about 250 prisoners guarded by just one soldier sitting on a wheelbarrow with a Bren gun across his knees. When I asked if I could have one or two to dig slit trenches his reply was 'Take your pick…' When I asked him if he was worried about guarding so many prisoners on his own he replied 'I think its all right…' I replied 'Its just as well you have got that machine gun,' pointing at the Bren gun. Then the soldier said, 'Yes, but what they don't know is that it has no firing pin!'

"I chose six Germans, all Luftwaffe ground crew and only about 16 years old. They were very anxious to please and dug excellent trenches. I also tried to milk the cows but did not know how. I was helped by a soldier who was looking around for loot. I didn't find any, but at least I found out how to milk a cow, so we were able to have fresh milk that night and the next morning…

"The time came to move out and it was suggested to Major Ian Toler, the commanding officer of 'B' Squadron, that we harness up the horse and connect it to the wagon to take all our equipment to the Rhine. He did not think it a good idea and the horse and cart were left behind. We arrived at a tented area and it was here that the chance came to clean my rifle, which was filthy. I put a round in the breach and fired it to clear the muck out of the barrel, then used a pull-through and finished by oiling it…

"The next day we travelled by truck to Helmond and were put up in a hotel. While there we took in an ENSA party that was entertaining the troops…

When we arrived back at Earls Colne via Down Ampney an enquiry was set up to find out what had happened to the kit which had not come back. It was amazing how many service watches went missing on Operation Varsity! I then spent a month at the School of Infantry, Warminster. Here we spent a certain amount of time under fire, which proved a very valuable experience. I only wished I had been posted here before taking part in the Rhine Crossing…"

• • • • • • • • • •

St/Sgt Spowart and F/O Ankers of 'F' Squadron, flying glider number 273, landed in an open field near Rheinberg and immediately came under fire from a farmhouse thought to be a German HQ. Both pilots were shot through the head and killed. They were found later by the Americans, propped up against the main wheel of the glider. The glider hydraulics had been damaged so in an attempt to unload the Bren gun carrier it was driven through the doors of the glider. However, in doing so the carrier was damaged and rendered useless. The men on board formed a defensive ring around the glider but when they were down to three they had no alternative but to surrender. Driver Harry Baker was also killed. Private Bates was wounded and died 4 days later.

Ken Selley of the Parachute Regiment and a post-war Mayor of Torquay had been attached to this glider at the last moment. He was taken prisoner and ended up at POW Camp 11b at Fallingbostel where he discovered that many of the men captured at Arnhem were prisoners. The camp was not far from Belsen...

• • • • • • • • • •

John Herold found Sgt Geoffrey Grant approximately 10 yards from his glider. He had a number of bullet wounds in his back. He was only 20 years old and had undergone his pilots training in Miami, Oklahoma. He and his wife Barbara had been married only three months when he was killed. After his death, Barbara gave birth to twin sons, Geoffrey and Anthony.

John was only able to secure Geoffrey's pay book and wallet from his right hand breast pocket

Sergeant Geoffrey Grant. [Mrs Grant]

as he was under fire himself from small arms and light anti-aircraft cannon fire.

John came to the conclusion that both pilots had been killed in flight by machine gun fire. Their glider, No 69, had fallen out of the sky, out of control, and crashed into the side of a farmhouse. It then caught fire and exploded, catching

Geoffrey Grant's crashed glider. [Mrs Grant]

the farmhouse alight in the process. There were seven other bodies in the wreckage, including the first pilot F/O Robert Jamieson. It was thought that the glider crashed at about 11.15am.

"Shortly before we left the battlefield," John remembers "an army padre conducted a short service in the corner of a tented area. I was very moved and still remember the padre's eloquence, sense of occasion and understanding. I was later told that this padre had done much to help the injured and dying in the open on the battlefield, the enemy included. I felt his job was far more arduous then ours…

"When I arrived back in the UK I was posted to 296 Halifax Squadron at Earls Colne. Having had the experience of being tugged, I was now a tug pilot. We also did parachute dropping and acted as the GPO, carrying mail to the Far East…"

John went on to become a group captain, serving in the Engineering Branch and became the senior member of his branch, finally retiring in 1974.

• • • • • • • • • • •

Maurice Laing and his second pilot Sgt Derek Hammerton were pinned down by enemy fire after landing.

Maurice tells the story as follows:

"We decided the only thing to do was get out the Piat gun. This, however, was still in the glider, so we arranged with the troops we had carried to cause as much diversion as possible while we went back into the glider to get the Piat gun, together with the ammunition. We were able to do so before any serious fire came our way, but as the Lieutenant in charge of the troops got out of the glider he was killed. The senior NCO, a St/Sgt, set off with two or three of the party to take the level crossing house and silence the fire coming from that direction. This they did, but they were killed in doing so.

This left Maurice and Derek Hammerton, who were not soldiers but airmen, in charge of the troops who were left, all privates who had not been in action before. They came under fire from the canal bridge (the canal at that position was contained in an embankment about ten to twelve feet high).

No other gliders arrived on Maurice and Derek's LZ. They later found that one had landed with the main force and the other three had been lost.

"We soon set up the Piat gun, but not being soldiers, we forgot to fuse the first round of ammunition, with the result that our first shot hit a wire fence only 15 feet away. Realising our mistake the next round of ammunition was fused and our firepower directed at a house 200 yards beyond the bridge, from which most of the enemy fire was coming. We scored a hit and the fire from the house ceased, enabling us and the remaining troops to proceed to the bank of the canal and the bridge. Here, all opposition from the enemy was silenced by the use of hand grenades."

"Allied motorised infantry soon arrived and we were told to make for our rendezvous or RV point – a farm near Hamminkeln. When we arrived we found our commanding officer, S/Ldr Reynolds, riding around on a farm horse, far too busy to worry about our arrival. After a good meal supplied by the farmer's wife we were shown to comfortable beds and had a good 12 hours sleep.

"On arriving back in the UK via Eindhoven 'F' Squadron merged with 'E' Squadron and here I stayed until April when I became ill and ended up in at RAF Wroughton in an isolation ward. I was diagnosed as having glandular fever. Here I spent six weeks and during this time I was transferred to 'N' Squadron at Fairford. In June 1945 I was discharged back to civilian life…"

For Maurice, Operation Varsity proved to be the beginning of a lifetime friendship with his second pilot Derek Hammerton which continued until Derek's death in 1997.

Maurice, now Sir Maurice, has always remembered Operation Varsity in some detail, but had forgotten that he was never de-briefed by his squadron commander S/Ldr Reynolds, nor was he ever aware of what happened to the 'Coup de Main' party he carried to the Rhine.

A crashed glider on the railway line at Hamminkeln.

• • • • • • • • • •

Jim Rudkin having been thrown through the front of his glider cockpit, was taken to a field hospital and from there by ambulance to Eindhoven.

"After an operation I came to with Plaster of Paris on both legs. I was transferred to Brussels and after a few days, being a priority case, flown in a Dakota to RAF Lyneham, and from there to RAF Hospital Wroughton. It was here that I was operated on by S/Ldr Evans, whose skill I am certain saved my right foot. I remember hearing Evans explaining to visiting doctors how my ankle had been badly infected and how, by making two incisions on the other side, he had drained the ankle.

"I awoke after the first operation with plaster up to the top of my right leg and a half plaster on my left leg. I lay in bed for about two weeks, not taking any interest in anything around until suddenly I felt somewhat better and began to communicate with the other patients. After five months in bed and six months convalescence, I was discharged from the RAF in April 1946."

• • • • • • • • • •

Sydney Grieve's memories of the aftermath of the Operation Varsity landings is as follows:

"I remember that as we dug holes for cover the water seeped in quite rapidly so we were directed down the road to a farm by a senior NCO. Having done our job as pilots we were now available for any duties that came along…

"The damage to the forests in the region over the River Rhine was devastating, as though a huge scythe had been used to cut the trees approximately 15 to 20 feet from the ground…

"After two or three days the 51st Highland Division came striding along in single file, followed by tanks. Just prior to leaving the battlefield area we endeavoured to have a look around on a German two-stroke motorbike, but despite a long search we could not find our glider…

"We were flown back to a base on Salisbury Plain and then taken to Larkhill Camp where our kit from Great Dunmow had been forwarded and was waiting for us when we arrived…"

• • • • • • • • • •

Cy Henson decided that they were not going to be any further use to the operation by staying in the house they had occupied. The other problem was the prisoners.

"We decided to take them with us and made for the railway line. This was going to be a cross-country trip, and to the prisoners this was a gentle stroll, as they had no kit to carry. I suggested to a GPR St/Sgt that these former members of the master race should assist with the load, but I was told that it was against the Geneva Convention and we would suffer dire consequences if captured. When we reached the railway line we found that the signal box had a Horsa glider stuck in its roof." [Any historical record of this does not appear to have survived.]

"When I heard that other members of my squadron were in the town of Hamminkeln I set off with an army padre to find them. Despite sniper fire I found my flight holed up in a bakery at Hamminkeln. The family who owned the bakery were also in the cellar with them...

"In the evening, a Lieutenant in the Intelligence Corps came to see us, wearing a white sheepskin jacket with the wool on the outside. Thinking he would not last long dressed in such a way I saw fit to relieved him of his very up-market Sten gun, which had a beautiful polished butt and a camouflaged barrel; in return I left my standard Sten gun, which had got slightly bent in the landing...

"I spent the night with my flight commander, Cpt Mike Corrie. We shared a double bed in the upstairs bedroom to get some well-earned and much-needed sleep...

"As we looked around the town I found a very nice tailor's shop in which I spotted a bow tie, which I promptly put on and became a source of amusement until a senior officer came along whereupon the bow tie vanished...

"At a butcher's shop I saw what I thought was a tin of bully beef, which I took back for the evening meal. However, it turned out to be a block of wood with a picture stuck on it, used for display purposes only...

"There were a lot of bikes around the town and I thought that the section could make use of them, but any that did not have three speed gears were rejected. The next plan was to get a cart to carry all our kit, which included six silk parachutes. Soon an NCO turned up with a horse and cart which he parked in the yard along with the bikes...

"However, as we set off, a jeep pulled up sharply alongside and having put on my bow tie once again, I rapidly pulled the zip of my smock up to cover it, then threw up one of my best airborne salutes – with the hand quivering in front of the forehead – but all to no avail...

"In the jeep was a very senior officer, all red tabs, red-faced and furious. It was bad enough that we looked like Fred Carno's army with a mixture of RAF and Army uniforms, but the bikes and horse and cart just did it for him. He said, 'You flew in here... now march out like soldiers!'

"The cart had to be unloaded and we each had to carry our own kit. We were about 20 minutes behind the rest of the men who had gone on foot. We arrived at a tented area outside Nijmegen, having been picked up by lorries on the way. My only regret is that I never did find out who that senior officer was...

"The next day we flew back to Down Ampney and then in a 3-ton truck drove to Fargo. En route we stopped at a pub to telephone our folks that we were safe. The locals were amazed to see 15 men getting out of a truck wearing German military hats, all brandishing weapons and wanting a drink immediately! The journey was a cold one, as the truck did not have a cover on it. However, when we arrived it transpired that the effects of the alcohol had allowed most to sleep as we hugged the floor to avoid the effects of the cold slipstream.

Some years ago, Cy presented the up-market Sten gun to the Army Aviation Museum at Middle Wallop. Having been deactivated and repainted it looked like new and was put on display in the museum.

● ● ● ● ● ● ● ● ● ● ●

Ivan Lancaster remembers setting off across the fields with his first pilot Ted Barton for their allotted RV point.

"As we trotted past some farm outbuildings, a paratrooper drew our attention to a spray of machine gun bullets which had hit the brick wall behind us without us hearing a thing...

"Around the corner, a party of about 40 paratroopers had gathered. We saw a German soldier face down on the ground, protesting fiercely. Sitting astride him was a paramedic, who was using a knife to dig a bullet from the protesting German's backside. It was a such bizarre sight that we fell about laughing...

"Having established our whereabouts we made our way to the arranged rendezvous. Here it had been planned that some 45 glider pilots would meet up and with the Royal Ulsters proceed to and then attack a nearby bridge. In the event, less than half the men turned up and only 8 were left to hold a farmhouse 500 yards away. Before we moved off, a German soldier came down the earthen road. He was wearing only his boots and trousers and had his hands in the air. One of the glider pilots shouted to him and then shot him. [A photograph of the dead German appeared in the *London Illustrated News* a week later.]...

"When we arrived at the farm we were met by an elderly housewife and her young daughter. After going into the ground floor cattle pens, one of the glider pilots heard a noise, kicked open the door and opened fire. The result – one dead cow...

"A German SS Colonel was put in an empty pen and guarded by a paratrooper Lance Corporal who was all for taking him out and shooting him, risking any possible reprisals. The German was later highly delighted to be moved to a POW compound in one piece. Everybody was very tense and strung up...

"A German fighter had attacked a party of paratroopers guarding a T-Junction when it was in turn attacked by six Typhoons and three Tempests. The German pilot turned his aircraft upside down and baled out, but it did not save him, he was shot by the paratroopers on his way down by parachute...

"Later Ted and I located the very gun battery we had flown in with and were given hot tea and sweets. Then came the re-supply drop. Chutes of all colours began to come down, one a bright red. I thought this must be special and went out to retrieve it. I tried to open it with my army knife, taking some 20 minutes, during which I came under sniper fire. I finally got the container open to discover it was loaded with six 25lb shells...

"I was then asked, as the sole glider pilot, to join a parachute officer with six jeeps and 12 men. Their task was to visit their crashed Hamilcar glider and retrieve its load of 650 25lb shells, which were urgently needed. We arrived at the glider safely, where as a glider pilot I was expected to advise them to how to unload it. Even though I had never even been near a Hamilcar, let alone flown one, we managed to get a side hatch open to find a stack of large wicker baskets, secured by ropes and tied down inside the glider. Once again my army knife came in handy and I got to work cutting the securing ropes. As each was undone, the paratroopers began to load the jeeps...

"I took a rest and let one of the other men carry on. I and the parachute officer were

Help is at hand.

standing under the port wing of the glider when suddenly a burst of tracer from the nearby woods shot over the wing, followed by a second burst along the ground between the portside of the glider and us. Without a word being said, everybody boarded the jeeps and set off back to the farmhouse…

"While I was away, the farmhouse had been attacked by a large party of about 80 German infantry. An RAF Glider pilot officer had opened fire with a Bren gun and killed about six Germans, including an officer and a senior NCO, whereupon the reminder had decided to lay down their arms. All, apart from a few, were taken away as prisoners. Two of those left behind were allocated to me to dig slit trenches – one a middle aged sergeant and the other a 'cocky' young private.

En route to dig the trenches I had 'liberated' a few eggs and placed them on a concrete path next to the farmhouse. The private, having seen the eggs, altered his line of march intending to stamp on them, but as he raised his foot, I slapped the butt of my rifle. The German very slowly and carefully withdrew his foot and we marched on…

"Would I have shot him? At that moment in time I think I would have. As it was, I told the sergeant that if the private misbehaved neither of them would see the war out, upon which the sergeant tore into the private and made him do the lion's share of the digging…

"As dusk came I managed to get hold of three American parachutes to line the slit trenches and was looking forward to a good night's sleep amongst all that silk. But I was given another task, to accompany a lieutenant colonel in his jeep, as his personal bodyguard. He was a tall man and I am 5 foot 6. His driving was something else. With lights out on the jeep, he ignored all challenges from the guards at their various posts, then got out and roared at each of them for not shooting at us! I was glad to get back to the farmhouse in one piece…

"However, I had a good meal of eggs and potatoes and an excellent nights sleep in my silk-lined slit trench. One of the parachutes I brought home with me, as many others did, was made into underwear for my mother and sister…

"I had, by now, acquired an MP40 machine pistol – something like a superior Sten gun. It had two triggers – one for single shot and one for rapid fire. It was a very well made weapon with only one fault, the magazine went vertically down, making crawling very difficult…

"When out on patrol we came across a patrol of paras who showed great interest in my newly acquired weapon. However, when I decided to give them a demonstration, things went slight wrong. I released the magazine, dropping it perhaps by half an inch but not taking it out of the weapon. Pointing it at the ground in the correct manner I pressed the single shot trigger only to find the weapon fired off nearly half a magazine of about 20 cartridges. The response from the paras was, 'I suppose you think that was effing funny Serge…'

"We went to check a Horsa glider in a position that was known to see if it contained a jeep. Moving left of the woods we made for the ditch on the far side of an earthen roadway. We could see the crashed Horsa in the distance near a farmhouse. Cautiously, two glider pilots made their way to the glider while the remainder prepared to give them covering fire. We returned with the news that the jeep was not in the Horsa as hoped. Just then, six tanks came up the lane. They had come across the Rhine and each had a pair of bronze propellers at the rear. They drove over the embankment in two groups, each of three tanks. The German 88mm guns opened fire and after only three shots three tanks were blown up – or as it was known 'brewed up'…

"A sergeant of the 50th Lowland Division came up the lane driving one of our jeeps. Although it was ours he would not hand it over. He explained that he had taken it from German troops and with his squad being short of transport, he had to keep it. But he did offer to drive us back to group HQ, which we accepted. En route back to HQ we ran over the bodies of eight or nine Germans that the squad had killed earlier that day. It is an experience that I have with me to this day…

Mk II Horsa glider on Landing Zone 'P' – 26th March 1945. German POWs in the foreground.

"Earlier in the day I remember coming across a stick of British paratroopers still hanging in their parachutes from the trees, obviously they had sustained injuries dropping through the trees, and it was believed that they had then been bayoneted by the Germans as they hung there, injured…

"The next farmhouse was the residence of the Mayor of Hamminkeln. As we arrived at the house, a wounded horse began screaming and I was asked to put it out of its misery. An RAF Glider pilot NCO obliged – and shot all the other cattle and horses just to make sure…

"Ted and I made our way to the dining room on the first floor where we found the Mayor in a tail coat and top hat. Ted stuffed his beret down inside his smock and took the top hat from the Mayor to try it on, which deflated the Mayor. Ted later wore the top hat when they marched out of the Landing Zone…

"Feeling hungry I set up my 'Tommy cooker' on the Mayor's large and beautiful dining table and cooked a meal, much to my dismay. The solid fuel burnt a large hole in the table top but did I care? I did not…

"We also suffered the indignity on our return to the UK of having H.M. Customs ask us where we had been and under whose authority! Among the men in front of us, there were wounded and many in a very dirty state. The glider pilots were getting very annoyed at their attitude and had plenty of ammunition left. One spark and a very serious incident could have erupted. Fortunately, common sense prevailed and we were soon on our way, I with my American silk parachute…"

Ian was destined later to be sent to RAF Shobdon to train on Hotspurs before becoming a 1st Pilot in preparation for the anticipated landings in Japan, which, of course, did not happen. His one regret is that he did not get to fly a fighter in combat, although post-war he did fly a Spitfire, and also Vampire and Meteor jet fighters whilst still on active service.

• • • • • • • • • •

Bill Sampson was also heading for the baker's shop in Hamminkeln, but did not know in which direction the village was, let alone the shop. He joined a party of about a dozen American paratroopers and spent the first night near a farmhouse in very wet slit trenches. The next day he managed to find the baker's shop. The baker had been baking extra bread for a week, so he said, as they had been expecting us. Perhaps he received an early copy of the London Illustrated News or had just put two and two together. The Illustrated News had a photograph of a jeep and six-pounder gun being unloaded with the caption 'Unloaded in two minutes.'

• • • • • • • • • •

The saddest part of the Operation for Ken Malet was the death of his friend Geoffrey Grant. Geoff had been best man at Ken's wedding to Barbara. Ken heard that Geoffrey, flying a Hamilcar in 'C' Squadron, had mistakenly landed in a park which, in the briefing, they had been told to avoid as the Germans were expecting them there and had ringed the area with their deadly 88mm guns.

• • • • • • • • • •

Eddie Wiggin and his first pilot, F/O Roger Topp, teamed up on the PIAT gun and scored a hit with their third shot on a German gun emplacement, upon which its crew surrendered. Roger Topp went on to command the Black Diamonds display team, the forerunner of the Red Arrows and finished his RAF career as an Air Commodore with no less than three AFCs.

• • • • • • • • • •

John Love, having been hit, was lying flat in a stream when a German machine gun strafed his wrecked glider. He suffered a further eight superficial scratches from the onslaught. Two field dressings were stuck in the hole in his leg, with a bandage over us to keep them in place. They were pinned down for a time until some Americans turned up and, with the aid of a bazooka and some grenades managed to persuade the Germans that they ought to be somewhere else… The medical men were soon on the scene and he and Lieutenant Starkey were carried off to a First Aid Station at a farm."

This left his second pilot, F/Sgt McEwan as senior man, the task of getting the soldiers back to their units. He did a wonderful job, but it was not without its moments.

"At one point we came across a large house full of German prisoners and were ordered by a senior officer to guard them. This we did until we came under intense fire from the Americans, who could see the Germans but not the British guarding them. However, by waving our yellow identity dusters we managed to convince the Americans that we were on their side."

John, in the meantime, was taken to hospital at Eindhoven and from there to Brussels. After operations at both these locations, he was flown to the hospital at RAF Wroughton.

"When I fell asleep, the bed next to me was empty," he remembers, "but when I woke up in the morning I found it was occupied by my good friend 'Chuck' Barker, who, in landing his Horsa, had attracted a peppering of German shrapnel in his legs."

John Love DFC. [John Love]

John was sent from Wroughton to RAF St Athan. By the time he was well again, the war was over. When he did get back to flying it was in a Halifax bomber, dropping parachutists and towing gliders rather than flying them. He was demobbed in 1947 and became a professional footballer. After a spell in Scotland, he was transferred to Nottingham Forest, where he spent four years. A bad knee injury finally ruined his career and he went into soccer management.

On 18th May 1945 he was recommended for the DFC. The full account of his flying and landing his glider despite being wounded was in the recommendation. Although the first recommending officer was Lt-Col Murray, who commanded No.1 Wing of the Glider Pilot Regiment, an error was made in the recommendation in that it stated he was flying a Horsa glider, whereas he was, in fact, flying a Hamilcar.

• • • • • • • • • •

Phil Johnson was also wounded. He had been hit three times and was more or less helpless. He was soon a prisoner and taken on a stretcher to a German Field Hospital.

"More field than hospital," he remembers. "After a couple of weeks I was repatriated, given an emergency operation in Belgium, and flown back to the UK…

"In the UK I was taken by ambulance to RAF St Athan where they did an excellent, job of patching me up. By November 1945 I was up and walking again."

• • • • • • • • • •

F/O Geoffrey Atkinson spent the night of the 24/25th in a Dutch barn with other British wounded and German prisoners. Having been flown back to the UK and then to Wroughton he was then taken to the RAF Officers Hospital, Cleveleys Hydro, near Blackpool where he spent "three to four very enjoyable months" receiving physiotherapy treatment. RAF Glider pilot Atkinson had received 16 bullets through both feet and legs and had also been wounded in the arm. Despite this, he had successfully landed his glider without it sustaining any further damage.

Flying Officer Geoffrey Atkinson DFC of 'F' Sqn GPR. [Geoffrey Atkinson DFC]

Geoffrey Atkinson was recommended for and awarded the DFC.

• • • • • • • • • •

Colin Miller remembers having set off to his designated RV point when he came across a British soldier lying prone on the ground with a bullet wound in his left thigh, spouting blood. Colin proceeded to put a field dressing on the soldier's wound and then prepared to run after the group he was with. As he did so, he was shot in the right leg and fell to the ground. He was then pinned down by rifle fire and could hear mortar bombs coming nearer and nearer. He tried to crawl to cover under hedgerows and trees but the rifle fire continued to keep him pinned down. He tried to scrape a hole in the sandy earth but a mortar bomb fell within a few feet of him. It blew him into the air and he lapsed into unconsciousness. When he came round, he heard voices in the distance, which he identified as American. He shouted to them and they put him on stretcher and took him to a field where many other stretchers were laid out. After some medical treatment he was loaded into a Dakota along with other wounded men and ferried across the Rhine. Like many others he spent many months in hospital. He lost an eye and some toes and the medical board were of the opinion that he should be discharged.

••••••••••

Rick Brown looked around the field at the scene of the fighting. Smashed equipment and motionless bodies told all. Several gliders loaded with ammunition, burned and crackled nearby. Only twenty yards away a German 88mm gun pointed its barrel mutely to the sky. Its crew were spread-eagled over its sandbagged emplacement. Of his particular group, only one had survived. Standing over temporary graves he reflected that his earlier casual exchange of second pilots had meant that he had been among the first British troops to stand on German soil, rather than being among those who did not even make it to their landing zones on Operation Varsity...

••••••••••

When Len Jordan saw the troops of the 51st Highlanders coming up the road he knew his job on Operation Varsity was over. They were followed by tanks. Nearby was a deserted farmhouse where a couple of hundred German prisoners were being held. Len and the other gliders pilots were ordered to stand guard over them.

"By the look on their faces," he remembers, "they knew the war was over – for them and for Germany. But it was difficult to abide the arrogant young German officers, and with our Sten guns at the ready we rather hoped that some of them would try to make a run for it. As the British tanks went by we got a cheer from them; they must have thought we had just captured the Germans, so we swaggered somewhat as we marched our prisoners towards the Rhine. The damage to the countryside and the number of dead cattle was appalling...

"The Dakota we came back in landed at Fairford on the 30th March, just six days after we had taken off from Shepherd's Grove on the 24th. Before taking off for Varsity we had separated our kit into two kitbags; one held our personal belongings and the other our RAF kit, which was waiting for us at Fairford on our arrival. That night we had a few beers and drank a toast to the men who had not returned…"

••••••••••

Gordon Procter knew that he and his second pilot were looked upon as 'sprog' soldiers.

"One severe criticism of Army allocation of weapons was the utter stupidity of my being equipped with only a .38 calibre Smith & Wesson revolver – quite useless – and Sgt Reed with only a rifle. We also carried a 2-inch airborne mortar and six shells, but we had had only one practice session with it before the operation…

"Why we were not issued with Sten guns has always been a mystery to me. If we had been, as other GPs were, I feel we would have suffered fewer casualties on the ground and would have been far more effective in mopping up German resistance…

"One of the German prisoners I was involved in capturing was a young officer who had been educated at Cambridge before the war. He queried the RAF insignia on my smock and mockingly told me that they had been bringing in additional anti-aircraft battalions for over a week and showed me a map with my landing zone marked on it. He also asked why we were late, referring to our late take-off from the UK! It became clear that there had been a serious security leak and that the Germans had prepared a hot reception for us.

"One off-beat moment I remember was some Americans running out of their gliders wearing top hats, although these were soon cast aside when the firing started…"

••••••••••

John Perry was soon taken prisoner and singled out as the pilot of the glider.

"I was ordered to follow one of the guards into a field where I was confronted with a Hamilcar glider which seemed to be intact with a field gun off-loaded and two British gunners leaning over it in the process of loading it. It was

Entries in Gordon Procter's log book.

only when I went to touch one of them that I realised they were both dead. I shook my head and returned to where the German guards were standing. As we marched off, across the field, out of the smoke came a lone US Waco glider. As it landed, the German guards became very confused and lowered their rifles, which Pete and I promptly grabbed and the Germans now became our prisoners…

"The Americans jumped out of the Waco and formed a semi-circle in crouched positions with their guns pointed in the direction of Pete and I and our prisoners. I quickly got out my yellow duster and waved it furiously. They ran over to be greeted by our congratulations on the arrival of the US Cavalry…

"As a novice RAF pilot turned khaki by a twist of fate, I now look back with pride on my involvement with the men of the GPR. I joined them, flew with them, fought with them and admired them. I shared their sorrow at the casualties they suffered, not only on Operation Varsity, but on all the other expert operations undertaken by this prestigious band of men…"

• • • • • • • • • •

F/Sgt Billingham's glider crashed into a hedge, which provided useful cover behind which the survivors crouched before making their way to their respective RV points. F/Sgt Billingham managed to reach the bakery in Hamminkeln.

"Here I guarded young boys and old men of the *Volksturm* who had clearly decided that all was lost. A service was held in a field for those that had fallen, although at that time I had no idea that so many had been killed…"

• • • • • • • • • •

Sid Edwards, having been helped out of his glider by Eddie Raspison, was loaded onto a jeep which then drove him across the fields.

"When we came under fire, a captain gave the order to get off the jeep and take cover. At this point I again passed out and when I regained consciousness I found that I was lying in a field. The jeep and soldiers had gone; I never saw them again. I pulled off my flying helmet and discarded it. An RAF pilot was coming across the field, he was on his own and had come to see if he could help me. He tried to patch me up with his first aid pack but then said, 'I am sorry, I shall have to go.' I never did find out who he was. I then lapsed into an unconscious state again and when I woke up I was in a farmyard lying on a handcart. I saw a tall German lady with an apron down to her ankles surrendering a hand gun to a British soldier. On each side of him was a wounded German soldier. Tied to a wall was a big farm horse, like a shire. During the night, I was told, it strangled itself during the shelling. My memory from there on is hazy…"

At a British General hospital in Belgium, a Red Cross officer, Mrs Driver, wrote to a WAAF friend of Sid's at Earls Colne and she was able to tell his parents that he was OK, but wounded. After treatment at a hospital in Brussels he was flown home and taken to RAF Hospital Wroughton. In May 1945, he was given a full bill of good health and after leave was given permission to return to full flying duties. He rejoined the squadron in July and was commissioned in October.

"However," he remembers, "in 1946, I suddenly went giddy, lost the vision in my left eye and my limbs started to shake. The medical officer I saw asked if I had been thinking about anything when I had the attack. I replied that I had not, whereupon he said to me, "Do you realise it is 12 months to the day since you were shot down?"

In 1947, he was discharged with a 30% disability pension, having served 7 years ands 8 months in the RAF.

His first pilot, St/Sgt Eddie Raspison, was recommended for the DFM in May 1945.

In April 1945 Major Ian Toler wrote to Sid's mother and asked if she could tell him which hospital Sid was in and how he was progressing.

"A nice gesture," remembers Sid, "making sure one of his flock was okay."

• • • • • • • • • •

Stan Jarvis and his co-pilot Pete Geddes had to leave their troops and work their way up the railway track to a pre-arranged rendezvous point. Their instructions were to report to a farmhouse 150 yards west of the railway station, but it was necessary to dash across an open field to reach it. This they did, safely, and found it had already been captured. The glider pilots' job, once down, was to guard German prisoners and to search them for weapons, maps, money or anything that could be of some benefit to the allies.

"Each prisoner was covered by another pilot with a Sten gun as they were searched. A table had been provided on which to put the articles discovered. I was astonished at the amount of Dutch Guilders already on the table. It transpired that the Germans had ransacked a bank and that the money they had in bundles had come from there…

"Another young German had a handful of contraceptives in his pocket and someone joked that, as a prisoner of war, it would be some time before he got the chance to use them. When this was explained in German the other prisoners roared with laughter! When the number of prisoners became too great for the farmhouse to hold, they were marched to the village, which had by now been captured by the 12th Devons...

"As we waited to return to the UK in a Dakota, the loadmaster asked if anyone had any information about Stan Jarvis and Pete Geddes. The reply was "Why don't you ask them yourself, pointing at me. There was great jubilation on board – it was the same crew, led by Alex Blythe, who had towed us out..."

• • • • • • • • • • •

John Codd eventually made it to safety at Hamminkeln, after which he and his co-pilot had to march some 500 prisoners across country to the Rhine. En route they met allied tanks followed by troops. The prisoners were handed over to the Americans near a pontoon bridge over the Rhine.

"When I arrived back at the aerodrome I had taken off from, the worst moment was when a roll call was made and we realised how many of our comrades had failed to return, having been either killed, wounded or taken prisoner. Those of us who survived later received letters from relatives and sweethearts all over the country, begging us to tell them what had happened to their loved ones."

• • • • • • • • • • •

Kenneth Ross found it good to be back on the ground again.

"Even though we were holed up in a forest and I was still lugging a 2-inch mortar around – without ammunition! Eventually it was noticed by an officer of the 6th Airborne, who told one of his men to take it and give me a Bren gun in return. However, I was only slightly better off, having just one magazine of ammo...

"For five days my home was a former German slit trench, which I lined with confiscated carpets; a door served as a roof. By now I only had a Sten gun, my Bren having been taken off me. The prisoners I was guarding thought me an ardent paratrooper with my dirty face, camouflage jacket, three stripes and a crown (F/Sgt) and red beret."

Ken must have been favoured, having a red beret, which only airborne forces wore; the standard issue beret to RAF glider pilots was Air Force blue.

"Nearby was a first-aid post and when I crossed over to it I found a man lying there who had lost his legs. He was so badly wounded he could not be moved for surgery. A short distance away was an even sadder sight. In neat lines lay row after row of dead bodies, among them a paratrooper who had been pitch-forked as he landed. Close by were the bodies of the women who had killed him."

• • • • • • • • • • •

Alan Kingston, after unloading his glider, made towards his designated assembly place.

"As the Americans were landing in their Wacos, a large German force of armoured vehicles came down the road with everything firing. The allied tanks stopped them with one shot...

"I remember seeing a Hamilcar glider shot up as it came in and the tank inside falling out of the nose. How the operation succeeded and was a success I still wonder even to this day...

"On the third day we RAF glider pilots went back to Hamminkeln. We thought we would soon be back in the UK but the Germans started to shell Hamminkeln and hit the church where the women and children were taking shelter. We rushed to help when another shell landed in the square and a piece of shrapnel hit me in the right leg. After hospital treatment at Nijmegen and Brussels, I was taken to RAF Wroughton for skin grafts.

• • • • • • • • • • •

John Crane and his first pilot, F/O John Arnold made their way to Hamminkeln station.

"We found four gliders that had hit power lines and crashed on their backs. All the occupants had been electrocuted and were still inside their gliders…

"An hour after we landed, Liberators came over, dropping supplies to the troops. Up to the time we left and despite being attacked three times a day by fighters, one 88mm anti-aircraft gun was still firing. This gun one day shot down a Piper Cub spotter plane, which crash landed in front of me. The pilot promptly got out, picked up part of the wing that had been shot away and walked away with it down the road…

● ● ● ● ● ● ● ● ● ●

F/Sgt Worrall was a little apprehensive about what the Germans who had captured him might do with him.

"But when I spoke to one of the guards, he showed some sympathy towards us and said in broken English 'Flying gliders? You must be mad!' Considering my own flight, I was inclined to agree with him. The German then added, 'We learned our lesson in Crete'…

"Like many allied prisoners I ended up marching on the road, often being attacked by allied aircraft firing rockets. We covered about 30 kilometres a day and at night camped out in farmyards. Escape would have been difficult because the guards kept the barrels of their guns clean, plugging them with small pieces of wood and rags so they were always ready for use…

"After ten days we reached Nienburg, a small town on the river Weser to the South of Bremen, where we were herded into cattle trucks attached to a train. There were about 50 men in each truck and we were told we were being taken to a prisoner of war camp. By nightfall we reached Fallingbostel – Stalag 356 – a camp that had not only British prisoners but also Russians…

"The camp was grim: crowded huts, little food and nonexistent toilet facilities. We had been better off on the road. There were daily deaths, mainly Russians, who were carried to their graves in wooden coffins which were stacked up outside a hut and returned each day for further use. The Russians were not protected by the Geneva Convention and so suffered harsher treatment than the British.

"After a week, to avoid the advancing allies, we were again moved in an easterly direction, en route passing Belsen…

"On 13th April the Germans made an announcement – '*Roosevelt ist tod*' (he had died the day before). The news of his death left the prisoners feeling even more depressed…

"We eventually reached the River Elbe at Bleckede and crossed to the Eastern side on a large raft…

"There were occasional Red Cross parcels, but in the main food was very short; watery soup and bread was the normal diet. I was by now suffering from dysentery and as a consequence lost a lot of weight. All the prisoners were infested with lice as the result of sleeping in farmyards and spent many hours each day removing and killing them. Toilet arrangements were abysmal and it was difficult to have a daily wash and impossible to shave. All in all I was in a sorry state and felt utterly degraded…

"When the German guards heard Russian gunfire in the distance they were persuaded to turn and make for the west. We reached Zaaentin on 1st May and camped down in a farmyard…

"All around there was gunfire and we knew that the day would be critical and we would be caught up in the crossfire. We saw several army vehicles pass by, and thought at first they were German – but then we saw the familiar uniform of the 6th Airborne Division…

"Some of the advancing forces were detached to look after our needs. We were dowsed with DDT for the lice, had a welcome shave, a haircut and food and drink. Then we were told to make for Lüneburg about 60 kilometres away, a long trip which we didn't intend to make on foot. When a German in a Mercedes staff car turned up to surrender we turfed him out and drove off, heading for Lauenburg on the Elbe. Here we found a pontoon bridge that had been constructed across the river. After a while we were allowed to cross and got to Lüneburg at about mid-afternoon. Some British soldiers took a fancy to the car and said they would take us to the local

Men of the Royal Engineers digging in a field gun.

barracks if we gave it to them. A deal was struck and we were soon installed in a large dormitory in the barracks…

"Here I met another glider pilot, Dick Jestico, who had just been liberated and had managed to obtain a flight home that day. I asked Dick to post a letter for me when he got to the UK. This he did and my parents received it on 10th May 1945, much to their relief and joy; they had been told that I was missing in action and had assumed that I had been killed…"

• • • • • • • • • •

Maurice Thirkettle was part of a 6-man patrol – two army and four RAF – given the task of making contact with the airborne forces at the western perimeter of the landing zone, facing the German positions in the forest near the Rhine.

"When we reached the railway line, about 100 yards from the forest, the Army sergeant in charge of the patrol said on his signal to clamber up and over the railway line, down the other side and to run like mad over the open land to the edge of the forest.

"As we did, a sniper opened up and the four RAF chaps dropped to the ground, whereas the two army chaps kept running. After a few choice words from the sergeant we got up and followed. Going to ground, we were told later, was exactly what the sniper wanted – he would then have us pinned down and could pick us off if we tried to move, whereas hitting running man was extremely difficult…

"When the allies broke through, we Glider Pilots were told to get to hell out of it. As we waited for transport, Major Bartlett, the 'A' Squadron Commander, said we would march back towards the Rhine. It was a long march through the forest and we saw many bodies strewn around…"

• • • • • • • • • •

After landing Ron Watson headed for a farmhouse, from which the owners had fled.

"Inside we came across photographs of the family – one showed the husband in the uniform of an SS officer, together with his wife and two children. The wardrobes were full of ladies' furs, men's suits; bottles of preserved fruit and vegetables lined the kitchen walls…

"Snipers were the worst problem. One 17-year-old German had made his lair in a nearby deserted glider…"

• • • • • • • • • •

Tony Spicer found his Flight Commander in a farmhouse, where he was looking after the troops who he had been carrying in his glider, all of whom had been badly hurt when it crash landed after his controls were shot away in mid-air.

"We dug ourselves well in and then witnessed our first artillery fire from the enemy. The small village of Dingenberg, north east of Hamminkeln, was the target and the shells were flying directly overhead – luckily none fell short…

"The officer in charge of the anti-tank platoon had positioned a gun at the farmhouse they were defending. It was dug in just in front of us. A German self-propelled 88mm anti-tank gun came down the road towards us. It seemed quite ignorant of our presence but was soon made aware of it. The anti-tank gunner held his fire until the Germans were about 100 to 200 yards away and then fired three rounds in quick succession. The target suffered three direct hits and was soon burning fiercely…

"A small German patrol advanced under the cover of darkness across the field in front of us. This attack was at first repulsed but later it resumed on a larger scale. The farmhouse behind us was set on fire and we were silhouetted against the flames. The attack developed and the Germans advanced, hiding behind a number of British troops who had already been taken prisoner…

"It was soon time to call it a day and we too were taken prisoner. Dawn was breaking as we were marched away into Germany, carrying a German paratrooper, an Ober-Lieutenant, on an improvised stretcher. He had a serious wound in his back, sustained during the attack…"

• • • • • • • • • •

Howard Hansford landed in a small wood with his load of two jeeps, radio equipment and signallers. He was slowed down by the trees which chopped off the wings and tail of his glider before it came to rest near a farmhouse.

"The success of the operation," Howard says, "can be judged by the number of German prisoners that were taken. One abiding memory is of a long line of German prisoners guarded by a lone British soldier marching at their head and of piles of rifles, knives and bayonets lying alongside the road having been taken from the prisoners as they surrendered…

"Three days after landing, I and about 100 other glider pilots returned to Eindhoven, about 30 miles, by force marching and running. I was pleased that the RAF had trained us well and that I had kept myself fit, so much so that I became a physical training instructor at the end of the war until I was demobbed in September 1946. Six of the men I trained with at No.4 FTS were killed on Varsity."

• • • • • • • • • •

Fred Meek was with 'G' Squadron, but at the time of Varsity was in hospital at RAF Ely. He had trained for the operation but because of recurring bouts of tonsillitis his flying time was restricted. On 14th March 1945 he flew as second pilot to John Haig in Exercise Vulture with a live load of men of the Air Landing Brigade. It was the last time the were to fly together. Fred was saddened to learn in April that his squadron had suffered a number of casualties and that John Haig was among those who had been killed.

• • • • • • • • • •

When Ian Toler looked around the landing zone he saw what appeared to be nothing but a mass of crashed and broken gliders. Many had been attacked on the ground as soon as they landed. He tried to asses the casualties; they appeared to be high. Cpt Rex Norton had been killed; he and Ian were the only officers of the squadron to have survived Arnhem. Ian visited the spot where Rex had been buried in a temporary grave. He had been killed by a mortar burst. During the morning more pilots were brought in dead and Ian realised that his casualties were about 20%.

•••••••••••

Rosemary Britten found herself in hot water. The group captain at her station had been in a flap and told her he was furious that she had gone. Apparently, he had instructed S/Ldr Mayer to fix the ballot so that she would think she was in it, when in fact she was not. Now that she had returned unscathed he was pacified, however, and even expressed the hope that she had enjoyed her little excursion. Keeping it from the papers was now the important thing…

•••••••••••

After his glider had been unloaded, Leslie Norris made his way to a house across a field and a road where German wounded were being tended by US medical orderlies.

"When an American officer saw I had maps and photographs of the area he asked me where he was," remembers Leslie.

"Later a sergeant in charge of the seven men we had transported in our glider asked if I thought they should drive down the road towards Hamminkeln. I replied 'Don't do it sergeant…' I had no sooner uttered the words when two German armoured cars packed with German troops appeared, driving up the road from Hamminkeln. The sergeant looked at me and said, 'You were dead right to tell me not to go down *that* road!'

"Major Jackson, commanding 'E' Squadron, had a batman who had been a regular soldier and had risen to the rank of sergeant major but then been demoted back down to a private.

"He turned up, amongst all the firing, with a mug of tea on a saucer and said, 'Tea Sir?' When I told him to take cover, he said not to worry, it was just allied 25 pounder guns shelling the Germans across the canal…"

•••••••••••

Ken Scolding found the village of Hamminkeln a hive of activity.

"Male civilians were rounded up under the guard of glider pilots, while women and children were taken to the church in the village square. They were all in a state of shock. One minute they had been going about their daily business and the next they were caught up in the middle of the biggest airborne operation of WWII. One woman gave birth prematurely and another suffered appendicitis and was operated on in primitive conditions in the brewery cellars by the light of torches supplied by glider pilots.

"When the dawn of the next day came up I decided to clean my Sten gun. In the back room of a shop, I emptied the magazine, cleaned each bullet individually and then the magazine, making sure that the spring was not full of sand. I then cleaned the weapon itself…

"A glider pilot arrived who they called 'the indestructible one'. He had taken off from the UK but his tow-rope had broken. Seeing an airfield below, both glider and tug landed and without delay another aircraft was laid on to collect a replacement tow-rope from their home base. Their subsequent take-off and flight to the Rhine was uneventful but they were hours behind the rest of the force. I will always regret not seeing this lone glider land in what was, by now, a deserted landing zone."

•••••••••••

F/Lt Howard Curry regained consciousness on a stretcher.

"I was in large room with a high ceiling and a big window. It would appear that it was the local Schloss, which had been taken over by the Allies as a first-aid post. Most of my clothing had been cut off and I was now wearing a grey woollen shirt. After being ferried across the Rhine I was transported to a hospital in Brussels, where I lay on a stretcher in a hallway for ages while other casualties came and went. When the call of nature came I asked a man in a white coat if I could have a bottle. He turned out to be an English doctor, who was surprised to find out that I too was English. 'Good God!' he exclaimed, "I thought you were a bloody German!" With my blonde hair and grey shirt I suppose it was a reasonable assumption…

I was soon treated and on my way back to the UK, but it was 24th March 1947, exactly two years later, before I was pronounced fit to fly again. My second pilot, Sgt Graham, was killed during the operation."

• • • • • • • • • •

Sgt Dan Richards, an RAF Glider pilot, told his son Richard that an American Division who were off course saved his life. Apparently, one of the Americans was naked except for trunks, boots, a Mohican haircut and war paint. He landed alongside Dan and said, "Say Buddy, where's the Enemy?"

• • • • • • • • • •

F/O David Richards [no relation to Dan] and his second pilot Sgt Jeff Cohen, having got down safely, soon found there was still a lot of accurate enemy firepower around. [German flak guns could be elevated horizontally and used as ground weapons as well as anti-aircraft.]

"We saw an enemy flak gun bring down a couple of gliders and decided we had to do something to silence it," David remembers. After an abortive attempt with a 2-inch mortar, that we didn't really know how to use, Jeff Cohen and I retrieved our Bren gun and Jeff volunteered to give me covering fire. After a couple of bursts a message came back from the British attacking force to stop; apparently he was frightening them more than the enemy! They then fired a round from a 6-pound gun, which had been placed in a nearby pigsty. This scored a direct hit on the German gun pits which resulted in the immediate surrender of the surviving occupants...

"By nightfall, all the glider pilots, those who were not casualties, were collected together and all 'F' Squadron members were told to rendezvous at Hamminkeln station, where they were to defend part of the perimeter facing the Issel Canal. This meant yet another slit trench being dug and in the dark – on a sandbank below a very prickly hedge...

"After a couple of days, when things had become quiet, we went back to our glider to retrieve or attempt to retrieve a few belongings, in particular a steel helmet. At the time I was wearing a 'liberated' German helmet...

"There was a great deal of air activity from both sides, night and day, and the amount of artillery fire being put up by the 2nd Army on both sides of the Rhine was remarkable...

"On the third morning we were ordered to rendezvous at Hamminkeln Station and then marched back under spasmodic shell fire through the village to Brigade Headquarters, which was in landing zone 'B' to the west of the village. That night we were glad to leave our waterlogged slit trenches and sleep in straw-filled barns. There were about 700 men in the barn and the fire risk, although orders about smoking had been issued, was considerable. After a couple of days we marched back to Dierfordter Wald where we were picked up in lorries and driven back over the Rhine by way of a pontoon bridge and finally to the village of Kaervalier near Xanten. The tented base camp's official name was Twisterden but its unofficial name was 'Camp Cornucopia' where we stayed for a week...

"Finally, we were driven once again in lorries into Holland where a decent meal at the Red Cross Centre at Helmond awaited us. From there to Eindhoven and a flight home in a 46 Group Dakota to RAF Fairford."

• • • • • • • • • •

Alan Hartley was at Down Ampney on the 22nd March 1945 and was among about 30 mechanics, engineers and airframe fitters who were told to report with small kit at the airmen's mess.

"Having duly reported we all climbed aboard the awaiting lorries and set off, not knowing where we were heading," he remembers. "After about two or three hours driving we arrived at what looked like a disused airfield where we were allocated billets, which we thought strange because they had no light bulbs in them. We were told that from the next day we were to inspect daily the 271 Squadron Dakotas. I and the other engine mechanics would look after the engines and the airframe mechanics would look after the flying controls and fuel contents."

Men of 'B' Flight, No.12 RAF glider pilots course including Ken Ashurst, later second-in-command to Major Ivan Toler.

"On the 24th" Alan remembers, "the air around the airfield was full of all manner of aircraft – Spitfires and Mustangs swept over, escorting Bostons and Marauders high in the sky. A lone Flying Fortress dropped orange flares and other Fortresses formatted on it and then as a formation flew off towards the east, then another would do the same thing. The Dakotas of 271 Squadron started to tow off the gliders and by lunch time I was on my way back to Down Ampney. The reason, I was later told, for not flying direct from Down Ampney, was due to the extra towing distance and fuel consumption."

It was 40 years before Alan discovered that the airfield they had been taken to was Gosfield.

• • • • • • • • • •

Ken Ashurst was a flight commander with 'B' Squadron and later second in command to Major Ian Toler. His second pilot was Sgt Hickson, known as 'Hick'.

"The American Waco gliders landed virtually in the same place as us and helped us," he remembers. "I shared a slit trench with an American paratrooper with a painted face and Mohican haircut. 'Hick' and I spent the night of the 24th in a farmhouse. One of the great joys were the supply drops by American Liberators on the following days. Four pilots in my flight were killed on Operation Varsity."

After the operation Ken took over command of 'M' Squadron of the GPR and had an Army captain as his second in command.

• • • • • • • • • •

After casting off the glider he had been towing, tug pilot Dick Wynne performed a 180-degree turn to drop off the tow-rope on his way back across the Rhine.

"I had forgotten to pull back the throttles after the cast off," he remembers, "so we were travelling quite fast and climbing. With my earphones covered by a flak helmet I was not able to move the right one forward of my ear as I usually did in order to hear the crew conversation in the cockpit. We were flying below other gliders and, not wanting someone to drop a rope on us, I went a little wider than them in my turn. My wireless operator, who was talking through the intercom from the astrodome, told me there was tracer coming up over the tail of our aircraft. I headed for B75 at Niveless, France, where we were scheduled to land and stand by, ready to drop supplies. In the aircraft we had a roller-conveyer for pannier dropping, which weighed about 1000lbs. As it turned out it was not needed, as the American B24 Liberators of the 8th US Air Force undertook the task of dropping supplies…"

"We flew back to Blakenhill Farm on the 26th and here we stayed until the damage to my aircraft had been repaired. A bullet had gone through the a main hydraulic line, which was leaking fluid, although neither in flight nor in the landing had I noticed anything amiss; the brakes and flaps had worked perfectly…"

It would appear that the pilot of the glider that Dick towed was F/O Geoffrey Atkinson DFC. Even today Dick says that he finds it incredible that Geoffrey and the other glider pilots were able to find their landing zones, given all the haze and smoke in the area.

••••••••••

F/O White AFC of 233 Squadron was from New South Wales, Australia. His Dakota was holed three times by flak before he slipped his tow-rope.

"F/O Jungwirth, my navigator, reported seeing the RAF Dakotas towing their gliders in three gigantic streams. Over to one side we saw the American Dakotas carrying paratroopers. Ahead and below were the Typhoons blasting German positions while above were the Tempests, Spitfires and Thunderbolts. We released our glider, pulled up sharp to dodge the pieces of another Dakota which blew up in front of us, and then turned back," he remembers.

••••••••••

Australain pilot F/Lt Vanrenen DFC of 196 Squadron arrived after German gunners had recovered from the initial attacks on their positions. His aircraft was badly shot up over the landing zone; two of his four engines failed and he, his navigator and wireless operator were all wounded. Undaunted, he struggled back across the Rhine, where he made a masterly landing in friendly territory and refused any assistance for himself until his wounded comrades had been given medical treatment.

••••••••••

F/O O'Donnell from New South Wales, Australia was flying with 271 Squadron and was the first Dakota back to base. His navigator, F/O Holdsworth, from Victoria, Australia, reported seeing 40 gliders released in one batch within 30 seconds.

"We saw the gun flashes from the east bank of the Rhine. The noise of the battle was so great that I heard it even above the roar of our engines."

They were the first Dakota from 271 Squadron to arrive back at base.

••••••••••

General Eisenhower later commended "…the courage of the transport pilots, flying relatively slow aircraft steadily along the allotted route, in spite of heavy flak barrage…"

••••••••••

By 11am, 402 British gliders were down successfully.

••••••••••

One man who had arrived by glider met a particularly tragic fate. Lt Cox, having crawled clear of his blazing Horsa, was struck and killed by another glider as it came into land.

••••••••••

Two gliders collided in mid-air and, locked together, plunged into a house. Pilots Sgt Andrew Bell and Sgt Angus Skeldon were killed in the crash.

••••••••••

One Horsa, carrying men of the 12th Devons, a jeep and a trailer full of explosives cast off at 2,500 feet. As they came in they were followed by a trail of flak which soon set the centre section of the glider on fire, which in turn set the jeep's petrol tank on fire. Not having parachutes, their only hope was to get down to the ground as quickly as possible before the whole lot went up. Sadly, as the pilot made his final turn to come in to land with his flaps down, the trailer carrying the explosives blew up. Horsa, jeep and wreckage were strewn all over the field and farm buildings. Miraculously, there was one survivor, the jeep driver, who somehow was blown clear and found himself lying in a haystack. It was obviously his lucky day...

• • • • • • • • • •

Within minutes of the last airborne troops hitting the ground, formations of B-24's of the 8th US Air Force arrived. Two hundred and forty aircraft hit the assigned area with 598 tons of supplies, dropped from between 200 and 600 feet. The drop was exceedingly accurate, with an estimated 85% of supplies falling into the areas occupied by the division. However, the large Liberators offered a tempting target to the German gunners and 15 of them were shot down.

• • • • • • • • • •

During the afternoon of the 24th, medium bombers of the 9th US Air Force returned to the attack in an effort to completely destroy all remaining bridges along the line. Four attacks were made, with 340 tons of bombs being dropped. Two of the attacks were made on the bridge at Colbe. The bridge, which had been previously been listed as 'possibly usable' was completely destroyed. Other bridges attacked included those at Pracht and Vlotho.

• • • • • • • • • •

The splendid work of Coastal Command in flying day and night diversionary operations along the Dutch Coast and in carrying out air-sea rescue operations along the English Channel during the flight of the airborne train contributed substantially to the success of the operation.

• • • • • • • • • •

The American paratroopers were dropped more than two miles from their assigned drop zone. Instead of making for the correct area, they went into action there and then, killing some 55 Germans and taking over 300 prisoners and a battery of 150 mm Howitzer guns. Two American Generals, General Josiah Dulbey and General Ridgeley Gaither, who had received special permission to take part in the parachute drop, came down on top of a battery of 20 mm guns reinforced by machine-guns and German troops. They soon organised an attack with whatever troops were available, including US and British glider pilots. The German emplacements were rushed and the battery eliminated. The make-do force became known as the 'Chattahoochee Task Force', named after the river that runs past Fort Benning, Georgia, where the Generals were based.

• • • • • • • • • •

Harry Clark was given a message by CSM Stephenson to take to Lt-Col Darrel-Brown, the Commanding Officer of the 2nd Ox & Bucks, as communications had broken down, probably owing to the number of casualties among radio operators suffered in the landings. As Harry picked his way to the railway station he noticed that stretcher bearer parties were searching and recovering large numbers of casualties.

"Several American parachutists lay among the dead," he remembers. "They had landed in the wrong drop zone and were immediately attacked by German troops in the vicinity of the station. To the front of one burning Horsa lay the burnt and blackened body of the pilot, his arms outstretched in the shape of a crucifix, on his head, and still in position, his headphones."

By a stroke of good luck Harry soon contacted Lt-Col Darrel-Brown who came towards him riding a fold-up airborne-issue bike. Harry delivered the message, informing the Colonel that Major Tillet and 'D' Company were moving forward to the area of the railway bridge.

"I asked him what the casualty situation was, and he said that out of the 630 men who had been engaged in landing, 62 were either dead, wounded or missing. He then wished me a safe journey back to 'D' Company lines and rode off on his bike...

"I made my way towards the railway bridge, waded across the river to the east bank, crawled to the top of the embankment and then saw that 'D' Company were in position some 25 yards to

Major (later Colonel) Tillet, commander of 'D' Company. [Colonel Tillet]

my front. They had come under direct fire from enemy positions and I found out that one of my closest friends had been killed only minutes before."

At 10pm that night Lt Shaw, a platoon commander, sent a patrol out under the cover of darkness to investigate the noise of movement to the immediate front of the platoon's position. Harry was selected to go on this patrol, carrying just a rifle and several grenades.

"As we neared the autobahn and a clump of bushes we settled down to watch and listen. It was obvious that there were a lot of Germans around on the eastern side of the road. After an hour we made our way back to the safety of our own lines. When the enemy began to move towards us there were about 700 of them. When they were about 400 yards away, our artillery opened up from the far side of the Rhine. A number of the enemy appeared out of the smoke and were immediately despatched by a concentrated volley of fire. When the German medical team began to collect up their casualties, a cease fire existed. It was the custom of the Ox & Bucks never to fire in such circumstances. It was like the Battle of Normandy all over again. On the 26th, with the enemy broken, we were relieved by a battalion of Scottish troops…

"A number of houses had been taken over on the outskirts of Hamminkeln and a German family was still living in the one in which I was billeted. I was dirty and covered in mud and found the house spotless. I could not bring myself to use the bed with its beautiful blue quilt, so I removed my boots and slept on the floor…"

• • • • • • • • • •

Of the 630 men of the 2nd (Airborne) Ox & Bucks who had taken off from Birch and Gosfield at 6am on the morning of the 24th, the number left in a fighting condition on the morning of the 26th was just 200. They had lost 110 men killed and 300 wounded.

• • • • • • • • • •

Richard Dunkley, after his Normandy experiences, decided to 'look after number one' and ran to the farmhouse they had landed near, passing a deserted German slit trench as he did so.

"The first Germans I encountered were two old ladies in their sixties, who stood there holding hands. In broken English I asked them if there were any German soldiers in the farm and one of them pointed upstairs. I called for whoever was up there to come down. When we failed to appear I pulled out a No.36 grenade and pulled the pin, scaring my fellow soldiers as much as anyone. Then one of the ladies shouted up through a trapdoor and two faces appeared. When they saw the grenade they very quickly came downstairs. They were anti-aircraft troops being used as infantry, so they were only too glad to surrender. When an officer arrived he told me to hand them over to the Padre who was outside with a jeep…

"We then set off for the church pulling hand carts across a field. By now the whole mortar crew was together. As 'Number 1' I was responsible for laying (aiming) the mortar…

"When we arrived at the church in Hamminkeln we met a group of glider pilots who had occupied the farm beside the church and were in the process of searching about a hundred prisoners…

"We then set up, making a mortar pit six feet by six feet by four feet deep. As we did, one of the glider pilots, who spoke excellent German and who we later found out to be Jewish, came over and asked us to come with him. He took us to where the German prisoners were standing and asked for three volunteers to help dig trenches. I heard him mention cigarettes, so there was some bribery going on. A crowd of prisoners stepped forward and we picked three to help with the digging. When they had finished they were paid off with cigarettes and chocolate…"

• • • • • • • • • •

Private Aldis was a soldier in an infantry division and one of the first to get to the Rhine at Rees.

"When we got there it was quiet, but as the officer commanding the 51st Highland Division,

Lance Corporal Richard Dunkley and colleagues.

Maj-Gen Tom Rennie, arrived in a jeep to have a look around, the Germans opened up with mortar bombs," Aldis remembers.

Rennie's jeep was hit and he was killed. He is now buried in the Reichswald War Cemetery, Cleve.

• • • • • • • • • •

The smoke screen laid down by the Royal Artillery was kept up for the whole of the daylight hours, making many of the soldiers violently sick. The bridges that the 3rd Division were to cross were called, London, Blackfriars, Waterloo and Westminster.

• • • • • • • • • •

Winston Churchill was taken to an observation point at Ginberich, overlooking the Rhine. Here he and his party remained for about two hours until departing in two armoured cars. The one that Churchill drove in had the name 'Sheila' written in white on the side. They made their way to Xanten and on to Calcar, where earlier that morning Maj-Gen Rennie had been killed.

The next day, the 25th, Churchill managed to persuade them to take him over to the eastern bank on a landing ship tank. They spent some time looking at the smashed Buerich road bridge where Churchill apparently put both his arms around a twisted girder when they came under fire from shelling. General Simpson, the 9th US Army commander, told Churchill that he could not take the responsibility for his safety and that they must leave the area. As Churchill hung on to the girder it became obvious he did not want to leave. When General Eisenhower heard about the expedition he said that if he had been present Churchill would not have been permitted to cross the Rhine.

It was the 26th before Churchill returned from Venlo in a Dakota – escorted by 12 Spitfires – and landed at Northolt. After his weekend in the glorious weather of Germany he seemed in much better spirits.

•••••••••

Major Michael Graham crashed outside a farmhouse at Tellmannshof – north of Hamminkeln and west of the road.

"The fit men helped the injured into the house where the farmer's wife and her servant girl, a smashing Teutonic blonde," as Michael describes her, "put the wounded to bed and gave them milk to drink. Denis Hardy, my second pilot, said he was going to refuse his, as he thought it might be poisoned. When the farmer's wife asked us to stay to lunch Michael was also suspicious and refused again."

•••••••••

Major Tillett's glider landed in an open field. It had been hit in the tail but without suffering any major damage.

"As we came in one of the pilots shouted "Cables!" and we jumped over high electric cables. This slowed us down and we hit the ground with a thump, tore through a couple of fences and other obstacles but still ended up in one piece. Once down, we took up an all-round defensive position, while I tried to find out where we were. There was a line of trees, but no sign of the buildings that were to be 'D' Company's objective. After setting off under the cover of the trees we came across some US Parachutists who had landed miles from their northern dropping zone.

When they finally found 'D' Company's position it was occupied by Lt Dennis Fox and the remains of one of 'D' Company's platoons. They had landed at about 10.30 am and at 11.30 were ordered by the Commanding Officer of the 2nd Ox & Bucks, Lt-Col Mark Darrell-Brown DSO, to send a platoon to help 'B' Company at the road bridge over the river Issel and then to move with two other platoons of 'D' Company to assist 'C' company at the railway bridge.

By the time they had fended off heavy German attacks and held their position at the railway bridge, 60 hours had elapsed since taking off from the UK. The company were now down to 63 men out of the 140 who had set out.

A few hours later they started off on a 300-mile advance across Germany to meet the Russians in the Baltic early in May 1945.

•••••••••

Sgt Jack Harris went all the way to Hamburg, now an open city, the Germans having surrendered without a fight. They were billeted in a hotel that had been used by Lord Haw-Haw for his propaganda broadcasts throughout the war. Until recent times Jack says that he firmly believed that all glider pilots were from the army and had no idea that a good number were from the RAF.

•••••••••

One unit carried by the gliders and based at RAF Woodbridge was 716 Company of the Royal Army Service Corps (Airborne Light) under Major G.P.R. Crane. When a roll-call was made on the morning of the 25th, they found that four glider crews and part of a fifth who had carried them to the Rhine were missing. The gliders they flew in were 267 to 278. No.267 made a good landing but was hit by a shell on the ground, set on fire and destroyed. No's 268, 269 and 273 were missing. No.270 flown by P/O Stone and Sgt Radcliffe was hit by flak in the tail; the Bren gun carrier inside broke loose but was not damaged but the public relations man being carried was wounded. No.271 was hit by flak and crashed, breaking up on impact.

No.272 flown by St/Sgt Pearson and Sgt Hugh Carling was hit by flak but still made a fairly good landing, crashing through a fence and losing a wheel in the process. Sgt Carling saw a Hamilcar blown apart and a tank fall with the crew inside and hit a hillside at about 200mph. It bounced and turned over a number of times, killing all the crew but one. Miraculously, he survived, although every bone in his body was broken. After a long time in hospital he recovered to work post war at the Teeside shipyards with Swan Hunter, who were renowned for looking after ex-servicemen. No.274 was hit by flak and the right wing torn off just before landing.

No 275, flown by P/O John Love and Sgt McEwan has already been written about in an earlier chapter. No 276 was hit by flak and set on fire but although making a good landing was destroyed by fire on the ground. The Bren gun carrier inside was removed intact but two of the crew were wounded. It reached its allotted position with only two of the four man crew on board.

No 277 carried the War Correspondent Marsland Gander and has already been mentioned. No 278 was hit by flak but was able to make a good landing.

One Horsa glider was seen to crash in a wood that was held by the 8th Battalion and was also the 9th Battalion RV point, at 1035am. The glider crashed into trees near 8th Battalion HQ of the Parachute Regiment, hurling out its load, including a jeep, which killed ten men on the ground – Lt John K. England, an Intelligence Officer, and nine others – and wounded the Commanding Officer, Lt G. Hewetson. His second in command, Major John Tillett, took over the Battalion for the next few days.

●●●●●●●●●●

Ex-POW Gerry Coughlan started to make his way towards Lüneburg, en route commandeering a small car from a party of disarmed German officers.

"When we arrived we found thousands like ourselves and decided to keep going, eventually arriving at an RAF airfield at Celle. We were flown to Brussels the next day to another repatriation centre. Here I met a Spitfire pilot with whom I had trained, who was flying back that day. He agreed to send a telegram to my parents to let them know I was safe and well. I later learned that when it arrived my mother would not take it from the telegram boy. She had already received an official telegram to say I was missing and she was certain that this one would say I had been killed. But the telegram boy was aware of the contents and persuaded her to take it, saying it was 'good news'…"

Within days Gerry had arrived back in the UK and was taken by train to RAF Cosford, Wolverhampton which had been set up as a reception centre for ex-POWs.

"The hard part was to come," he remembers, "when I visited Edwin Cook's widow, Ellen. She just would not accept that he was not coming back. By some miracle she thought he would return…"

Shortly after the war, Gerry met a colleague who told him that a WAAF who had 'taken a shine to him' at Rivenhall had 'cried her eyes out' when she learned he was missing.

"Apparently she had referred to me as her 'little blond pilot', Gerry says. "I now wish I had been nicer to her. It seems everybody but me knew she was sweet on me – and I never even knew her name…"

The words of a song came to him as he travelled home on the train…

The longest mile is the last mile home
When you've been away
the dearest dream is a dream of home
When you've been away
You travel far over land and sea
Then one day it's as a clear as can be
The sweetest mile you'll ever roam
Is the last mile home.

THE COST OF WAR
Graves at Hamminkeln in 1945. (above)
The graves of Major General T.G. Rennie of the Black Watch and Sergeant A.B.C. Love of the RAF
in the Reichswald Cemetery. (below)

CHAPTER 17

Post-Mortem

Despite heavy casualties how successful was Operation Varsity? Lieutenant Murray, the Officer Commanding No.1 Wing of the Glider Pilot Regiment made a report regarding the airborne glider landings and raised some of the following points:

1. Incorrect loading of gliders was caused by air landing units putting extra ammunition in the trailers after the landing manifest had been completed and without the Glider pilots knowledge

(a) Trouble was experienced with the lashings for the Hamilcar loads. The types of loads were constantly being changed and required different kinds of lashings.

(b) Old types of loads underwent modifications which were not notified.

(c) Modifications to loads were made without notification of the new lashing requirements.

(d) A great deal of delay and unnecessary work could have been avoided had it been possible to decide on standard loads for Hamilcars and the responsibility for ensuring that these standards were adhered to and also that changes in load were notified in order that new lashings might be designed.

2. The Horsa Mark II was used principally for all vehicle loads and the Mark 1 for troops. The advantage of using the Mark II for equipment was that it could be unloaded through the nose as well as the tail and side. This saved valuable seconds on the ground after landing. The flight to the landing zones was generally uneventful and no enemy fighter opposition was experienced. Bunching on the final approach was evident and the tug pilots did not stick to briefed times and heights at landing zones with sufficient accuracy. The result was that the gliders carrying troops arrived 8 minutes early and the company of the 12th Devons who had been allotted the task of clearing the landing zones had insufficient time to do so. This caused unnecessary casualties to the gliders and personnel of Divisional HQ.

For future operations the following was to be noted:

(a) Considerably difficulty was experienced in loading and unloading the 25 Pounder gun.

(b) RAF Glider pilots should wear Airborne Berets. RAF Berets can easily be mistaken for the German Field Grey.

(c) Glider pilots should be used, more than has been the practice in the past, for the salvaging of equipment.

(d) The present scale of G.1098 equipment proved most satisfactory.

3. It appeared that a great many glider crashes were caused by excessive landing speeds.

(a) In spite of apparently clear spaces gliders were found wrecked against houses and orchards.

(b) Some of the these wrecks may have been caused through controls being shot away, but the impression was that the landing speed was excessively high in many cases.

To sum it up it is generally considered that a tactical air landing, although causing higher casualties in the initial stages, is more sound from the military point of view and ultimately means fewer casualties.

From all the evidence collected the gliders that suffered worst were those carrying equipment and explosives. To all opposed landings the first wave should carry troops only and the heavy equipment be put down after the opposition is distracted or overwhelmed.

Owing to little opposition after the first phase, glider pilots were not required or used to any great extent in combat but were employed in many other roles relieving the Air Landing units to get on with the main risks of the operation.

In the initial phase it was obvious that the RAF Glider pilots were not fully prepared for the ground battle. This was rapidly overcome and in many instances their conduct was good and they showed courage and determination. Considering the short period of military training they have had, it was only to be expected that they would be unnerved, it is, however, considered that more battle inoculation should be given in the future.

Withdrawal was effected by squadrons passing a checkpoint at quarter hour intervals and getting buses on to the east bank of the River Rhine. The whole withdrawal was well organised and every effort was made for the men's welfare at 12 Corps Transit Camp at Twisteden, and 8 Corps Rest Centre at Helmond.

The customs officials at Down Ampney had been asked, and had agreed to let glider pilots through the customs on the signature of the senior officer. This was not adhered to and some delay was caused by each glider pilot having to complete forms, luckily after 300 had done so, they ran out of forms.

Smoke by the Pioneer Corps to cover troops crossing the Rhine and from forest fires occasioned by shell fire, interfered with the airborne operation to some extent. The smoke drifted over the drop and landing zone area, resulting in haze that cut down visibility especially from the air. There was also smoke from burning farmhouses set on fire by artillery fire, and the enemy also used smoke candles.

The danger from flak had been considerably reduced by air and artillery attacks before the operation. The heaviest concentration against the 6th Airborne Division landings was the light flak to the RAF north of the landing zones. There were some scattered light flak on the run-in from the Rhine.

All losses were due to flak, but reports indicate that the amount experienced was not more than slight to moderate. The American parachute and tug aircraft had over 340 aircraft damaged by flak as opposed to the British tug aircraft of only 13 damaged.

Although the element of surprise as to timing and location had been achieved, and losses initially were light, hostile mobile anti-aircraft (20mm) batteries were quickly moved to the threatened area by the Germans. The incendiaries used by this lethal weapon together with accurate small arms fire began to take its toll of the low flying parachute aircraft at a height of 600 feet, the glider aircraft and the re-supply aircraft which flew at 200 feet. This occurred during the early stages of the drop. Approximately seventy-two per cent of the aircraft losses occurred during the first 30 minutes of the battle. The remainder were sustained in the next 2 hours.

The 6th Airborne had 347 men killed and 731 wounded on the first day. The US 17th Airborne had 159 killed and 522 men wounded, making a grand total of 506 killed and 1253 wounded, out of an overall total of 4,976 British and 9,387 American troops that made up the landing force.

The American tug aircraft lost 41 men killed, 163 missing and 623 damaged, but which did not include the 15 B-24 Liberators aircraft lost, flying supply missions.

In total the 17th US Airborne Divisions had 393 killed, 834 wounded and 80 missing making a total of 1307. From Bomber Command, Transport Command, Fighter Command on the

A US glider on fire on the battlefield during Operation Varsity.

23/24th March 1945, 129 aircraft were lost, including 46 from IX US Troop Carriers.

Some 416 gliders reached the landing zone, 88 landed undamaged and 37 were burnt out. The British casualties were 27% killed, wounded or missing and the Americans 10.9%. Of the force 416 tug aircraft released their gliders after 10am, and within 5 hours the 6th Airborne Division had captured all its objectives, including 6 undamaged bridges over the Issel, and had taken 600 prisoners of war.

The RAF had 61 glider pilots killed, 21 wounded and 21 taken prisoner. This was probably due to the fact that the British gliders were released from 2,500 feet or above and the Americans from 600 feet.

Thus the former were exposed to fire from the ground after a much longer period. However, the Americans suffered much greater proportion of parachutes and tug aircraft damage than did the British. The conclusion was that a low release height exposed the tug aircraft to damage, as opposed to the gliders, where as a high release had the opposite effect.

In selecting landing zones for gliders the aim was to land the troops in tactical groups as near as possible to their initial objectives. This was the first time this method had been used for a complete division. In addition the troop-carrying gliders were planned to land on the outside of the landing zones, and so give protection during the unloading of the heavy equipment which was to land in the centre of the landing zones. The planned tactics over the landing zones were different for British and American aircraft.

The British aircraft approached and released at 2,500 feet, where as the American aircraft were 500 feet. The greater height of release for British aircraft was made possible by a timed glider, turn and approach drill evolved and practised after Arnhem.

The re-supply operation was undertaken by selecting five supply dropping points beforehand, but which before any re-supply was undertaken the airborne troops were to signal which dropping point zone to be used. A lesson from the Arnhem operation.

Due to the fact that all wheeled loads were put into Mk II Horsas to facilitate unloading, much time was saved. There was still, however, individual cases of lack of knowledge on the part of glider pilots and/or airborne passengers of the elementary drill for unloading through the nose and tail.

The question of glider and equipment salvaged was considered before the operation.

Despite the success of the operation the percentage of material recovered was less than even the most conservative estimate. It has to be borne in mind that the majority of the gliders landed in areas where there was a large loss due to artillery fire, incendiary flak and burning inflammable loads.

The American plan for this was;

After preliminary survey it was decided to do emergency repairs at the landing zones, then lift as many gliders as possible and land them at a field on the west bank of the Rhine for complete overhaul and inspection. Of the 889 gliders landed in the operation, 148 or 16.6 per cent, were recovered.

In addition, forty seven, two and half-ton truck-loads, and thirty one-ton trailer loads of spare parts, including 2000 instruments and 1273 tyres and wheel assemblies, were reclaimed from the landing zone. There were 889 tow ropes, each 350 feet in length that were used in the operation of which 360 were recovered from the rope landing area. Of these 288 were found to be serviceable a recovery percentage of 32. per cent.

However, the British plan was far from successful.

Owing to the boggy terrain of the landing zones and a large number of ditches, it was found impossible to "snatch" any of the British gliders. It was, therefore, necessary to dismantle the gliders on the landing zones, transport them by road to a suitable airfield on the west bank of the Rhine and after re-assembly, fly them off in the normal manner.

Seven tug aircraft and ten gliders were shot down and 32 tugs and 300 gliders damaged.

Of the 416 gliders which landed in the landing zone during the operation only 24 were recoverable, a total of 5.8 per cent. Seven tug aircraft and 10 gliders were shot down and 132 tugs and 300 gliders damaged. With respect to the gliders that were not recovered, only instruments, wireless sets, tyres, etc of the Horsas were salvaged since the Ministry of Aircraft Production does not require salvaged assemblies for new production. On the other hand, major assemblies for Hamilcar production are required and were shipped to the UK after dismantling.

Over 198 American gliders were snatched from the ground after Varsity and 39 allied gliders were snatched after Normandy. The idea was invented by the Americans. The RAF set up a Glider Pick Up Flight at RAF Ibsley, Hampshire. The tug-aircraft had a wire drum in the fuselage from which hung a hook and the towing rope of the glider was attached to a looped nylon rope which hung between two poles, about 50 feet in front of the glider. The tug aircraft picked up the loop with its snatch hook and pulled the glider into the air.

The tug aircraft radio serviceability was 95.3 per cent and the tug-glider intercommunications serviceability was 94.3 per cent. The total serviceability was 89.9 per cent. There were many messages of congratulations after Varsity.

The AOC C in C RAF Transport Command sent a message: "Well Done 46 Group."

The AOC of 38 Group: " Please give my thanks to all your group who took part in two days operation whether in the air or on the ground."

The AOC of 46 Group: "To all ranks of air and ground crew on their work and devotion to duty."

From the Chief of the Imperial General Staff to General Gale Commanding 1st British Airborne Corps: "Please convey to the Glider Pilot Regiment my heartiest congratulations on their wonderful performance in operations connected with the crossing of the Rhine. The skill and bravery displayed by them in this magnificent action of airborne forces will pass down into history as one of the highlights amongst the deeds of valour of the war."

The GOC 6th Airborne's message to the Chief of the General Staff: "Feel sure you will like to know Glider Pilot Regiment has done magnificent work for the 6th Airborne Division. Their skill and bravery are spoken of by all."

From General Eisenhower: "The great operation of forcing the Lower Rhine proved successful to the fullest extent of my desire."

• • • • • • • • • • •

Another report was made by Lt-Col W.J. Kirwan-Taylor of the Rifle Brigade, a staff officer to General Bols. He took off in a glider from Rivenhall at 7am in glider 'Smiling Sylvia' carrying Defence Platoon 2. With Defence Platoon 1 and a company of the Devons carried in seven gliders, their task was to capture a farmhouse in an orchard for use as a Divisional HQ, and to clear the area.

Approaching the Rhine, the glider doors were opened. The far side was covered in a thick pall of smoke, due to the bombing of Wesel, gunfire, and to burning houses, also a view that the Germans had laid an artificial fog to increase the difficulties of glider landings. After crossing the Rhine under some ground flak but which did not perturb the glider in anyway and they made a perfect landing.

They had landed in the middle of hundreds of American parachutists of 513 Regiment, who had dropped a mile or two too far north. Having checked if they were in the correct place, which in fact they were by about 100 yards they made for the orchard. There was some firing going on in and around the house, and several Germans ran out with their hands up. There was, however, no sign of any of the company of the Devons, nor of the other Defence Platoon, but as the Americans had largely done a clearing up job it was of no great consequence. They reached the house a minute or so before General Bols arrived — his glider had dropped him on the doorstep of the house.

Divisional HQ was set up and by 1300 (1pm) reports had come in by wireless from each of the brigades that the first objectives had been captured. By 1330 (1.30pm) 6 Air Landing Brigade further reported that they had captured Hamminkeln. Meanwhile, the glider pilots were being used for local defence of HQ:- slit trenches were dug and the airborne bulldozer was used to make a pit for the larger wireless sets. During the later afternoon Colonel Kirwan-Taylor, with the Chief Royal Engineer visited 6th Air Landing Brigade on their forward bridges over the Issel. The parachute squadron Royal Engineers was very depleted, and the Chief Engineer made arrangements for sending up a special party to prepare the bridge for demolition in an emergency. Later that night in the course of an enemy counterattack, it became necessary to blow one of these bridges, at the very moment a German tank was crossing. Later that night General Ridgeway called at Div HQ. On his way back to 17 Divisional HQ he and his party had a sharp skirmish with a party of about 40 Germans.

The report said that there was no doubt that the enemy expected the airborne landing in this area.

This may have been he commented an intelligent anticipation, but he did hear it said that they knew the fly-in route and the actual areas to be used.

Casualties were heavy-estimated at about 30-35% in the Air Landing Brigade in the fly-in and initial assault. There were four main reasons for this:-

(a) Heavy flak, including the use of incendiary shells and bullets.

(b) Crash landings, due to the heavy smoke screen.

(c) Landing in fairly strongly defended areas, often right under enemy batteries of 88mm or 20 mm guns.

(d) The enemy held prepared positions from which they could inflict heavy casualties on attacking troops

Casualties in the Parachute Brigades were comparatively light-estimated at about 5-20% in the different units. Each parachute brigade had an allotment of some 15 gliders but it was understood that none of the gliders for 5 Parachute Brigade arrived.

Casualties in weapons and vehicles were very much heavier-often over 50%. This was largely due to destruction of the gliders on landing, especially the burning of gliders before the equipment had been extracted.

Only a few Hamilcars arrived, probably due to broken tow ropes.

Overall the operation was an outstanding success and enabled the ground assault troops to establish a firm bridgehead from which the advance could immediately be continued.

Nevertheless, he went on to say that he did not consider that it was an operation which disproves the principle that it is unsound to land glider borne troops in a defended area. It succeeded this time because the enemy were partly demoralized and unwilling to fight to a finish. In his view, the principal that gliders cannot be landed in daylight in the middle of enemy troops still held good. If it was necessary to make an airborne landing in such an area, the gliders must be landed under cover of darkness or preceded by parachute troops. It was understood that a considerable number of American parachute troops were killed in the air as they came down, but the losses inflicted in this way were nothing like so heavy as they were in the case of gliders. Many gliders were raked with enemy fire as they touched down and often set alight: others were mortared before they stopped running.

During the early stages of the advance, the lack of transport was no disadvantage. The roads were bad, often little more than sandy tracks.

Losses in wireless sets were very heavy in the initial fly-in, only about 40% being in use on the 24th. Fortunately, 100% reserve had been provided, and this over-insurance would seem always to be essential. Personnel casualties were about 50 out of strength of 270. The parachute 62 set was regarded as being most successful.

Casualties in guns was heavy. It was thought that 25 pounders would be better provided if the division was to operate for more than three weeks. Casualties in artillery personnel were approximately 5 officers and 50 other ranks in the Light Regiment and 5 officers and 80 other ranks in the Anti-Tank.

The re-supply by air on D-Day was most successful. The Liberators flew over in formation at about 100 feet, and dropped their loads accurately. About 80% was recovered-by carriers and captured German half-track vehicles.

Generally speaking, the enemy fought well from prepared positions, but surrendered when attacked or on a show of force.

The civilian population were eager and anxious to surrender and to disclaim Nazi faith. In the area, which was strongly Catholic, there may have been some slight truth in this. There was no sign of food shortage or discomfort, that is until the airborne assault arrived. White flags were prolific and were waved and hung from every window.

General Ridegway decorated General Bols, Bridagier Hill and Lt-Col Roberts with the US Silver Star.

Harry Clark of the 2nd (Airborne) Ox & Bucks has this to say:

"I owe my life to the skill and courage of two RAF sergeant pilots, Sgts Jarvis and Geddes, who took part in an action for which they had never been properly trained. They flew us into hell and in the face of fearsome anti-aircraft fire and a smoke screen that obscured the landing area. I survived that day and 54 years and four bullet holes later still marvel at the nerve, skill and courage of these two wonderful pilots."

Harry was wounded in April 1945 and lost his right hand.

• • • • • • • • • • •

There were many acts of individual gallantry.

F/O Edgar Ince landed his glider within 50 yards of his briefed position despite heavy and accurate anti-aircraft fire and in very poor visibility.

P/O Michael Odlum was wounded in the back, but in spite of this he landed his glider successfully on the correct landing zone and then supervised the unloading of his glider under considerable fire. He refused despite being wounded to be evacuated and remained with his section until the 26th March.

Acting F/Lt John Lodge was engaged by anti-aircraft and small arms fire over the landing zone which damaged the elevator controls and caused the glider to build up excessive speed. He applied half-flap at which point a burst of enemy machine gun fire struck the glider penetrating the compressed air bottle making the flaps inoperative and killing one, and wounding another of his passengers. The air speed of the glider again built up excessively and a further burst of small arms fire practically severing the starboard aileron controls, the glider striking the ground at high speed. After travelling through two fields on the ground the aircraft came to a standstill almost a total wreck. Although severely shaken after this accident F/Lt Lodge remained with his flight throughout the operation. They along with F/O Love and Atkinson were recommended for the Distinguished Flying Cross. The final countersigning officer was Field Marshal Bernard Montgomery.

St/Sgt Eddie Raspison GPR was awarded the Distinguished Flying Medal for his great skill, getting his glider down and his second pilot Sgt Edwards RAF out of the burning glider.

St/Sgt Albert (Bert) Bowman who flew with C Squadron was also awarded the Distinguished Flying Medal, for saving the life of his second pilot Sgt Peter Davies RAF. With the elevator controls shot away by flak, the flaps on his glider became unserviceable and the undercarriage was badly damaged. Despite this handicap, Bert was able to safely get his glider down, loaded with a tank, by using the elevator trimming device. He made what could only be described as an exceptionally good landing.

Lt-Col Ian Murray was awarded a bar to the DSO. Much of the success of No 1 Wing of the Glider Pilot Regiment was put down to his actions and training. In his glider he had carried

Stan Jarvis and Harry Clark. [Harry Clark]

the General Officer Commanding the 1st Airborne Division. During the landing, his glider had been hit several times Also, owing to casualties on the ground he had taken over command of the 9th Parachute Brigade which he led to safety over the Rhine.

One glider pilot of the Glider Pilot Regiment worthy of mention, particularly as he was awarded an Air Force award, was Acting Squadron Sgt-Maj Lawrence William Turnbull, known as 'Buck'. As he came in to land carrying a heavy load of personnel and medical equipment at a height of 2,000 feet, a loose tow-rope smashed across his cockpit, destroying most of the controls and breaking the fin and rudder. Subsequently his glider went out of control and in a vertical dive, but he remained at the control column and managed to bring the glider under control. His glider was hit at least five times, killing the second pilot and wounding two of his passengers. One of the wingtips was shot away and the fuselage badly damaged. Despite all this he managed to get his glider and its load down to the landing zone only a 100 yards from its correct position.

On the ground he organised a stretcher party and got the wounded out of the stricken glider. For his great efforts on this occasion he was recommended and awarded the Conspicuous Gallantry Medal (Flying), the second highest award in the Royal Air Force to other ranks to the Victoria Cross. This was the only CGM (Flying) awarded to a soldier in WWII and still the only one out of 112 awarded since its inception in 1943.

••••••••••

The tug crews were also remembered.

F/Lt Donald Campbell from Canada was awarded a bar to his DFC, awarded in August 1944. He had taken part in the operations to Arnhem with 196 Squadron, and on an operation in February 1945, after a combat with an enemy fighter came back with his rear gunner dead. On the 24th March, he lost one of his engines but continued to tow a fully loaded Horsa glider at a greatly reduced speed for two hours and forty five minutes and delivered his glider at the correct landing zone with the minimum of loss of time.

Wg/Cdr Trenham Musgrave OBE was awarded the DFC. At the time he was commanding 296 Squadron at Earls Colne having been in command since the 10th September 1944. On the 24th August 1943, he had been involved in an accident flying a Horsa glider and lost his left leg. Despite this considerable handicap he was flying again by December 1943. He also took part in the Arnhem operations towing a glider on the subsequent and re-supply operations. In between this and Operation Varsity, in which he led 296 Squadron with great leadership and skill, he also took part in tactical bombing and SAS sorties.

Wg/Cdr Roy Dutton DFC commanding officer of 512 Squadron was awarded the DSO. On Varsity he led 120 aircraft and glider combinations from 46 Group, and 320 aircraft and glider combinations from 38 Group. His own glider was the first to reach the enemy occupied area in broad daylight and under heavy and accurate flak. In spite of this and the fact his aircraft was totally unarmed, a straight and steady course was steered to the glider landing zone, 6 miles behind enemy lines, and only when he was sure did he give the word to the glider pilot to release.

Sgt-Major Turnbull accompanied by his wife and mother at Buckingham Palace to receive his Conspicuous Gallantry Medal (Flying). [Museum Middle Wallop]

He had flown 103 hours with Transport Command and previously to that 340 with Fighter Command.

Lt-Col Pierre Joubert AFC of the South African Air Force commanded 271 Squadron on Operation Varsity. He had taken part in the D-Day and Arnhem operations. One of his pilots at Arnhem, F/Lt David Lord, was posthumously awarded the Victoria Cross, and F/Lt Jimmy Edwards the DFC after being shot down and escaping back to allied lines. Jimmy was later to become a well known voice on the radio and an actor on television.

Pierre was, at 48, much older than most aircrew and more the age of senior officers in the Royal Air Force. He had flown over 4,000 hours of which 600 were with 271 Squadron. On this occasion and after Varsity he was recommended for the DFC but which was later upgraded to the DSO. It is sad to record that Pierre died in an accident on the 8th May 1945. It is said that, while attempting to make fireworks to celebrate Victory in Europe he was blown to pieces.

● ● ● ● ● ● ● ● ● ●

There were a number of other awards to members of 38 and 46 Groups. A report on the role and performance of the tug crews of 296 and 297 Squadrons was made by Wg/Cdr Musgrave.

Of the 60 Horsa gliders delivered 59 released at the correct height the remaining one suffered a broken tow-rope and landed behind allied lines. The failure was due to slipstream from a preceding aircraft, and the remnants of the rope still attached to the Halifax were brought back for examination in accordance with the briefing. He also mentioned the tendency to overload by way of soldiers, and after Arnhem not unnaturally adding ammunition. This practice, it was said, would happen again in the future.

He found the east bank of the Rhine fairly thick with grey/white smoke, streaked with black in places. The head of the stream was eight minutes early, and it was almost impossible to loose this without some sort of dog-leg course being made. The cause was partially a tail wind, and partially a slight miscalculation of airspeed in the planning stage. The flak was being directed at the incoming gliders and not the tug aircraft, the losses of only 7 tug aircraft and the 29% losses to glider pilots confirmed this.

● ● ● ● ● ● ● ● ● ●

There were many strange happenings during this vast operation… At one point, a canoe paddled by an RAF Wing Commander was seen coming across the Rhine from Gray Island, near Wesel. He called to troops of the Scottish Division, saying, "I have come to ask you to come and get my 120 German prisoners."

He had been shot down flying a Typhoon and landed on the island by the edge of the river. A German had invited him into a dug-out, where he found the German officer commanding the units in the area. The question of surrender came up and the German had said to him, "I will take you to Wesel."

"You can't," said the Wing Commander, "We have already captured it."

"Then *we* shall surrender to *you*," replied the German.

● ● ● ● ● ● ● ● ● ●

It was the courage and skill of the 300 men of the Royal Engineers that took the first British tanks across the Rhine. They used a bold experiment using ferry-rafts. These 30-ton rafts were constructed from pontoons and weighed four and half tons each. The pontoons were drawn up to the Rhine by trailers, gutted Bren carriers and armoured sledges, all this was done under four hours of intense enemy fire. Personnel of the RAF were there to operate balloon winches which dragged the rafts from one side of the river to the other.

Corporal E. Rideout of the Royal Marines was the first man to hoist the Royal Navy's White Ensign on German soil. The Navy were there to supply a ferry-service to carry tanks, bulldozers, and mobile guns across the Rhine.

A front line was established and a large pocket of enemy troops, 800 to 1000 strong caught between the 6th Airborne Division and the

17th US Airborne Division in the area of Diersfordter Wald were eliminated.

• • • • • • • • • •

The thoughts of some RAF Glider pilots are worth recording, and one in particular, F/Sgt Worrell, does not mince his words…

"I think that although Varsity was regarded as a success I have misgiving about its value. There were no vital strategic features in the area where the landings took place and I doubt very much whether we speeded up the breakout from the bridgehead across the Rhine.

I think that more would have been achieved if the landings had taken place nearer the Rhine. Nothing seemed to have been learned from Arnhem. The opposition which might be expected from the Germans was sadly underestimated by the organisers, who should have had better intelligence and insight."

• • • • • • • • • •

The airborne troops also had a poor opinion of the glider as a means of transport. Norman (Nobby) Hall, an airborne corporal who had previously parachuted into Normandy but had been transported by glider on Varsity said to Worrell shortly after they had been captured and taken prisoner: "F*** gliders, I'll jump next time!"

Charles Stewart had the following comment about the difference in parachuting out of an aircraft as opposed to flying in a glider.

"Ask any para what he would rather do and he will say 'Me? Go up in those bloody flying coffins? Not likely!'

But the boys who flew in gliders would say the same about parachuting."

S/Ldr 'Duke' Kent was even more scathing. He said that there was no real effort to toughen up the RAF Glider pilots, route marches were a laugh and the rest of the day off. There was a lot of foot stamping and saluting but no daily PT. He never once flew a loaded glider and no effort was made to give the pilots the experience of being in a battle. The mass landings were done by numbers and the timing bad. The only real danger was being run over by some clot who had come in to fast in an empty glider, but never laden.

Whoever was responsible for training the RAF pilots should have been shot, but was probably given a medal by Group. 'Duke' had served in North Africa and Malta so had been in a number of battle areas. He tried to make his feelings known before Varsity, but only days before the operation began he was promoted to squadron leader, made a squadron commander and posted on to a company commanders' course to the School of Infantry, thus missing the operation.

• • • • • • • • • •

Gordon Procter has never really forgiven the Glider Pilot Regiment for sending him into action on the Rhine Crossing armed with only with a Smith and Wesson revolver.

"A sten gun would have been so much more practical, let alone the superb sub-machine guns carried by the American airborne troops," he says.

• • • • • • • • • •

Ken Scolding regards the part played in Varsity as highly important.

"I lost a number of friends, amongst them many army pilots for whom I had the highest regard. They had done it before and knew what it was all about."

• • • • • • • • • •

Pete Culley just missed Varsity. He was an air gunner with 296 Squadron at Earls Colne. On the 24th, and having attended the briefing for Varsity his pilot became unwell and was put in the sick bay with temperature of 102. Pete waited with his flying kit in his hand until the last aircraft and glider had left, hoping, that at the last moment someone in one of the crews would drop out, they didn't.

• • • • • • • • • •

Operation Varsity constituted the greatest air-lift in any one airborne operation ever.

In support of the Allied air forces flew 7000 sorties in the battle area and in attacks on targets in North-West Germany during the 24th March.

By Sunday the 25th, British and American troops had joined up into one solid front, 30 miles long and 9 miles deep.

The King sent telegrams of congratulations to General Eisenhower and Field Marshal Montgomery, referring to the crossing of the lower Rhine as "a military achievement of incalculable significance to the whole world."

• • • • • • • • • • •

The opinions expressed by German spokesmen after the war regarding the pros and cons of airborne operations are worthy of mention.

Field Marshal Albrecht Kesselring commented on the airborne operations in Holland…

"In Holland 1940, on the whole, the German airborne operations must be classified as a success, especially the capture of bridges which were strategically important to the attacking ground forces. Very large forces could penetrate deep behind Dutch lines, saving the German Army the possible cost of a serious fight in capturing Holland. The element of surprise was the main element success."

As this was the first airborne operation in history it should be treated in somewhat greater detail. The operation was under the command of the Second Air Force, the Commander, General Student.

The operation was divided into the following parts:

1. An operation with gliders alone against Fort Eben Emael and the Maas Bridge.

2. A major airborne operation by two divisions to capture the Moordijk Bridge, the Rotterdam Airport, the City of Rotterdam, and the Dutch capital, The Hague and its airfields.

The operation was a masterpiece in

the deployment of troops and troop carrier formations, among the only airfields near the border, just within range of the distant objectives.

The incorporation of escort fighter wings in the transport movement, for which General Osterkamp can claim both the responsibility and the credit.

The failures and losses can be attributed to the following:

Interference with the plan of attack by the Commander-in-Chief of the Luftwaffe, mentioned above.

The inadequate strength of parachutists in the air attack group of the 22nd Infantry Division. Defects in training and other technical defects were also responsible.

The next attack was on Corinth in 1941, by parachute troops and troop-carrier units.

The actual tactical success was limited to the capture of the Isthmus of Corinth. It is true that if the attack had been undertaken a few days earlier it would have been far more successful and a large number of the British Expeditionary Force would have been cut off from access to their embarkation ports on the Peleponessus.

The capture of Crete in 1941, proved to be the most interesting and certainly the most eventful German airborne operation. It resulted in very serious losses, which percentage-wise greatly exceeded those sustained by the Germans in previous World War II campaigns.

The German High Command began to doubt whether such operations could continue to pay – the Crete success had cost too much. As this point Hitler himself lost confidence in operations of this nature.

In 1944, came the Ardennes offensive in which the airborne operations were definitely a failure. The force committed was far to small and the training of the parachute troops and troop carrier squadrons was inadequate.

To sum up, from the German point of view, airborne operations which are to achieve success on a large scale require a great outlay of material, outstanding personnel, and time for training and preparation. Such operations are accordingly 'expensive'. From 1941, Germany, in comparison to its enemies, in this respect, was 'poor'.

German records show that the allied landings in Normandy in June 1944 caught them by surprise. They were expecting the air landings to take place further inland and to be aimed at more strategically important objectives, whereas, in fact, they were closely tied in with the amphibious landings. The German defence plan was tailored for the former eventuality.

At Arnhem the allied troops found by pure chance two worn-out SS Panzer Divisions in the vicinity.

They were able to hold the bridge at Nijmegen for a further four days and prevented the allied troops from establishing contact with the northernmost airborne troops at Arnhem.

The counter attacks were successfully conducted under the unified commands of Army Group B, whose operations staff were stationed there. With the Panzer Divisions they were the only troops there at the time. The Germans had done enough to prevent the Allies breaking through and it was six months before they were able to launch another attack across the Rhine.

The Germans were impressed by the operation in March 1945. It was practically a mass crossing of the river by air. The worn out German Divisions with limited fighting strength defended their positions for a short time before they were defeated, their only reserves were one training division, whose troops were widely dispersed to escape incessant air attacks, This division were given orders to launch a counter attack, and one German regimental group did temporarily achieve a minor success against the landed airborne troops. The rest of the divisions were not committed at all owing to allied low level aeroplanes completely wrecking all means of transportation.

● ● ● ● ● ● ● ● ● ● ●

The military glider had shown that it had two major advantages, silence and the ability to land a concentrated body of troops on a specific target en masse. Recommendations for the future were issued by Allied commanders. The provision of glider pilots should be the responsibility of the Army and airborne development work was to be centralised in the UK.

CHAPTER 18

South-East Asia

In the Far East, No.344 glider Wing of the Royal Air Force was commanded by a Wing Commander G. Lillywhite AFC, AFM, at Royal Air Force Bikram. The other glider wing was No.343 Base near, Rawalpindi. The distance between the two was 600 miles.

The gliders used were American Wacos identical to those used on Operation Varsity by the American Airborne Forces. Wooden gliders like the Horsa tended to warp in the humid tropical atmosphere and the four-engined aircraft needed to tow the large gliders were rare in the Far East. Wacos towed by Dakotas, which were already in service in the Far East, were ideal.

There were six further RAF glider squadrons in India.

The gliders were assembled at RAF Bihta and then ferried by Dakota and Halifax to airfields in the Central Provinces. No 96 Squadron was used for glider towing duties.

The first glider operations were in February 1944, when Hadrian gliders towed by the 1st Air Commando USAF were landed behind Japanese lines. Some 51 gliders were landed in jungle landing zones carrying troops who cleared landing strips for Dakota aircraft to land with further equipment and men.

Gliders were used for getting casualties out of remote jungle areas. This was done by the 'snatch pick-up, technique. One end of the tow-rope was attached to the glider while the other, which ended in a large loop, was suspended from two poles not much taller than goal posts. On the tail of the tug aircraft was a hook which was at the end of a boom and rather like a giant fishing hook. Within the tug the tow-rope was wound around a drum which had a friction brake. When the rope was pulled out rapidly, heat was produced which caused a brake to come on which rapidly slowed down the rate which the tow-rope unwound. However, on occasions tow ropes could not stand the sudden strain of the snatch and snapped and on other occasions whipped backwards with such violence that they smashed the flimsy, plywood gliders to smithereens.

The 44th (Indian) Airborne Division was based in the Bilaspur area and some 600 lifts were made before the first accident when a Waco with an RAF crew crashed on approach and a number of the passengers and crew were injured.

When the news came of the Japanese surrender in August 1945, the 6th Airborne Division with Horsa gliders were due to arrive. The airfields were primitive, a couple of shacks and six bell tents for accommodation. The men were issued with 'Pith' helmets previous to this they had been wearing bush hats.

By about December 1944 there were approximately 500 RAF and Army glider pilots in the Far East, some of whom had served at Arnhem. The training consisted of jungle school, survival courses and Army weapons training assault courses. These camps were good, and well organised with good food and accommodation. The Jungle School of Self Preservation was run by Mrs Graham-Bower MBE, assisted by the Naga Hill people. Here they were reminded that their purpose in being in India was to fly troops into Singapore, and then if they landed in one piece to become patrol leader. The infantry training was given for this role by the Wiltshire Regiment.

The dropping of the Atomic Bomb saved many glider/tug crews in the Far East from a nasty experience in the shape of any airborne invasion of Japan.

• • • • • • • • • • •

Peter Bailey, having been trained in Canada, found himself flying in a Dakota, via Sardinia, Malta, Egypt, Palestine, Iraq, Persian Gulf and Karachi ending up in what he described as a "god-forsaken dump called Fatherjang" about 30 miles from Rawalpindi, where training continued on Wacos. This was followed by a spell with 31 Squadron on a supply dropping course in the Cachar Hills, Assam.

• • • • • • • • • • •

John Rayson undertook his pilot training on Tiger Moth's and Ansons in Canada. He returned to the UK in April 1944 with the chance of flying with the Fleet Air Arm or becoming a glider pilot, the latter won. After courses on Hotspurs, Hadrians and Horsas he was flown to India by Dakota and joined 670 Squadron in December, 1944. He joined Army glider pilots who became second pilots or 'second dickies' as they were known.

As an example the percentages – in 668 Squadron there were 65 RAF Glider pilots to only 35 Army pilots.

After VE Day 15th August 1945, the squadron was disbanded and he was posted to Heliopolis, Cairo for a flying control course. On completion of this course he became a flying control officer at Palam Airport, Delhi until he was demobbed in November 1946.

The one main problem was gliders that were meant to carry 3,750 pounds of supplies, but often British and Ghurkha troops smuggled extra food and ammunition on board, pushing the weight up to 4,500 pounds. One pilot reported having an all up weight of 6,400 pounds, which meant he took two hours to reach a height of 4,000 feet in a double tow!

One of the glider pilots from the USA was Flight Officer Jackie Coogan, the Hollywood actor who, on a number of occasions, flew in Ghurkha troops into jungle areas.

CHAPTER 19

Further Planned Operations

As the Canadian First Army advanced into Holland, 21st Army Group proposed to use SAS troops to create confusion in enemy rear areas, stimulate local resistance and generally assist the Canadian First Army. SHAEF did not consider that the operation could be launched before the 5th April 1945. A meeting was convened on the 15th March, 1945.

The first of the conferences was held on the 2nd and 3rd April 1945, and the plan finalised on the 5th April 1945, and operational instructions were by Headquarters, First Canadian Army, the date the 1st May 1945.

General Eisenhower said he would like one more big airborne operation before the war ended.

• • • • • • • • • •

Operation 'Amherst' was a plan to drop in 47 Stirlings of 38 Group French parachutists of the 2nd and 3rd Regiments de Chasseurs on 20 selected dropping points with the task of securing airfields at Steenwijk, Helve and Leeuwarden along with 15 roads and 3 railway bridges. At the same time 18 Halifaxes of No 38 Group were to drop the same number of jeeps on six of these dropping zones.

• • • • • • • • • •

Operation 'Keystone' was a plan to convey troops of the 2nd SAS Regiment with two Jedburgh wireless teams and three jeeps carried in three Halifaxes to four previously selected dropping zones. Their task to take the airfield at Teure and 7 road bridges.

• • • • • • • • • •

Operation 'Schnapps' on the 8th May 1945, was an operation to carry troops and equipment of the 1st Airborne Division, 7000 troops and 2000 tons of supplies to Copenhagen in 33 Stirlings, 9 Halifax's and 10 Dakotas of 38 Group.

• • • • • • • • • •

Jospeh Cadden of 'H' Squadron was in the operations room, at Newbold Revel waiting to be briefed for another ' Balbo' around the airfields of the UK, when the CO came in and called out the names of some of the crews.

They were told, including Joe to report to the armaments hut and draw what ever they needed – no advice or information was given as to why.

When the men who had been at Arnhem heard this, there were many subdued mutterings, as far as they were concerned the war was at an end and another operation spelt danger. Joe's second pilot was St/Sgt ' Jock' Carcary, who had served at Arnhem. When they got to the runway the Albemarles were ticking over ready to be hitched onto the Horsas. We took off and landed somewhere in the East of England and awaited the arrival of the SAS troops.

"We were confined to a hut but soon found out from an 'old soldier' the target was Templehof airfield, Berlin. When we heard the operation had been cancelled we broke into our 'K' rations and had a good smoke."

• • • • • • • • • •

When Frank Haddock returned to the UK he heard that their next trip was to cross the Kiel Canal but nothing ever came of it. This was to support the battle for Kiel as the German Navy was delaying the Canadian forces along the northern flank.

Towards the end of April 1945, 10 Hamilcar crews were briefed for an operation intending to carry full loads of petrol to the outskirts of Berlin. This also was later cancelled.

• • • • • • • • • •

John Herold remembers two operations similar to Varsity were set up but cancelled because of the speed of the allied advance into Germany and the ultimate ending of the war in May 1945.

One operation was to fill the gliders with fuel and land forward of the advance areas to support the advance of the leading allied tanks. The second operation was support of the battle of Kiel as the German Navy were delaying the Canadian forces along the northern flank.

• • • • • • • • • •

Lieutenant General Lewis H. Brereton and his staff of the First Allied Airborne Army after Varsity were continuing to search for an opportunity to launch a genuinely strategic airborne operation. This they thought they had been found in Operation 'Arena' – a plan to land six to ten divisions by parachute, glider and aircraft in the vicinity of Kassel, more than a 100 miles beyond the Rhine.

On the 27th March 1945, information on Operation Arena was received from Brigadier Flavell, Deputy Chief of Staff First Allied Airborne Army. The task was to seize and hold the area of Kassel in conjunction with a thrust of north-eastwards via Frankfurt and Fula by 6th Army Group, and an advance eastwards by 12th Army Group. The original date was the 1st June 1945, but this was brought forward to the 15th May 1945. The Estimated glider serviceability on the 1st May 1945, was 736 Horsas and 89 Hamilcars. The estimated maximum recovery from Varsity was say 25-100%.

A second plan was to seize control of Berlin should German resistance suddenly collapse, the plan would involve 1500 transport aircraft, over 1,000 gliders, 20,000 paratroopers, and escorted by 3,000 fighters, a force larger then had landed in Normandy on D-Day would be landed at two airfields Tempelhof and Gatow, Berlin, Germany.

The plan with the code name Operation 'Eclipse' was to capture Berlin against a rear-guard action of a force said to be 200,000 die-hard Nazis with parachutists and glider troops.

But as history now shows the decision came for the taking of Berlin to be left entirely to the Russians. This they did, but at a cost of 100,000 casualties. It was said that if the plan to capture Berlin with parachutists and gliders had gone ahead, the Russians also had a huge number of gliders amassed on airfields behind Russian lines ready to go as soon Eclipse had been given the word to go.

The first suggestion of an air landing in Norway was made at a conference held at Headquarters Scottish Command on the 21st November 1944. Arising out of this meeting came a special planning committee who prepared a draft plan for a landing in Norway. On the 23rd April 1945, at a conference of the 1st British Airborne Corps it was decided, as the S.A.S would be fully employed at the time to use one of the British Airborne Divisions.

Final orders for Operation 'Doomsday' as the landing in Norway was to be known were received by the First Allied Airborne from Supreme Command on the 5th May 1945, No 38 Group were ordered to furnish the lift assisted by Dakota aircraft from the Troop Carrier Command.

The Air Officer No 88 Group was appointed Air Commander to co-ordinate and control all air forces from the operation. The Air Officer commanding No 38 Group was also appointed commander of the Troop Carrier Forces.

The main objectives were as follows:

(a) Oslo, capital of Norway and centre of administration:-both German and Norwegian;

(b) Stavanger, because of its good airfield and having one of the nearest good harbours to the United Kingdom. It was also suitable for the operation of fighter aircraft;

(c) Kristiansands, because of its importance as a minesweeping bases in the Skagerrak, because they were the only suitable airfields on which four-engine transport aircraft might safely land.

Any troops intended for the Kristiansands area were to be landed at Sola and make the rest of the journey by road. The operation was carried out in four phases between the 9th and 13th May, delay was caused by unfavourable weather conditions and the operation took 36 hours longer than had been intended. As no enemy opposition was expected, the shortest possible route was taken by the aircraft and the landings were successful. Only two aircraft were lost one contained as part of the crew the Air Officer Commanding No 38 Group, Air Vice Marshal James Rowland Scarlett-Streatfield CBE on the 10th May 1945, he was flying in Stirling LK 566-G of 190 Squadron flown by S/Ldr Douglas R. Robertson DFC RCAF, from Kamloops, British Columbia, Canada, who had flown this aircraft on Operation Varsity, March 1945. All the crew of seven and the 30 passengers from the 1st Airborne, and Border Regiment were killed.

The aircraft was not found until 2nd July 1945 and all the casualties were buried in the War Graves Cemetery, Oslo. It had crashed in bad weather on its way to Gardermoen airfield. One other aircraft from 196 Squadron also crashed on the 10th May 1945; 18 other aircraft turned back because of the weather conditions.

Between March and May 1945, 700 men of the 6th Airborne were killed, 750 wounded and 400 missing making a total of 3,092 men killed in WWII. The cost to the 6th Airborne Division was high; glider pilots from other programmes and the men they carried had possibly less chance of surviving then the men who came down in parachutes.

The conclusion was that airborne forces in the Second World War was a luxury-spectacular, impressive and often highly useful, as many luxuries can be. The expense of training specialist airborne troops, the diversion of resources from other programs, the leadership denied regular units by the diversion of highly qualified and motivated men into elite units, and the cost of providing special equipment such as aircraft, gliders, and parachutes-all those would have to be weighed against the results.

(above) Veterans of the Glider Pilot Regiment gather at Hamminkeln in 1997: (l to r) Elliott, Mills, Haddock, Henson, Thirkettle, Scolding, Meek, Jarvis, Buckle, Procter, Angell (Tug Pilot), Scott (Tug Pilot). [Cy Henson]
(below) The Reichswald war cemetry. [Alan Cooper]

CHAPTER 20

Reunions

In 1981, a visit back to Hamminkeln was made, the first of many to come. The village, now more a town, is 8 km north west of Wesel and 13 km east of the Rhine.

Over those 36 years the village had changed considerably, although the front gardens of the houses and the allotment-lined back gardens still had the same look that the glider pilots remembered so well from the briefing photographs taken by the RAF Photograph Reconnaissance Units. The brewery had been extended and had flourished. The shops had large plate-glass windows, some displaying fashions which would do justice to an Oxford Street store in London.

The windmill stood immaculate, although now overlooked by a modern block of flats, which for some reason of design did not look out of place.

The tall-spired church, into which on that fateful day in March 1945, the women and children were placed for safety, still dominates the village/town centre.

One lady who was 16 years of age in March 1945 remembered hearing the sound of heavy aircraft, which could only mean one thing, an air raid, upon which she and her family hurried to the cellar. Unbeknown to us, at the time they were in the cellar the gliders were making a 'circuit' of the village. The raid was obviously a large one for the noise was deafening but, unlike other raids, no sound of bombs was heard; only the continuous firing of the local field guns and rifles. Post-war she ran a café in the village.

In 1985 John Rayson revisited Hamminkeln. He had difficulty in recognising the area that he had landed in, but as he drove on he came to a farm where he recognised the spinney just beyond and could see the bank which he had climbed over to get into the spinney, so he was sure that this was the first farmhouse he had gone to. However, when he drove on to find the second and third, he found the whole area to be covered in farms and it was impossible to decide which were the ones he had stopped at 40 years previously.

In 1987, Brigadier Chatterton died at the age of 75.

On the 24th March 1995 members of the 6th Airborne Division with their families and friends gathered at Hamminkeln. They included Colonel John Tillet of the Ox & Bucks Regiment. They were welcomed by Burgemeister Heinreich Meyers and given a civic reception followed by a tour of the Divisional landing zones.

A copper beech tree was planted alongside a memorial stone close to the railway station at Hamminkeln which had been the regimental headquarters of the Ox & Bucks in March 1945. This was to commemorate the allied dead and also the German civilians who died as a result of the battle. The memorial is an attractive granite boulder which has a brass plaque with an inscription, in both German and English.

52nd Light Infantry
In Memory of all those who gave their lives during the Airborne Landing at Hamminkeln on 24th March 1945.
This tree has been planted by comrades on the 50th Pilgrimage-Rhine Crossing 1995.

The memorial was covered with both the Union and German National Flags and was unveiled jointly by the Burgemeister, Heinrich Meyers and Howard Wright who then both proceeded to plant the copper beech tree. Twenty veterans of the regiment then planted 140 Poppy Crosses in front of the memorial. Each cross bore the name of a member of the regiment who had given their lives in the landing and in subsequent actions across Germany up to VE Day, 8th May 1945.

Out of a total of around 630 men in the Battalion 110 were killed and over 300 wounded on 24th March 1945, whilst a further 30 lost their lives in the advance across Germany to meeting the Russians near Lake Schwerin, close to the Baltic Sea . A film of Operation Varsity was shown to the veterans. A visit was made to Kopenhof Farm which was landing Zone 'P' Stallmanshoff Drop Zone 'A' , and finally the area of Drop Zone 'B' the site of 5 Para Brigade operations.

Next to the Church in Hamminkeln is a fully operational red GPO telephone box.

A visit was made to the Reichswald War Cemetery at Kleve where the great majority of casualties from Operation Varsity are buried. A service was conducted, and led by the band of the Parachute Regiment.

In March 1999, a further visit, on this occasion to unveil a plaque to the memory of glider pilots from the Glider Pilot Regiment, and the Royal Air Force. This was attended by one Army glider pilot Alan Smith, and five ex-RAF Glider pilots, John Love DFC, John Herold MBE, Len MacDonald, Bill Holdsworth and the irrepressible Cy Henson who organised the RAF element on this occasion.

Also present were former members of the 2nd Ox & Bucks, Royal Ulster Rifles, and the Parachute Regiment, plus the twin sons Geoffrey and Antony of the late F/Sgt Geoffrey Grant killed on Operation Varsity.

On Monday the 22nd March 1999, a reception was given by the Burgemeister Herr Heinrich Meyers prior to the unveiling of the plaque which was done in pouring rain, but which on this occasion went unnoticed. A second plaque, in brass was unveiled to the memory of the Royal Ulster Rifles.

On returning to the reception the veterans of Varsity were joined by a dozen pupils from a school in Hamminkeln, there were fewer boys than girls and the reason given was that the girls

Former RAF glider pilots (most of whom are featured in this book) attending a reception at the RAF Club, Piccadilly after a church service at St Clement Danes, London. (l to r) back: Hudson, Macdonald, Johnson, Atkinson, Lancaster, Scolding, Elliott, Brown, Sims, Procter; front: Herold, Giddings, Henson.

were better at learning English than the boys. They were undertaking a project on the landings in March 1945, when their village/town became a battleground.

They began to ask the veterans questions about the battle, the first going to Colonel Tod Sweeney MC, who in 1945 was a Company Commander with the 2nd Ox & Bucks. He was asked where he would have rather been at the time of the battle, his reply, "Home in Bed." This seemed to break any ice there had been, as everyone roared with laughter, although his reply was written down with great precision and used in the project they were doing.

Former F/O John Love DFC, when asked by author Alan Cooper how the wounded were treated, gave a graphic account of how they were graded according to the severity of their wounds.

"A coloured tab was placed on each wounded man and the colour of the tab determined if you were treated first or last."

He had been badly wounded coming into land but made a full recovery and went on to play professional football, post-war, for Nottingham Forest and later went into football management. Having made a full recovery from his war wounds he is now suffering from his footballing 'wear and tear' over a number of years.

In the afternoon of the 22nd March 1999, a tour of the landing zones around Hamminkeln including the railway station, where John Herold had landed his glider 54 years before and found the body of F/Sgt Geoffrey Grant still in his own glider.

The Issel Bridge was taken by the 2nd Ox & Bucks under the leadership of Sgt John Burns, who took over the platoon when his platoon commander was killed while landing by glider. He was on the visit and although now a senior citizen still looked very much the soldier he obviously had been in March 1945, when he won a well-deserved Military Medal. At the memorial, on the site of the former headquarters of the 2nd Ox & Bucks, a short but moving service of remembrance and poppy laying in memory of the many men of the regiment who fell during the operation.

1998. Cy Henson and Alan Cooper at Geoffrey Grant's grave in the Reichswald war cemetery. [Hilda Cooper]

On Tuesday the 23rd March 1999, the main party left for the UK, where as the RAF Glider pilot element stayed on for a further two days. Another visit was made to landing zones, and the site where Cy Henson found a glider with its nose in a railway signal box. A fence was found with three former Horsa undercarriage legs being used as fence posts.

On Wednesday 24th March 1999, a pilgrimage took place to the Reichswald War Cemetery at Kleve. A wreath was laid in memory of the 61 RAF Glider pilots killed during Operation Varsity, of whom 48 lay in peace in the cemetery.

The author Alan Cooper was honoured and proud to be able to play on the bugle, Last Post and Reveille to give a little colour and atmosphere to the ceremony. The gravestone of Sgt Andrew Love had an alteration on it. In the cemetery register he is recorded as a glider pilot whereas on his gravestone, in 1999 this has been changed to pilot. An enquiry to the Commonwealth War Graves resulted in them not being

Nephews of John Nash (Andy, Kit & Pete) at his grave in the Reichswald war cemetery. [Paddy Nash]

In 1985, Paddy Nash and his three son's visited the Reichswald Cemetery, the 40th Anniversary of the battle. He was there to visit his brother Jack's grave. His other brother Kevin had also been a pilot and survived the war. Jack's middle son Kit looked very much like his Uncle Jack, who he never met.

Harry Clark often wondered about the 19-year-old RAF Glider pilot who had safely got him down on the 24th March 1945. It turned out that Stan Jarvis, his pilot, was living only a few miles away from Harry in Essex. Both have since met up and talked about that day over 50 years ago. They met when Harry was asked to give a talk on Operation Varsity at a meeting of the Essex Branch of the Aircrew Association.

Eddie Raspison had not seen his RAF co-pilot Sid Edwards since the day he pulled him out of their crashed glider and he was taken away badly wounded, when both in their 70s they wrote to the author and he found their memories were similar and realise that Sid Edwards and not 'Tom' Edwards as Eddie remembered him, was his second pilot. He then put them in touch. Sid was flabbergasted to receive a call from Eddie.

aware of this alteration, or after investigation knowing the reason other than it may have been an error when routine maintenance was made on the grave.

The result is the headstone is now to be replaced.

Still flying, former RAF pilot Ken Elwood, who is now the proud owner of the very same Tiger Moth aircraft in which he learned to fly during World War II. [both photos, Ken Elwood]

He could not remember much of the operation, but had always believed that he had fallen out of the glider after landing, whereas, in fact, Eddie had carried him out. Eddie then told him he had been awarded the DFM, which he shared with Sid.

For one former RAF glider pilot flying is still a part of his life... Doctor Ken Ellwood now owns and flies the very Tiger Moth that he flew at Carlisle Elementary Flying School in 1945.

Alan Hartley was the organiser of the stained glass memorial window at Down Ampney. This originated from a meeting with the late Jimmy Edwards DFC at Down Ampney in 1971. In 1974, the window was unveiled included in the design of the window is the portrait of the late F/Lt David Lord VC, killed flying supplies from Down Ampney to Arnhem in September 1944. When Jimmy Edwards died a few years ago he bequeathed his flying log books to Alan.

Jack Harris, who went all the way to Hamburg in 1945, post-war was a guest of the Burgemeister of Hamburg at the time of a visit by Prince Charles to the German city. He was, in his own words, 'given a wonderful reception'. Up to recent times I believed all the glider pilots on Varsity were from the Army.

Padre Jimmy Mack joined the 2nd Ox & Bucks in 1945 but when the war in the Far East came to an end he was posted to the 9th Parachute Regiment and told to report to Ringway for parachute training. They were divided up into sticks of six and trained by a pint-sized Ulster Protestant F/Sgt.

After balloon training came the time to jump from an aircraft, Jimmy found himself at No 1.

Later, after jumping successfully, he asked the F/Sgt why he had put him at No.1 in the stick.

"Well Padre," replied the sergeant, "when you had gone I looked at the others and said, 'If the padre can do it; you can do it! No.2 stand at the door, get ready, go!' And he did, followed by the others..."

When the 9th Parachute Regiment were posted to Palestine with the task to control the Jewish Freedom Fighters who refused to accept any international quota of Jewish immigrants into Palestine, Jimmy went with them.

He first revisited Hamminkeln for the 50th Anniversary in 1995. The village had grown and become a town but he did recognise the railway station, railway lines, the river, bridges and a farmhouse with a wall still pitted with bullet holes. The small church had also grown and the churchyard and military graves had vanished.

Jimmy later found out that the soldiers buried in the churchyard had been re-interred in the crypt when the church was rebuilt. This was to remove any signs of war in Hamminkeln.

At the unveiling of the memorial to the 2nd Ox & Bucks, one ex-Ox & Bucks officer said that compared with taking Hamminkeln, the taking of the Pegasus Bridge in Normandy had been 'a dawdle'.

There is a Memorial Tree growing in the Hamminkeln Railway Station another at Sedgefield Village Green in the UK, Sedgefield having been twinned with Hamminkeln.

Jimmy assisted Padre Cheadle – who in 1945 had been a glider pilot – in the services at the Reichswald and Groesbeek cemeteries.

In 1999, Jimmy again returned to Hamminkeln and then back to the UK for the Remembrance Service for the Rhine Crossing at Marks Hall, which previously had been RAF Earls Colne when he travelled on the road which had once been part of the runway in 1945.

"As I approached the old airfield where the service was to be held I heard music and thought "It's a military band." I realised it was a recording of the tune 'Ein Feste Burg', the German Chorale I had recognised in the hymn book I picked up in the church at Hamminkeln in 1945, fifty four years before."

When his brother-in-law – a territorial who had served in the Royal Artillery in North Africa and Italy – heard of Jimmie's experiences on the Rhine Crossing, he nicknamed him "the Weekend Warrior."

His two nephews who were schoolboys at the time and later became regular officers in Highland Regiments improved somewhat on that and his experiences are now known in the family as "

Uncle Jamie's Weekend War". Another name for him is "Sky Pilot".

Ivan Lancaster, who later became a squadron leader in the RAF Auxiliary Air Force, flew in 1995 with his son David, a serving F/Lt in the RAF and a staff pilot at RAF Cranwell in a Dominie aircraft on a low-level training sortie around the Scottish Highlands.

In the USA, the pilots who trained at No.1 BFTS at Terrell Texas and flew on Varsity were remembered on the 24th March 1995. The American 'Silent Wings' museum at Terrell gave them space for a memorial alongside a large model Horsa glider.

In 1997, after a service at St Clement Danes, the RAF Church in the Strand, London, in which No 38 Group were mentioned a small reunion of ex RAF Glider pilots followed at the RAF Club, Piccadilly (see photo, page 222).

Charles Stewart who had flown in the back of a glider on Varsity was, in 1998, made a Member of the British Empire (MBE) for his services to his local community, he was also in the same year a subject for the TV show *This Is Your Life*.

In Salisbury Cathedral there is a memorial window to the Glider Pilot Regiment by Harry Stammers, a memorial to 551 officers and NCOs who were casualties in WWII. This was unveiled in 1950 by Field Marshal Lord Allenbrook.

In the Memorial Chapel lies a book of the Roll of Honour. On the cover three badges: The Army Air Corps, The Glider Pilot Regiment and the Royal Air Force. This is fitting in that the men from the RAF who flew gliders with the GPR on the Rhine are remembered.

Those RAF pilots, who in March 1945 flew aircraft without engines on Operation Varsity to enable ground forces to get across the Rhine and into Germany and within less than two months end the war, must never been forgotten for their efforts and courage at that time.

For the men who took part in that operation, and for the 61 who did not return, we owe our deepest gratitude, so when we say each year those immortal words "We will remember them" lets really mean it...

The great majority never did get to fly the aircraft that they had hoped they would on returning to the UK from pilot training in the USA, Canada, and South Africa. Many are still very bitter at having to fly gliders and not powered aircraft. Others felt it was their only chance of getting into the war and seeing some action. Others still, accept that destiny is destiny and they made the best of it.

One thing is for certain – we should all be very proud to have taken part in Operation Varsity. I hope this book will go some way to show the vital part they played in WWII and the ultimate victory of the Allied forces in Europe.

REMEMBER

We must remember those who died,
Remember them for going to war,
Remember them for leaving home,
Remember them for their bravery,
Remember them for giving us freedom,
Remember they fought to the end,
We remember them in our silence
Remember them and the violence.

Paul Ramshaw, aged 10 years and 6 month
Stanhope Barrington School C.E. Primary School, Durham

To live in the hearts we leave behind is not to die.

APPENDIX

Statistics

RAF and GPR personnel involved

	Officers	NCOs	Total
	409	2,893	3,303

Casualties

	Officers	NCOs	Total
Killed	35	115	150
Missing	58	425	483
POWs	21	349	370
Totals	114	889	1003

These figures later changed to:

	Officers	NCOs	Total
Killed	60	254	314
Missing	12	96	108
POW	36	515	551
Totals	108	865	973

37 Officers and 161 men were wounded but returned to unit.

Percentage losses from the operation

Returned unharmed	2,131	64.537%
Killed	314	9.505%
Missing	108	3.270%
Repatriated	551	16.687%
Wounded/Evacuated	198	5.997%

6 Officers and 78 men were killed during training.

SQUADRONS BY STATIONS

- A. Earls Colne
- B. Earls Colne
- C. Woodbridge
- D. Shepherds Grove / Shenfold
- E. Birch
- F. Broadwell & Blakewell / Earls Colne
- G. Gt Dumow
- J. Rivenhall
- K. Gt Dumow

AIRCRAFT USED

38 Group

Station	Squadrons	Aircraft
Great Dunmow	190/620	Stirling
Shephers Grove	196/299	Stirling
Rivenall	295/570	Stirling
Earls Colne	296/297	Halifax
Woodbridge	298/644	Halifax

120 Halifaxes   200 Stirlings
48 Hamilcars   272 Horsas

46 Group

Station	Squadrons	Aircraft
Birch	48/233	Dakota
Gosfield	271/512/575	Dakota

120 Dakotas   120 Horsas

Total of 440 Aircraft to tow 440 Gliders

EQUIPMENT LOSSES

	taken	lost
5 cwt cars	323	140
Trailers	283	125
Carriers	18	8
Tanks T9	8	4
Dodge 3/4 ton water carrier	16	4
Guns 75mm	24	7
25 pounder	2	1
17 pounder	16	9
6 pounder	34	10

GLIDER ALLOCATIONS

Unit	Tug Squadron	Chalk No	Airfield
2/Ox & Bucks	271, 512, 575	1 - 8	Gosfield
2/Ox & Bucks	271, 512, 575	16 - 30	Gosfield
2/Ox & Bucks	48, 233, 437	31 - 63	Birch
2/ Ox & Bucks	271, 512, 575	64 - 72	Gosfield
1/ RUR	48, 233, 437	94- 120	Birch
1/RUR	295, 570,	121 - 131	Rivenall
12 Devons	295, 570,	132 - 146	Rivenall
12 Devons	295, 570	147 - 152	Rivenall
12 Devons	190, 620	183- 206	Gt Dunmow
12 Devons	ORTU	207- 226	Matching

Artillery

Unit	Tug Squadron	Chalk No	Airfield
HQ 6/AL Bde	296/297	153 - 167	Earls Colne
3 A/TK Bty	296/297	168 - 172	Earls Colne
53 Lt Regt RA	296/297	173 - 175	Earls Colne
A/Tk Bty RA	298/644	227 - 238	Woodbridge
3 A/L A/TK Bty RA	298/644	239 - 244	Woodbridge
3 A/L A/TK RA	298/644	245 - 246	Woodbridge
3 A/L A/TK RA	298/644	247 - 254	Woodbridge
53 Lt Regt RA	298/644	255 - 258	Woodbridge
AAR Regt	298/644	259 - 266	Woodbridge
DIV HQ	298/ 644	267 - 278	Woodbridge
53 Lt Regt RA	196/299	287 - 314	Shepherds Grove
DIV HQ	295/ 570	315 - 342	Rivenall
53 Lt Regt RA	296/297	343 - 372	Earls Colne
4 A/L A/TK Bty	190/620	373 - 378	Great Dunmow
3 A/L A/TK Bty	190/620	379 - 384	Great Dunmow
3 A/L A/TK Bty	190/620	385 - 393	Great Dunmow
53 Lt Regt RA	190/620	394 - 402	Great Dunmow
AARR Mortars	190/620	403 - 408	Great Dunmow
Light Regt RA	190/620	436 - 438	Shepherds Grove

MISC

Unit	Tug Squadron	Chalk No	Airfield
195 Fld Amb	296/297	176 - 182	Earls Colne
4 Air Landing	298/644	227 - 238	Woodbridge
3 Para Bde	298/644	279 - 281	Woodbridge
5 Para Bde	298/644	282 - 284	Woodbridge
RE	298/644	285 - 286	Woodbridge

IMMEDIATE LOSSES OF GLIDERS OPERATION VARSITY

38 GROUP

Earls Colne	(Tug Sqns 296/297)
Glider No 177	Rope Broke

Gt Dunmow	(Tug Sqns 190/620)
Glider No 187	Tug aircraft shortage of petrol
Glider No 205	Rope Broke
Glider No 378	Glider Pilot in difficulty
Glider No 401	Rope Broke

Matching	(Tug Sqn ORTU)
Glider No 211	Rope Broke
Glider No 213	Rope Broke
Glider No 215	Returned to base
Glider No 221	Rope Broke
Glider No 222	Returned to base
Glider No 223	Rope Broke
Glider No 224	Rope Broke

Rivenhall	(Tug Sqns 295/570)
Glider No 133	Rope Broke
Glider No 316	Rope Broke
Glider No 341	Rope Broke

Shepherds Grove	(Tug Sqns 196/299)
Glider No 289	No record
Glider No 291	Plug pulled out of rope
Glider No 292	Rope Broke crash landed in France
Glider No 302	No record
Glider No 309	Returned to base Air Line Fracture
Glider No 313	Glider Pilot in difficulty force landed on west bank of the Rhine
Glider No 413	Engine failure crash landed in France
Glider No 421	Rope Broke crash landed in France
Glider No 438	Glider Pilot in difficulty crashed off French Coast
Glider no 440	Rope Broke crash landed in France

Woodbridge	(Tug Sqns 298/644)
Glider No 241	Force landed after take off
Glider No 246	Glider pilot in difficulty
Glider No 250	Engine failure
Glider No 253	Glider pilot in difficulty
Glider No 254	Rope Broke
Glider No 262	Distenregation
Glider No 268	Engine failure
Glider No 283	Glider pilot in difficulty

46 GROUP

Birch	Tug Sqns 48/233/437 (RCAF)
Glider No 56	Rope Broke
Glider No 61	Rope Broke

Gosfield	Tug Sqns 271/512/575
Glider No 16	Glider pilot in difficulty
Glider No 30	No report

GLIDERS DESPATCHED

46 GROUP

Sqn	Glider No	Station
48	55 to 63	Birch
233	31 to 54	Birch
271	25 to 30	Gosfield
	88 to 93	
437 RCAF	97 to 120	Birch
512	1 to 24	Gosfield
575	64 to 87	

38 GROUP

Sqn	Glider No	Station
296/297	343 to 372	Earls Colne
190/620	373 to 408	Great Dunmow
295/570	315 to 342	Rivenhall
196/299	287 to 314	Shepherds Grove
196/299	409 to 440	Shepherds Grove
ORTU	207 to 226	Matching
298/644	227 to 238	Woodbridge
298/644	239 to 286	Woodbridge

Total of	120 Dakotas	48 Hamilcars
	120 Halifaxes	392 Horsas
	200 Stirlings	440 Gliders
	440 Aircraft	

RAF GLIDER PILOTS BY CREWS – Operation Varsity

'A' SQUADRON

Cdr: Maj H.T. Bartlett DFC

(Sgt R Wilson)
(Sgt A Wadley)
S Weston
M Thirkettle
(Fg Off G Procter)
(Sgt Reed)
(Fg Off B Williams)
(Sgt G Richmond)
Flt Sgt K W Bowler (k)
Flt Lt M R Clark (k)
(Fg Off E Cook (k))
(Sgt J G Couglin (POW)
Sgt H H Denby (k)
(Fg Off H Currie) (W)
(F/Sgt G N Graham) (k)
(Flt Sgt W G McInnes) (k)
(S/Sgt L J T Catt) (k) GPR
(Fg Off G W Maddock (k)
(Sgt King)
P/O J Potter (W)
P/O T Woods (W)
(Sgt A R Kingston (W))
(Flt Sgt C S T Jacks)
Sgt M Matthews (W)
Sgt E Westwell (W)
(Fg Off A Rushworth)
(F/Sgt L Gillate)
Fg Off J Cuff
Fg Off C Haines
Fg Off S Bryant
Fg Off V Castle
Fg Off R E J Brown
Fg Off J E Lodge
Fg Off K Scolding
A Harley
(Flt Sgt A Anderson)
(Sgt J Jenkins GPR)

'B' SQUADRON

Cdr: Maj T.I.J. Toler DFC

(Fg Off J P Leavy) (k)
(Flt Sgt T Laidlaw) (k)
(Sgt J Barnsley) (POW)
(Sgt D Bruce) (POW)
(Flt Lt J Stringer) (W)
(Sgt J Newton) (W)
(Fg Off J W Rayson)
(Sgt Priddon)
I K Sillars
Sgt W G Matcham
(Fg Off E Barton)
(Sgt I Lancaster)

J Codd
K Malet
(Sgt J Barnsley) (POW)
(Sgt D Bruce) (POW)
Sgt R Bingham (POW)
(Flt Lt J Stringer) (W)
(Sgt J Newton) (W)
Fg Off P H Tupper (W)
(Sgt S Edwards) (W))
(S/Sgt E Raspinson)GPR
Sgt A M Morris) (W)
Fg Off Sharman (Flt Cdr)
Sgt R Stead
(Fg Off J Gregory)
(Sgt Jeffers)
(Flt K L Ashurst) (Flt Cdr)
(Sgt Hickson)
Fg Off Lineham
Fg D Heald
Flt Sgt J Codd
(Sgt T Brentini)
(Sgt G Elliott)
(J Perry)
(P Read)
(Major TIJ Toler)
(Fg Off G Telfer)
(S/Sgt R Howard)
(Fg Off Daniels)

'C' SQUADRON

Cdr: Major J.A. Dale

(S/Sgt W D Jackson) (W)
(Sgt Pease)
Sgt P Davies
(P/O J Love) (W)
(F/Sgt G McEwan)
Sgt (D Mills)
Sgt (A Pogson)
F/O (C Law)
F/O (D Leonard)
Sgt (J McKenzie)
(Sgt C Ellerington (k))
(Fg Off K M Johnson (k))
(Sgt T J A Stevens) (k)
(Sgt W Hayman) (k)
Sgt F Hedley (k)
(F/Sgt F Haddock)
(Fg Off C Law)
Fg Off K M Johnson (k)
Sgt T Whiteley (k)
(Sgt J Smith) (POW)
(S/Sgt A B Holmes) (W)
(Sgt E Hardy) (W)
(S/Sgt Desbois)

Sgt J MacKenzie (W)
Sgt K Owens (W)
(Sgt D Tomlinson) (W)
(S/Sgt J Wallwork)GPR
Sgt L Waiters (W)
(Sgt W J Worall) (W)
(Sgt J E Lipscombe)
(POW)
Sgt A Warhurst (W)
(Flt Lt White)
(Capt Akenhead) GPR
(Fg Off Duke)
(Sgt Hyland)
Fg Off JL Brebner
Fg Off Mockerridge
(Fg Off C JW Herold)
(Sgt Jones)
Sgt W Tombleson
(F/Sgt Alwyn)
(F/Sgt Baily)
(S/Sgt Bowman GPR)
(Sgt Davies)
(P/O Stone)
(Sgt Radcliffe)
(Sgt Jestico)
(Sgt Smith)
(P/O Hanson)
(Sgt Sarjeant)
(P/OWalker)
(Sgt Knox)
(F/Sgt Forsyth)
(S/Sgt H Carlin)

'D' SQUADRON

Cdr: Maj J.F. Lyne MC

(Fg Off JKP Nash) (k)
(Sgt RAF Rowley) (k)
(Fg Off JVA Welply) (k)
(Sgt R Day) (W)
(Ssgt Neilson) (k)
(Flt Sgt RJ Shepherd) (k)
(Flt Sgt G Dines) (k)
(Sgt CG Irons)
T Hasset
J Fretwell
J Newton
(Fg Off S P A Mansell) (k)
(Sgt L A Morl) (W)
Flt R Gray (k)
(Flt Lt P N Hyde) (k)
(Sgt F A Taylor) (k)
Fg Off E J Knowles (k)
Fg Off Q McGregor) (k)
(Sgt W McFadyen)

(Fg Off J K P Nash) (k)
(Sgt R A F Rowley) (k)
(Flt Sgt J M O'Sullivan (k)
Fg Off R W Morrison)
(W)
Sgt J A Shore (k)
(Fg Off J V A Welply) (k)
(Sgt DAJ Ray RAF) (W)
Sgt A Bourne (POW)
Sgt C W Dines (POW)
(Sgt T Henshall (POW))
(Sgt G Cove (POW))
Sgt J Kelly (POW)
Sgt D Williams (POW)
Sgt G Cove (POW)
Sgt H Clark (POW)
Sgt E Macrae (POW)
Fg Off B Kenfield (W)
Fg Off R Merrison (W)
Sgt J Bessford (W)
Flt Sgt N G Fletcher (W)
Sgt W Hay (W)
Sgt P A Johnson (W)
Sgt L Pillings (W)
Sgt H Sparrow (W)
Sqn Ldr G L Huntley
(Sgt M H Hudspith)
(Flt Sgt R Taylor)
(Flt Lt L Jordan)
(Sgt N Cambridge)

'E' SQUADRON

Cdr: Maj P.H. Jackson DFC

(Fg Off R Topp)
(Flt Sgt E Wiggin)
(Sgt W Martin)
(Flt Sgt W Davies)
(Sgt A S J Ford)
(Sgt R Trussler)
F Meek
Fg Off C A E Miller
Sgt T Obbe
Fg Off M Austin (k)
Flt Sgt D L Bond (k)
(Flt Sgt M F Essen) (k)
(Flt Lt Whetter)
Sgt D L Hutchens (k)
Fg Off S McLean (k)
Sgt W F Murphy (k)
Sgt T A Parkinson (k)
(Fg Off W H Paul) (k)
(Flt Sgt R Dormer) (k)
Sgt R J Beare
Fg Off J King (POW)

RAF GLIDER PILOTS BY CREWS – Operation Varsity

(Fg Off W A Spicer)
(POW)
(Sgt H Cooper) (POW))
Sgt P Fairhall (POW)
Sgt A Grieve (POW)
Flt Lt D Phillips (W)
Fg Off W Hamilton (W)
Fg Off A B Kyle (W)
(Fg Off C A E Miller (W))
(Sgt E Obel)
Fg Off I Scott (W)
P/O C R Barker (W)
P/O M J Odlum (W)
Sgt W A King (W)
Sgt B Parkinson (W)
Sgt W Pritchard (W)
Sgt E Richmond (W)
Sgt M Walker (W)
Sgt D Neilson (W)
(Sgt S Jarvis)
(Sgt P Geddes)
(Fg Off L Norris)
(Sgt Scott)

'F' SQUADRON
Cdr: S/Ldr V.H. Reynolds

(Fg Off DW Edwards) (k)
(Sgt JE Ramsden) (w)
(Flt Sgt JGC Grant) (k)
(Fg Off RW Jamieson) (k)
(Sgt ABC Love) (k)
(Sgt A W Skeldon) (k)
Fg Off WJ Wates (k)
(Sgt K A Kelsall) (k)
(Sgt E Ayliffe)
Fg Off G Atkinson (W)

Sgt W S E Lowman (k)
Sgt K C Sparkes (k)
(Sgt W J Tyson) (k)
(S/Sgt W Pavitt) (k) GPR
Fg Off F Sewell (W)
Fg Off B C Bruce-Gardner (W)
Sgt J T Baker (W)
Sgt J Dobson (W)
Sgt J E Ramsden (W)
Sgt E B Clarke (W)
Sgt F N Cole (W)
Sgt K A Kelsall (k)
(Fg Off A M Ankers) (k)
(Staff Sgt Spowart) (k)
Fg Off F H Cusworth (k)
Flt Lt K P Ince
Fg Off Bailey
Sgt Antonodowlos
(Fg Off D R Richards)
(Sgt J Cohen)
(Flt Sgt J Crane)
(Fg Off J Arnold)
R Bowers
(Fg Off E Giles)
(Sgt L Gearing)
Flt Sgt L S Ince
M Laing
Fg Off B S Evenden
P/O Barker (W)
Captain R Ford GPR

'G' SQUADRON
Cdr: Maj W.D. Priest DFC

(Fg Off AS Ledbrook) (k)
(Sgt A Stredwick) (W)

G Dobson
(Fg Off H A Fowler) (k)
(Sgt A R L Logie) (k)
Flt Lt J W Freeman (k))
(Sgt Graham)
Flt Lt J S Haigh (k)
(Flt Sgt R Heads) (k)
Sgt R Podmore (k)
(Fg Off R A Scrase) (k)
(Sgt J Hartfield) (W)
Flt Lt J R Sherwood (k)
Sgt J W Stubbings (k)
(P/O G B Hanson) (k)
(Sgt G A Sargent)
Flt Lt P Parsons (W) Trp Cdr
P/O H Crinham (W)
Sgt W Dowling (W)
Sgt W Hodson (W)
Sgt A Mills (W)
Sgt A Parkham (W)
(Sgt J W Rudkin) (W)
(Sgt J K Smith) (k)
Sgt K Wright (W)
Sgt R E Hall (W)
Fg Off R Grubb
Sgt D L Bond (k)
P Johnson
F Meek
P/O J Haigh
(A G Head)
(S/Sgt P Young)
(Fg Off C K Henson)
(Sgt K Wright)
(Fg Off P W Edwards)
(W Fleming)

(S/S V Miller) GPR
(Sgt McGordon)
P/O Castle
(Sgt L Macdonald)
(S/Sgt Penketh)
(Flt Sgt W Billingham)
(P/O Tranter)
(Fg Off E Hart)
(Fg Laidland)

'H' SQUADRON
H.R Hunt
J Cadden
R Drean
A Diamond
V Davis
Fg Off J B W Bower

'J' SQUADRON
F Wilson
W Middleton
J M Barden
H J S Buckle
A Brooke

'K' SQUADRON
D Jefferies
(P/O R Dodsworth)
(F/Sgt R Watson)
R E Wilson
Flt Lt R H Sims

* (Same Crew)

This is not an official nominal roll, as one was never compiled by the Glider Pilot Regiment. This list has been compiled from information supplied by former Royal Air Force and Glider Pilot Regiment personnel with whom contact has been made.

ROLL OF HONOUR: RAF TUG CREWS KILLED ON OPERATION VARSITY – 24TH MARCH 1945

196 SQUADRON

Stirling LJ 979 – Force landed 3 miles east of Overlook having been hit badly over the landing zone and losing two engines.

F/Lt H.P. Vanrenen DFC	Pilot	wounded
F/Sgt Holmes	–	uninjured
WO Hadley	–	uninjured
P/O Jones	–	uninjured
WO R.B. Tammas	Nav	wounded
WO J.E. Chalk	WOP/AG	wounded

295 SQUADRON

Stirling 136 – Port inner engine on fire after being hit by heavy flak. Crashed in flames at approx 10.33am.

W/O H.C. Symons	Pilot	Killed after baling out
Fg Off R. Joy	B/A	Safe
F/Sgt P.D. Waterman	WOP/AG	Safe
W/O B.G. Sallis	AG	Safe
Sgt J.H. Ellis	F/E	Safe

296 SQUADRON

Halifax NA 131 – Crashed in flames on the East Bank 4km west of Mehr at 10.30am.

Flt Lt H S Priest	Pilot	Killed
Sgt R Armstrong	F/E	Killed
F/Sgt R Brothwood	AG	Killed
W/O M.E.N. Allen	Nav	Safe in Hospital
W/O K.F. Rogers	WOP/AG	Safe in Hospital
F/Sgt G.E.J. Holmes	A/B.	Killed

298 SQUADRON

Halifax NA 113-8AQ – Shot down and crashed 7 miles south east of Bocholt.

F/O D.R. McGillivary RCAF	Pilot	Killed
F/Sgt A.A. Aherne	F/E	Killed
WO II J.E. Bunn RCAF	A/G	Killed
Fg Off G.Dixon	W/Op	Killed
Fg Off E.M. Hales	A/B	Killed
F/S J.B. Walker	Nav	Killed

512 SQUADRON

Dakota F2 649 AK *Hit by flak on the port side fuel tanks and caught fire. One seen to bale out and parachute open the aircraft broke in two and fell to the ground.*

Flt Lt C.A. Chew	Pilot	Killed
F/Sgt H. Gravett	2nd pilot	Killed
W/O G.C. Newman	Nav	Killed
W/O P.J. Hughes	Wop/AG	Safe

644 SQUADRON

Halifax 2P 'M' – Aircraft broke up in two on fire having been hit by flak and crashed on the west bank of the Rhine.

F/Sgt J P Hughes	Pilot	Killed
F/Sgt L Attewell	A/B	Killed
F/Sgt W.G. Lawrence	WOp/AG	Killed
Sgt C. Main	F/E	Killed
Sgt L.A. Dutton		Killed
F/S T.B. Nicholson		Killed

Halifax III 2P 'T'

F/O H Mc Conville RAAF	Pilot	Injured
F/O D R Locke	Nav	Safe
F/S A S Munro RAAF	B/A	Safe
P/O K R Bruce RAAF	WOP/AG	Killed
F/S J H Harris	A/G	Safe
F/S R H Smith	F/E	Safe

Missing
P/O Bruce is recorded on the Runneymede Memorial

REICHSWALD WAR CEMETERY CASUALTIES

Operatation Varsity March 1945

2 Ox/Bucks	1 Ulsters	12 Devons	9 Para	8 Para	7 Para	GPR	RAF(GP)
116	64	68	18	40	23	26	48

TOTAL 403

The Reichswald Forest War Cemetery, at Kleve or Cleves is situated in the middle of the Reichswald Forest and is two and half miles from the German/Dutch border. It lies three miles south-west of the town of Cleves and six and half miles from Gennep in Holland. Some 7,640 British Commonwealth and Allied servicemen are buried in the cemetery. Of this 3,558 are from the Army and 3,899 from the Royal Air Force.
Inside the cemetery in a small cloister are six books which cover alphabetically the names of those buried in the cemetery. The plot, row and grave numbers are given for each burial. Also a complete plan of the cemetery.

ROLL OF HONOUR: RAF GLIDER PILOTS KILLED ON OPERATION VARSITY 24TH MARCH 1945

Flying Officer Alfred Michael Ankers Age 23 from Margaraten, Venray, Holland Served in 'F' Squadron shot by a sniper just after landing his glider. Found propped up against the wheel of the glider No 273 by American troops. Buried US Military Cemetery

Fg Officer Maurice Austin Age 21 (Waterhouse, Staffs) Served in 'E' Squadron Killed by friendly fire. Originally buried at Hamminkeln but later moved to the Reichswald War Cemetery, Cleve, Germany

Flt Sgt Dennis Langdown Bond Age 22 Served in 'G' Squadron Found near the wreckage of his glider. Buried Reichswald War Cemetery

Flt Sgt Kenneth W Bowler age 20 (Hadfield, Derbys) Served in 'A' Squadron Flying glider No PW 231 when hit by anti-aircraft fire and crashed he and his second pilot were killed by advancing enemy forces. Buried Reichswald War Cemetery

Flt Lt Maurice Robert Clark Age 24(Darlington, Co Durham) Served in 'A' Squadron Flying glider RN 375 when it crashed in the area of Hamminkeln, 4 miles south of Dingen, 4 miles due south of Bochult. Buried Reichswald War Cemetery

Fg Officer Edwin Cook Age 21 (Crail, Fife) Served in 'A' Squadron Flying glider No EX 931 which crashed at Hamminkeln, 5 miles North of Wesel Buried Reichswald War Cemetery

Fg Officer Frank Horrower Cusworth Age 23 (Cullercoats, Northumberland) Served in 'F' Squadron Killed instantly by a bullet fired by a sniper as he went to get his rifle out of the back of the glider after landing at Hamminkeln. Buried Reichswald War Cemetery

Sgt Herbert Hartley Denby Age 31 Served in 'A' Squadron Hit by enemy flak while flying horsa glider PW 231 over the landing ground at Hamminkeln. Buried Reichswald War Cemetery

Flt Sgt Reginald Dormer Age 22 Served in 'E' Squadron Found dead underneath his wrecked glider on a landing zone at Hamminkeln. Buried Reichswald War Cemetery

Fg Officer Derek Wallace Edwards Buried Reichswald War Cemetery Age 27 (Newington, Kent) Served in 'F' Squadron Flew glider No 7 hit by flak in free flight and crashed near Hamminkeln. 6 members of the RE flying in the glider were also killed. Originally buried 1 mile NNE of of the centre of Emmerich and later reburied in the Reichswald.

Sgt Claude Ellerington Age 20 (Knottingnly, Yorks) Served in 'C' Squadron Originally buried 100 yards west of Ringenburg. Map Ref 220500 and later reburied in the Reichswald.

Flt Sgt Malcolm Frederick Essen Age 21(South Hackney, London) Served in 'E' Squadron His glider was hit several times by light anti-aircraft fire, before crashing near Hamminkeln. He died later of his injuries. Buried Reichswald War Cemetery

Fg Officer Hubert Aleaxander Fowler Age 28(Llandaff, Cardiff, Glam) Served in 'G' Squadron Glider crashed at Hamminkeln. Buried Reichswald War Cemetery

Fg Officer John William Freeman No known grave on Panel 266 of the Runneymede Memorial Age 20(Fulwell, Co Durham) Served in 'G' Squadron

Sgt Gordon Noel Graham Age 24(Bramham Park, Yorks) Served in 'A' Squadron Flying in Glider No RZ 142 which crash landed at Hamminkeln. In flight the tail of the glider was blown off. Buried Reichswald War Cemetery

Flt Sgt Geoffrey John Cradross Grant Buried Reichswald War Cemetery Age 20 Served in 'F' Squadron Seen flying past Hamminkeln in glider No 69 after landing encountered heavy intense enemy fire on the ground. Buried in Hamminkeln but later reburied in the Reichswald.

Flt Lt Robert Gray No Known Grave on panel 265 at the Runneymede Memorial Age 27 (Ballymena, Co Antrim) Served in 'D' Squadron Crash landed in the Hamminkeln area and was taken prisoner. Later reported to have been shot at the begining of April near Wesel/Emmerich.

Fg Officer John Sutherland Haigh Age 20 (Edinburgh, Scotland) Served in 'G' Squadron Flew with Sgt Bond and found lying by the wreckage of his glider. Buried Reichswald War Cemetery

Fg Officer Geoffrey Bernard Hanson Age 20 (East Barnett, Herts) Served in 'G' Squadron Killed by enemy fire after his glider had crash landed. Buried Reichswald War Cemetery.

Sgt William Hayman Age 23 Served in 'C' Squadron Flew with Sgt Stevens in Glider No 230. Originally buried in the Bocholt area, map ref 1.50.000, later reburied in Reichswald War Cemetery.

Flt Sgt Robert Heads Age 21 (Thornley, Co Durham) Served in 'G' Squadron No Known Grave panel 271 Runneymede Memorial

Sgt David Leslie Hutchens Age 22 (Comwood, Devon) Served in 'E' Squadron Made a successful landing a mile from the rendevous area but then fired upon from a wood 50 yards south of the landing area and killed. No Known Grave – on panel 275 Runneymede Memorial

Flt Sgt Percy Nicholas Hyde Age 22 (Gravesend, Kent) Served in 'D' Squadron Flew in glider no 134 and made a successful landing at zone 'B' but later reported missing. No Known Grave – on panel 271 Runneymede

Fg Officer Robert William Charles Jamieson Age 21 (St Denys, Southampton) Served with 'F' Squadron Shot down by intense enemy fire near Hamminkeln while flying glider No 69. Buried Reichswald War Cemetery

Fg Officer Kenneth Maurice Johnson Age 22(Ewell, Surrey) Served in 'C' Squadron Flew with Ellerington same details. Buried Reichswald War Cemetery

Sgt Kenneth Albert Kelsall Served in 'F' Squadron Originally buried in a field on the west side of the railway station at Hamminkeln by a Army Chaplain. Buried Reichswald War Cemetery.

Fg Officer Edwin James Knowles Served in 'D' Squadron Successfully landed his glider No 295 at landing zone 'P'. Nothing further is known. Buried Groes Beek Canadian War Cemetery

Flt Sgt Thomas Laidlaw Age 23(Whitfield, Lancs) Served in 'B' Squadron Hit by flak in mid air at 10.30am and his glider No RX 534 blew up and crashed. Buried at Hamminkeln but later reburied in the Reichswald.

Fg Officer Joseph Patrick Leavy Age 21 (Whatley Range, Manchester) Served in 'B' Squadron Flew with Laidlaw same details. Buried Reichswald War Cemetery

Fg Officer Arthur Sydney Ledbrook Served with 'G' Squadron Crashed near Hamminkeln Buried in the Divisional Cemetery at Hamminkeln but later reburied in the Reichswald

Sgt Alexander Randolph Logie Age 26 (East Wenyss, Fife) Served with 'G' Squadron Crashed near Hamminkeln. Buried Reichswald War Cemetery

Sgt Andrew Bell Colville Love Age 21 Served in 'F' Squadron Glider No 67 crashed into a house on landing. Buried Reichswald War Cemetery

Sgt William Samuel Edgar Lowman Age 20 (Welling, Kent) Served in 'F' Squadron His glider No 5 crashed near Hamminkeln, he was originally buried at Volgelsang, and later reburied in the Reichswald.

Fg Officer Geoffrey William Maddock Age 22 (Barnsley, Yorks) Served in 'A Squadron Crashed flying glider No RX234 in the Hamminkeln area. Buried Reichswald War Cemetery

Fg Officer Stephane Peter Anthony Mansell Age 20 (Paris, France) Served in 'D' Squadron His glider no 293 crashed at landing zone 'P' he was taken prisoner by the Germans but escaped two days later. On the 29th March 1945, he was recaptured and shot by two members of the German Police Battalion. His parent's address was given as Paris, France. His brother a tank commander found his brothers body in the village of Weldar which he had liberated. Buried Reichswald War Cemetery

Fg Officer Andrew McGregor Age 29. Served in 'D' Squadron He landed at landing zone 'A' and was killed in the crash. Originally buried in No 5 Para Brigade Cemetery but later reburied in the Reichswald.

Flt Sgt William George McInnes Age 21 .Served in 'A' Squadron Flew glider XX 909 when hit by flak and crashed in the Hamminkeln area. He was originally buried at the site of the crash but later reburied in the Reichswald.

Fg Officer Samuel McLean Age 21 (Daunmir, Dunbartonshire) Served in 'E' Squadron Crashed in the Hamminkeln area. Buried by an army padre in a field west of Hamminkeln railway station. Later reburied in the Reichswald.

Sgt Walter Francis Murphy Age 33. Served in 'E' Squadron Last seen passing Hamminkeln. Buried in a field by an army chaplain in a field west of Hamminkeln railway station. Later reburied in the Reichswald.

Fg Officer John Kenneth Patrick Nash Age 20 (Hounslow, Middx) Served in 'D' Squadron Shot down in the air and on fire. Glider No 431 crashed near landing zone 'B' killed in the crash. Originally buried in No 5 Para Brigade Cemetery later reburied in the Reichswald.

Flt Sgt John Mortimer O'Sullivan Age 22. Served in 'D' Squadron Crash landed at landing zone 'B'. First pilot F/O R W Morrison (wounded). Buried Reichswald War Cemetery

Sgt Thomas Athony Parkinson Age 21. Served on 'E' Squadron Originally buried at Hamminkeln. Buried Reichswald War Cemetery.

Fg Officer William Henry Paul Age 26 (Waterloo, Liverpool) Served in 'E' Squadron Found underheath his Horsa glider which had crashed landed. Buried Reichswald War Cemetery

Sgt Roland Podmore Age 25 Served in 'G' Squadron Crashed at Hamminkeln. Originally buried at map ref 169518. Later reburied in the Reichswald.

Sgt Reginald Albert Rowley Buried Reichswald War Cemetery Age 21. Served with 'D' Squadron Flew with Nash same details. Crashed while flying Horsa glider No 431 near Hamminkeln. Originally buried in No 5 Para Brigade Cemetery, reburied Reichswald War Cemetery.

Fg Officer Robert Alfred Scrase Age 20 (Burgess Hill, Sussex) Served with 'G' Squadron Originally buried in a roadside field near Komderhof. Later reburied in the Reichswald.

Flt Sgt Robert James Shepherd Age 22 Served in 'D' Squadron Crashed at landing zone 'B' missing No Known Grave – panel 272 Runnymede Memorial

Flt Lt John Richard Sherwood Age 21 (Sale, Cheshire) Served in 'G' Squadron Crashed near Hamminkeln originally buried No 5 Para Regiment Cemetery later reburied in the Reichswald.

Sgt James Alphonsus Shore Age 25 Served on 'D' Squadron Glider No 302 crashed in landing zone 'P' Died while a prisoner of war. No Known Grave – panel 276 Runneymede Memorial

Sgt Angus Wallis Skeldon Age 20(Cambridge) Served on 'F' Squadron Flew with Love same details. Buried Reichswald War Cemetery

Sgt John Kenneth Smith Age 23 (Brinstead, IOW) Served on 'G' Squadron Crashed near Hamminkeln originally buried 6th Airborne Divisional Cemetery later reburied Reichswald.

Sgt Kenneth Charles Sparkes Age 20 (Grangetown, Cardiff) Served on 'F' Squadron Flew with Lowman same details.

Sgt Thomas John Alfred Stevens Age 22 (Rough Common, Kent) Served ' C ' Squadron. His glider safely landed at the landing zone but he was later killed in the ground fighting. Flew with Sgt Hayman in Glider No 230. Originally buried at Bosholt Map Ref 228 479, reburied Reichswald War Cemetery.

Sgt Jack William Stubbings Age 21 (Bishop Stortford, Herts) Served on 'G' Squadron Flew with Podmore same details.

Sgt Frederick Arthur Taylor Age 23. Served on 'D' Squadron Flying glider No 434 safely landed on landing zone B but later killed in the ensuing battle. No Known Grave panel 277 Runneymede Memorial

Sgt William John Tyson Age 20. Served on 'F' Squadron Originally buried in a field on the west side of the railway station at Hamminkeln. Later reburied in the Reichswald.

Sgt Kenneth John Warren Age 20 Served on 'G' Squadron Crashed near Hamminkeln. No Known Grave – panel 277 Runneymede War Memorial.

Fg Officer William John Wates Age 20 (Purley, Surrey) Served on 'F' Squadron Crashed in glider No 19 near Hamminkeln at 10.30am. Originally buried by an army chaplain in a field on the west side of the railway station. Later reburied in the Reichswald.

Fg Officer James Victor Alton Welply Age 20 (Limerick) Served on 'D' Squadron Crashed at landing zone 'B'. Buried Reichswald War Cemetery

Sgt Tom Whiteley Age 20 (Marsh, Huddersfield) Served on 'C' Squadron Buried Reichswald War Cemetery

Totals: Officers 26. NCOs 34. Overall 61.

RAF GLIDER PILOTS KILLED DURING TRAINING 1942 TO 1945.

Sgt Royston John Beare
Served on 'E' Squadron. Committed suicide 15th June 1945. Took part in Operation Varsity.

F/O Jack Lucien Brebner
Served with 'C' Squadron on Operation Varsity. Seriously injured in a road accident on 9th May 1945 near the Horse and Jockey Hotel on the Bournemouth-Winton Road in Hampshire, returning from Bournemouth. Died of his injuries on the 11th May 1945. Based at Tarrant Rushton. Took part in Operation Varsity.

F/O John Bernard William Bower
Served with 'H' Squadron. Killed in a road accident with a 15 cwt lorry at Golders Green 8th May 1945. Based at Birch.

Sgt Neil Cook
Serving with RAF Element GPR. Admited to station hospital at Yatesbury on 3rd June 1945, with Cerebral Spine Meningitis. Later transfered to St Hugh's Hospital, Oxford suffering from Xstaplyloticial Meningitis, where he died on the 21st June 1945.

T/WO Thomas Arthur Edward Tobias AFM
Served at HGCU Brize Norton. Seriously injured 31st August 1942 when flying Horsza DF 755 towed by Whitley BD 438 that hit a tree on takeoff at Black Bourton, Oxon. He was medically discharged from the RAF 10th December 1943. Died on the 3rd June 1945. Two others in the glider were seriously injured. Two of the Whitley crew, F/O Thornely and Sgt R.W.J Hisson killed.

T/ F/Sgt Kenneth John Williams
Served with 1 HGSU. On the 11th February 1945, when flying a Hamilcar LA 737 he crashed 2 miles west of Tarrant Rushton airfield. The other member of the glider crew Sgt R A W Foster was injured in the crash.

CASUALTIES – Glider Pilots – Rhine Crossing March 1945

KILLED

RAF	Glider Pilot Regt
A Squadron	
F/Sgt K W Bowler	S/Sgt G Bright
*Flt Lt M R Clark	**S/Sgt LJT Catt
F/O E Cook	*S/Sgt GR Evans
Sgt H H Denby	Lt L Harrison
Sgt G N Graham	
**F/Sgt W G McInnes	
F/O G W Maddock	
* Same Crew ** Same Crew	
B Squadron	
(F/O J P Leavy)	(Capt HMR Norton)
(F/Sgt T Laidlaw)	(S/Sgt J RHebden)
	Wounded
	S/Sgt D Harrison
	S/Sgt JF Smith
C Squadron	
Sgt C Ellerington	(Lt R L Graefe)
Sgt W Hayman	(S/Sgt E L Jarvis)
Sgt TJA Stevens	Lt D C Kenward
F/O K M Johnson	
Sgt T Whiteley	
D Squadron	
*Flt Lt R Gray	Sgt JF Astor
(S/Sgt J Neilson)	
F/O E J Knowles	Capt KF Strathern
F/O SPA Mansell BSc	
F/O A McGregor	
(F/O JKP Nash)	
(Sgt RAF Rowley)	
F/Sgt JM O'Sullivan	
*Sgt JA Shore Died a POW	
(F/O JVA Welply)	
(Sgt D A J Ray POW)	
(Sgt P N Hyde)	
(F/Sgt RJ Shepherd)	
(Sgt F A Taylor)	
E Squadron	
F/O M Austin	Sgt E O Bruce
	S/Sgt WB Denholm
F/Sgt MF Essen (DOW)	Sgt J Doughty
Sgt DL Hutchens	S/Sgt G Duns
F/O S McLean	Sgt HJ Gordon
Sgt WF Murphy	S/Sgt DR Montgomery
Sgt T A Parkinson	S/Sgt S Roberts
F/O WH Paul	Sgt WL Ross
F/Sgt R Dormer	

RAF	Glider Pilot Regt
F Squadron	
	Tpr J Amstrong
F/O A M Ankers **	
	Sgt JP Bennett
(F/O DW Edwards)	(Sgt GH Collins)
(Sgt JE Ramsden)	(S/Sgt WF Rowlands)
Wounded	Wounded
(F/Sgt JGC Grant)	Sgt HW Comber
(F/O RW Jamieson)	(Lt G J D'Archy-Clark)
	(Capt AM Carr)
(Sgt ABC Love)	S/Sgt PA McLaren
(Sgt AW Skeldon)	S/Sgt WC Pavitt *
(Sgt WSE Lowman)	Sgt PJ Read
(Sgt KC Sparkes)	Pte AC Robertson ACC
Sgt WJ Tyson *	Sgt CV Roche
(Shot by German SS)	
(F/O WJ Wates)	Sgt JH Stevens
(Shot by German SS)	S/Sgt H Wright
(Sgt K A Kelsall)	S/Sgt J B Spowart **
(Shot by German SS)	
G Squadron	
*F/O HA Fowler	S/Sgt JL Ellison
Flt Lt JW Freeman	Sgt D Nuttall
	Sgt GK Richardson
**F/Sgt R Heads	S/Sgt G Duns
(F/O AS Ledbrook)	
(A Stredwick (W))	
*Sgt AR Logie	
Sgt R Podmore	
(F/O RA Scrase)	
(Sgt G Hatfield (W))	
Flt Lt JR Sherwood	
Sgt JK Smith	
(Sgt JW Stubbings)	
**Sgt KJ Warren	
P/O G B Hanson	
(F/O J S Haig)	
F/Sgt DL Bond	

Total RAF 61   **Total GPR 38**

Overall Total 102

* Same Crew ** Same Crew

WOUNDED

RAF	Glider Pilot Regt	RAF	Glider Pilot Regt
A Squadron		**E Squadron**	
F/O H Curries	Lt Hall	Flt Lt D Phillips	WO2 BR Holt
P/O J Potter	Lt Tuppen	F/O W Hamilton	Sgt PJ Walford
P/O T Woods	Lt J Weir	F/O AB Kyle	Sgt L D Brook
Sgt AR Kingston	S/Sgt LF Haines	F/O CAE Miller	S/Sgt WC Herbert
Sgt M Matthews	S/Sgt G Lawson	F/O I Scott	Sgt DC Deliss
Sgt E Westwell	Sgt R Shipley	P/O CR Barker	Sgt DG Hardy
Flt Lt Halley	Sgt RA Dine-Hart	P/O MJ Odlum	Sgt LH Martin
Sgt T O'Brien		Sgt WA King	Sgt SW Moore
		Sgt B Parkinson	
B Squadron		Sgt W Pritchard	
(Flt Lt J Stringer)*	Capt GR Millar	Sgt E Richmond	
(Sgt J Newton) *	S/Sgt JR Hebden	Sgt M Walker	
F/O PH Tupper	S/Sgt J Pickles	Sgt D Neilson	
Sgt S Edwards	S/Sgt F Richards		
Sgt AM Morris		**F Squadron**	
Sgt A Harne		F/O F Sewell	S/Sgt R Percival
Sgt CEL Mee		F/O BC Bruce-Gardner	S/Sgt EJ Farmer
Sgt R Glover		Sgt JT Baker	Sgt WF Rowland
		Sgt J Dobson	Sgt J Vose
C Squadron		Sgt JE Ramsden	Sgt J Kitchener
P/O J Love	Lt KG Guest	Sgt EB Clarke	
Sgt E Hardy	S/Sgt JWR Bonome	Sgt FN Cole	
Sgt J MacKenzie	Sgt R Desbois	F/O G Atkinson	
Sgt K Owens	S/Sgt AB Holmes	P/O Barker (W)	
Sgt W Tombleson	Sgt JD Hulse		
Sgt L Waiters	Sgt WJ Worrall	**G Squadron**	
Sgt A Warhurst		Flt Lt P Parsons	Lt C Horace
		P/O H Crinham	Capt AF Boucher-Giles
D Squadron		Sgt W Dowling	Sgt R E Hall
F/O B Kenfield	Capt B Murdoch	Sgt G Hartfield	
F/O R Merrision	Capt BD Hich	Sgt W Hodson	
Sgt J Bessford	Sgt TE Housley	Sgt A Mills	
F/Sgt NG Fletcher	Sgt W Tuck-Brown	Sgt A Parkham	
Sgt W Hay		Sgt J Rudkin	
Sgt CG Irons		Sgt K Wright	
Sgt PA Johnson		Sgt A Stredwick	
Sgt W McFadyen			
Sgt L Morl		**MISC**	
Sgt L Pillings			W/O IK Mew
Sgt H Sparrow			S/Sgt CP Ashling
		Wg HQ	Lt D Abott
			Sgt G Wagg

Total RAF 60   **Total GPR 42**

PRISONERS OF WAR

RAF	Glider Pilot Regt
A Squadron	
Sgt J G Coughlin	Sgt JE Watkins
B Squadron	
(Sgt J Barnsley)	Sgt RE Block
(Sgt D Bruce)	Sgt A Parker
Sgt R Bingham	
C Squadron	
Sgt JE Lipscombe	Sgt PA Attwood
Sgt J Smith	Sgt HG Harget
Sgt WD Jackson	
Sgt RG Perkins	
Sgt RR Wedge	
Sgt M Wicks	
Sgt J Barnes	
Sgt Lymbarn-Ferguson	
Sgt DG Rogers	
D Squadron	
Sgt A Bourne	S/Sgt HAJ Gibbons
Sgt CW Dines	
Sgt T Henshall	
Sgt J Kelly	
Sgt D Ray	
Sgt D Williams	
Sgt G Cove	
Sgt H Clark	
Sgt E Macrae	
E Squadron	
F/O J King	S/Sgt D Conway
(F/O WA Spicer)*	S/Sgt J Jones
(Sgt H Cooper)*	Sgt J Smith
Sgt P Fairhall	
Sgt A Grieve	
F Squadron	
Sgt GW Baston	Sgt B J Delahunty
Sgt DFV Dance	
S/Sgt JD Smith	
Sgt A S Brown	
Lt I D Abbott Misc	

Total RAF 21   Total GPR 21

MISCELLANEOUS

RAF Glider Pilots Killed or died 1942 to 1945

WO Tobias AFM Died of his injuries recieved when serving with HGCU at Brize Norton. His glider DP 755 crashed at Black Bourton, Oxon, on the 31st August 1942. The tug aircraft a Whitley hit a tree on take off, two of the crew were killed and three of the glider crew including Tobias were seriously injured. He was medically discharged on the 10th December 1943, and died on the 3rd June 1945. He is buried in Newport, Gwent.

Sgt E T Pettit Killed 22nd June 1945, at Witney in a traffic accident.

F/O J L Brebner Took part in the Varsity operation with C Squadron. Seriously injured in a road accident 9th May 1945, in Hampshire. Died on the 11th May of his injuries.

F/O J B W Bower Served with H Squadron at the time of Varsity. Killed in an accident at Golders Green, London 8th May 1945.

Sgt R J Beare Served on Varsity with E Squadron. Committed suicide on the 15th June 1945.

Sgt N Cook Died of an illness on the 21st June 1945.

T/Sgt K J Williams Serving with No 1 HGSU and while flying a Hamilcar glider No LA 737 crashed 2 miles west of Tarrant Rushton airfield on the 11th February 1945. He was killed and his co-pilot Sgt R.A.W Foster injured in the crash.

PERSONAL THANKS

Dame Barbra Cartland DBE | K A Merrick, Author | Air Historical Branch, Mr Graham Day | Public Records Office, Kew | References Air 20, Air 40, Air 27, Air 29, Air 2, Air 5, WO 208, Defe 2, Cab 106 | Newspapers all over the UK | RAF News | Flypast Magazine | After The Battle Magazine | Commonwealth War Graves | PMC RAF Innsworth | Glider Pilot Regiment Association, David Brook | MOD Library Whitehall, Miss M.M. Simpson | Cavendish Morton | Mrs E. Payne | Mrs B. Grant | David Hall | Bob Randall | Sqn Ldr Chris Goss

RAF Glider Pilots

Cy Henson | Len Jordan | Tony Wadley | Geoffrey Atkinson DFC | Ken Ashurst | Sid Edwards | Bleddwyn Williams | Eric Ayliffe | Len Macdonald | John Rayson | John Codd | Jack Newton | Geoff Dines | William Davies | Gp Capt John Herold MBE | Frank Haddock | Duke Kent | W. Worrall | Phil Johnson | Alan Kingston | John Barnsley | Stanley Weston | F.E. Meek | Alan Hoad | Ian Sillars | Howard Hansford | Gordon Procter | David Richards | Bill Rayston | M.H. Hodspith | Ken Scolding | John Crane | Jim Rudkin | Ivan Lancaster MBE | Kenneth Ross | R.E. Wilson | A.G. Head | Peter Davies | Rick Brown | A.J. Allam | Graham Edward | Alan Stredwick | Air Cdr Roger Topp AFC ** | Tom Haslett | Maurice Thirkettle | Ron Watson | John Love DFC | W J. Billingham | Ted Giles | Leslie W. Norris | Joe Cadden | Sqn Ldr Reg Leach | Sqn Ldr M F.H Dobson AFC | P Nash | C A E Miller | C Penn | S Grieve | G Burn | J Cornish | D Payne | W Sampson | W Matchham | J Fretwell | J Baker | K Malet | W Worrall | A J Allam | P Bailey | A O'Shea | N Cowling | G Telfe | K Ellwood | F Hendy | E Wiggan | A Aldis | R Sims | W Howell | W Davies | F Wilson | H Mould | J Harris | P Davies | J Hudd | F Turner | G Procter | C Hargraves | P A Davies | W A G Spicer | J Gregory | D Richards | A Wadley | R Watson | W Rayson | Sqn Ldr K I Ashurst | John Perry | Stan Jarvis | Denis Mills | John Lodge DFC | Gerard Coughlan | Sir Maurice Laing

Tug Crews

Jimmie Stark | Bill Angell DFC | George Edwards | John Gray | Doug Coxell | Gp Capt A C Blythe DFC* | Dr Dick Wynne | Pete Culley | Alan Hartley | Ron McQuaker | Jack Cottam | Jim Davis

GPR Pilots

Joe Kitchener | Eddie Raspison DFM | H.Mould | Laurence J. Minall DFM | Roy Howard DFM | Eric Duguid | James Wallwork DFM | Major Michael Graham | Lt Col Ian Toler DFC | Hugh Carling | George Burn - With thanks for his excellent illustrations.

Army Personnel

Harry Clarke 2/Ox & Bucks Regiment | C Stuart 6th Airborne | Colonel John Tillett 2/Ox & Bucks Regiment | Jack Harris REME | Padre Jimmy Mack

Others

Mrs J.Porter | Clifford W. Witt | Sqn Ldr Steve Forster | Rosemary Brittan WAAF | Mr V K Benkon

SOURCES / BIBLIOGRAPHY

Airborne Warfare 1918-45, Harry Gregory & John Batchelor

Aircrew Unlimited, John Golley

Bounce the Rhine, Charles Whiting

History of the World's Glider Forces, Alan Wood

Lion with Blue Wings, Ronald Seth

Memoirs, Montgomery of Alamein KG

Nothing is Impossible, Victor Miller

Over The Rhine, Brian Jewell

Pilot, Joe Patient DFC

Richard Dimbleby, Jonathan Dimbleby

Stars at War, Michael Munn

Suffolk Airfields in the Second World War, Graham Smith

The Bloody Eleventh - History of the Devonshire Regiment, W.G.P Aggett

The Eagle - Newsletter of the Glider Pilot Regiment

The Glider Gang, Milton Dank

The Glider Pilot Regiment, Claude Smith

The Glider Soldiers

The Glider War, Colonel J.E Mrazek

The Glider, Alan Lloyd

The Marines Were There, Sir Robert Bruce Lockhart KCMG

The Red Beret, Max Arthur

The Red Devils, G.G. Norton

The Wings of Pegasus

The Wooden Sword, Lawrence Wright

Upside Down Again: another collection of RAF Humour, Lars Torders (ed), Woodfield (1999)

Victoria Cross: Bravest of the Brave, Woodfield (in press)

MEDALS & AWARDS FOR OPERATION VARSITY

RAF AND ARMY GLIDER PILOTS

Bar to DSO 1
DSO 1
CGM (Flying) 1
DFC 11
DFM 11

RGM (FLYING)
S/SM W Turnbull (GPR)

DFC (GPR) | **DFC (RAF)**
Capt F C Aston | Fg Off G Atkinson
Major H T Bartlett | Fg Off P Ince
SSM B R Holt | Fg Off J E Lodge
Major R H P Jackson | P/O J T Love
RSM K Mew | P/O M J Odlum
Major N W D Priest

DFM (GPR)
S/Sgt A Bowman
S/Sgt J E Edwards
S/Sgt I W Evans
S/Sgt T Gray
S/Sgt L J Minall
S/Sgt G E Moorcroft
S/Sgt E Raspison
S/Sgt F A Richards
S/Sgt D Ryans
S/Sgt J R Taylor
S/Sgt L Wright

RAF TUG CREWS

No 46 Group

DSO

W/C R G Dutton DFC	512 Sqn
Lt Col P S Joubert AFC SAAF	271 Sqn

DFC

S/L R D Daniel AFC	233 Sqn
F/L R E Charlton DFM	575 Sqn
F/L P W Smith	48 Sqn
F/O F J Andrews RCAF	437 Sqn
WO J H Golton	48 Sqn
D/L R R C Hyne RAAF	233 Sqn
A/S/L J T Reed RCAF	437 Sqn
F/L J W Atkin	575 Sqn
WO H Farrar later P/O	271 Sqn
A/S/L P A Clarke	512 Sqn
P/O N A E Mills	233 Sqn
F/O J E Seary RCAF	437 Sqn
F/L R A Davis	512 Sqn
P/O F A Prior	575 Sqn
P/O G S Wright	233 Sqn
F/O J M Syrness RCAF	437 Sqn
F/O R S Purkis RCAF	437 Sqn

DFM
F/S R Seddon	575 Sqn
F/S G W Jackson	575 Sqn

MID
F/L C H McLeod	575 Sqn

Index

Aaron, F/Sgt Arthur L. VC 53
Ainsworth, Sgt Johnnie 39
Aldis, Private 199
Aldworth, Bill 164
Allam, Bert 107
Allanson, Lt 164
Allenbrook, Field Marshal 106, 226
Angell, Wg Cdr Bill 91, 92, 115
Ankers, F/O 176
Archer, Wing Commander AFC 115
Arnold, John 189
Ash, Lieutenant 150
Ashurst, Ken 143, 176, 195
Atkinson, F/O Geoffrey DFC 78, 125, 156, 185, 196, 209
Attwood, Sgt P 31
Austin, Bunny 152
Ayliffe, Eric 79, 143, 175

Bailey, Captain 127
Bangay, Wg/Cdr R.J M. 115
Barker, 'Chuck' 184
Barnsley, John 63, 69, 141, 173
Barrow, Major Wallie 164
Bartlett, Major 191
Barton, Ted 129, 180
Beardmore, Lissart 13
Bell, Andrew 196
Bellamy, Brigadier R.H. DSO 97
Bertram, Grp Cpt 157
Bick, Jimmy 148
Billingham, F/Sgt 57, 133, 188
Bird, P/O E.R. 47
Blakehill Farm 84, 85, 157
Bliss, Flt Lt USAF 114
Blythe, Alex 145, 189
Boland, Sgt 147
Bols, Major-General E.L. DSO 97, 207, 208
Boon, Sgt J.F. 47
Bowman, St/Sgt Bert 129, 130
Bradley, General Omar 95
Brereton, General Lewis H. 99, 218
British Aircraft Company 12
British Gliding Association 12
Britten, Flt Off Rosemary 157, 193
Brize Norton 23, 24, 27, 28, 47, 56, 65, 66, 69, 70, 73, 74, 76, 77, 78, 80, 83, 85, 110
Brodie, RSM 76
Brown, Rick 55, 115, 130, 186
Browning, Maj-Gen Frederick 23, 27, 42, 47
Bruce, Danny 141, 173
Bruce, Michael 72
Buchanan, F/O RCAF 115
Bunker, Wg Cdr R.H. 113

Calder, S/Ldr Jock 102
Caley, George 11
Cambridge, Sgt Norman 78, 122

Cameron, Rev A.P. 116, 136
Campbell, F/Lt Donald 210
Carling, Hugh 200
Carr, Cpt A.M.D 120, 143
Carson, Lt-Col Jack 140, 163
Cartland, Barbara 12
Chattahoochee Task Force 197
Chatterton, Brigadier George DSO 23, 25, 27, 29, 31, 32, 39, 47, 138, 221
Cheadle, Padre 225
Christie, John 165
Churchill, Sir Winston 15, 17, 22, 66, 106, 107, 171, 199
Clark, Harry 145, 146, 197, 208, 224
Clarke, Sqn/Ldr 116
Codd, John 143, 189
Cohen, Sgt Jeff 161, 194
Connell, F/O 114, 130
Cook, Edwin 117
Cooper, Alan 223
Cooper, Grp Cpt Tom B. DFC 25, 92
Cooper, Maj Alastair 33
Cooper, Sgt Jock 149
Corrie, Cpt Mike 180
Cottam, Jack 93, 113
Coughlan, Gerard 117, 201
Cox, Lieutenant 196
Coxell, Doug 92, 156
Crane, Major John 73, 136, 189, 200
Crawford, Lt Col Charles 33
Cross, Flt/Sgt 115
Culley, Pete 212
Cunningham, Air Marshal 40
Curry, Flt/Lt Howard 115, 154, 193

Dalby, General Josiah T. 111
Dale, Maj Alec 144
Darell-Brown, Lt Col 150, 164, 197, 200
Darvall, Air Commodore L, MC 115
Davie, F/O 16
Davies, F/O Bill 57, 82, 139, 151, 170
Davies, 'Jock' 175
Davies, P/O Norman A. 25
Davies, Sgt Peter 129, 209
Davis, Sq/Ldr P.B.N. 25
De Gency, P/O Garard W.S. 25
Dean, Wg/Cdr R. DFC 113
Deanesley, Wg/Cdr E.C. DFC 113, 164
Dempsey, General 99
Dimbleby, Richard 135, 136
Dines, Geoff 153
Doig, Sgt Peter 25, 27
Drummond, ACM Sir Peter 47
du Maurier, Daphne 23
Dulbey, Josiah 197
Dunkley, L/Cpl Richard 147, 198
Dunne, John 11
Dutton, Wg/Cdr DFC* 115, 210

Dutton, Wg/Cdr R.G. DFC* 113
Dyball, Major Tony 163

Edwards, Flt Lt Jimmy DFC 211, 225
Edwards, Percy M 150
Edwards, Sid 79, 153, 188, 209, 224
Eisenhower, Gen Dwight D. 36, 42, 97, 157, 159, 196, 199, 207, 213, 217
Elliott, Sgt 70
Ellwood, Ken 65, 225
England, Lt John K. 201
Espelawl, Herr 12
Evans, Sq Ldr 179
Exercise Token 82

Ferguson, F/Lt 151
Fiddament, Air Cdr L.A. 35
Fitzgerald, Dennis 160
Flavell, Brigadier 218
Fleming, Bill 150
Flynn, Sgt H 31
Fogarty, Flying Officer 114
Ford, Roger 161
Fox, Lt Dennis 200
Fraser, P/O Herber J. 25
Fretwell, John 154, 155

Gaither, General Ridgeway M. 111, 197
Gale, Gen Richard, DSO OBE MC 35, 40, 157, 206
Galland, Adolf 11
Gander, L. Marsland 116, 136, 201
Geddes, Pete 145, 188, 189
Giles, Ted 153
Gillets, F/Sgt 163
Gleadell, Lt-Col Paul 163
Graham, Major Michael 134, 159, 200
Graham, Sgt 124, 154, 194
Graham-Bower, Mrs 215
Grant, Sgt Geoffrey 33, 126, 177, 184
Gray, John 92, 157
Grieve, Sydney 137, 179
Griffiths F/O, RCAF 115
Guthrie, F/O 57

Haddock, Frank 86, 144, 169, 217
Haig, John 76, 192
Hall, Cpt J.W. 148
Hall, Norman (Nobby) 212
Halley, Flt Lt Len DFC 70, 71, 78, 82, 137
Hambly, Fred 158, 159
Hamilton, Bill 152
Hammerton, Derek 178
Hansford, Howard 192
Hardy, Dennis 159
Hargraves, Sgt Cyril 'Cy' 149
Harper, CSM 77
Harris, Jack, St Sgt 200, 225

Harrop, Sgt 137, 138
Hartley, Alan 194, 225
Head, Alan 130, 155
Heath-Smith, Major 147
Hendry, Frank 140, 171
Henson, Cyril (Cy) 56, 67, 72, 75, 120, 179, 222, 223
Herold, John 61, 85, 125, 177, 218, 222
Hewetson, Lt G. 201
Hicks, Brigadier 32
Hickson, Sergeant 195
Hill, Bridagier 208
Hill, F/Lt 27
Hobbs, Sgt 147
Holdsworth, F/O Bill 196, 222
Hollinghurst, AVM L.N. CBE DFC 35
Hook, F/O 114
Hopkinson, Maj-Gen 29, 32
Horrocks, Gen 40
Howard, Major John 39
Howard, Roy 159
Hudspith, Sgt 128
Hughes, F/Lt 27
Hughes, Sgt 173

Ince, F/O Edgar 143, 208

Jack, Sq/Ldr W.A. 152
Jackson, Major Peter DFC 84, 140, 193
Jacques, W/O 148
Jarvis, Stan 145, 188, 189, 208, 224
Jenkins, Norman 89
Jennings, Wg/Cdr P. I. N. 115
Jestico, Dick 191
Johnson, Phil 52, 77, 119, 185
Jones, Sgt 125
Jordan, Len 77, 122, 186
Joubert, Lt-Col Pierre S. AFC 113, 211
Jungwirth, F/O 196
Jury, W/O 115

Kean, Wg Cdr Tom AFC 23, 24, 27, 28, 46, 47, 50, 71
Kent, F/Lt Stanley (Duke) 64, 87, 212
Kerr, Andy 145
Kingston, Alan 122, 189
Kirwan-Taylor, Lt Col W.J 207
Kitchener, Joe 65
Koch, Captain 15
Kronfeld, F/O Robert 13, 16, 24

Laing, Maurice 120, 178
Laird, Lt 163
Lancaster, Ivan 62, 71, 128, 180, 226
Law, F/O Cecil 86, 144
Law-Wright, Wing Commander DSO, DFC 115
Le Bouvier, Flt Lt 82
Leach, S/Ldr Reg 24
Ledbrook, 'Tiny' 131
Lee, Pte 162
Leigh-Mallory, Air Marshall Sir Trafford 39
Lodge, F/Lt John 209

London Gliding Club 12
Lord, Flt Lt David, VC 211, 225
Lord Haw-Haw 200
Love, John 57, 148, 184, 201, 209, 222, 223
Love, Sgt Andrew 223
Lowe-Wylde, C.H. 12

Macdonald, Len 47, 56, 152, 222
MacIntyre, Grp Cpt 77
Mack, Padre Jimmy 166, 225
Mackrill, Warrant Officer 115
Malet, Ken 184
Mansell, Gerald 160
Mansell, John 162
Martin, Wally 83, 170
Maxted, Stanley 135, 165
May, Peter 24, 27
Mayer, Sq/Ldr 157, 193
McEwan, F/Sgt 'Mac' 148, 184, 201
McGillivary, F/O 115
McMillen, Cpt 164
McQuaker, Ron 92
Meek, Sgt Fred 66, 76, 192
Mellor, Wg/Cdr K.G. DFC* 113
Methven, Lt GM 26
Meyers, Heinrich 222
Miller, F/O Colin 150, 185
Mills, Dennis 88, 150, 170
Mills-Roberts, Brigadier 108
Milton, F/O 151
Mole, F/O Edward 12, 13
Montgomery, Field Marshal Sir Bernard 40, 42, 98, 99, 105, 106, 107, 130, 173, 209, 213
Moorehead, Alan 107
Mostyn-Brown, Sq/Ldr 115
Mountbatten, Admiral Lord Louis 27
Murdock, Capt Barry 78
Murray, Lt-Col Ian 23, 167, 185, 203, 209
Musgrave, Wg/Cdr Trenham C, OBE 112, 115, 210, 211

Nash, Flt/Lt John 154
Nash, Paddy 224
Newton, Jack 81, 160
Nicolson, Nick 134, 151
Nightingale, LAC 47
Norman, F/O Arthur 33
Norman, Gp Cpt Sir Nigel Bt CBE 15, 31
Norris, Leslie 151, 193
Norton, Cpt Harold 138
Norton, Cpt Rex 192

Oakes, Harry 165
Odlum, P/O Michael 140, 171, 208
O'Donnell, F/O 196
Operation 'Arena' 218
Operation 'Doomsday' 218
Operation 'Eclipse' 218
Operation Fustian 32
Osterkamp, General 213
O'Sullivan, Johnny 169

Palmer, Major 164
Pare, Padre George 166

Parkinson, Fl Lt Arthur R. 25
Parr, Wally 40, 145
Pearson 200
Penketh, St Sgt 152, 153
Perry, John 56, 65, 138, 186
Pogson, Arthur 88, 150, 170
Poole, Sgt R 77
Priddin, Sgt 80, 141, 142
Priest, Major Maurice 77, 113, 163
Procter, Gordon 53, 56, 127, 186, 212
Prout, Lt J.R. 33

Radcliffe, Sgt Jack 170, 200
Raspison, St/Sgt Edgar (Eddie) 65, 79, 88, 153, 188, 209, 224
Rayson, John 56, 65, 80, 141, 176, 216, 221
Read, Pete 65
Reed, Sgt 127, 186
Reid, Flying Officer RAAF 115
Rennie, Maj-Gen Tom 199
Reynolds, S/Ldr V.H. 150, 161, 164, 178
Rice, Lieutenant 153
Richards, Dan 194
Richards, David 56, 161, 194
Richmond, Sgt Graham 79, 142
Rigby, Cpt Robin 163
Roberts, Lt-Col 208
Robertson, S/Ldr Douglas R. DFC RCAF 82, 114, 219
Robinson, Lieutenant 150
Rock, Lt-Col John F. 15, 23
Ross, Kenneth 62, 70, 82, 137, 189
Rostron, Harry 158
Royal Aero Club 11
Rudkin, Jim 62, 128, 179
Ruhr Interdiction Line 103
Rushworth, F/O 163

Sabourine, Flt/Sgt 115
Sampson, Bill 151, 183
Sayers, Captain 11
Scarlett-Streatfield, AVM James R. CBE 48, 99, 219
Scolding, F/Lt Ken 63, 73, 134, 151, 193, 212
Scott, S/Ldr 136
Selley, Ken 177
Shannon, F/O 70
Shaw, Lieutenant 198
Shipway, Sgt 160
Shore, Peter 62
Sidebottom, S/Ldr John 28
Simpson, F/O 157
Simpson, General 105, 199
Sinclair, Sir Archibald 112, 157
Skeldon, Angus 196
Slade, Lt 164
Smith, F/O Alan 115, 222
Spicer, Tony 133, 192
Spowart, Sergeant 176
Sproule, W/Cdr J DFC 113
Spruell, Flt Lt 115
Squires, Wg Cdr DFC 113
Stammers, Harry 226
Stark, Jimmie 92
Starkey, Lt 148, 184

Stephenson, CSM 197
Stevens, Sgt 164
Stewart, Charles 158, 165, 212, 226
Stone, P/O John 170, 200
Strange, Wg Cdr L.A. DSO MC DFC 15
Strathdee, S/Sgt Malcolm F. 18, 25, 27
Strathen, Jock 128
Stredwick, Alan 131
Stringer, Mike 81
Student, General 213
Sweeney, Col Tod, MC 164, 223
Symmons, W/O 114, 115

Taylor, Richard 128
Tedder, Air Chief Marshal Sir Arthur 110, 112, 138, 157
Telfer, F/O 112
Thirkettle, Maurice 132, 191
Thompson, F/O 123
Tillett, Maj John 147, 164, 197, 200, 201, 221
Toler, Major Ian DFC 70, 82, 110, 112, 116, 143, 158, 176, 188, 192, 195

Topham, Cpl Frederick VC 166
Topp, Roger 133, 184
Turnbull, Sgt-Maj Lawrence William (Buck) 210
Turner, Wg/Cdr RT 115

Urquhart, General 42
Ursihus, Dr 11

Vanrenen, Lt H.P. 115, 133, 196
Vickery, Major Charles 140, 163
von Kesselring, Field Marshal Albrecht 98, 213
von Rundstedt, Fld Marshal 98

Wadley, Tony 78, 124
Waitz, General 11
Walden, Flying Officer 114
Walker, Sgt J.W. 47
Wallwork, Sgt James DFM 39, 43
Wanliss, F/O Ewan 13
Watkins, F/O 115
Watson, Ron 56, 132, 191
Watts, Colonel 165
Webb, F/Sgt 150
Webster, F/O 115

Weldon, Flying Officer 114
Weston, Sgt Stanley 63
White, F/O 196
White, St Sgt 33
Whiteley, F/O Tom 114, 167
Whitfield, Flt Lt DFM 116
Wiggan, Eric 133
Wiggin, Eddie 184
Wilkinson, S/Ldr A.M.B. DFC 25, 33
Williams, F/O Bleddwyn 55, 79, 115, 142, 174
Williams, Maj-Gen Paul L. 110
Wilmot Ragdale 115
Wilson, Sgt 'Tug' 78
Worrall, Sgt 155, 190
Wright, George 158
Wright, Sq/Ldr 11
Wright, Wilbur & Orville 11
Wynne, Dick 156, 195
Wynne-Powell, Wg Cdr T. DFC 113

Young, St/Sgt P. 130, 155

Zogling 12

THE ORIGINS OF 'MR CHAD'

During the early days of the war, RAF Wireless and Radar Mechanics were trained at RAF Yatesbury. In their early days of training they were taught basic AC (Alternating Current) theory which involved drawing a 'sine wave' showing how AC voltages varied over a cycle, thus:

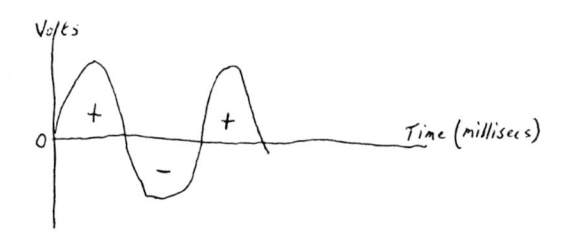

Before long, keen trainees were practising drawing sine waves on the lavatory walls and it was not long before some clever airman spotted that the sine wave could be made to resemble a character looking over a wall – the top of which was made by the timebase of the graph, thus:

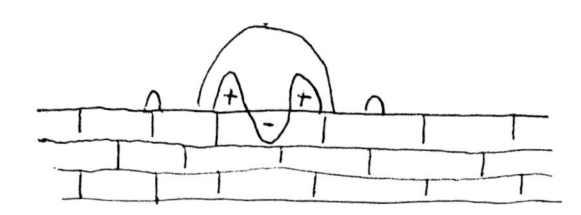

Pretty soon, the character was given the name "Doomie" and lavatory walls all over Yatesbury were decorated with cartoons with the caption "Doomie says ...." followed by a topical or apposite quote.

At that time there was a Wing Warrant Officer at Yatesbury by the name of Chadwick (known affectionately as 'Mr Chad') who issued an ultimatum to the effect that, if the Graffiti did not cease, the doors of all the lavatories would be removed. The next day, several lavatories carried the final "Doomie" cartoon which read: "Wot no doors?" and was signed 'Chad'.

The rest, I think, is history...

Before this, however, Doomie had spread far and wide throughout the RAF, in the same way as the later 'Kilroy' amongst US armed forces. I first saw him on a lavatory wall at RAF Aboukir, Egypt in mid-1940.

Mr Chadwick achieved fame in his own right several years later, when a new generation of Yatesbury trainees started to send some of his utterances to the *Daily Mirror* 'Live Letters' column. Most of these were, I think apocryphal, and I believe he ended up deliberately uttering malapropisms for trainees to send up to the paper!

One quote that I remember was when all leave was cancelled at the start of the Korean War. One airman asked if he could have a day pass, as he had already booked to see Dr Malcolm Sergeant.

"What's wrong with the Medical Officer on camp?" was allegedly Mr Chad's reply.

J. Bennett

Extract from *Upside Down Again: another book of RAF humour*, Woodfield Publishing (1999).